ActiveX™ Web Programming

ISAPI, Controls, and Scripting

Adam Blum

WILEY COMPUTER PUBLISHING

John Wiley & Sons, Inc.

New York • Chichester • Brisbane • Toronto • Singapore • Weinheim

Publisher: Katherine Schowalter
Editor: Tim Ryan
Assistant Editor: Kathryn A. Malm
Managing Editor: Angela Murphy
Text Design & Composition: North Market Street Graphics

This text is printed on acid-free paper.

Library of Congress Cataloging-in-Publication Data:
Blum, Adam.
    ActiveX Web programming : ISAPI, controls, and scripting /
Adam Blum.
        p.   cm.
    Includes index.
    ISBN 0-471-16177-2 (pbk. : alk. paper)
    1. Web sites. 2. Web servers—Computer programs.   3. Interactive multimedia. I. Title.
TK5105.888.B58   1997
005.2'76—dc21   96-44768

Printed in the United States of America
10 9 8 7 6 5 4 3 2 1

CONTENTS

PART 2
WEB CLIENT-SIDE PROGRAMMING

INTRODUCTION:

WHAT IS ACTIVEX?

Microsoft has recently introduced the ActiveX family of technologies to enable Internet developers to build more advanced, better Web-based applications. ActiveX includes server-side technology in the form of the ActiveX server framework: both the Internet Services API (ISAPI) specification and the ISAPI filter specification. It includes a variety of client-side technologies. Of particular importance, especially as presented in this book, are ActiveX Controls for embedded client-side functionality in Web pages or Visual Basic applications, Active Scripts, a standard for VB Script to provide client-side scripting functionality in Web browsers, and Java applets, specifically those developed with Microsoft's new Java development environment, currently called Jakarta.

ActiveX Web Programming covers gateway programming to Common Gateway Interface (CGI) and Microsoft's new ISAPI standards. Programs will be demonstrated in C++ and Perl. This book covers both server or gateway applications and client-side development using OLE Controls and VBScript. With the new capabilities of the

ActiveX server and client-side technologies, a given set of functionality can often be provided with either ISAPI gateways, OLE Controls, VB Scripts, or Java applets. Most applications will benefit from a combination of the available programming techniques, and indeed I will try to demonstrate how this combination produces better Web-based applications than any of the techniques alone.

Web Development History

Building Web sites by assembling static HTML content has become a commonplace skill. The best Web sites are now distinguished by their level of interactivity, that is, the ability to allow the user to respond to the content, post his or her own feedback, search for desired information, or just view information that is more dynamic than a static HTML page. This requires the participation of a developer to either program a Web gateway or a client application (a program that runs on the user's Web browser). More precisely, it requires building Web-based applications that are ideally combinations of these techniques.

First-generation approaches to building Web server-side functionality were CGI programs. While CGI is an important standard covered in this book, it has many limitations, which the ISAPI (part of the ActiveX Server Framework) addresses. Eventually even the powerful capabilities of ISAPI gateways run into limitations—functionality that can best be performed on the user's workstation. For this ActiveX introduces OLE Controls and Active Scripts.

Goals of This Book

If all you have is a hammer the whole world looks like a nail. If that hammer is server-side gateway programming, you will build your applications with gateways, and most applications *can* be built that way. But it's not always the right way, and doing all the work on the server may be causing unnecessary data traffic between the server and the client. If the user requests an operation with locally available data they should be able to get the answer locally without making a CGI gateway on the server do the work. If the hammer is client-side scripting you may build applications that do all the computational and data transformation work on the client, when that is not necessarily the best way to structure the application. My goal with this book is to present all of the new ActiveX technologies available for Web development so the reader can select the right tools, or more likely the right *combination* of tools, and use those tools effectively to create advanced, dynamic Web applications.

There is a wide variety of technology introduced in Microsoft's ActiveX Software Development Kit (SDK). All of this technology is new. The context where each technology is applied has not completely gelled. Further, guidance on and knowledge of how to combine these technologies to make comprehensive Web-based applications is almost nonexistent at this point. This book will use many small sample applications, and some larger ones, to illustrate use of a technology, and when a particular technology is most effective. The larger applications will often be a mix of technologies to illustrate how to apply multiple tools in creating Web applications. One larger application that we will be demonstrating is a Web-based online store. This uses ISAPI gateways (a C++ class library allows it to be configured to use either gateway protocol) to display products and enter orders. It uses ActiveX Controls to manipulate this data on the client. It uses VBScript to perform client-side validation of data before submitting order forms. Traditionally this might have been done all with gateways, but at the cost of possibly redundant trips to the server due to faulty data. As another example, ActiveX Controls can be used to graph data on a client browser without shipping the entire chart to the user, just shipping the data, and allowing the control to receive and display data. This can save many large image downloads for a Web-based application, and result in pages that display data graphically but still load up quickly. With technology like ActiveX Controls (a simplification of the COM standard for controls), there is no reason not to perform computational work on the client browser, as long as the data is already located there on the workstation. Finally Java applets can do much of the same client-side work, and are easily downloaded and executed on client browsers on the fly. Microsoft's Java VM implementation has the unique feature of being able to invoke the functionality of existing COM objects. Indeed the Java model maps closer to the COM model than C++ does. So the discussion of Microsoft's Java implementation is very much appropriate to this book on ActiveX.

An overarching goal of this book is to make it self-contained enough to act as a reference source, but also present material and utilities not found in any of the ActiveX

SDK reference material: either the SDK itself, the Visual C++/MFC documentation on various portions of ActiveX (such as VC's enhancements to assist in ISAPI programming), or on the www.microsoft.com/intdev Web site. These are all great resources referred to over and over again in the book. But throughout the book are sample programs using each technology that are useful in and of themselves *and that can't be found anywhere else.* Also presented are programming tools, such as C++ class libraries, that assist in the creation of such programs. Many of these tools were written just for this book to provide examples of various technologies and techniques. Others emerged from the crucible of solving real client problems as a Web development consultant. Almost every tool presented is now in production use on one Web site or another.

The book attempts to present enough information to act as a reference to each of the important new specifications and technologies in ActiveX. It's also long on thorough explanations of the whys and wherefores of each API. It shows sample programs that attempt to do useful, productive tasks for each technology. It does not attempt to show lots of HTML pages or full working sites that incorporate the sample programs. The assumption here is that the reader is a developer. Lots of HTML in the text and on the book's Web site that incorporates the sample programs to make more full-fledged examples would obscure the purpose and structure of each program. I mention this somewhat obvious caveat, because every so often in my Web development seminars a Webmaster sneaks in and asks, "Where's the HTML?" The answer is usually, "Well . . . generated by this Internet Server Application or ISAPI filter or Perl script or whatever." If you see much static HTML presented anywhere, you'll know the book is straying from its original goal of being an authoritative programmer's reference for the host of technologies in ActiveX, with lots of useful example source code, reusable class libraries, and utility programs.

Structure of This Book

The first part of this book covers Web server-side programming. First I briefly introduce the capabilities of Microsoft's new Internet Information Server (IIS), in particular, the IIS Internet Database Connector, which allows small applications to be built that collect data for storage into databases or reporting from databases with no true programming. Next is the CGI standard for extending Web server capabilities (still important to know even with the introduction of ActiveX and ISAPI), and how to program CGI in C++. Also presented here is a class (unique to this book) to alleviate CGI forms processing. The next chapter covers how to build gateways in Perl, useful for both CGI- and ISAPI-based gateways. The next chapters cover the ActiveX Server Framework for extending the capabilities of IIS, as well as the new ISAPI standard and several example uses of the ISAPI interface, including a C++ class framework to assist in building ISAPI programs (another tool unique to this text). The last chapter in this part covers the ISAPI filter specification and examples of how this allows a Web server's capabilities to be dramatically expanded. All of the sample ISAPI filters presented here were written just for this book, and the ISAPI filter for enhanced IIS access control can only be found here.

The next part of the book discusses Web client-side technologies introduced by ActiveX. The foremost of these is ActiveX Controls, which is a standard for creating OLE Controls that can be easily distributed over the Internet. It also covers a standard for client-side scripting to create interactive Web pages. This standard is called Active Scripts, the primary instantiation of which is VBScript.

Note: This symbol ↳ is used to indicate a break in code due to the restrictions of the printed page. When programming, these lines should be continuous.

ActiveX™ Web Programming

1

INTERNET INFORMATION SERVER FOR PROGRAMMERS

Microsoft's new Web server, Internet Information Server (IIS), contains three major distinguishing features over a basic HTTP server: the Internet Database Connector (IDC), which provides built-in access to ODBC databases; security integrated with Windows NT; and ISAPI, a robust, high-performance method of communicating with gateway programs. IIS is very strong product and has many other features to recommend it, but these are the true differentiators. From a developer's perspective, what is significant about IIS? Certainly the big one is ISAPI (also known as the ActiveX Server Framework), which opens the door to building robust, high-performance, easily scaleable, full-fledged Web applications that interoperate tightly with the IIS Web server. This book will focus on this last feature and give a great deal of attention to techniques for developing ISAPI-based applications, also known as Internet Service Applications (ISAs).

However, before plunging into our multichapter description of ISAPI, I would like to give some attention to the IDC. Although this component was developed to allow access to databases by nonprogrammer Webmasters, this can actually be a quite useful tool for Web developers. The IDC can be used to supplement existing SQL-based systems with easy ad-hoc reporting and querying from Web pages. Web pages that collect data via HTML forms and enter them as records in the ODBC database can also be constructed with very little effort with nothing resembling conventional programming. These Web pages can be built from any HTML authoring tool, with just a little syntactic sugar added to identify database field names. The process is so easy and straightforward that it's difficult to think of this as programming, and in fact it probably shouldn't be thought of that way. Nevertheless it is possible to supplant many a custom development effort with this approach, so the true ActiveX Web developer should be well aware of how to utilize the IDC to maximum effect.

The Internet Database Connector

The IDC is actually an instantiation of an ISAPI DLL, an Internet Server Application, designed to provide access to ODBC datasources from the IIS HTTP server. The specific DLL is httpodbc.dll. The architecture of the IDC is shown in Figure 1.1.

The Internet Database Connector is automatically invoked by IIS whenever a file with the extension .IDC is referenced. How is this done? IIS ships with several script mappings. These are maintained in the registry key HKEY_LOCAL_MACHINE\ SYSTEM\CurrentControlSet\Services\W3SVC\Parameters\Script Map.

Figure 1.2 shows the script mappings that IIS ships with. You can add to this list to make, for example, IIS run perl.exe when it encounters a .pl file.

To make the Internet Database Connector run, you create an IDC file with an extension of .IDC that contains the necessary SQL to add a record to your database (generally an INSERT statement), or retrieve a table of records or a particular record from the database (generally via a SELECT statement).

Preparing to Use the Internet Database Connector

To use the IDC, you will need to have ODBC installed on your IIS server machine. This is an option during install of IIS, and hopefully you have selected it and can just proceed. Otherwise you will need to perform the install by rerunning the IIS install.

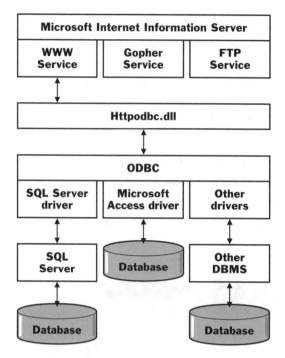

▬▬▬▬▬ **Figure 1.1** Internet Database Connector architecture.

The first step in getting the IDC running, assuming ODBC is already present, is to create a *system datasource*. To do this, click on the ODBC applet in Control Panel. Click on the System DSN button. If you are running SQL Server 6.5, a System DSN will already exist, called Local Server. ODBC of course works against other databases such as Microsoft Access and RDBMS from many other vendors. If you have the choice of working with either SQL Server or Access, I urge you to use SQL Server if only for the

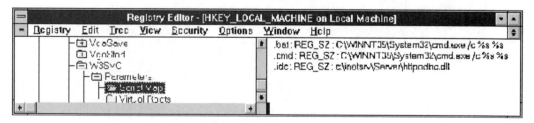

▬▬▬▬▬ **Figure 1.2** Registry key for script mappings.

scalability to high levels of transactions that it offers. This book will use SQL Server for almost all examples. If you are planning to always use the IDC to communicate with a particular database, you may wish to set the database name in that database. Figure 1.3 shows modifying the Local Server DSN to always use the pubs database.

Authoring Internet Database Connector Files

Once configured you can then create Internet Database Connector files. This involves writing a .idc file that determines what command is sent to the database, and the user and ODBC drivers used to submit the command. It also involves building an HTML template file that controls the display of the data coming back from the Internet Database Connector.

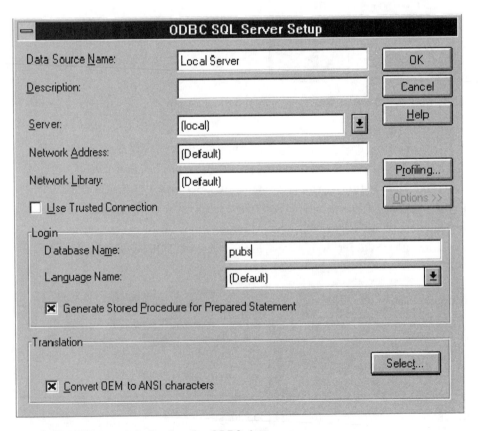

■■■■■■ **Figure 1.3** Configuring ODBC datasource.

Here is an example IDC file, the sample.idc that ships with IIS. It will work against the Microsoft SQL Server sample pubs database.

```
Datasource: Local Server
Username: sa
Template: sample.htx
SQLStatement:
+SELECT au_lname, ytd_sales from pubs.dbo.titleview where
+ytd_sales>5000
```

Note that the Datasource: field indicates a System DSN that should have been set up with the ODBC applet. The Username: is an SQL username with sufficient privileges to effect the SQL statement. You may not want to use sa as the username. The IDC sample files that ship with IIS do use that ID, but you may want to be more selective. The Template: name is the name of a file that contains HTML for presentation and embedded field codes to determine the formatting of the data coming back from the server. By convention, the extension is .htx (connoting presumably HTML eXtensions), but this is not required. We urge you to use the same basename for your template as you used for the .IDC file, if only for ease of management. The final field in the file is the SQL Statement: field. The data in this field is the full SQL statement that will be sent to the backend database. Note the plus (+) signs at the beginning of each line. We urge you to develop and test the SQL statement interactively using Microsoft SQL Server's ISQL tool or Access's query builder. Then paste into this file and prepend the plus signs to each line. SQL statements employed in .idc files will generally be a SELECT to list records, an INSERT to add records, a SELECT with a WHERE clause to retrieve a particular record, and an UPDATE statement to modify a record.

Now we need to build an HTML template file to accept the results back from the database. Following is the sample.htx that displays the results of the IDC file just shown.

```
<HTML>
<HEAD><TITLE>Authors and YTD Sales</TITLE></HEAD>
<TABLE BORDER>
<B><TR><TH>Author<TH>YTD Sales</B>
<%begindetail%>
<TR><TD><%au_lname%><TD>$<%ytd_sales%>
<%enddetail%>
```

```
</TABLE>
</BODY>
</HTML>
```

This looks like any other generic HTML page, but look at the fifth, sixth, and seventh lines. They contain a number of <% . . . %> tags that do not look like generic HTML. They are IDC extensions to HTML that determine the placement of the data coming back from the database on the HTML page. The tags <%begindetail%> and <%end-detail%> allow you to handle the occurrence of an unknown number of rows coming back from the database system. Each row is formatted using the HTML and embedded field names in between these tags. A common way of handling this is to place it inside an HTML table row as shown. This is not required, however, and you could just as easily place the field codes all on a line and use a paragraph (<P>) tag to move the browser to a new line after each data row. The field data for each row is retrieved with a tag <%fieldname%>. Generally, for a SELECT statement IDC such as used in this example, there are field codes for each field mentioned in the SELECT statement. Note that though similar to the sample.idc file that ships with IIS, this example is *considerably* simplified, and I believe much easier for you to understand and begin using as a base for your efforts.

The IDC Extended HTML Tags

Full documentation of the IDC appears in the IIS help file. For quick reference, and because it's not laid out in an easy-to-read table format in the help file, some of the commonly used tags and variables you have available to you when authoring HTML template (.htx) files are shown in Table 1.1.

What You Can Use the IDC For

The Internet Database Connector is valuable even outside the context of applications that must be Web-based. Why? Because it provides a no-programming, very easy-to-maintain interface to relational database data. The only skills required to maintain the system (for example, modifying a report page) are HTML authoring and knowing the field names of the tables in question. Usually it is not even required to change the SQL statements on an ongoing basis. It's ideal to provide a system to a customer that is maintainable as possible with skills close to end user level.

▬▬▬▬▬ **Table 1.1** HTX Tags and Variables

Tag	Description
<%begindetail%> <%enddetail%>	<%begindetail%>, <%enddetail%> keywords surround a section of the HTML extension file in which the data output from the database will be merged.

<%if%>..<%else%>..< %endif%>	Conditionally display one set of HTML or another. Example:
	
	`<%if CurrentRecord EQ 0 %>`
	`No records returned!<P>`
	`<%endif%>`

CurrentRecord	Used as argument to <%if%> tag.
MaxRecord	The maximum number of records that can be returned by the IDC. This is an option in the IDC file. If not set, it is essentially infinite (4 billion).
EQ	Condition test used in <%if%> statements. True if value1 equals value2.
LT	Another condition test. True if value1 is less than value2.
GT	True if value1 is greater than value2.
CONTAINS	True if any part of value1 contains the string value2.

▬▬▬▬▬

It's particularly useful in situations where you need to provide Web browser access to existing data that has been populated by some other application. It's more useful on the reporting and searching side than the data entry side, because it is difficult to provide sophisticated (or any) validation logic in the HTML form for data entry. For some applications that just facilitate simple data collection, this is acceptable. For most it probably isn't. Luckily there is a ray of hope on the horizon for this limitation: client-side validation. This means putting logic on the client's browser to check each field, meaning that the record entry is much more likely to succeed. In later chapters, we'll show you how VBScript, and active scripting in general, can facilitate this.

To give you an example of this, that may also serve as the basis for your own systems, let's show you a simple order entry system built with the Internet Database Connector.

A Web-Based Ordering System Using IIS, the IDC, and SQL Server

The classic example of using this technology is a Web-based system for ordering products. We will introduce this example here and make it work with only the Internet Database Connector (no programming necessary!). Over the course of this book, we will enhance it with other features, to demonstrate the various programming technologies available with ActiveX.

The Database Definition

The initial Web ordering system will be based on two main tables: a *products* table and an *orders* table. Figure 1.4 shows the definition of the products table in the Microsoft SQL Server 6.5 Enterprise Manager. Note that since the IDC talks to any ODBC datasource, you can replicate this database definition in your database of choice.

There is the key field of *prodno* that uniquely identifies the product. The product text name is in the *product* field. The field names that are likely to be used in the HTML templates and maintained by nonprogrammer Webmaster/administrator staff are kept as simple and readable as possible. Thus *price* is the price the product can be purchased for. *Available* indicates amount of product left to sell. *Discount,* if present, indicates a percentage to reduce the price, allowing easy implementation of sales by doing a global update of the table on that column. The next two fields anticipate some future enhancements to the system, by providing indexes into a future *categories* table and a *manufacturer* table. The *imagefile* field allows the path name to a GIF or JPEG file for displaying a picture of the product.

Following is the definition of the orders table (see Figure 1.5).

The *orderno* field is the unique key. The *prodno* field is the index into the products table. The *price* is the price the product was purchased for per unit. The price paid is computed from *price* × *quantity.* The *paymethod* is a numeric index into a payment method table, for example, 0—cash, 1—check, 2—VISA, 3—MC, 4—Amex. The next five fields refer

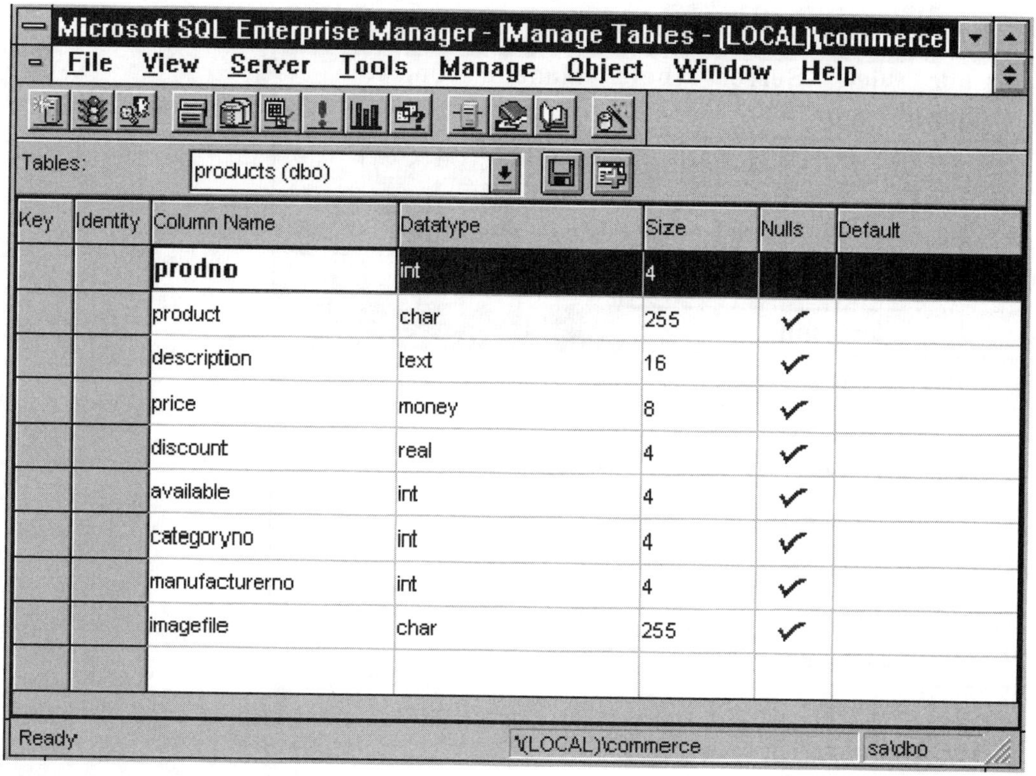

Key	Identity	Column Name	Datatype	Size	Nulls	Default
		prodno	int	4		
		product	char	255	✓	
		description	text	16	✓	
		price	money	8	✓	
		discount	real	4	✓	
		available	int	4	✓	
		categoryno	int	4	✓	
		manufacturerno	int	4	✓	
		imagefile	char	255	✓	

Figure 1.4 Products table.

to the shipping address. They cannot just be grabbed from the stored customer table (once we implement one) since we are assuming that it can be shipped to any address. There is also a customer ID number field and a customer name field, making the database less normalized, but useful for our simple example. The table might get more complex as we progress through the book, but this should serve as a useful base for our immediate examples.

Simple Set of Pages

Now we will want to put together some HTML pages that will allow users to pick from the list of available products, listed in the products table, and place an order for that product into the orders table. Here is the top-level page that allows us to invoke the products.idc file that displays all of the products.

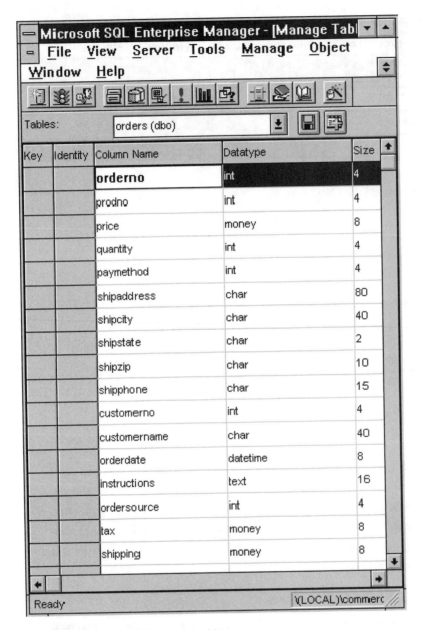

Figure 1.5 Orders table.

```
<HTML><HEAD><TITLE>Welcome to the CyberStore</TITLE></HEAD>
<BODY>
This is the list of <A HREF="/scripts/products.idc">products
available</A>.
</BODY></HTML>
```

To generate the list we want to retrieve all records in the products table. Here is the products.idc file.

```
Datasource: Local Server
Username: sa
Template: products.htx
SQLStatement:
+SELECT prodno, product, description, price FROM products
```

Note that the SQL statement can, and probably should, be generated and tested in any interactive SQL front end. Many people use Microsoft Access for this purpose to work against arbitrary ODBC backends. If the backend is Microsoft SQL Server, the ISQL interactive query tool can be used to build and test the SQL statement. The statement can then be copied and pasted into the text editor (e.g., Notepad) used to create the .IDC file.

Below is the listing of the products from the products table. This enhanced HTML (HTML with field codes embedded) will be stored as file products.htx.

```
<HTML><HEAD><TITLE>CyberStore Products</TITLE></HEAD>
<BODY>
Click on the product of your choice.
<TABLE BORDER>
<TR><TH>Product<TH>Description<TH>Price
<%begindetail%>
<TR>
<TD>
<A HREF="/scripts/vieword.idc?product=<%prodno%>"><%product%></A>
<TD><%description%>
<TD><%price%>
```

```
<%enddetail%>
</TABLE>
</BODY>
</HTML>
```

This is written so that each product comes back on its own row in the table. An example of the display, with a very small products table, is shown in Figure 1.6.

Clicking on a particular product invokes another Internet Database Connector file, vieword.idc. Here are the contents of that file:

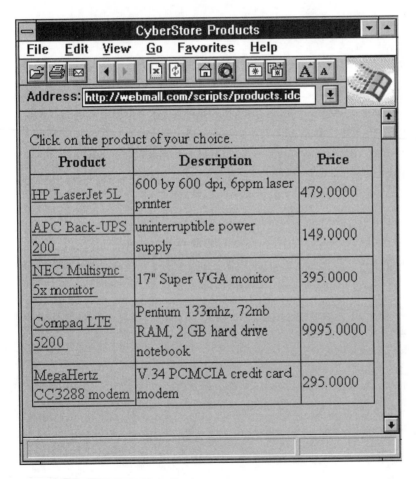

■■■■■ **Figure 1.6** Product list display.

```
Datasource: Local Server
Username: sa
Template: orderprd.htx
SQLStatement:
+SELECT product, description, price,
+ available, discount, available, imagefile,
+FROM products
+WHERE prodno=%prodno%
```

To display it we'll use a product ordering form, orderprd.htx, as shown here.

```
<HTML><HEAD><TITLE>Ordering <%product%></TITLE></HEAD>
<BODY>
<FORM ACTION="/scripts/orderprd.idc">
<TABLE>
<B>
<TR><TD>Product<TD><%product%>
<TR><TD>Description<TD><%description%>
<TR><TD>Available<TD><%available%>
<TR><TD>Price<TD><%price%>
</B>
<INPUT TYPE="hidden" NAME="prodno" VALUE="<%prodno%>">
<INPUT TYPE="hidden" NAME="price" VALUE="<%price%>">
<TR><TD>Quantity<TD><INPUT NAME="quantity" SIZE="2" VALUE="1">
<TR><TD>Name<TD><INPUT NAME="customername" SIZE=20>
<TR><TD>Payment Method:
<TD><SELECT NAME="paymethod"><OPTION VALUE="1">Visa<OPTION
VALUE="2">MC<OPTION VALUE="3">Amex</SELECT>
<TR><TD>Number<TD><INPUT NAME="credcardnum"
SIZE=20><TD>Expires<TD><INPUT NAME="expires" SIZE=4>
<TR><TD>Shipping Address<TD><INPUT NAME="shipaddress" SIZE=20>
<TR><TD>City<TD><INPUT NAME="city" SIZE=20><TD>State<TD><INPUT
NAME="state" SIZE="2"><TD>Zip<TD><INPUT NAME="zip" SIZE="10">
<TR><TD><INPUT TYPE="submit" VALUE="Order Product"><TD><INPUT
TYPE="reset" VALUE="Cancel Order">
```

```
</TABLE>
</FORM>
</BODY>
</HTML>
```

Clicking on a product from the list above will result in an order form as shown in Figure 1.7.

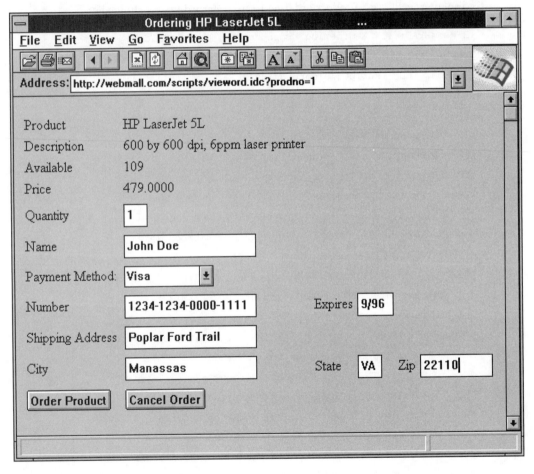

■■■■■ **Figure 1.7** Order form.

Now we need to write orderprd.idc that contains the SQL statement to submit this data to the database. The SQL statement below is definitely one that should be tested interactively first. Note that type conversions are necessary for many of the fields.

```
Datasource: Local Server
Username: sa
Template: ordresult.htx
SQLStatement:
+INSERT INTO orders (
+ prodno,price,quantity,customername,paymethod,credcardnum,
+ expires,shipaddress,shipcity,shipstate,shipzip)
+VALUES (
+ CONVERT(int,'%prodno%'),CONVERT(money,'%price%'),
+ CONVERT(int,'%quantity%','%customername%',CONVERT(int,'%paymethod%'),
+'%credcardnum%','%expires%','%shipaddress%','%shipcity%','%shipstate%',
  '%shipzip
+)
```

This will result in the contents of the form being stored in the orders table.

There are many more enhancements that can be made to this simple system. In the meantime, this is meant to be a programming book, so I would like to go on to show you some of the programming techniques that can be used to build and enhance such Web-based applications. Knowing the IDC will be useful even though it is a nonprogramming interface, because many Web development efforts will involve enhancing the IDC and other nonprogramming Web-database interface tools.

Let's go on to developing gateways to link Web servers to other applications and databases. We'll start by presenting the CGI interface and how to program to it in C++ and Perl in Chapters 3 and 4.

CHAPTER

2

GATEWAYS AND THE COMMON GATEWAY INTERFACE

Why You Need to Know CGI

This chapter discusses the CGI standard—the original method of writing Web gateways and other programs to extend the functionality of Web servers. After reading the discussion of the advantages of IIS, the foremost of which is support for a new standard for server add-on development called ISAPI, you may be asking: "Why do I need to learn CGI? I only plan on writing ISAPI gateway programs."

Understanding CGI is still necessary, even if you write all of your gateways to Microsoft's new ISAPI standard (covered in Chapters 5 and 6). Why? Because ISAPI maintains many CGI artifacts, and in many cases uses CGI as the foundation upon which to build its functionality. For example, ISAPI does not use its own set of error codes. It adopts the CGI set of error codes. You need to know and understand these to develop for ISAPI effectively. ISAPI uses all of the header name conventions invented by CGI to pass data directly from the client to the backend program. ISAPI dispenses with the environment variables that CGI uses to communicate data from the

Web server to the gateway program. However, it maintains all of the same names as handles to the same sets of data. It just communicates this information more efficiently. You'll need to know what each of the CGI environment variables does, because they live on in ISAPI, but as just fields within an ISAPI control block. Despite the vast improvement that ISAPI makes over CGI for most Web applications, it really is fair to think of ISAPI as a CGI enhancement rather than a completely new standard.

There are even occasions where not just understanding but also developing a CGI application is warranted. CGI is a standard for communicating with an external process. ISAPI is a standard for supplying an in-process extension, a DLL. There may in fact be occasions when having a separate process is in fact appropriate. For one thing, it's much safer to have the gateway function in a separate process.

Finally, there is a huge installed base of freely available CGI gateways. Many of these you may be able to convert to ISAPI, and you will see how to do that later. But you'll need to understand CGI thoroughly to effect the conversion. In many cases, a conversion may not be necessary, and sometimes, if the CGI gateway is written in a language in which ISAPI DLLs cannot be created, it will not be possible to port it. In other cases, such as those where the scaleability benefits of ISAPI don't pay off for the intended application, it is just not worth it to port the script. This means that you will be maintaining the script as a CGI program for some time, and you'll need to be just as conversant with CGI as you will become expert with ISAPI later on.

This chapter discuss how to do CGI programming in C++, and the next one covers CGI programming in Perl (along with an introduction to Perl). If you feel you already know CGI very well, and are looking to concentrate on the new ActiveX Web programming features, please skip ahead to Chapter 5 on ISAPI.

What Is a Gateway?

Writing HTML allows you to create static Web content before placing it on the Web server for viewing. This book is oriented to creating interactive webs, which generate the information that the user views on the fly in response to user actions. One of the ways to do this is to use a *gateway*—a program that the HTTP server invokes in response to user actions or when the user clicks on a link that calls the gateway.

Gateways provide real-time access to information, without the necessity of a priori conversion to or creation of an HTML text file. For example, a gateway to a SQL server might retrieve current product price and availability information. Another gateway program might store data supplied in a form into a database format of choice. Typically any form that the user fills out will need to be processed by a gateway program to store the data, or retrieve other data for display in response to the form request.

The scenario of using a gateway is as follows:

1. The user points browser at (or selects a link for) a URL that represents a program or script instead of an existing HTML page.

2. The HTTP server identified in the URL invokes the program, with whatever arguments are supplied in the URL, and other information supplied by environment variables to the invoked program.

3. The gateway program stores the information supplied by the server to it, if necessary. This is most common if the gateway is the ACTION of a form.

4. The program creates an HTML page on the fly and sends it back to the server.

5. The server sends newly created page to browser, which displays it.

This book covers gateway development to both the CGI and new Microsoft ISAPI standards separately. But the syntax of embedding references to gateways into your HTML documents is the same:

```
<gateway>[/<supplementary path>][?<query>]
```

where <supplementary path> and <query> are optional arguments. The following HTML embeds a reference to the Internet Database Connector gateway program as a link.

```
Here is the <A HREF="monthrpt.idc">monthly report</A>.
```

Gateways can be configured to process form data, as in the statement:

```
<FORM METHOD=POST ACTION="cgi-bin/formstor.exe">
```

This is how you embed references to gateways into your HTML page. But this book is about Web programming, and how to develop your own gateways. Let's look at the CGI standard in more detail so that you are prepared to write your own CGI programs.

The CGI Standard

From the very first HTTP servers, there was often the need for these servers to run external programs. These programs might have been to store information from an HTML form, to retrieve information from an external database, or to create an HTML page dynamically. From the very beginning these programs were called gateways, but there was no standard for them. Each Web server (there were two primary Web servers at the time from NCSA and CERN) communicated with gateways differently.

The CGI interface attempted to standardize how information was communicated from servers to gateways, so that gateways could be written that functioned on more than one server. The standard consists of a set of *environment variables* that will be created by the server for each gateway invocation, a set of command-line arguments to the gateway program, and the input and output files to and from the program.

Also note that we use the term standard loosely, because that's just what CGI has become: a loose standard. Many of the environment variables in CGI are available on all servers, because they have to be. In general, however, each server has introduced its own environment variables for its own needs. Some servers don't implement parts of the documented standard. We will try to navigate this maze for you so that you implement to the workable subset of the standard that will make your gateway programs portable amongst the many popular Web servers. Where using a nonstandard environment variable is necessary, the information we present should let you include conditional logic in your programs that checks for the server used (through a CGI environment variable!) and use the appropriate extension environment variable in each case, depending on which server the gateway is installed on.

CGI URLs

To begin our presentation of how CGI gateway programs are developed, we'd first like to cover how to embed references to CGI programs in your HTML pages. This syntax applies to ISAPI programs as well. The format is:

```
<CGI gateway program> [/<supplementary path information>] [?<query>]
```

<CGI gateway program> is a path to the CGI gateway itself, such as http://ourstore.com/cgi-bin/order.exe or just cgi-bin/order.exe. In the case of ISAPI programs, the name will end with .DLL. <supplementary path information> is an optional argu-

ment that follows the gateway name after an intervening slash (/). It can be retrieved from the PATH_INFO environment variable. It is often the name of a file that the gateway program operates upon.

The query is another optional argument appended to the gateway program and supplementary path info (if present). The query is available in URL-encoded form in the QUERY_STRING environment variable. If there is no equal (=) sign in the query, it will also be available in the command line arguments to the program.

A common use of gateways is to process data from a form, as in the statement:

```
<FORM METHOD=POST ACTION="cgi-bin/order.exe/products.db?widget">
```

In this example, the gateway program is order.exe, the PATH_INFO is products.db, and the command line argument (and QUERY_STRING) is widget. Standard input is all of the form data (field names and values) in URL-encoded form.

Invocations of CGI gateways can also be embedded into your HTML with simple hypertext links. In this form, the method is always GET, and there is no standard input to the program.

```
<A HREF="cgi-bin/order.exe/products.db?widget">Order this Product</A>
```

Now let's go on to show you how to develop programs that process the input that you have specified with this format.

Input

If the CGI program has been invoked with the POST method, data will be supplied to your program via standard input. The CONTENT_LENGTH environment variable determines the size of the data. If the CGI program has been invoked with the GET method, this information appears in the QUERY_INFO environment variable (see the following section on CGI environment variables). Of course, the data is then limited to the size of environment variables, so this is not an ideal way to pass data to your program. Ideally your gateway should be prepared to handle data from either QUERY_INFO or standard input, determining at run time which is actually present. The REQUEST_METHOD environment variable determines where to get the information from.

The CONTENT_TYPE environment variable determines what form this data is sent in. Currently, the only standard content type used is *application/x-www-form-*

urlencoded. This means that the information has been URL-encoded: spaces have been replaced with plus (+) signs, and non-alphanumeric characters have been replaced with %xx codes. You will have to URL-decode this information to use it within your program. The following C function will decode a character buffer of URL-encoded information.

```c
// decode URL-encoded text
void UrlDecode(char *p)
{
    char *p2 = p;
    while (*p) {
        if (*p == '%') {
            // next 2 chars are hex representation
            ++p;
            if (!isxdigit(p[0]) || !isxdigit(p[1]))
                throw "corrupted hex encoding";
            char hold = p[2];
            p[2] = '\0';
            *p2++ = char(strtoul(p, 0, 16));
            p[2] = hold;
            p += 2;
        }
        else if (*p == '+') {
            *p2++ = ' ';
            ++p;
        }
        else
            *p2++ = *p++;
    }
    *p2 = '\0';
}
```

For form data, the input will be a series of field names and field values. Subsequent sections will present some reusable code to parse out this data format, and do useful things with it, such as store it in text files.

Command-Line Arguments

Command-line arguments are often used in programs that are written to respond to ISINDEX queries, but they can be used in other programs that take arguments, but little data. They aren't usually necessary for form processing programs, which should interpret their data from standard input. They are useful in search programs, or programs that generate pages based on some criteria.

The query, which is all of the text following the question mark, is split at the plus (+) signs, URL-decoded, and placed into successive command-line arguments. The query is also available in undecoded form in the QUERY_STRING environment variable. If the query contains any unencoded equal (=) signs, the query is only accessible from the QUERY_STRING environment variable.

Output

Output from the CGI program is returned to the user via standard output. Output should be in valid HTTP format. As mentioned earlier, HTTP is the Web transport protocol. Web browsers submit requests to Web servers via HTTP, and receive responses back in HTTP. As you start to write your own gateway programs to communicate back to the Web browser, you will need to generate HTTP format output. This is very similar to HTML, with a few additional responsibilities outlined in the following discussion.

The output begins with a set of headers, which is terminated with a blank line.

Content-length and Content-type

First the gateway should tell the server and the client what format it is displaying the data in. This is done with the Content-type. directive followed by the MIME type. Common values are text/html to return HTML, and text/plain for plain text. Content length is a less necessary header but may be supplied if you wish.

Status

Another common header is the status line. The status header is in the format Status: <number> <text>. A common response is Status: 200 OK. You should attempt to follow the conventions for reporting CGI program status. Available status codes are shown in Table 2.1.

Other headers that may be supplied in your returned data are described in the following sections.

■■■■■ **Table 2.1** CGI Error and Status Codes

Code	Text	Meaning
200–204	SUCCESS	
200	OK	Succeeded.
201	CREATED	Text part of response line indicates the URI by which the new document should be known.
202	ACCEPTED	Accepted for processing, but processing has not yet been completed. This is useful for asynchronous processing requests: The work is submitted but the user can continue with Web browsing.
203	Partial Information	Returned information is not definitive or complete.
204	No Response	Server received request but nothing to send back. This is to allow script input without changing documents.
300–304	REDIRECTION	
301	Moved	Data requested has been permanently moved. Header lines that follow show the new location(s) with URI: <url>
302	Found	Data requested has been found at following other locations: URI: <url>
303	Method	Suggests client try different URL or method to access (for example POST rather than get): Method: <method> <url>
304	Not Modified	Client has performed condition GET but document has not been changed since the time specified in the If-Modified-Since Field.
400–404	CLIENT ERRORS	
400	Bad Request	For example, bad syntax.
401	Unauthorized	Needs good authorization header.
402	Payment Required	Client should respond with valid ChargeTo header.

▉▉▉▉▉ **Table 2.1** Continued

Code	Text	Meaning
403	Forbidden	Request will not be granted even with valid authorization or payment.
404	Not found	Could not find specified document, query, or URL.
500–503	SERVER ERRORS	
500	Internal Error	Server experienced internal error.
501	Not implemented	This particular server does not support function requested.
502	Service temporarily overloaded	Due to current high load on server, the service is temporarily unavailable.
503	Gateway timeout	If your gateway is using another gateway or service, that other service took longer than you were configured to wait.

Expires

This header indicates by what date the data is no longer valid.

Content-encoding

You can return data in compressed form if the client has indicated that they can accept the particular content type. (See the Accept-Encoded request header in Table 2.3.)

Location

This is the location of a URL for the server to retrieve to present to the client. You can think of it as shorthand for you actually opening that file, reading all of the data in it, and outputting it for the client to read.

The server will check all of these headers for validity before returning the information to the client. If you wish to bypass this checking, begin your script name with nph- (standing for "no parse headers"). There is little reason to do this with modern Web servers: the performance hit of the checking is not significant and the verification of your output is a worthwhile safety net.

Following is a short sample C++ program that returns a document to the Web browser user. Subsequent sections will show you how to install these programs on your server and invoke them in your HTML documents.

```
// simple CGI output
#include <iostream.h>
void main()
{
    cout   << "Content-type: text/html\n" //_returning HTML
           << "Status: 200 OK\n" // indicate success of gateway
           << "\n"     // blank line indicates end of headers
           << "Order entered successfully!\n"
           << "Go back to <A HREF=\"http://ourstore.com\">"
           << "home page</A>\n"

           ;
}
```

Environment Variables

Table 2.2 documents the available environment variables. For the sake of completeness, an environment variable is a variable name and some text associated with that variable name. Each process or program in Unix, MS-DOS, Windows, or Windows NT has an *environment* associated with it, which is just a collection of environment variables. Generally there is a global environment that contains environment variables such as PATH (the list of directories to look for an executable command in) and COMSPEC (the directory for the command processor). But each program or process can be supplied with additional environment variables that are only valid for it and its child processes. Environment variables were chosen to communicate information to CGI programs, since they are a simple mechanism of communication of data to invoked programs that is available on all popular modern operating systems. I emphasize simple and available since it is hardly the most advanced. If one could assume Windows NT or Unix, one could use other techniques such as shared memory, but at the cost of the ability to write scripts that run on any platform.

Generally in gateway programs I will use the contents of environment variables to get information from the server. In C or C++ that is performed with the getenv() run-time library command, and in Perl with the $ENV associative array, but I will cover these details later in showing you how to create CGI programs in Perl and C++. Note in the previous discussion that since there is a global environment, there will be environment variables that have nothing whatsoever to do with the gateway program or the HTTP server that will nevertheless show up if we do a dump of the environment, which can be performed with the following code in Visual C++. Note that the code below, unlike most examples I present, is not portable to other platforms, due to the nonstandard _environ array. If you aren't a programmer you should still be able to understand what is going on.

```
#include <stdlib.h>
#include <iostream.h>
main()
{
    cout  << "Content-type: text/html\n" // returning HTML
          << "Status: 200 OK\n"
          << "\n";   // indicate success of gateway
    for (int i=0;_environ[i];i++)
          cout << _environ[i] << "\n";
}
```

I will present all the details of building and testing gateway programs in C++ or Perl in coming sections. Such a dump will always result in the following environment variables on Windows NT: PATH, COMSPEC, and SystemRoot. You can use the contents of these environment variables if you wish, but be aware that they aren't really related to the Web, and haven't been generated for your use by the HTTP server.

HTTP Request Headers

HTTP request headers may be supplied by the Web client, and passed through the server to be available to the gateway program you may write. Note the following statement from Table 2.2: Any header lines received from the client are placed by the server into the environment for processing by the gateway, with the header name prepended with HTTP_ as a direct pass-through.

This includes the Referer, User_Agent, and Accept headers mentioned when discussing CGI environment variables. It also includes the Charge-To, Authorization, and If-

■■■■■ **Table 2.2** CGI Environment Variables

VARIABLE	DESCRIPTION	EXAMPLE
GATEWAY_INTERFACE	CGI/version; does not vary per invocation.	CGI/1.1
PATH_INFO	Additional arguments following slash after the script name and before the question mark.	/document.htm
PATH_TRANSLATED	The translated physical path corresponding to a virtual path. Of course, doesn't exist on servers that do not provide path translation.	d:\docs\document.htm
QUERY_STRING	The arguments supplied to the gateway following the question mark. In some cases, the server may choose to send the information here on the command line as well. For safety, you may wish to have your script check the command line for information if QUERY_STRING is blank. Data from a form is placed here if the request method is GET.	arg1+arg2+arg3
REMOTE_ADDR	IP address of remote host.	192.177.42.2
REQUEST_METHOD	GET or POST. GET means that form data is placed in QUERY_STRING. POST means that it goes into standard input.	GET
SCRIPT_NAME	Name of CGI gateway program. Useful for gateway program to create URLs that reference the current program or even current site.	cgi-bin\formstor.exe
SERVER_NAME	Hostname or IP address; does not vary per invocation.	204.192.45.2
SERVER_PROTOCOL	Name and revision of format of gateway request, varies per invocation.	HTTP/1.0
SERVER_PORT	Port that Web server was accessed from. Usually 80 by default. Sometimes 443 with Netscape's secure HTTP server.	80

■■■■■■ **Table 2.2** Continued

VARIABLE	DESCRIPTION	EXAMPLE
SERVER_SOFTWARE	Name/version of server; does not vary per invocation.	HTTPS/1.0
REMOTE_HOST	The host corresponding to REMOTE_ADDR. Not set if server doesn't have this information.	http://users.host.com
REMOTE_USER	If user authentication is performed, the remote user name will be supplied here.	jdoe
AUTH_TYPE	The type of user authentication performed (if user authentication was performed before invoking your gateway).	
CONTENT_TYPE	If POST method is used to send data to our gateway, the MIME type used to send. Currently can only be: application/x-www-form-urlencoded.	application/x-www-form-urlencoded
CONTENT_LENGTH	Length of packet sent via POST method.	156
HTTP HEADERS		
HTTP_*	Any header lines received from the client are placed by the server into the environment for processing by the gateway, with the header name prepended with HTTP_ as a direct pass-through. Complete list in Table 11.3.	
HTTP_REFERER	The name of the document that links to or invokes the gateway.	http://somewhere.else.com/cool_links.html
HTTP_USER_AGENT	What Web browser the reader is using. Very useful to create pages with content conditional on what browser they are using.	Mozilla/1.1N (Windows; I; 32bit)
HTTP_ACCEPT	Type/subtype. The MIME formats the client will accept. Useful for the gateway program to determine what format to return information in.	*/*,image/gif,image/x-xbitmap,image/jpeg

Modified-Since headers mentioned in the status code table. For completeness, I should present all the HTTP request fields that you have available to you. If the header is present, that is, if it is created by the Web client, you should be able to use the contents of these headers by accessing the CGI environment variable that has the same name as the request header, prefixed with HTTP_. Also note that the CGI environment variable will also be in all caps, and hyphens (-) will be replaced with underscores (_).

Typically these headers are created by the HTTP client, the Web browser. However, you can have a gateway program generate these headers for use by another gateway program. The headers below that are almost always created by a Web browser are: User-Agent (the HTTP_USER_AGENT environment variable), Referer (the HTTP_REFERER environment variable), and Accept (the HTTP_ACCEPT environment). However, you should not assume the presence of any of the headers in your programs. That is, your programs should gracefully handle the absence of any of these variables.

For a complete and current list of request headers, see http://www.w3.org/hypertext/WWW/Protocols/HTTP/HTRQ_Headers.html.

CGI Programming in C++

Now that I've shown you what the standard is, I'd like to arm you to begin your gateway programming in C++. This section does assume knowledge of C++. If you are not a C++ developer (this book in general does not require it), you can develop gateways in Perl. The next chapter contains a variety of information that will be helpful in building gateways with Perl. This includes an introduction to the Perl language.

The HTMLForm Class

By far the most common gateway program written is one that stores information that a user has entered into a form. The tasks involved in writing this are the URL decoding previously described, parsing out the form field names and values, and storing them in some format. It also involves taking some action based upon the contents of one or more of the fields. This usually requires keeping the field names and values available in some form to the gateway program. Very often each gateway developer writes this code as a "one-off," duplicating this effort over and over.

HTMLForm is my attempt to provide a C++ class that alleviates most of the work of building a CGI gateway for processing forms. It's worth following this discussion even

████ **Table 2.3** HTTP Request Headers

HTTP Request Header	Description
From	Name of the requesting user.
Accept	List the types of output that the HTTP client will accept in response to a request. HTTP requests are generally accompanied by one or more accept directives. By default, Accept: text/plain, text/html is assumed.
Accept-Encoding	Similar to Accept, but lists the Content-Encoding types acceptable in the response.
Accept-Language	Lists the Language values preferable in the response in ISO 3316.
User-Agent	The HTTP client (the Web browser).
Referer	The URL of the page or program that refers to this gateway.
Authorization	Formats still emerging and being specified. For example, the user format: user username:password.
Charge-To	The account which will be charged (no browsers that we know of supply this header yet).
If-Modified-Since	This will have a date, and when invoked with a conditional GET, will not return the document if not modified since the supplied date.
Pragma	Used for extensions to this list. Only one pragma currently exists: no-cache. This should indicate to your program not to return any cached copy of the document the user requests. Pragma: no-cache

████

if you are going to be using ISAPI only for gateway development. With the magic of C++ inheritance, you will inherit all of the capabilities of the HTMLForm class into the ISAPIForm class. ISAPIForm provides the same high level forms processing facilities to ISAPI DLLs. I haven't covered ISAPI yet, but it's essentially a better interface for gateways than is provided with CGI. Any CGI tools developed are implemented with a view toward using them with ISAPI as well. So the HTMLForm class you learn here can be used for all of your forms processing, whether you use CGI or not.

The HTMLForm constructor reads all of the form data in from standard input, URL-decodes it, and parses the field names and values. It then takes those field names and values and stores them in an *associative array*. An associative array allows you to retrieve the contents by the named index. For example, to retrieve the array value named Quantity from the array a, you would use the following code:

```
int price = a["Quantity"];
```

This eliminates the need to have two parallel arrays, one with field names and one with values, or have an array of structures, each with a name and a value. That method also requires the C programmer to loop through all the names to find a match and then grab the associated value. Associative arrays are a great high-level way of manipulating large amounts of data and eliminating the need to write code to search for data once it's stored. The associative array feature exists in Perl, and is one reason why Perl is so popular for CGI programming.

But wait! C++ doesn't have an associative array data type, so how can you store the form's fields in such a construct? Luckily, C++ is great at creating new abstract data types, replete with operators (such as the array indexing []) and everything you would expect if the data type was part of the language. The HTMLForm class uses my associative array class, AssocArray, to store form fields for easy retrieval and manipulation. The AssocArray class is a template class, which means that it can represent any kind of data for its key or value. For representing HTMLForm objects, the AssocArray template class is instantiated to use String objects for field names and values. I won't discuss all of the AssocArray implementation here, but the full source for the class (which may be useful to you in other contexts) is in file assocarr.h, listed in the appendix of source listings.

Once the form data is in the associative array, it is easy to access any field's value by just subscripting the variable with the field name as shown above (a[Quantity]). Other natural operations one might want to perform with a form variable would be to display all of the form's contents, store the form's contents into a text file, create an HTML form that prompts for form field values, and perhaps add other name/value associations to the array. It would also be useful to be able to stream the form contents out to a C++ ostream. If the class provides these facilities we should be able to write gateway code as simple as the following:

```
#include "htmlform.h"
main()
{
```

```
CGIForm x;  //parse out the form contents from

x.Header();  // put out some header information to allow us to
⌐display other info

cout << "Ordered " << x["Quantity"] << " of product: "
⌐<< x["Product"] << "\n";

cout << "Full form contents below: \n";

x.Display(); // display all form fields

x.Store();  // store the form data into a comma separated value
⌐file
}
```

It's not important exactly what this tiny gateway program does. The point is that you can do a large amount of functionality with very little code. Note that the actual class used is CGIForm. This is because most of the necessary code is common to both CGI gateway form processing and ISAPI gateway form processing. The common code is kept in the base class HTMLForm. The class CGIForm is then used in CGI gateways and ISAPIForm is used in ISAPI Internet Server applications.

Below is the class definition for HTMLForm. This class definition can also be found in source listings appendix in the listing for htmlform.h. Notice the public interface portion of the HTMLForm class. There is the standard C++ orthodox canonical class form (functions that should be part of any class): a constructor, a destructor, a copy constructor, and an assignment operator (operator=). Discussion of good C++ programming practices is beyond the scope of this book; for a good reference on why you really should have all of these functions defined see Coplien's *Advanced C++*.

Beyond these are the interesting methods that the class provides. The most commonly used function is likely to be the array index operator (operator[]). The operator[]() functions allow a field name to be supplied inside the square brackets as either a String variable or a char * data type. Notice that this is a String variable, not an MFC variable. Using CString would bring in a very large MFC library. For some applications this might be okay. But this is meant to be general purpose for any CGI gateway, and a CGI gateway should be as lean and mean as possible. So the String variables used in this class are all based on a small String class implementation embedded in the htmlform.h file. Feel free to substitute your own String class definition for this. The AddField() functions, one taking a pair of String variables and the other taking a pair of character pointers, allow field/value associations to be added to the form variable. The Display() function display the contents of the form in HTML format. The Header() function should be called one time before using any of the other functions (currently just Display() and the stream insertion operator) that display data back to the Web browser. The Store() function stores all of the form's field values as a record appended to the end of a comma-separated-value (CSV) text file. CSV files are directly editable with Microsoft Excel and importable by most database packages, so this can be a useful lowend store for testing purposes. There is a nonmember function for stream insertion, operator<<(). This takes all of the fields in the form and sends it to an C++ ostream. Almost all streams insertion operators are nonmember functions, since the output stream itself must be the lefthand operand of the insertion operator. This set of methods should allow you to build most gateways with considerably less code.

Now for the representation: This is the set of data structures that comprises the HTMLForm object. The HTMLForm object is represented as an associative array with a String for the field name and a String as the contents of each field. This is stored in the aFields data member. The only other data member is a field called nError used to track the error state of the object.

```
class HTMLForm {
protected:
        AssocArray<String,String> aFields;
        int nError;
        int Size() {return aFields.Size();}
        int Parse(char *pszData);
        friend ostream& operator<<(ostream& os,HTMLForm& form);
public:
        HTMLForm();
        HTMLForm(AssocArray<String,String> init);
        HTMLForm(const HTMLForm& form);
        operator=(const HTMLForm& form);
        virtual HTMLForm::~HTMLForm(){}
        String operator[](const String& sFieldName);
        char *operator[](const char *pszFieldName);
        void AddField(char *pszFieldName,char *pszFieldValue);
        void AddField(const String& sFieldName,const String& sFieldValue);
        int Display(); // displays form contents on HTML page
```

```
virtual void Header();
int Store(char *pszCSVFileName); // appends field values to
⌐specified CSV file
};
```

The class definition following is for CGIForm. This is the class specifically tied to using the CGI interface. Notice that it only overrides two methods of HTMLForm: Header() and Display(). The overrides are necessary because the communication mechanism back to the Web browser with CGI is just writing to standard output and with ISAPI it is via special function calls. For all other methods, the HTMLForm class is identical for both gateway interfaces.

```
class CGIForm: public HTMLForm {
public:
     void Header()
     {
         cout << "Content-type: text/html\r\n";
             cout <<"Status: 200 OK\r\n";
         cout <<"\r\n"; // finished sending headers
     }
     int Display()
     {
             Header();
             cout << "<H1>Form Data</H1>\n";
             aFields.First();
             while (aFields.Current() ) {
                     cout << aFields.Current()->Key() << ": "
                         << (aFields.Current() )->Value() << "<p>\n";
                     ++aFields;
             }
             return 1;
     }
     CGIForm();
     ~CGIForm(){}
};
```

At this point you already have some code that should save you a lot of time in your gateway programming efforts. Chapter 5 will extend this class library to work via the new ActiveX standard for communicating with backend programs: ISAPI. This again involves just inheriting from CGIForm and overriding the Header( ) and Display( ) methods.

The source code for HTMLForm is in files htmlform.h, htmlform.cpp and assocarr.h. All of these files appear in the listings in Appendix A. They also appear on the Web page for this book: http://www.wiley.com/compbooks/.

3

GATEWAY

PROGRAMMING

IN PERL

D ue to some of the unique features of the Perl language, it is a very useful tool for building Web gateways. In fact, it's fair to say that right now it is the predominant tool used by Web gateway developers. The C++ classes I just showed you were actually inspired by Perl language features, especially the HTMLForm class's use of associative arrays, a feature very central to Perl.

This book's emphasis is certainly on the C++ developer. This is rightly so, since many of the more advanced features of the various technologies we present can only be truly leveraged in C++. Perl however has many practical strengths for CGI development (though nothing that C++ cannot do). If you feel strongly that you would not use another language, so be it. Please skip ahead to Chapter 5 where we introduce ISAPI programming.

Use of the classes shown earlier gives C++ many of the features of Perl for gateway development, evening out the usefulness of the two languages. However, there remain other reasons why Perl is a great tool for gateways. For those that are not already fluent in either Perl or C++, the learning curve is lower for the Perl language than it is for C++. Also, Perl is somewhat higher-level and Perl programs tend to be smaller than their equivalent in C++. This means that, often, Perl programs can be faster to develop and easier to maintain. For large, serious development efforts, C++ is still the tool of choice, especially since it gives the most direct access to the advanced capabilities of ActiveX presented in a later chapter. Nevertheless, a familiarity with Perl is very useful both for ad hoc small script development, for those maintaining existing Perl scripts, and for those who want to get a quick start in gateway development without learning C++ right away. The benefits of Perl as a gateway development tool carry over to the ISAPI world, since there is now an ISAPI-compliant Perl available from the developer of Windows NT Perl.

Perl is also now available for Windows NT in several forms. Among these are the Perl 5.0 included with the Microsoft Windows NT 3.51 Resource Kit. It is also available directly from the developer, hip communications, at http://www.perl.hip.com. This version of Perl can control OLE servers, making it a scripting tool for Win32 applications in general, a status previously reserved primarily for Visual Basic. The hip Web site also features a version that allows Perl scripts to be run using ISAPI.

As I traverse through Perl describing its various elegant features, you may start to think that I'm a Perl zealot. Not really: I actually do most of my Web development in C++, because C++'s capacity for abstraction is stronger. As programs get larger and larger, I find this ability to abstract out the fundamental objects in classes to be more and more important. Also, integration of third party DLLs and function libraries is more possible in C++, and when talking to other data formats that is sometimes important. Both Perl and C++ have their advantages for gateway programming. You will want to know the strengths of both tools so that you can make an informed decision about which tool to use for a given task. With that caveat out of the way, let's go on to explain how to use this very valuable tool.

An Introduction to Programming in Perl

Covering all of the capabilities and nuances of Perl is far beyond the scope of this book. What I want to do here is teach you just enough Perl to be able to modify existing Perl-based CGI gateways, and potentially write your own. Another goal is to give you a sense of the power and flexibility of the language, and in some cases its limitations, to help you to decide between Perl and C++ for various tasks in your gateway development.

An excellent book on Perl is *Programming Perl* by Larry Wall (the creator of Perl) and Randal Schwartz. Another good book, more geared to the beginning programmer, is *Learning Perl* by Randal Schwartz. As good as these books are, they really take their time in giving you the knowledge you need to program productively or modify Perl scripts. For example in *Programming Perl,* to get the overview of all of Perl's capabilities, you have to wade through an extensive set of scenarios of Job using Perl to automate his camel farming operation. While these examples are well presented and entertaining, it may at times seem to knowledgeable programmers like a slow-moving caravan across a desert of less than relevant problems. So informally I'll title this treatment "Perl for the Impatient: Mastering Perl Without the Trials of Job."

In this section, I present the significant elements of the language that you are likely to find useful and encounter in CGI scripts written by others, and bypass the more obscure portions of the language as well as in depth nuances not necessary to get your code written. Hopefully this introduction will let you be productive in Perl very quickly. If you decide you need to know everything about the language you can pick up *Programming Perl* to expand your knowledge on individual topics.

Hello, Perl

Typically we will be supplying Perl with scripts that are written and stored in files. We then invoke Perl with an argument of the file name. All programming tutorials seem to begin with printing "Hello, world!" and who are we to buck tradition? So (presuming you have installed a Perl of your choice on your system), create a file called hello.pl. Place in the file the following text:

```
print "Hello, world\n";
```

Now run the program by invoking perl hello.pl from the command line. This assumes you have made your Perl directory part of your path, which you should do anyway.

Data Types

Now let's look at the various available data types so that we can make our programs start to process data. The first example showed the most common data type used in Perl: strings. Strings enclosed in double quotes (") as shown above may have escape sequences operate on them and embedded variables will be replaced with their content. Strings inside apostrophes (') will have no substitutions done on them. Perl also has numbers in the form of integers (a string of digits with no decimal point), floating point (a string of digits containing a decimal point or in scientific notation), hex (prefixed with 0x), or octal (digits with a leading zero). Examples include:

'hello'   literal string

"hello\n"   string allowing escapes (such as \n) and variable interpolation

100   integer

100.5   floating point

Complex data types include arrays that are represented as comma delimited sequences of values or variables inside parentheses. For example:

```
(1,2,3)
```

File handles in Perl are represented as a literal or variable inside angle brackets, for example, <FILE>. Predefined file handles include <STDIN>, the input supplied to the program on the command; <STDOUT>, the output of the program; <STDERR>, the error output of the program, which always goes to the screen even if the standard output is redirected; and <ARGV>, a special file handle that combines all files mentioned on the command line. For example, in the following invocation:

```
PERL PROGRAM.PL ARG1.DAT ARG2.DAT <INPUT1.DAT >OUTPUT.DAT
```

<STDIN> contains the contents of the INPUT.DAT file. <STDOUT> writes out to OUTPUT.DAT and <STDERR> writes to the console. <ARGV> reads from ARG1. DAT until exhaused and then reads from ARG2.DAT. If input is not redirected to the program on the command line (e.g., <INPUT1.DAT), input is obtained by prompting the user.

Variables

In order to build useful programs, you'll need to use variables as well as data type literals. Variables are prefixed with a dollar sign (e.g., $var1). All data types use the same notation for variable references. The data type of the variable is determined by its contents. For example:

```
$var1=1
```

makes the $var1 variable an integer. It can become a string as quickly as it is assigned:

```
$var1="hello"
```

An array variable is referred to by prefixing the name with an at sign (@). Array items are referenced by subscripting the variable name in square brackets. The last item of an array can be accessed using the built-in value, #<arrayname>. In the following example, #array is 2, since an array is indexed beginning with zero.

```
    # simple array manipulation example - note that # begins a
comment line
    @array=(5,10,15);
    $firstitem=@array[0];
    $lastitem=@array[#array];
```

The values of an array can also be treated as a list and Perl has several functions available to operate on the array as a list, which I will present shortly. Perl has a built-in array variable called @*ARGV* that contains all of the arguments to Perl that are present on the command line.

Perl also introduces a concept known as an *associative array.* That is an array that is retrieved by supplying the value of a key rather than an index. An associative array is referred to with a variable name prefixed with %. Individual elements are accessed by including the key value inside braces (e.g., {"key"}). The contents of an associative array are specified as a list of key value pairs. For example:

```
%capitals=("Israel", "Jerusalem",
             "Egypt", "Cairo",
             "Saudi Arabia", "Riyadh");
$city=%capitals{"Egypt"};
print $city;
```

This will print out "Cairo." Perl has a built-in associative array called %*ENV* that has all of the environment variables available to the Perl program. Since environment variables play a prominent role in communicating information to CGI gateways, this is a very useful feature. The following code will retrieve the contents of the QUERY_STRING environment variable:

```
$query_string=%ENV("QUERY_STRING");
```

Special Variables

Perl has several built-in variables supplied for you which you do not need to declare or set values. some of the more important built-in variables are shown in Table 3.1.

Operators

The following operators are available in Perl to work on the data and variable types presented previously.

Numeric Operators

These operators work on numeric data types. You will want to restrict the bitwise and shift operators to work on integer data or variables. There are of course traditional arithmetic operators (+ − / *) and the modulo division remainder operator (%). Perl includes the exponentation operator (**) to raise the lefthand argument to the right-hand number power. Bitwise operators for or (|), and (&), and exclusive-OR (^), and for left and right shift (<<and>>) are also available.

Table 3.1 Perl Special Variables

Variable	Description
$_	default inout
$@	error message from last eval or do command
$ARGV	name of current file
$&	string matched by last pattern match (see pattern match section)
$'	string preceding match
$`	string following match
$+	last bracket matched by last search
$1 . . . $9	subpattern in parens from last match
@ARG	command line arguments for script
V	(not including script name)
@INC	where to look for Perl scripts (typically set by programmer)
%ENV	associative array of current set of environment variables and their values

Appending any of the preceding operators with = assigns the resulting value to the lefthand operand. For example:

```
$a=1; $a += 2; print $a;
```

This will print out 3.

There are operators to perform comparison on numeric data types: ==, !=, <, >, <=, >=, <=>. The last operator returns a number depending on whether the first operand is less than (returns −1), equal to (returns 0), or greater than (returns 1) than the second operand. The ++ and — operators take a variable as argument and increment or decrement that variable. For example, $I++ increments the variable $I.

String Operators

String operators include the period (.) operator for string concatenation, and the various string comparison operators: eq,ne,lt,gt,le,ge,cmp. Like <=>, cmp returns −1, 0, or 1 based on the comparison between the strings on the left and right side of the operator.

Functions

Perl includes many built-in functions, though not nearly as many as those of you that are C and C++ programmers may be used to. There are time functions: time, taking no arguments, returns number of seconds since January 1, 1970. Localtime( ) converts the value return by time into a nine-element array representing seconds, minutes, hour, day of month, month, year, weekday, and Julian day of year, for the local time zone. The following use is an example:

```
@ltime=localtime(time);
$wday=@ltime[6];
```

There are trig functions (sin( ), cos( ), atan2( )), logarithmic functions (exp( ), log( ), and sqrt( )), and random number generation (srand( ), rand( )). All of these functions take one argument, whose meaning is usually obvious from the purpose of the function.

There are functions to operate on strings that include a length( ) function, taking one argument and returning the number of characters in the expression. The chop( ) function takes off the last character of all elements of the supplied list, which may be just one variable. The index( ) function returns the position of the second string argument in the first string argument at or after the position specified in the optional third argument (which is the first element if left unspecified). As with all Perl strings, indices are zero-based. The substr( ) function returns the string given by an offset specified in the second argument, into the string specified in the first argument.

These can be used as in the following code:

```
$string="Hello, world.";
$indx=index($string,",");
$substring=substr($string,$indx);
print $len=length(chop $substring);
```

This will display the length of ", world" or 7.

There is also a special string function called eval( ). It evaluates the argument and executes it as if it were Perl code. An alternate form of eval is invoked as eval followed by Perl code surrounded by braces ({). If there are runtime errors the $@ variable contains the error message.

List and Array Functions

There are several functions to operate on arrays and lists. As mentioned, they are represented the same way in Perl, as array variables, but you can operate on them as either arrays, using subscripting to access individual elements or set individual elements, or setting all of the values of the array variable by setting the variable equal to a parenthesized list of values.

But there is also a set of functions that treat an array more abstractly as a list. This permits performing list-oriented operations, such as adding to the end of a list or to the beginning of a list, accessing and/or removing the first element of the list, reversing the order of the list, and sorting the list. This level of abstraction saves a lot of code from having to do all of these operations with raw arrays.

The list functions that operate on array variables are as follows (square brackets indicate optional arguments):

- **push** (@array, list)—This pushes the elements of list onto the end of @array; list can be a single item.

- **pop** (@array)—Removes and return the last (#array-th) element of the array list.

- **shift**(@array)—Removes and returns the first element of the array. For example, to process the elements of the @ARGV array successively, you would use code such as the following:

```
while (@ARGV) {
        $arg= shift @ARGV;
    # do stuff with $arg
    }
```

- **unshift**(@array,list)—Adds the elements of list, which can be a single item, to the beginning of the array.

- **splice** (@array,offset,[length],[list])—Removes elements of @array specified by offset and length and replaces them with list (if present). You will rarely use this, but it's worth noting that the other list functions can be implemented with splice().

- **reverse**(list)—Returns the list in reversed order.

- **sort** (list)—Returns the sorted list.

- **split**(pattern,expression)—Splits expression (a string variable or literal) on specified pattern into a list which is then returned.

- **join** (expr,list)—This joins all of the items in the list, separated by the value in expr, into one string, which is returned.

The following are examples of using various list operations:

```
@fruits=split(',',"apple,orange,lemon,kumquat,mango");
push(@fruits,("tangerine",'kiwi',"lime"));
$lostfruit op(@fruits);
@fruits=reverse(sort(@fruits));
$firstfruit=@fruits(#fruits);
```

The first statement splits the literal string of fruit names and puts it into the @fruits list. The second statement pushes three fruits to the end of the list, by listing the three fruits in a parenthesized literal list. Note that the use of apostrophes or quotes in that list are interchangeable. The third statement pops the last item ("lime") off the list and puts the contents into the $lostfruit variable. The list is then sorted in reverse alphabetic order with the reverse() and sort() functions. Finally the $firstfruit variable is assigned the last item of the list, "apple", using the #fruits subscript on the @fruits array.

Flow Control

Perl statements are delimited by semicolons and can be conditionally executed or repeatedly executed using a modifier such as if, unless, while, or until. For example:

```
$a=1 unless $b<>0
```

Multiple statements can be combined by surrounding them with braces. The same modifier can then precede the block of statements, and more looping modifiers are available. These include the following:

- **while** (<expression>) {<block of statements>}

  Among the statements that can be used are the **continue** statement, which will skip to the top of the loop without executing the rest of the statements in the block. Typically **continue** is executed conditionally with an **if** or **unless** statement.

- **until** (<expression>) {<block>}

- **for** (<expression>;<expression>;<expression>) {<block>}

  The **for** statement operates just like its C equivalent. The first expression is executed only once when the statement is first encountered, and is typically used to initialize variables. The second expression is used to test whether to continue the loop. The block of statements will only be executed again if it returns true. The third expression is executed after each time through the block of statements. It is typically used to increment index variables for the next pass through the loop.

- **foreach** <variable>(<array reference>) {<block>}

  This construct loops over all items in the specified <array reference>. The <variable> is used to place each element of the array into on successive iterations.

- **do** {<block>} **while**<expression>

  This will execute the block of statements while <expression> is true.

- **do** {<block>} **until** <expression>

  This will execute the block of statement until <expression> is true.

Input and Output

As stated earlier, Perl gives you several file handles for free. The most common one to use is <ARGV>. This file handle will supply all of the contents of files specified on the Perl command line successively. Another file handle is <STDIN>, which will read either from the user or from a file that is supplied to Perl as standard input. How do you read from a file handle? Just assign a variable to the input operator for the file handle (e.g., $arg=<FILEHANDLE>). Or evaluate the file handle reference by itself, as in the condition of a while loop. This will read the next line from the file and put it into the variable on the left hand side of the assignment, or just test if another line is available.

For example, the following code reads successive strings from the user until they enter a null string.

```
while ($_=<STDIN>) {
    print;
}
```

The print with no argument actually prints $_, which we have assigned to be the line supplied from standard input. The $_ variable is a special variable that is supplied by default to many operations that expect an argument or a variable to assign their result to. The operations that work with $_ include input from file handle. So the above loop can be written even shorter as:

```
while (<STDIN>) { print;}
```

Or even:

```
print while <STDIN>;
```

If the input operator is assigned to an array, an array will be built that contains the rest of the file handle contents, one line to an array item. For example, the following code will read the entire contents of all files supplied on the command line and make each line an item in @array.

```
@array=<ARGV>
```

This is often done inadvertently, and can lead to huge arrays that use up gobs of memory in places where its not anticipated or needed. On Windows NT and Unix, this will work, but your system may slow significantly as it pages to make enough virtual memory available for the full contents of all the files.

There is also a special file handle called the *null filehandle* whose notation is <>. <> reads from the files specified on the command line, if there are any present. Otherwise it reads from standard input. So, assuming that no files are supplied on the command line, we can shorten the code presented above (print while <STDIN>,) to:

```
print while <>;
```

To use the input operator on other files besides <ARGV> and <STDIN>, you should open the file with:

```
open(filehandle, filename);
```

If filename is not specified, it is obtained from a variable named $filehandle (whatever the filehandle name may be). Prefixing the filename (either in the variable contents or in the open statement) with a greater than sign (>) opens a file for output. Placing two greater than signs (>>) in front of the name opens the file for append. For example the following code opens a log file to add information to it.

```
$LOG=">>RESULTS.LOG";
open(LOG);
```

Output can be written to an output filehandle with any of the following commands:

- **print**(filehandle, list)

  If the filehandle is not specified, then STDOUT is used by default.

- **printf**(filehandle, list)

  This assumes that the first element of the list is a C printf style format string, and allows you to create more formatted output. For example:

  ```
  open(OUT,">OUTPUT.TXT");
  @list=('Value in hex is: %x');
  push(@array,16);
  printf(OUT,@list);
  ```

  The %x flag prints out a digit in hexadecimal format. For details of the available C printf format flags see any C manual.

- **write**(filehandle)

  Writes out a formatted record. The format is set for a filehandle with the format statement.

  ```
  format <filehandle>=<formlist>
  ```

  <filehandle> specifies which filehandle the format statement affects. If unspecified, it applies to STDOUT. <formlist> consists of a sequence of picture lines to format the output, and argument lines, which supply values or variables to insert into the previous picture line. As in other Perl code, comment lines can be created beginning with #. The picture line will contain multiple @ codes, one for each value to be placed on the line. The @ code will be followed by a

number of justification characters, the number of which determines the width of the field. Less than (<) indicates left justification, vertical bar (|) indicates centering, and greater than (>) indicates right justification. A sample format statement is:

```
format STDOUT =
@<<<<<<<<<<<<<<<< @<<<<<<<<<<<<<< @<<<<<<< @>> @>>>>>> @>>>>>>>>>>
$name,          $address,       $city,   $st,$zip,  $phone
```

Note that since STDOUT was the default its presence was not necessary in the format statement above.

Pattern Matching

Perl's pattern matching capabilities for searching, text substitution, parsing input formats, and translation are one of its greatest strengths. You can write a parser for any text oriented file format with a small fraction of the code that it would require in C or C++.

Perl incorporates all of the regular expression-based pattern-matching and substitution capabilities that are present in various Unix tools such as awk, flex, sed, and vi. Among the regular expressions available are:

.	any character
[a–z]	any character of set
[^a–z]	any character not in set
\d	digit
\D	nondigit
\w	alphanumeric
\W	nonalphanumeric
\s	whitespace
\S	nonwhitespace
\n	newline (any C backslash escape sequence is valid)
\t	tab
\0	null
\nnn	ASCII character of octal value

\xnn	ASCII character of hex value
\<character>	character itself (e.g., \(is left paren, \. is period)
(pattern)	any parenthesized portion of expression saved to be referred to later with $n, where n is order of subexpression in overall pattern
x?	0 or 1 x's
x*	0 or more x's
x+	1 or more x's
this|that	matches first pattern or second pattern
\b	word boundary
\B	nonword boundary
^	beginning of line
$	end of line

There are two pattern-matching operators: the matching operator, m//, which can also be invoked with just //, and the substitution operator, s///. The matching operator lets you test for matches to a regular expression, and if the match occurs, put matching parenthesized subexpressions into variables (number $1 through $n, where n is the order of the subexpression) known as *backreferences* that you can then access and manipulate. The matching operator can be invoked with the expression to be searched followed by the =~ operator followed by the matching operator (with or without the preceding m). If operating on the $_ default variable the =~ is unnecessary (as is the default variable itself).

For example, the following code matches the $_ variable containing an email address:

```
if ( /(\w*)@([a-z\.]+)/ )
{
     $user=$1;
     $domain=$2;
}
```

This expression will match any string with alphanumerics followed by an at (@) sign followed by a sequence of letters or periods (the \. specifies the literal period). The expression returns true or false depending on whether the pattern is matched in the $_ variable. The block within the if will only be executed if the pattern is matched. The backreferences are assigned in the order the parentheses are encountered. For example, if $_ contains "webmaster@www.ourstore.com", $1 is "webmaster" and $2 is "www.ourstore.com."

The replacement operator works very similarly except that an additional pattern is specified after the second slash (/), which is to be used to replace the matching pattern in the original expression. If we wanted to parse out the name and domain of the email address and create a string containing them, the following code would suffice:

```
$string ~=s/(\w*)@([a-z\.]+)/Name: $1, Domain: $2/g;
```

This will replace all strings in $string matching the pattern inside the first pair of slashes with the text between the second and third slash, and the trailing g will make it do so globally across $string's contents.

Subroutines

Perl creates subroutines with a sub keyword followed by the name of the subroutine followed by the block of statements enclosed in braces. In naming your subroutines and trying to avoid naming conflicts, remember that Perl reserved words are lowercase and that identifiers in Perl are case-sensitive. For example:

```
# prints contents of filename specified in $_ to stdout
sub  print_file_contents
{
    open (INPUT,$_);
    # note that we don't use $_ default so we leave $_ intact
    while ($arg=<INPUT>)
    {
        print $arg;
    }
}
```

To invoke a subroutine, just supply the subroutine name prefixed with an ampersand (&). For example, &print_file_contents would display the contents of the file specified in the $_ variable. You can also call subroutines with the do command but this is less common.

To pass arguments to subroutines by value, make a local copy of the arguments. You should assign the argument list variable, @_, containing the list of actual arguments, to a list of variables representing the formal parameters using the local function. For example, the local statement in the following source assigns the arguments from the call to the $src and $dest variables:

```perl
sub file_copy
{
    local($src,$dest)=@_;
    open(SRC,$src);
    open(DEST,">".$dest);
    while (<SRC>)
    {
        print DEST $_ ;
    }
    close SRC;
    close DEST;
}
```

Call-by-value arguments only allow the use of the values locally in the procedure. If you want the ability to modify the arguments that you pass, you will need to call by name. The exact way that Perl does this is slightly different than call-by-reference, which Perl also supports, but the use of true call-by-reference is deprecated in Perl. I would not even explain call by name, except that you will often see it in some of the more popular publicly available Perl code. I actually recommend avoiding the technique as much as possible in your own programs.

Call-by-name is performed by assigning the argument list (@_) to a *type glob,* which is an asterisk (*) followed by a name. The type glob can than be referenced later in the subroutine with an at sign (@) followed by the name. For example, the following subroutine removes all trailing whitespace from the supplied argument, which is passed by name with the code local(*arg)=@_:

```perl
# removes all trailing whitespace
sub rtrim
{
```

```
        local(*arg) = @_;
        while ($arg~=/.*\s/)
            chop $arg;
    }
```

This function is invoked by passing the name of the variable used to the rtrim subroutine. The name is passed by supplying an asterisk preceding the variable to the subroutine call:

```
$x="a string with trailing whitespace    ";
&rtrim(*x);
print $x." chopped.\n";
```

In order to successfully reuse subroutines (which is the main purpose of writing them), we will need to have some way of including them from existing files. This mechanism is the Perl require statement, which takes an argument of a filename, and then executes all of the code found in the specified file. In that sense, it's very similar to the eval statement except that it works on a filename rather than a literal string, and is smart enough not to execute code that has been required earlier. For example, if you include the previous subroutine and other related ones into a set of string subroutines, you could use them in other programs with the statement:

```
require "string.pl";
```

Perl has even more sophisticated tools for reuse and abstraction: *packages*. Packages provide a separate namespace for variables. Packages are created by simply invoking the package statement with the package name, as in:

```
package string_handling;
```

This provides a rudimentary form of data hiding: the variables associated with a package are not accessible to other routines unless they explicitly set their package to string_handling (which of course they shouldn't do). It also provides a tool that helps in building abstract data types, or that overused term *objects*. That is, building a related set of routines that all operate on the same data. The data is hidden from outside code (that is, well-behaved outside code), and is accessible only through the defined set of routines, usually called *methods*. The subroutines may each invoke the package statement, or be in a file with the package statement at the top. Data shared among package routines are referenced as if it was global data. This falls short of the protection mechanisms available in most object-oriented programming languages: you can't actually package all of the data into its own explicit object, and invoke the methods on the object directly. But it has more support for abstraction and reusability than you would expect in a scripting-oriented language.

Perl as an OLE Automation Controller

Windows NT Perl 5.001 as released on the Microsoft Windows NT Resource Kit allows Perl to control and utilize OLE Automation servers. This warrants extensive coverage here, since you will not find this documented in any other books at this point. If you aren't running Windows NT, you may want to skip on to the next section, since everything we discuss here is specific to this product and to Windows NT.

OLE Automation is the method under Microsoft's OLE 2.0 specification of a program exposing a set of capabilities (which might also be called methods) to other programs. I am definitely not going to try to describe OLE here, a task far beyond the scope of this subject. However, you should know that all Microsoft desktop applications, and a large and growing set of applications from other vendors are OLE automation servers. They expose capabilities that can be used by other programs and applications, including programs that you write. This means that you can write programs that, for example, grab information from Excel or Access through the OLE automation interfaces exposed by those programs. OLE automation controllers that do this can be written very easily in Visual Basic and Excel, and with a bit more work in Visual C++.

But as you've been reading this section, you may have started to like Perl for many scripting-like applications—a category that controlling an OLE automation server would probably fall into. Wouldn't it be great if Perl could be an OLE automation controller? Well, with NT Perl 5.001 for NT, this is now possible. In fact, NT Perl ships out of the box with Perl packages to control Excel, Word Basic, and Netscape. The Word Basic and Excel packages are particularly relevant. You could use the Excel package to grab selected parts of an Excel spreadsheet that is updated frequently and dump the contents to a Web page.

These Perl packages are created by a script called MkOLEx.BAT. MkOLEx can be supplied with just the object class of an OLE automation server that has been installed on your NT system, or with a type library. What does that mean? Well, the *object class* is the name of the class associated with the particular OLE automation server whose services you wish to access, such as Word.Basic or Excel.Application.

How do you find this out? Typically it can be found in your product documentation, but you can also use the Registry Editor to find it. In your \WINNT\SYSTEM32 directory is a program called REGEDT32.EXE. Invoke this program and you'll be surfing the NT registry. You'll want to use the *Windows NT Resource Kit,* or Richter's *Advanced Windows,* or another Windows NT-oriented book to understand all aspects of the registry. For now, to find the class name of the application which you want to control from Perl, go to the HKEY_CLASSES_ROOT portion of the registry (using the Window command if necessary). Scroll down past all of the extensions listed (e.g., .ASC, .AVI, etc.). Then you'll see a bunch of class names that correspond to your applications with OLE automation interfaces. For example, if you have Microsoft Office installed, you'll see Access.Database.2, Excel.Application, and Word.Basic. You can run MkOLEx.BAT and supply it with any of the names of the classes in the registry, and it will determine the methods available for that program and create a Perl package that exposes the capabilities of that automation server. At the same time it creates an HTML document that describes the available methods of the package.

MkOLEx can also create Perl packages from type libraries. In this case, if you're not familiar with what that means, you probably can't use one. A type library is a file (typically with a .TLB extension, although groups of type libraries can appear in .OLB files) containing information about the methods and properties available for a class object. Most commercial software that provides an OLE automation server interface still does not ship with type libraries. Once installed, however, the information that MkOLEx needs is available in the registry, and the script can then be run with the class name as described. When would you use a type library? Possibly on your own OLE automation servers, if you wanted to make manual changes to the .TLB files rather than the registry, and then quickly regenerate the Perl packages to correspond with this.

MkOLEx does not support every type of method, property, or parameter. However, it graciously reports those methods and properties that it cannot convert. MkOLEx is a very exciting capability: giving Perl the ability to control any OLE automation server. This truly opens up the door to access to all types of information from your Web server, without the necessity of writing a full-fledged special-purpose gateway program for each type of data you need to access. Now, when you encounter a new type of data that you need to make available, possibly dynamically, on your Web server, you can ask: Is there an OLE automation server that can provide this data? If so you can use NT Perl to serve that data directly to your Web clients.

A Perl Script for Web Form Data Collection

Collecting data from Web forms requires a fair amount of parsing through the submitted data, breaking it into field names and values, and then URL-decoding the values. This is a fairly significant amount of code in either C, C++, or Visual Basic. Due to Perl's pattern-matching and associative array capabilities, it's very little Perl code. Here is the code to read the data from standard input (which assumes the POST method in the HTML form action):

```
read(STDIN, $buffer, $ENV{'CONTENT_LENGTH'});
# Split the name-value pairs
@pairs = split(/&/, $buffer);
foreach $pair (@pairs){
        ($name, $value) = split (/=/, $pair);
        $value =~ tr/+//;
        $value =~ s/%([a-fA-F0-9] [a-fA-F0-9])/
                pack("C", hex($1))/eg;
        $form{$name}=$value;
}
```

At the end of this code, the %form associative array will contain all of the field values. The value of a particular field can be retrieved with $form{<fieldname>}. For example, to retrieve the product cost, use $form{'Cost'}. If you wish to store the data as a single record, to a comma-separated value (CSV) file, here's the code to do that:

```
open(ORDERS, ">>orders.csv");
foreach $value (sort values (%form))
```

```
        print ORDERS $value, ",";
    print ORDERS "\n"
```

Although HTML form writing is beyond the scope of this book, just for completeness here's how this would be embedded into an HTML form (assuming that Perl script mapping has been performed on the server):

```
<FORM ACTION="store.pl">
<PRE>
<INPUT NAME="Product">
<INPUT NAME="PartNo">
<INPUT NAME="Cost">
<INPUT TYPE="submit">
</PRE>
</FORM>
```

A Perl Package for Web Programming

At this point, in keeping with the theme of the rest of the book, I would develop and present a class library for Perl Web programming. In fact, there is little point in doing this myself since there is already an excellent one available as freeware: Lincoln Stein's CGI.pm. This is a *package* (Perl's term for a class or collection of related routines that operate on the same data) of routines that automates both generation of HTML and retrieving information from HTML forms. It uses the latest Perl standard and is a well-thought-out effort to create an object-oriented reusable library of routines for various HTML tasks. To use it install the CGI.PM file in your Perl library path, and include use CGI at the top of your script.

Creating HTML Forms

You will normally begin outputting your form with the header call, which will generate "Content-type: text/html:"

```
print $query->header ;
```

The next call you will usually make in displaying a form is to create an HTML document template with start_html, of which the first argument is the title of the document, the second argument is the author of the document, and the third argument is 'true' or 'false' and controls whether a BASE element is created that allows relative addresses to be converted to absolute addresses:

```
print $query->start_html('Order
Form','webmaster@ourstore.com','true');
```

This will generate an HTML document that looks something like this:

```
<HTML><HEAD><TITLE>Order Form</TITLE>
<LINK REV=MADE HREF="mailto:webmaster@ourstore.com">
<BASE HREF="http://www.ourstore.com:80">
</HEAD><BODY>
```

The startform call generates a <FORM> tag. It takes arguments of the FORM method (GET or POST with default of POST) and the form action, which defaults to none. Since you will almost always want something to be done with your data, you shouldn't rely on the default of no action (though Lincoln Stein's example script does invoke startform with no arguments):

```
print $query->startform('GET','cgi-bin/formstor.exe');
```

There are methods to generate each field type: textfield, checkbox, textarea, radio_group, popup_menu, scrolling_list. Text input fields are created with the textfield call. The first argument is the name of the field. The second argument is the initial default value of the field. The third optional argument is the size of the field in characters. The fourth optional argument is the maximum number of characters the field will accept:

```
print $query->textfield('Part Number','123-001',40,80);
```

The textarea call is identical but the third and fourth argument specify the number of rows and columns:

```
print $query->textarea('Part Number','123-001',5,40);
```

The package also lets you create menus with the popup_menu call. The first argument names the menu, the second argument is an array reference with the available selections, and the optional last argument indicates the default choice:

```
    print $query->popup_menu('Credit
Card',['Visa','MasterCard','Amex'],'Visa');
```

You can create multiple select lists with the scrolling_list call. The first argument is the field name, the second argument is the list of possible choices, the optional third argument is a list of selected items (or single selected item), the optional fourth argument is the size of the list, and the last argument enables multiple selection (it should be 'TRUE' if you wish to select multiple items):

```
    print $query->scrolling_list('Toppings',
['pepperoni','mushrooms','sausage',green peppers','hot peppers','onions',
 ⌐'anchovies'],
['pepperoni','mushrooms'],7,'true');
```

An individual checkbox can be created with the checkbox call. The first argument specifies the checkbox name. The second argument indicates whether the checkbox is on by default. The third argument indicates the value that is set if the checkbox is on. The last argument is the label used to prompt the user, which is just the checkbox name if not supplied:

```
    print $query->checkbox('Mailing List','checked','ON','Would you
like to be on our mailing list');
```

You can create a group of checkboxes with the checkbox_group call. The scrolling_list pizza topping example above translates to the following for a checkbox group. The first argument is the field name. The second argument is the list of checkbox values. The optional third argument is the list of checkboxes that are selected (default is none). The optional fourth argument is 'TRUE' if you wish line breaks to appear between the boxes (defaults to no line breaks). The optional fifth argument is an associative array that relates the checkbox values to labels for display to the user (defaults to labeling with the values themselves):

```
    print $query->checkbox_group('Toppings',
['pepperoni','mushrooms','sausage','green peppers','hot peppers','onions',
 ⌐'anchovies'],
['pepperoni','mushrooms'],'true');
```

Radio button groups can be created with the radio_group call, which has the same calling convention as the checkbox_group, with the exception that the third argument can only have one item selected:

```
    print $query->radio_group('Credit
Card',['Visa','MasterCard','Amex'],
'Visa','true');
```

Your form should include one submit field, which will generate a submit button. It has optional arguments for the button label and a value that can be submitted to the form processing script.

```
    print $query->submit('Order');
```

Processing HTML Forms

CGI.pm supports processing user responses from HTML forms. To begin processing a form, create a CGI form object with the new method in your Perl script that you create to process a form:

```
$query = new CGI;
```

$query will then contain the contents of the form filled out by the user. The names of the fields can be retrieved with the $query->param method:

```
@fieldname = $query->param;
```

Individual field values can be retrieved by supplying the param method with a field name:

```
$emailaddr = $query->param('Email Address');
```

Field values can be set with by supplying the param call with additional parameters:

```
$query->param('Total amount',$totamt);
```

You can save the state of a form to a file with the save method:

```
$FORMSTORE='ORDER.TXT';
$query->save(FORMSTORE);
```

The values can be retrieved from the file with the new method:

```
$query->new(FORMSTORE);
```

An Example Form

Following is an example that uses most of the major calls of the library:

```perl
use CGI;
$query = new CGI;
print $query->header;
print $query->start_html("Order Form");
print $query->startform('GET','FORMSTOR.EXE');
print $query->textfield('Name')
print $query->checkbox('Ship Overnight?');
print $query->submit('Order');
print $query->endform;
foreach $key ($query->param) {
        print "Field Name: $key, Value: ";
        @values = $query->param($key);
        print join(", ",@values),"<BR>\n";
}
print $query->end_html;
```

CGI.pm is presented in Appendix A in its entirety. Current versions can be retrieved at http://www-genome.wi.mit.edu/ftp/pub/software/WWW/cgi_docs.html.

Perl is an excellent tool for developing CGI gateways. Nevertheless, there are significant problems with CGI as a standard for developing gateways. In the next chapter I will show you how the ISAPI standard addresses these problems. You can still use Perl in the ISAPI world (though some capabilities will require the use of C++), so this background has not been wasted.

Specifically, the preeminent Windows NT implementation is from hip communications at http://www.perl.hip.com (this is also the version that ships with the Windows NT Resource Kit). Located on the hip Web site is an ISAPI DLL version of their Perl implementation, that will let us take advantage of the cool capabilities of ISAPI presented in the next chapter.

4

THE ACTIVEX SERVER FRAMEWORK: THE ISAPI SPECIFICATION

Microsoft's new Internet Information Server product (also known as Gibraltar) introduces several new capabilities to the Web development world, most of them stemming from a new interface to external programs known as the Internet Services API (ISAPI). ISAPI is a more efficient, robust protocol for server-to-gateway program communication. The Common Gateway Interface certainly allows you to build scripts and programs that receive and transmit information to and from Web servers. CGI provides a minimal, portable interface between an HTTP server and an external application that is functional and usable as long as there are not too many simultaneous invocations of the program, and the data communication needs are modest. But there are major problems with CGI that ISAPI was specifically designed to address.

Problems with CGI

Among the problems with CGI are:

- Lack of support for many external program development tools, operating systems, and environments

- The data transfer method is not robust or efficient even when supported by the development tool
- Unnecessarily low-level interface to common facilities
- Scalability

CGI transmits data from the server and indirectly from the user's Web browser to the standalone external gateway program in two ways: environment variables and the program's standard input. The external program transmits data back to the server primarily with standard output.

One problem with this is that an application may not have the concept of *standard input* and *standard output*. Windows programs do not have these *automatic file handles*. Thus, Visual Basic programmers cannot generate CGI programs directly. Individual Web application developers and Web server vendors attempted to address this problem by modifying the CGI interface slightly, or providing a CGI-compliant *wrapper*. For example, the O'Reilly WebSite Web server provides an interface they call WinCGI. It takes all of its input from a particular named file on disk, and sends output to another file. However, this is even worse than CGI from a system overhead perspective. Not only is one creating an entirely new process each time a file is executed, but one is also creating intermediate files, and reading from them in the WinCGI program, each time the gateway program is executed. Invoking several copies of a WinCGI gateway has even greater scalability problems than conventional CGI gateways.

Data is transferred to CGI programs through standard input and through a host of different environment variables (as presented in Chapter 3). Of course, this is an inherently fragile mechanism. The environment in DOS, Windows, Windows NT, and OS/2 is of limited size. This means, for example, if there is too much data passed from the server to the gateway program using the GET method (which passes data via the QUERY_STRING environment variable), it can easily fail if there is too much data.

Finally, the CGI standard forces developers to memorize all of the environment variables that are relevant to gateway processing. For example, as a developer you may need to use the CONTENT_LENGTH environment variable, the QUERY_STRING environment variable, and others. But these are all related (to determining the data coming in from a form). They are also always in text form even if, as with CONTENT_LENGTH, they are numeric data. Why not put them all together in a single structure with structure members of the correct datatype? The programming interface for CGI is needlessly indirect.

Finally, and most importantly, CGI does not scale to high levels of simultaneous transactions. Firing off an entire separate program or process each time a user clicks on the Purchase button of an HTML order form is the online equivalent of a large discount warehouse packed with customers, waiting in line at a single cash register. The Web server may be able to handle up to hundreds of simultaneous order program invocations, but certainly won't be able to handle thousands of them. What would be better is some way to have each gateway program or server application be just a separate thread that runs in the process space of the Web server. This creates much less overhead for the gateway, no more than a function call.

ISAPI Architecture

The ISAPI standard addresses each of the previous limitations. Instead of having the HTTP server call each gateway as a separate process, it calls them as DLLs that run within the same process space, as shown in Figure 4.1.

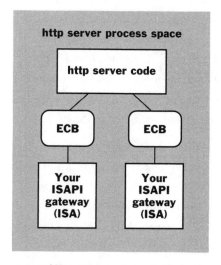

▰▰▰▰▰▰ **Figure 4.1** ISAPI architecture.

Communication with the gateway application, now referred to as Internet Server Applications (ISAs), in deference to their now more robust capabilities, is via Extension Control Blocks (ECBs), rather than via environment variables. There is also no reading from standard input to get supplied data. This is also supplied in the Extension Control Block. Communication back to the server is not performed by just writing to standard output any more. It is done via support functions callable from the ECB. Using the ISAPI architecture, ISAs will work on any Win32 operating system, although the standard is open enough to be used on other platforms. Process Software (who helped to formulate the ISAPI specification) has vowed to make ISAPI available on their Unix-based Web servers.

Having ISAs run within the HTTP server process space, with the overhead of merely a thread creation call, makes ISAs scale to a degree impossible via the one process per invocation CGI model. There are some additional programming burdens that come with writing ISAs. First of all they must be multithread-safe. See any book on Win32 programming (e.g., Richter's Advanced Windows) for details on how to do this. More seriously, there is a higher level of trust and verification that must take place to run ISAs on a server. An ISAPI DLL that crashes can take down the whole server. This is a limitation that should not be minimized. It means that for some purposes you may still want use CGI-based gateways. For example, an Internet Service Provider (ISP) or Web hosting service would probably only allow their users to run CGI programs. Even in an internal corporate setting, if Web servers are centralized, and departments rent space for pages and scripts, allowing use of only CGI programs may be appropriate. This was one of the reasons I went into such detail on CGI in general, and particularly Perl scripts for CGI development. However, in most cases, the huge advantages of scalability, more robust interface, and ease of programming do outweigh the negatives of potential for server crashes with insufficiently tested ISAs.

Before we go much further in discussing ISAPI, let's address the issue of what to call these cool ISAPI programs. The preferred term is ISA, for Internet Server Application. However, they are referred to in Microsoft product literature by many different names. Visual C++'s documentation on MFC ISAPI support calls them *ISAPI Extensions*. So many programmers whose introduction to ISAPI is via the MFC classes refer to ISAs as ISAPI Extensions or sometimes just *extensions*. Others refer to ISAs as *ISAPI DLLs*, and indeed this can be a very descriptive term that indicates the difference between ISAs and CGI programs: The ISAPI version is a DLL, and the CGI version is a separate executable program. (I will often call an ISA an ISAPI DLL when comparing it with a CGI version of some utility or application.) Even the ActiveX SDK occasionally refers to ISAs as *Internet Web Server Applications,* instead of ISA.

Since this is a book on ActiveX and programming with this new set of standards, I will tend towards the term used most often in the ActiveX SDK: Internet Server Application. However, when comparing ISAs to other technologies, or when discussing utilities and class libraries to assist in creating ISAs, I may use other terms. For example, since MFC refers to ISAs as ISAPI Extensions, I'll use that term there.

Let's now go on to describe the programming interface you need to use to write your own ISAs.

ISAPI Programming Interface

The ISAPI programming interface requires writing just two main functions: GetExtensionVersion() and HttpExtensionProc(). GetExtensionVersion() merely requires providing some version information. It is called by the HTTP server (Internet Information Server) when the ISA is first loaded.

GetExtensionVersion() takes one argument of type HSE_VERSION_INFO. It populates this structure with both a major and minor version number and a text description of the ISA. The return of the function is BOOL, which means that unless you have some catastrophic failure in your code, you should return TRUE from the function. Here is the typical code for the function:

```
BOOL WINAPI GetExtensionVersion (HSE_VERSION_INFO *pVersionInfo)
{
    pVersionInfo->dwExtensionVersion =
            MAKELONG (HSE_VERSION_MINOR, HSE_VERSION_MAJOR);
    lstrcpyn ((LPTSTR) pVersionInfo->lpszExtensionDesc,
            TEXT("MYISA - Does cool stuff"),
            HSE_MAX_EXT_DLL_NAME_LEN);
    return TRUE;
}
```

The other call, HttpExtensionProc( ), is called on each invocation of your ISA. It is where most of the work in your ISA will probably be performed. HttpExtensionProc( ) takes one argument, a pointer to an EXTENSION_CONTROL_BLOCK. The extension control block is a way to rationalize the interface between the HTTP server (IIS) and the supporting backend application (what one would have once called a gateway). Instead of using the environment and the backend application's standard input, all of the information that the ISA needs is stored (or pointed to) by members of the extension control block structure. The important fields (the ones you are likely to actually use) of this structure are presented in Table 4.1. The table includes the CGI equivalents of each variable called out prominently. This should help your efforts to port CGI scripts to ISAPI. It also allows you to refer back to Table 2.2 and accompanying text for full descriptions of the purposes of each variable. The full definition of this structure is in the HttpExt.h file in the \INETSDK\INCLUDE directory installed by the ActiveX SDK.

Notice that there are four members of this structure that are functions, not data fields. These functions are actually members of the structure, so they are invoked by referencing the ECB variable (e.g., pECB->WriteClient (pECB->ConnID, (PVOID) lpsz, &dwBytesWritten, 0);)

WriteClient( ) is used to communicate information back to the browser. The specific syntax of the call is:

```
BOOL WriteClient(
    HCONN hConn,
    LPVOID lpvBuffer,
    LPDWORD lpdwSizeofBuffer,
    DWORD dwReserved
    );
```

where hConn is the connection ID, lpvBuffer is the string you want to write back, lpdwSizeofBuffer is a pointer to a DWORD that contains the length of the buffer (strlen(lpvBuffr)) going into the call, and the amount written coming out. The value should obviously not change, and it's not really clear what you would do to handle the value being different. You could try another WriteClient( ) with an offset into lpvBuffer of the changed value pointed to by lpdwSizeofBuffer, but it's not clear that this would work. Other things are probably bad if you have gotten this error.

Table 4.1 ISAPI Extension Control Block Fields

Field	Input/Output	CGI Equivalent	Description
cbSize	input		Size of structure
connID	input		Unique ID assigned by HTTP server. The connection ID is used by the ISAPI WriteClient() and ServerSupportFunction() calls to communicate back to the client.
dwVersion	input	GATEWAY_INTERFACE	HIWORD has major version, LOWORD minor
lpszMethod	input	REQUEST_METHOD	Typically GET or POST
lpszQueryString	input	QUERY_STRING	Contains the supplied data if and only if the method was GET
lpszPathInfo	input	PATH_INFO	Optional extra path information (alternate way of supplying arguments) supplied by client
lpszPathTranslated	input	PATH_TRANSLATED	The translated physical path of the URL of this ISAPI DLL
cbTotalBytes	input	CONTENT_LENGTH	Number of bytes of data to be retrieved from client
cbAvailable	input		If less than cbTotalBytes, then successive ReadClient() calls are required
lpbData	input		The data that we are going to be operating on! Points to buffer of size cbAvailable. Used in lieu of standard input.
lpszContentType	input	CONTENT_TYPE	Usually set to application/x-www-form-urlencoded.
dwHttpStatusCode	output		Set to the CGI status code. Refer to Table 3.1 for CGI error and status codes.
lpszLogData	output		Null-terminated string that is placed in HTTP server log.
WriteClient()	output		Function used to communicate information back to client (no longer just write to standard output as in CGI).
ServerSupportFunction()	output		General purpose function (controlled with flag variable) used to communicate information back to server
ReadClient	input		Used to read additional data from server when cbAvailable<cbTotalBytes
GetServerVariable()	input		Gets values of other CGI environment variables not presented in this structure. See Table 3.2 for full listing of CGI variables

ServerSupportFunction( ) communicates data back to the server, using different request codes for different functions. The prototype of the call is

```
BOOL ServerSupportFunction(
    HCONN hConn,
    DWORD dwHSERequest,
    LPVOID lpvBuffer,
    LPDWORD lpdwSizeofBuffer,
    LPDWORD lpdwDataType
);
```

The dwHSERequest argument contains a flag with instructions to the server. The available flags are shown in Table 4.2.

ReadClient( ) is used to read additional data from the client if the number of bytes available (cbAvailable) is less than the number of total bytes (cbTotalBytes).

■■■■■■ **Table 4.2** Server Support Function Flags

Flag	Description
HSE_REQ_SEND_URL_DIRECT_RESP	Send redirect message to client to URL specified in lpvBuffer.
HSE_REQ_SEND_URL	Pass back the data specified by URL in lpvBuffer. Must be a URL local to server (no hostname specified).
HSE_REQ_SEND_RESPONSE_HEADER	Send server response headers back to client. Automatically sends back server status. Your app should add headers such as content type and length. Can be used to change URL by sending back URL: header. Terminate headers with extra \r\n.
HSE_REQ_MAP_URL_TO_PATH	Request that server perform logical to physical path mapping for logical path specified as null terminated string in lpvBuffer. Physical path returned in lpvBuffer. LpdwSizeofBuffer contains allocated size of lpvBuffer (not length of logical path passed in!) on input and on return contains size of physical path placed in lpvBuffer. A very strange interface indeed.
HSE_REQ_DONE_WITH_SESSION	Finishes up session specified by prior return from HttpExtensionProc( ) of HSE_STATUS_PENDING. LpvBuffer ignored in this case.

```
BOOL ReadClient(
    HCONN hConn,
    LPVOID lpvBuffer,
    LPDWORD lpdwSize
);
```

lpvBuffer contains the data read from the client. lpdwSize contains number of bytes allocated for lpvBuffer on input, and number of bytes written to lpvBuffer when returned.

GetServerVariable( ) is used to retrieve the value of other CGI variables besides those directly available in the extension control block structure. The full list of CGI variables is presented in Table 4.2.

```
BOOL WINAPI GetServerVariable(
    HCONN hConn,
    LPSTR lpszVariableName,
    LPVOID lpvBuffer,
    LPDWORD lpdwSizeofBuffer
);
```

lpszVariableName is the variable name of the CGI environment variable. lpvBuffer contains the value returned. The DWORD pointed to by lpdwSizeofBuffer should be set by you before the call to the size allocated for lpvBuffer.

The typical ISA that processes data from the user has the following format. lpszMethod is checked to see if the data is in lpbData or lpszQueryString. The ISA then processes data from either field. It uses the connID field to communicate back with the client, sending back data or just status information. When it has done its work, it should set an appropriate status code in dwHttpStatusCode. This is important to mention since almost none of the supplied ISAPI samples set this field before returning. When complete, the ISA should set one of the following return values: HSE_STATUS_SUCCESS, HSE_STATUS_SUCCESS_AND_KEEP_CONN, HSE_STATUS_PENDING, or HSE_STATUS_ERROR. The return should usually be HSE_STATUS_SUCCESS or HSE_STATUS_ERROR. HSE_STATUS_SUCCESS_AND_KEEP_CONN should only be called if the ISA has sent back a keep-alive header back to the client. HSE_STATUS_PENDING implies that the ISA is still working, and will notify the server when completed by calling ServerSupportFunction( ) with the HSE_REQ_DONE_WITH_SESSION error.

So, given this information, what should your ISA do when it encounters an unrecoverable error (let's say a poorly formatted client request)? It should actually do three different things. It should call ServerSupportFunction to let the server know that an error occurred. It should set the status code in the extension control block structure. And it should return HSE_STATUS_ERROR. Very few (if any) of the ISAPI sample do all three, so I think it's worth emphasizing here. The code below shows an example of these three actions being taken when an error occurs.

```
pECB->ServerSupportFunction(pECB->ConnID,

HSE_REQ_SEND_RESPONSE_HEADER,

(LPDWORD) "400 Bad Request",

        NULL, (LPDWORD) "Poorly formatted request\r\n\r\n");

pECB->dwHttpStatusCode=400;

return HSE_STATUS_ERROR;
```

That covers writing the required GetExtensionVersion() and HttpExtensionProc() functions. You can also write a DllMain() function to provide initialization code if your application requires it. This is not often done, since CGI had no such initialization mechanism built-in (it was in effect stateless). It is useful to know that this capability exists. An example where this could be quite useful is to establish a session with a database on initialization, store the session handle in a variable, and then use the session handle on each ISA invocation (within HttpExtensionProc()). Note that the Internet Database Connector described earlier does *not* do this, but it would be a very useful enhancement. Another sample initialization task might be to set up the event logging that your application will perform with the RegisterEventSource() call.

The full extension control block structure definition and prototypes for all functions are presented in the file HTTPEXT.H in the INCLUDE subdirectory of the ActiveX SDK (generally installed to \INETSDK by default).

Using ISAs

How does embedding Internet Server Applications into your HTML pages compare with what is necessary for CGI programs? The invocation process is exactly the same. You will incorporate a reference to the ISAPI DLL in your HTML just as you did with the CGI programs presented earlier: as the ACTION attribute of a FORM tag (<FORM ACTION="/scripts/sendform.dll">), or as the destination of a hyperlink specified as <A HREF="/scripts/foobar.dll">. The only noticeable difference is the .dll extension instead of the usual CGI .exe or .pl extension.

To see some good sample ISAs, complete with source code, and how they are embedded into HTML pages, see the \INETSDK\SAMPLES\ISAPI directory on the ActiveX SDK. It's filled with sample ISAPI applications, complete with source code and makefiles. Several of the samples are ISAPI Filter DLLs, which I cover in a later chapter. A particularly useful sample is OLEISAPI, which allows you to invoke the methods of an OLE Automation server from an HTTP server. This is a particularly good way to allow Visual Basic developers to develop applications that can be used from Web servers. VB allows very easy creation of OLE Automation servers that could be invoked from the OLEISAPI ISAPI DLL. Chapter 5 demonstrates the construction of OLEISAPI as an sample ISA. The next chapter also presents SENDFORM, an ISA for sending the contents of HTML forms via Microsoft Exchange. This is another example that you may be able to use as the basis of your own efforts. SENDFORM is also useful since it incorporates HTMLForm for form field processing. I recommend using this class in lieu of the FORMDUMP sample that ships with the ActiveX SDK: It's much more straightforward to use.

This finishes the summary of the ISAPI specification and architecture. In the next chapter we present some guidelines on C++ ISA development, tools to assist in developing ISAs, some sample Internet Server Applications, and some reusable C++ code that should make your ISA development much easier.

5

INTERNET SERVER APPLICATIONS IN VISUAL C++

L et's now give some guidelines on how to productively build ISAPI applications, starting with some advice on porting your existing CGI programs to ISAPI, followed by some development tools to ease your C++ ISA programming, and then some classes to aid in ISA development.

Porting CGI C++ Programs to ISAPI

Porting C and C++-based CGI programs to ISAPI involves the following steps.

Read Data from pECB->lpbData Instead of Standard Input

Most good CGI scripts use the POST method for data instead of the GET method. Porting these scripts means removing all references to reading from standard input. Usually these are getc() calls. These need to be converted to looping over the data pointed to by the lpbData, up to a limit of cbAvailable. If cbAvailable is not equal to cbTotBytes, then subsequent ReadClient calls need to be made to get all of the data. This situation is relatively rare and should only occur if truly large amounts of data are being sent back from the client.

The methodology should be scanned for all occurrences of getc( ), getchar( ), or fgetc(stdin) and replace with lpbData[index]. Loops that check for this character being NULL or index<atoi(getenv("CONTENT_LENGTH")) should be replaced with loops for index<cbAvailable.

Environment Variable Use Converted to ECB Fields or GetServerVariable( )

All references to CGI environment variables should be converted to either: (1) the equivalent extension control block field (e.g., pECB->cbAvailable instead of getenv("CONTENT_LENGTH"), or (2) a GetServerVariable( ) call. Scanning for getenv( ) calls and then making the changes manually should work well.

Change All Standard Output Writes to WriteClient( )

If the CGI program is an old-style C program, this means searching for printf( ) and puts( ) calls. If the program is a C++ program that uses iostreams, this means searching for cout<< . . . statements. These all need to be changed to WriteClient( ) calls. This means formatting the output string buffer with wsprintf( ), strcpy( ), and strcat( ), or character by character string manipulation. My experience is that this tends to be the most labor-intensive of the steps.

Change Return of Status to ServerSupportFunction( ) Calls

The typical CGI program starts its dialog with client something like this:

```
cout << "Content-type: text/html\r\n";
cout <<"Status: 200 OK\r\n";
cout <<"\r\n"; // finished sending headers
```

These calls need to be changed to ServerSupportFunction( ) calls that communicate the status back to the server. The equivalent call for the previous code is:

```
pECB->ServerSupportFunction(pECB->ConnID,
        HSE_REQ_SEND_RESPONSE_HEADER, "200 OK", NULL,
        (LPDWORD)"Content-type: text/html\r\n\r\n");
```

Remove the Main() Function and Write HttpExtensionProc()

This is really just building the housing for your new ISAPI-based application. Obviously since you are now creating a DLL, you should remove the main() function for your old CGI executable. You will want to embed your functionality primarily in HttpExtensionProc(). If you have any one-time initialization code (how did you do this in CGI anyway?) you would write a DllMain() function. You will need to write a GetExtensionVersion as well, which can be very close to the sample functions already presented. Then build a makefile for your ISA starting with any of the makefiles for the ISAPI samples on the ActiveX SDK or presented in this book. Build with your favorite C++ compiler and serve.

That's it! Once you've made these changes your CGI application can become an ISAPI-based Internet Server Application. These steps are predictable enough that perhaps there should be a CGI conversion wizard supplied with Visual C++ and the Microsoft Foundation Classes (MFC). Unfortunately, there is no such sorcery yet provided. But a script that just identified the lines in a source that needed conversion would be a rather modest Perl spell to write.

Speaking of wizards, there are some wizards available with Visual C++ to alleviate the process of writing ISAs. In the next section we look at Visual C++ and MFC support for ISAPI.

MFC ISAPI Support

The ISAPI Extension Wizard

If you select File/New/Project Workspace from the Microsoft Visual C++ 4.1 (or greater) Developer Studio menu, you can select ISAPI Extension (I told you to watch out for inconsistent terminology) as one of the choices. Before clicking on the Create button, supply a name for the project, and a location to place it in. Figure 5.1 shows the dialog that you are prompted with.

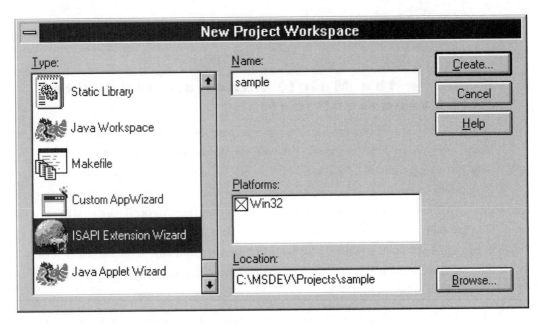

The location by default is C:\MSDEV\Projects (the Projects subdirectory of your VC++ installation). You can change that to whatever directory you wish. When you type in the project name it changes the location to the project named subdirectory of the Projects subdirectory. Be careful that you don't start out with a Location that already is tied to your specific project. It's very easy to end up with your work in a directory called, for example, C:\MSDEV\Projects\Sample\Sample.

After clicking Create, you will see the dialog shown in Figure 5.2.

Notice that the Server Extension object checkbox is checked by default. That's good because I haven't covered ISAPI Filters yet (which is what the Filter object checkbox creates). For the purposes of this example, you will leave the MFC library radio button set to shared DLL. For this to work, you have to assume that the IIS server machine that has MFC installed (specifically the DLL entitled MFC40.DLL) in its \WINNT\SYSTEM32 directory, or that the install program for your ISA will install it for you. If this isn't a reasonable assumption, then you should choose the statically linked library option.

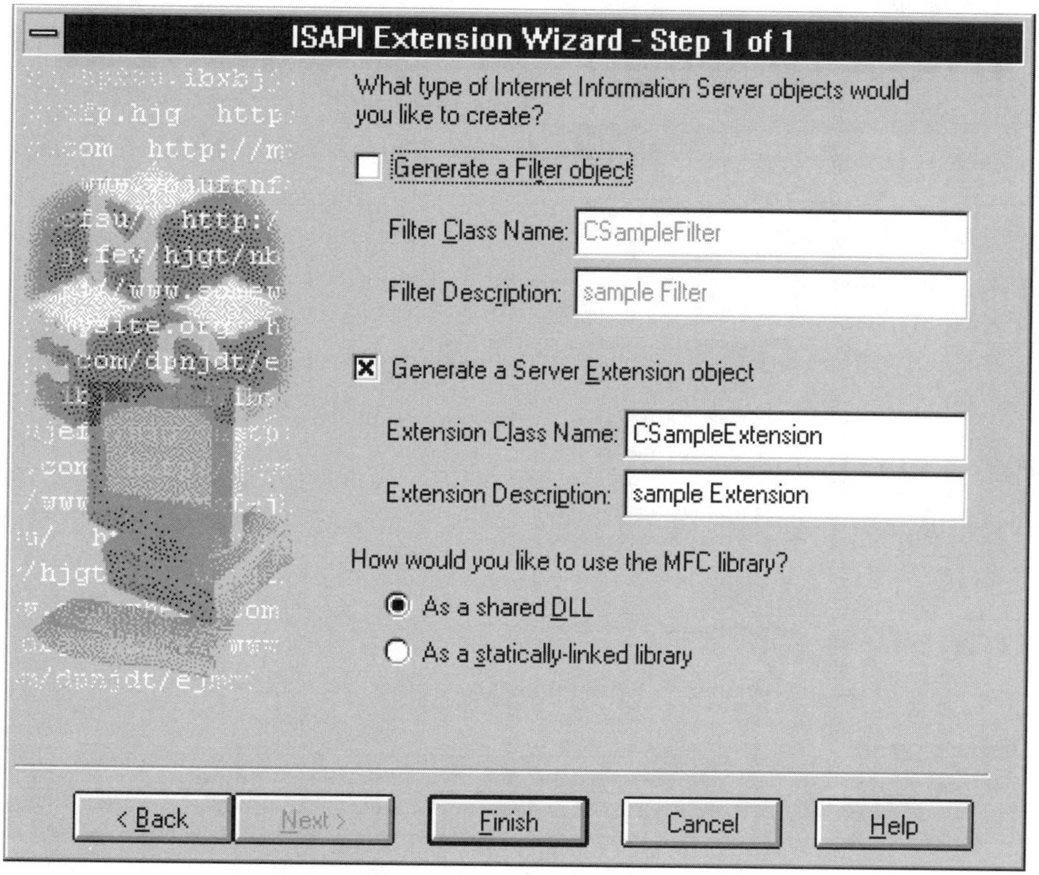

Figure 5.2 ISAPI extension wizard step 1.

The result of running the Wizard is that a new project is created, with a C++ source file, C++ header file, .RC resource file, .DEF file, and .MDP VC project file that implements a skeleton Internet Server Application. You can then edit the skeleton code to create your ISA. The project files and source file for a project called SAMPLE are shown in Figure 5.3.

Notice that the ISAPI Extension Wizard creates a command map that initially just contains the command called Default. This command will be invoked by the Internet Server Application when the application is invoked with no parameters, for example:

```
<A HREF="/scripts/sample.dll">Click here<</A>.
```

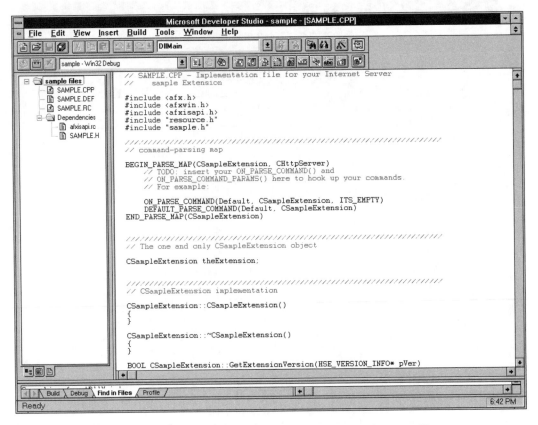

Figure 5.3 ISAPI extension wizard-created project and source files.

It can also be invoked with the argument named Default, as in:

```
<FORM ACTION="/scripts/sample.dll?Default">
<INPUT TYPE="submit" VALUE="Run Script">
</FORM>
```

The implementation of this function in the sample ISA that is built by the ISAPI extension wizard results in the following text appearing on the user's browser as a result:

```
This default message was produced by the Internet.
Server DLL Wizard. Edit your CSampleExtension::Default().
implementation to change it.
```

To change the functionality of the default function, do as the text suggests: Edit the CSampleExtension::Default() method. Once you start this, the coding process is very similar to writing the HttpExtensionProc() function, as I showed in the last chapter. There are some higher-level MFC classes to assist in the ISAPI development process; I describe these in the next section.

But the extension wizard introduces a framework for an Internet Server Application (what it terms an ISAPI extension) that did not exist before in native ISAPI. This framework is the ability to have multiple commands for a given ISA. The Wizard generates a parse map to correlate commands supplied as arguments to the ISA with functions. The parse map is generated with one command already in place: the Default command, which is both the command that is invoked when no argument to the ISA is supplied in the HTML, and when the ISA is invoked with the named argument of Default. The generic skeleton parse map is shown here.

```
///////////////////////////////////////////////////////////////////
// command-parsing map
BEGIN_PARSE_MAP(CSampleExtension, CHttpServer)
        // TODO: insert your ON_PARSE_COMMAND() and
        // ON_PARSE_COMMAND_PARAMS() here to hook up your commands.
        // For example:

        ON_PARSE_COMMAND(Default, CSampleExtension, ITS_EMPTY)
        DEFAULT_PARSE_COMMAND(Default, CSampleExtension)
END_PARSE_MAP(CSampleExtension)
```

The default-created ON_PARSE_COMMAND() macro shown previously requires there to be a function CSampleExtension::Default() to handle the Default command. This function (and command) takes no arguments (ITS_EMPTY is the argument list). As mentioned, you can start your ISAPI development process by just editing this function. But if you want to add additional commands (kind of the point of having a parse map), you'll need to understand how to add them to the parse map.

This is done by adding ON_PARSE_COMMAND macros to the parse map. The generic syntax for these macros is:

```
ON_PARSE_COMMAND(Command,Class,Arguments)
```

where Command is the name of the member function. Class is the name of the C++ class for your ISA (which is derived by the wizard from the CHttpServer class presented in the next section). Arguments is a space-delimited list of flags that specify the argument types that this command can take (if any). The possible values for this are:

ITS_EMPTY	Command takes no arguments
ITS_I2	A short
ITS_I4	A long
ITS_R4	A float
ITS_R8	A double

If the ON_PARSE_COMMAND macro specifies that the command takes arguments (anything but ITS_EMPTY), then an ON_PARSE_COMMAND_PARAMS macro needs to be added to the map, right after the ON_PARSE_COMMAND macro. The ON_PARSE_COMMAND_PARAMS names each parameter, and optionally supplies default values for the rightmost parameters (which are used if no parameter for the command is supplied on invocation of the ISA).

Once you have added the command to the parse map, you need to write the function that it will call. This function name will be Class::Command(), and will need to have arguments whose types match those specified in the ON_PARSE_COMMAND macro.

Let's add a command the the sample ISA we created here. One very valid use of the multiple command approach would be to provide diagnostics or performance statistics for the ISA. Perhaps a Stats command would be appropriate. Let's add this to the parse map, and then write a function that implements the command. To add this new command to the parse map, add ON_PARSE_COMMAND(Stats,CSampleExtension, ITS_EMPTY).

Following is the new parse map:

```
BEGIN_PARSE_MAP(CSampleExtension, CHttpServer)
        ON_PARSE_COMMAND(Stats, CSampleExtension, ITS_EMPTY)
        ON_PARSE_COMMAND(Default, CSampleExtension, ITS_EMPTY)
        DEFAULT_PARSE_COMMAND(Default, CSampleExtension)
END_PARSE_MAP(CSampleExtension)
```

The function that you need to write is CSampleExtension::Stats(). Just to ridiculously oversimplify it, assume that the Stats command should retrieve an integer that is stored in the file SAMPLE.CTR. The Default command could also be modified to read the same file, increment the integer, and write the result back to the file. Anyway, here's the code for the Stats() function:

```
void CSampleExtension::Stats(CHttpServerContext* pCtxt)
{
        StartContent(pCtxt);
        WriteTitle(pCtxt);
        ifstream is("SAMPLE.CTR",ios::in);
        int nCounterValue;
        if (!is)
                nCounterValue=0;
        else
                is >> nCounterValue;
        char szBuf[16];
        sprintf(szBuf,"%d",nCounterValue);
        *pCtxt << _T(szBuf);
        EndContent(pCtxt);
}
```

Besides adding this code to the SAMPLE.CPP file, you will need to add the prototype of the function to the SAMPLE.H file. This command can then be executed by invoking SAMPLE.DLL with an argument of Stats. For example:

```
<FORM ACTION="/scripts/sample.dll?Stats" METHOD="POST">
```

This parse map approach to allowing ISAs to accept multiple commands is a pretty powerful way to embed a lot of functionality in one package. Sure, you could have coded this up yourself within the native ISAPI HttpExtensionProc() function. You might have even come up with a simpler command parsing, mapping, and execution mechanism. Perhaps something as simple as doing a C switch statement on the first letter of the argument to determine which command function to invoke. But the presence of this parse map simplifies the job for you considerably if you are going to write an ISA that handles multiple commands. It's also a fairly robust mechanism and probably outshines something you or I might have written from scratch, if we were trying to crank out a project for a deadline.

With all that said, if you do *not* need the multiple command within a single ISA capability, then this feature might be a bit of overkill. I sometimes find that this layer of abstraction removes me a bit too far from being able to see the flow from the entry point of HttpExtensionProc( ) very transparently. This is especially true if you are trying to write a small ISA that you know will never have any commands that vary how it's invoked. This decision is obviously made on a case-by-case basis, and I'm not expressing a strong preference one way or the other. I do feel strongly, however, that if you are a professional programmer who plans to be spending a good deal of your time doing Web development (a fair guess if you have read this far), then you *should* understand the mechanics of native ISAPI, and write at least one ISA without benefit of the wizard. If anything, you'll come away with a richer appreciation of the wizard's value. (As an implied endorsement of this approach, all of the ISAPI samples that ship on the ActiveX SDK are native ISAPI.) That is actually the rationale behind presenting the native ISAPI specification and ISAPI first in Chapter 4, before showing how to "crank 'em out with the wizard" in this chapter.

Anyway, the decision to use the wizard or not for a particular Internet Server Application is very much a fine-grained judgment call, and I'm not going to set out guidelines for it just yet. One of the things the wizard does very well is generate code that utilizes the MFC classes for ISAPI effectively. Let's take a closer look at those classes, since it may help us in the decision to go ISAPI native or not.

The MFC Classes for ISAPI

The Microsoft Foundation Classes were originally written to provide a rational, object-oriented, higher-level interface, in the form of C++ classes, to the often overwhelming Windows SDK. The benefits of MFC went well past the fact that it was a C++ interface: MFC made the complexity of Windows SDK much less daunting, by organizing the functionality in class form. The application classes did provide much of the framework for a Windows application that was previously built from scratch.

It's not clear to me that ISAPI applications (what we call Internet Server Applications and MFC calls ISAPI extensions) has anything approaching the same level of complexity that needs to be wrapped. Nevertheless, the MFC classes for ISAPI provide a

C++ interface, and a familiar way of working for developers that are already accustomed to MFC for Win32 programming.

The CHttpServer class packages the functions necessary to build an ISA (GetExtensionVersion() and HttpExtensionProc()). When an ISA is invoked, a CHttpServer object is created. There is just one instance of CHttpServer for each application (even if the ISA is invoked multiple times). To handle the data present in different invocations (the different extension control blocks), the CHttpServerContext class was created.

Each invocation has its own CHttpServerContext object. Your ISA uses information from CHttpServerContext to get information about the particular invocation, such as the information in the extension control block (using CHttpServerContext's data member of m_pECB). Note that in the ISAPI extension wizard generated code, each function in the parse map takes an argument that is a pointer to an object of type CHttpServerContext. CHttpServerContext's member functions are the toolbox that you will use in building your ISAs if you choose to use the MFC ISAPI classes.

All of the things that you did before in native ISAPI to get data from the server, and send data back to the server and the client, can be done with few syntactic changes with member functions of CHttpServerContext. For example, remember that you did your output to the browser with the ISAPI WriteClient() function? To use the MFC ISAPI classes to, for example, write out the string "Hello, world!" to the browser, you would write the following code:

```
DWORD dwLen=strlen("Hello, world");
pCtxt->WriteClient("Hello, world!",&dwLen,NULL);
```

This is not much different than the code in native ISAPI. Note that there is a documentation bug on this call. The native ISAPI ServerSupportFunction() call also becomes a member function call, as do ReadClient() and GetServerVariable().

CHttpServerContext does provide some greater functionality than native ISAPI. For example, you can use C++ stream insertion operators to write data out to the client. This can be done since CHttpServerContext has a data member, m_pStream of class CHTMLStream. CHttpServerContext has an overloaded streams insertion operator (operator<<) that writes to CHTMLStream member. This allows you to write code such as:

```
pCtxt<<_T("Hello, world!");
```

There are some additional member functions in the CHttpServer class that provide a higher level of functionality. These include the StartContent( ) member function, which writes out <html> and <body> tags to start the HTML page. EndContent( ) writes out </body></html> to end the page. WriteTitle( ) writes out the title returned by the GetTitle( ) member function between <head><title> and </title></head>. To write out a title of your choice, override the GetTitle( ) member function with your own. This of course assumes that you are using these functions from a class derived from CHttpServer. And if you are starting with code generated by the ISAPI extension wizard, that is exactly the case. In our sample ISA that we built above, CSampleExtension is derived from CHttpServer. If we want to use WriteTitle( ) to generate titles on pages generated by our ISA, we would write our own GetTitle( ) with an appropriate title string.

It's not clear to me why these member functions, which after all are aids to generating HTML and don't really need to know much about the ISA itself, are members of CHttpServer rather than CHTMLStream. All of these functions are given a pointer to a CHttpServerContext object anyway as an argument to allow them the context and connection ID to write data back to the client. The only justification for doing this is so that WriteTitle( ) can call the overridden method GetTitle( ) to display a title, and this keeps the programmer doing all method overrides within the same class (the derived class from CHttpServer). Still, there's no reason that WriteTitle( ) couldn't just take a string argument, and have all of the HTML helper functions be part of CHTMLStream. My other problem with the CHTMLStream class, is that it's half a loaf. There is only support for generating starting and ending HTML head and body tags, writing out titles, and managing the buffer of HTML before transmission back to the client. There are many other aspects of HTML creation that could be automated, and those C++ functions could provide a big value add over writing the HTML manually. These include such repetitive chores as HTML form and table generation. Still (to morph the metaphor) the glass if half full, and the support provided is certainly useful on its own.

There are a couple other MFC classes for ISAPI but they are for ISAPI filters, which will be covered in Chapter 6.

Other Classes for ISAPI Programming

The MFC ISAPI class are useful tools. But I think they missed an opportunity to automate some of the more repetitive, time-consuming Web programming chores. The biggest, and most common, of these is HTML form field processing

Extending the HTMLForm Class for ISAPI Development

One class we would definitely like to have is a class to alleviate form field processing. We already wrote one, but need extend it to work from ISAPI. Recalling our earlier C++ class (presented in Chapter 2) for form field development, it is only necessary to override the Header() method, which begins the process of writing data back to the client, and the Display() method, which writes the form's contents back to the client. The following code is the entire definition of the ISAPIForm class:

```
class ISAPIForm: public HTMLForm {
        EXTENSION_CONTROL_BLOCK *pECB;
public:
        ISAPIForm(const EXTENSION_CONTROL_BLOCK *pECB);
        ~ISAPIForm(){}
        void Write(LPCTSTR lpsz)
        {
                DWORD dwBytesWritten;
                dwBytesWritten = lstrlen (lpsz);
                pECB->WriteClient (pECB->ConnID, (PVOID) lpsz,
                &dwBytesWritten, 0);
        }
        virtual void Header(){
                pECB->ServerSupportFunction(pECB->ConnID,
                        HSE_REQ_SEND_RESPONSE_HEADER, "200 OK",
                        NULL, (LPDWORD)"Content-type: text/html\r\n\r\n");
        }
        int Display()
```

```
        {
                Header();
                Write(TEXT("<H1>Form Data</H1>\n"));
                aFields.First();
                char szText[256];
                while (aFields.Current()){
                        sprintf(szText,"%s: %s<br>\n",
                        (char *)aFields.Current()->Key(),
                        (char *) (aFields.Current()->Value() ));
                        Write(TEXT(szText));
                        ++aFields;
                }
                return 1;
        }
    };
```

Now if you want to use the ISAPIForm class to develop your forms processing ISA, just declare a variable of type ISAPIForm inside your HttpExtensionProc() function. For example, the following tiny program appends the values from a form as a comma-separated-value record in the RESULTS.CSV file:

```
#include "htmlform.h"
DWORD WINAPI HttpExtensionProc (EXTENSION_CONTROL_BLOCK *pECB)
{
        ISAPIForm form(pECB);
        form->Store("RESULTS.CSV");
}
```

The following SENDFORM program shows how this class can be used to develop Internet Server Applications.

Sample Programs: The SENDFORM ISA

If you are a Web developer who also happens to be a Webmaster, you may want to be able to take a form and instead of, or in addition to, stuffing it into a database, also mail the form to a fixed or user-specified recipient. There are some Perl utilities out there to do this to an SMTP user. But we'd like to be able to send the form via a more robust enterprise messaging system—Microsoft Exchange. The recipient can actually be an SMTP user after all, but this utility uses a copy of the Microsoft Exchange client installed on the Web server machine to effect the send.

The SENDFORM utility lets webmasters create Web forms whose contents can be sent to an address supplied by the user or to a fixed address embedded in the form (using the "hidden" tag for an INPUT field). Use of a utility like this is often requested by my clients. There are existing CGI scripts available, but using ISAPI, as you have seen, has very real benefits. I am making this application available with this book, and as far as I know, this book is the only place where you will find such a utility written for ISAPI.

Usage

SENDFORM should be embedded into your HTML forms in ACTION attribute of the FORM tag. No arguments are necessary. The syntax is usually ACTION="/scripts/ sendform.dll". The form itself controls the functionality. The form should have one field named "To" as the recipient. This is the only absolute requirement for successful operation. If you wish the form to always be sent to the same recipient, you can specify an INPUT field with attribute NAME ="To" with attribute TYPE="hidden" and supplying the recipient name as the VALUE attribute, for example, <INPUT NAME="To" TYPE="hidden" VALUE="webmaster@ourstore.com">. If a field named "Subject" is present, it will be used as the subject of the message. If a field named "Body" is present, it will be used as the body of the message. If no such field is present, then a message body will be created by bundling all of the fields in the form together. This can be very useful for things like user registration forms.

Following is an sample HTML form that incorporates SENDFORM:

```
<HTML>
<HEAD>
<TITLE>SendForm ISAPI Sample Test</TITLE>
</HEAD>
<BODY>
<FORM ACTION="/scripts/sendform.dll">
<PRE>
Recipient <INPUT NAME="To">
Subject <INPUT NAME="Subject">
```

```
Message <INPUT NAME="Body">
<INPUT TYPE="submit" VALUE="Send Form">
</PRE>
</FORM>
</BODY>
</HTML>
```

You may notice that there is no From: field specified. That is because we can't have an Exchange profile for each user that might fill out a form. So the From: will always be that of the default Exchange profile on the machine that IIS is running on. Also, due to some strange limitations of MAPI called from ISAPI running under IIS, the Exchange client must be actually up and running on the IIS box in question (a full discussion of the reasons why this is so is well beyond this book). Should this limitation prove infeasible for your intended use, SENDFORM can be compiled with the -DCGIFORM flag to create a CGI executable version that does not have this limitation.

Technology Used

The actual form field parsing is done via the HTMLForm class just presented, as extended for use with ISAPI. This makes the form parsing portion of the application very brief.

SENDFORM uses Common Messaging Calls (CMC) to effect the send. CMC is the successor to Simple MAPI for doing mail-enabled sending. Simple MAPI use is now discouraged in favor of CMC. Writing the mail-sending code in CMC is much simpler than writing it in full Extended MAPI. All of the code for doing the send is encapsulated in the function SendMsg( ), which could easily be rewritten with Simple MAPI or Extended MAPI. The code for SendMsg( ) is not presented in the text here since it is not really germane to an ISAPI discussion, but the the full source is in the Appendices, and on the book's Web page.

The Code

The following is the essence of the code for this utility: the HttpExtensionProc( ) function call of this ISA. Note that the use of the HTMLForm class (actually the derived ISAPIForm class) makes the code very tight. The entire form field parsing process is embedded in the definition of the form variable: ISAPIForm form(pECB). Then the form fields can all be accessed using the associative array capability of the HTMLForm. Notice that the actual sending of the message is as simple as:

```
SendMsg(form["To"],form["Subject"]?form["Subject"]:"(no
⌐subject)",lpszBody);
```

All of the form field values can be accessed by just subscripting the variable with the field name desired. Here is the HttpExtensionProc() function definition:

```
DWORD WINAPI HttpExtensionProc (EXTENSION_CONTROL_BLOCK *pECB)
{
        ISAPIForm form(pECB);
        char *lpszBody;
        // if there's a Body field, then use that for message
        if (!(lpszBody=form["Body"]))
        {// if there is no body field, then just bundle up all form fields
                ostrstream s;
                s << form;
                lpszBody=s.str();
        }
        if (!form["To"]){ // must have recipient specified
                pECB->ServerSupportFunction(pECB->ConnID,
                             HSE_REQ_SEND_RESPONSE_HEADER,
                             (LPDWORD) "400 Bad Request",
                             NULL,
                             (LPDWORD)"No recipient specified\r\r\r\n");
                form.Write("<H2>No recipient specified</H2>");
                pECB->dwHttpStatusCode=400;
                return HSE_STATUS_ERROR;
        }
        form.Display();
        BOOL bResult=
        SendMsg(form["To"],
                form["Subject"]?form["Subject"]:"(no subject)",lpszBody);
        if (bResult==TRUE)
                form.Write("<H2>Message sent successfully</H2>");
        else
                form.Write("<H2>Failed to send message</H2>");
        return bResult==TRUE?HSE_STATUS_SUCCESS:HSE_STATUS_ERROR;
}
```

There is only one error that can occur (or at least only one that is handled here!), a missing recipient to send the message to. All of the recommended error handling steps are shown: informing the server, informing the client, setting the status code, and returning HSE_STATUS_ERROR:

```
pECB->ServerSupportFunction(pECB->ConnID,
              HSE_REQ_SEND_RESPONSE_HEADER,
              (LPDWORD) "400 Bad Request",
              NULL,
              (LPDWORD)"No recipient specified\r\n\r\n");
form.Write("<H2>No recipient specified</H2>");
pECB->dwHttpStatusCode=400;
return HSE_STATUS_ERROR;
```

For completeness, I will show that other important exported function: GetExtension-Version(). SENDFORM copies information into the pVersionInfo structure. But it also does a little bit of initialization logic: It sets up a handle to the Windows NT Event Log. But wait a minute: doesn't ISAPI allow for very easy logging to the HTTP server log by merely setting the lpszLogData string? Yes, but you would like to have a location to log particularly critical errors. The HTTP server log can get quite full. You would like to have a repository for particularly critical errors, that will be considerably cleaner and smaller than IIS's verbose text log. The NT Event Log fills that need quite nicely. There is also a variety of NT utilities that allow you to generate messages and alarms based on certain events being logged to the Event Log. In summary, you may want to have your ISAs (and ISAPI filters that I discuss later) log some events to the NT Event Log. A good place to put the initialization work for that is in Get-ExtensionVersion(). The call RegisterEventSource() sets up the Event Log to receive later ReportEvent() calls in case of critical errors:

```
BOOL WINAPI GetExtensionVersion (HSE_VERSION_INFO *pVersionInfo)
{
      pVersionInfo->dwExtensionVersion = MAKELONG (HSE_VERSION_MINOR,
      ⌐HSE_VERSION_MAJOR);
      lstrcpyn ((LPTSTR) pVersionInfo->lpszExtensionDesc,
        TEXT("SENDFORM - Sends form to address specified in To: field"),
        HSE_MAX_EXT_DLL_NAME_LEN);
```

```
    hEvtLog=RegisterEventSource(NULL,"SENDFORM");

    return TRUE;

}
```

Below is the makefile for SENDFORM, which I present here just to reassure you about how simple this technology is. That is, the integration of HTMLFORM is straightforward, and even using CMC for messaging and making registry calls doesn't add much to the make process:

```
CC=cl -c
CVARS=-DWIN32 -DNDEBUG
LINK=link
LINKOPT=/DLL
LIBS=wininet.lib user32.lib mapi32.lib advapi32.lib
OBJS=sendform.obj htmlform.obj
LINKOUT=/OUT:sendform.dll
DEFS=sendform.def

all: sendform.dll

.cpp.obj:
    $(CC) $(CVARS) $*.cpp

sendform.dll: $(OBJS) $(DEFS)
    $(LINK) $(LINKOPT) /DEF:$(DEFS) $(LINKOUT) $(LIBS) $(OBJS)
```

The full source for SENDFORM is presented in Appendix A and on the Web page for this book: http://www.wiley.com/compbooks/.

OLEISAPI—Integrating OLE Automation Servers into Your Web System

There is a sample Internet Server Application that ships with the ActiveX SDK that allows you to invoke the methods of OLE Automation Servers. This is a particularly useful capability to incorporate the functionality of existing applications into your

Web-based system. It also allows Visual Basic programmers to participate in the Web development process. You can't write Web gateways or applications to either the CGI or the ISAPI standards in Visual Basic. CGI is eliminated since there is no such thing as *standard input* or *standard output* in VB. ISAPI is eliminated since VB cannot expose the required GetExtensionVersion( ) and HttpExtensionProc( ) functions. However, VB programmers can easily create OLE Automation Server, which can then be integrated into the Web site using OLEISAPI.

To integrate OLEISAPI in your pages, embed the reference to OLEISAPI.DLL into your hypertext link (the <A HREF= . . . tag) or the FORM tag ACTION attribute. After OLEISAPI.DLL include extra path info with the DLL name, the class name, and the method name delimited by periods. Include the method's arguments after the question mark in standard URL-encoded form (separate the arguments with ampersands). For example, to call OLEISAPI's sample OLE automation server, TESTOBJ.DLL, within a hypertext link, embed the following HTML code:

```
<A HREF="/scripts/oleisapi.dll/TestObj.TestClass.SimpleCall?arg1=
↳foo&arg2=bar">
```

To embed a call to the OLE automation server within a FORM ACTION, use a similar syntax, but you don't need to put the arguments to the method right next to the method. They can be gathered from the form fields. The form field names and values supplied will be supplied as arguments to the method:

```
<FORM ACTION="/scripts/oleisapi.dll/TestObj.TestClass.DoPost" METHOD=
↳"POST">
```

The methods that the OLE automation server exposes (or at least those to be called by OLEISAPI) must all have the following signature:

```
HRESULT SomeMethod(BSTR Request, BSTR Response)
```

Request will contain all of the argument names and values supplied as arguments to the OLEISAPI invocation, or all of the form field names and values if OLEISAPI is embedded as the FORM action. Response should be populated with a BSTR containing the output to be displayed back to the user. It should generally begin with Content-Type: text/html\r\n\r\n, followed by the HTML formatted response. This syntactic requirement for callable methods obviously implies that the OLE automation servers to be integrated with OLEISAPI need to be consciously written for this purpose. Using just any existing OLE automation server will not work.

How OLEISAPI Is Implemented

OLEISAPI first checks to see how it has been invoked by checking the request method in the extension control block (pECB->lpszMethod). If it was invoked with the POST method, it takes all of the field names and values that are present in standard input, puts them together into a BSTR ready to be the Request argument for any method. It then calls the method specified in the lpszPathInfo member of the extension control block (pECB->lpszPathInfo). If it was invoked with the GET method, it checks the lpszQueryString member of the ECB for field names and values and builds those up into a Request argument. It then takes the Response argument and displays it back to the user with ServerSupportFunction().

The code for the main function, HttpExtensionProc(), is shown here:

```
DWORD WINAPI HttpExtensionProc(EXTENSION_CONTROL_BLOCK *pECB)
{
    CHAR pszPathString[PARAMLEN];
    CHAR *pszProgid = NULL;
    CHAR *pszMethod = NULL;
    CHAR *pszTemp = NULL;

    if (FALSE == TlsGetValue(g_dwTLSIndex)) {
      OleInitialize(NULL);
      TlsSetValue(g_dwTLSIndex, (void*)TRUE);
    }

    // only GET and POST supported
    if (strcmp(pECB->lpszMethod, "GET") && strcmp(pECB->lpszMethod,
    ↳"POST"))
    {
      return HSE_STATUS_ERROR;
    }

    // extract progid & method name from path info
    strncpy(pszPathString, pECB->lpszPathInfo, PARAMLEN);
    if ('/' == *pszPathString) {
      pszProgid = pszPathString + 1;
    }
```

```
pszMethod = strchr(pszPathString, '.');
if (NULL != pszMethod) {
  // progids can have zero or one periods in them
  pszTemp = strchr(pszMethod + 1, '.');
  // separate progid from args
  if (NULL != pszTemp) {
   *pszTemp = '\0';
   pszMethod = pszTemp + 1;
  } else {
   *pszMethod = '\0';
   pszMethod++;
  }
}

// startup object, invoke method, and return results
if (FALSE == CallObject(pECB, pszProgid, pszMethod)) {
  ErrorResponse(pECB, pszProgid, pszMethod);
  return HSE_STATUS_ERROR;
}
return HSE_STATUS_SUCCESS;
}
```

I don't attempt to present all the source code for OLEISAPI itself here. That would be more of an exercise in teaching OLE/COM development than it would be in showing you how to build ISAs (which other much simpler samples already shown do well). The full source for the OLEISAPI sample is on the ActiveX SDK and is located in the SAMPLES\ISAPI\OLEISAPI directory.

6

ISAPI FILTERS

The ISAPI standard enables very robust, scalable, high-performance applications to be built that communicate with HTTP servers. Applications written to the ISAPI specification (i.e., Internet Server Applications) are a very important innovation in Web development. However, another major, but really entirely separate, standard in the ActiveX Server Framework is the ISAPI Filter specification, which has ramifications that are just as important as ISAPI itself. The ISAPI Filter spec allows a separate class of applications to be built: ISAPI Filters allow you to truly extend and replace the functionality of any HTTP server that supports the spec (such as Microsoft Internet Information Server). In fact, this means that the term that MFC uses for ISAs, ISAPI *extensions,* is even more of a misnomer, since it is *ISAPI filters* that are the true server extensions. Speaking of nomenclature problems, it would have been nice if ISAPI filters were just called *Internet Server Filters,* or some other term that made it clear that they were really quite separate from the ISAPI standard for ISAs. Failing that, at least this book will attempt to treat these two important technologies totally separately.

What Are Filters?

The ISAPI Filter Specification provides the capability of registering a DLL to intercept specific server events and perform appropriate actions. Unlike ISAPI itself, which is an improvement over the Common Gateway Interface (CGI) that Web servers have used for years, ISAPI Filters are an entirely new capability in the world of Web servers. In effect, ISAPI filters let you extend the capabilities of your Web server. The ISAPI filter you build says to the Web server, "Hey, when something like this happens, let me handle it." Your filter can then handle the event entirely, process the event and leave it available for the Web server and other filters to handle, or decide on the fly that it's not an event it needs to process at all. For example, you can create ISAPI filters to: provide enhanced logging capabilities for your Web server by tracking more information than the Web server does with potentially a different data storage format, provide custom authentication techniques by interposing your filter with its own userid and password method on access requests for a particular resource or type of resource, or even enhance the functionality of your Web server by serving data in a different way than the Web server would do by default.

This last, extremely powerful, capability is one that I'd like to show a detailed example of in this chapter. First I'll show you briefly what you need to do to write an ISAPI filter in general. Then I'll walk through the code of a sample filter that I wrote that enhances the capabilities of a Web server. The CVTDOC ISAPI filter sample allows your Web server to automatically publish files by converting them dynamically to HTML. Though CVTDOC is primarily meant as an example of ISAPI filters, you may find it useful in its own right. So in the final section, I'll show the details of how to actually install and use the CVTDOC sample.

Introduction to ISAPI Filters

ISAPI filter authors must create two main functions for export: GetFilterVersion() and HttpFilterProc(). GetFilterVersion() is called just once by the Web server: on server startup when loading all filters. GetFilterVersion() should:

- provide version information to the server
- set the priority of the filter (determines the order its called in for these events)

- register whats events the filter is interested in

GetFilterVersion( ) takes just one argument of a structure that will store this information (version info, priority, and event flags).

```
BOOL WINAPI GetFilterVersion(PHTTP_FILTER_VERSION pVer);
```

The HTTP_FILTER_VERSION structure looks like this:

```
typedef struct_HTTP_FILTER_VERSION {
        DWORD   dwServerFilterVersion;
        DWORD   dwFilterVersion;
        CHAR    lpszFilterDesc[SF_MAX_FILTER_DESC_LEN+1];
        DWORD   dwFlags;
}HTTP_FILTER_VERSION, *PHTTP_FILTER_VERSION;
```

The GetFilterVersion( ) function should fill in the dwFilterVersion, lpszFilterDesc, and dwFlags structure members. Most importantly, dwFlags needs to have all events that it is interested in registered for by turning that flag bit on.

The events available to register are listed in Table 6.1.

The SF_NOTIFY_READ_RAW_DATA and SF_NOTIFY_SEND_RAW_DATA flags allow the ISAPI filter DLL to intercept data going from the client to the server (READ) or from the server back to the client (SEND), and store and manipulate the data for its own purposes. Intercepting the SF_NOTIFY_AUTHENTICATION event allows the filter to insert its own authentication scheme for use with the server. The SF_NOTIFY_LOG event allows the filter to supplement or replace the IIS logging mechanism with its own logging method. The SF_NOTIFY_URL_MAP is a good event to intercept if you want to change how the server can respond to a request for a URL resource. For example, you can intercept the SF_NOTIFY_URL_MAP in the CVT-DOC filter to create the file requested by the URL. The SF_NOTIFY_SECURE_PORT and SF_NOTIFY_NON_SECURE_PORT flags can be ORed with the events requested allow your filter to restrict its operation to a situation where the HTTP server is running over a secure port or over a normal HTTP session.

The other externally available function, HttpFilterProc( ) is called by the HTTP server—for example, IIS—each time one of these events the filter has indicated interest in occurs:

■■■■■ **Table 6.1** ISAPI Event Flags

Event ID	Description
SF_NOTIFY_READ_RAW_DATA	Intercepts data going to the server.
SF_NOTIFY_SEND_RAW_DATA	Intercepts data going from the server back to the client.
SF_NOTIFY_AUTHENTICATION	Calls your filter when authentication event occurs. Used to implement custom password schemes.
SF_NOTIFY_LOG	Calls your filter when the server is about to log a resource access or other event. Lets you implement your own custom logging schemes.
SF_NOTIFY_URL_MAP	Calls your filter when the server is mapping a logical path to a physical path. In effect, this is called every time a resource on your server is accessed.
SF_NOTIFY_PREPROC_HEADERS	Called before server preprocesses headers coming from Web client.
SF_NOTIFY_END_OF_NET_SESSION	Calls your filter when the user's session is about to end.
SF_NOTIFY_SECURE_PORT	Include with other flags if you want filter called when running over secure port (e.g., https:// . . .).
SF_NOTIFY_NONSECURE_PORT	Include with other flags when running over normal HTTP connection (almost always included in your filter flags).

■■■■■

```
DWORD WINAPI HttpFilterProc(
      PHTTP_FILTER_CONTEXT pfc,
      DWORD NotificationType,
      LPVOID pvNotification
 );
```

The first argument is an *HTTP_FILTER_CONTEXT* structure that has information about the server session, and has function pointers available that can get more information about the server session, and add headers or data to the response going back to the client. In the CVTDOC sample, this argument is not used, and indeed you won't always have a need to use this argument. The next argument indicates the event notification type. This determines what event triggered the call of your filter. It is almost always used because, as good form, you will want to make sure that you are not processing events that you are not concerned with. Also a single filter may be registered for multiple events, and HttpFilterProc( ) may have conditional logic based upon the event that triggered its call. For example, a filter may be registered for the SF_NOTIFY_READ_RAW_DATA and SF_NOTIFY_SEND_RAW_DATA events, where it processes some of the data passing from the client to the server or from the server to the client. But the details of its actions will likely vary slightly depending on the direction, so it needs to know the triggering event. The third argument stores data associated with an event in a structure. Available structure types are listed in Table 6.2.

Once you have the information of the event type and the data associated with the event, your filter can do its work. Once it's complete, it should return a valid return code. If you are not concerned with the event, you should immediately return SF_STATUS_REQ_NEXT_NOTIFICATION. If you handle an event and do not want any other filter or the server to handle it, return SF_STATUS_REQ_HANDLED_NOTI-FICATION. If you handled an event, but it's all right for other filters and the server to deal with the event as well, return SF_STATUS_REQ_NEXT_NOTIFICATION. SF_STATUS_REQ_ERROR can be returned to indicate an error in the filter (should be reserved for fairly serious problems). SF_STATUS_REQ_READ_NEXT can be returned

■■■■ **Table 6.2** ISAPI Filter Event Structures

Structure Type	Description
HTTP_FILTER_RAW_DATA	Points to the data passed back by a read or send event.
HTTP_FILTER_PREPROC_HEADERS	Access to the client headers before the server processes them.
HTTP_FILTER_AUTHENT	User and password info from server about to authenticate client.
HTTP_FILTER_URL_MAP	The physical path resulting from the server mapping a logical path.
HTTP_FILTER_LOG	Variety of information about the client and their request that can be logged by the filter or changed to affect IIS's native logging.

■■■■

to request to see more of the data being passed back to the client or received by the server, expecting to be called again with more data in the HTTP_FILTER_RAW_DATA structure.

Once your filter is built, you can install it on IIS by running REGEDT32.EXE and adding the DLL name to the key: HKEY_LOCAL_MACHINE\System\CurrentControlSet\Services\W3Svc\Parameters\Filter DLLs. Of course, ideally this should be done by a SETUP program that accompanies your filter.

This is the essence of what's required to build and use an ISAPI filter. To give you an even better sense of what's involved in building an ISAPI filter, I'll describe the construction of an ISAPI filter sample that ships with ActiveX: CVTDOC. Along the way, this should also give you a sense of what types of problems ISAPI filters can be applied to.

Building the CVTDOC ISAPI Filter

First I'll briefly describe the purpose of CVTDOC, then describe how I developed the ISAPI filter itself, and finally present how each of the supplied conversion programs was built.

What CVTDOC Does

CVTDOC is a simple ISAPI filter I wrote in response to a need from several clients for *automatic file publishing:* generating HTML for specific document types on the fly. CVTDOC uses the capability of ISAPI filters to supplement server capabilities by registering itself as intercepting all URL map events, and then checking to see if the document type requested is one that it knows how to convert.

Web content creators and webmasters often want to "publish" a document or data file to the Web. However, it can be very inconvenient to constantly run a conversion program to generate new HTML each time the document or data file is updated. Relying on the webmaster to run the conversion program for data that is often updated is also prone to error. If you are positive that the user has the software to display the document in native form, no conversion is necessary, but this is dangerous to assume. It would be great to be able to leave the document in native form, and have the Web server (or a Web server add-in such as CVTDOC) convert the document to HTML on the fly as needed.

CVTDOC is an Internet Services API (ISAPI) filter that converts documents to HTML dynamically if required when the HTML file is accessed. If the HTML document is out of date (older than the source document) or missing, it is generated automatically from the ISAPI filter, based on "conversion programs" registered for the source document type in the registry. We provide sample conversion programs for Word documents, Excel spreadsheets, and text files, but it's important to remember that this can be used for any document type. The primary purpose of CVTDOC is to demonstrate the powerful capabilities of ISAPI filters. Nevertheless, we think you will find it useful in its own right.

The following section describes in detail how the filter was constructed. It's relatively easy to not see the forest for the trees here. A quick glance at the section in this chapter on installing and using the filter (both of which are really quite simple) may help remove any disorientation as you plow through the minutiae of how this was built.

Building the Filter

Now we know what's required we can proceed to develop the filter. The basic steps are:

- Specify precisely how the filter is invoked, including what events it is registered for.
- Write GetFilterVersion, registering for required events.
- Write HttpFilterProc, processing the required event.
- Build and test the filter.

Requirements

The filter needs to be able to intercept URL requests ending with a reference in the format:

```
filename.extension.htm
```

and convert the file filename.extension to filename.extension.htm if and only if the HTML file is missing or older than the source. For example, an HTML hyperlink reference such as

```
<A HREF="specials.doc.htm">
```

should result in CVTDOC conditionally converting the specials.doc file to HTML. CVTDOC should first check if the HTML for that document already exists. If not, or if the HTML file is older than the source data file, it is a candidate for automatic conversion to HTML. CVTDOC searches through a list of registered data file types and associated conversion programs, stored in the registry, looking for a conversion program for the given extension (e.g., .DOC, .XLS, .TXT). If it finds a conversion program, it is launched to generate the specified filename.extension.htm file (e.g., specials.doc.htm).

Why does the HTML author need to use the strange syntax of specials.doc.htm instead of just embedding the file reference specials.doc and somehow configuring CVTDOC to know to convert all .doc files to HTML? Well, first of all you may want to still embed references to a .doc file and have it launch Word, or in general embed a reference to the native file format and have it launch a viewer for that format if present. Using the syntax presented, references to the native format are still possible. More fundamentally, the Web browser is always going to attempt to launch a helper app if the URL ends with an extension of the native file format and not .htm or .html. The URL ending with .htm makes the browser expect HTML back, which is what it gets.

What you need is a filter that intercepts every request for a file of a type that your filter can perform a conversion for. From looking at Table 6.1, it might seem that there is no explicit file requested event, but in fact there is. As long as the request is for a file on your local site, a URL mapping event (which can be intercepted with the SF_NOTIFY_URL_MAP flag) takes place. That is, if the URL reference is specials.doc.htm or any other URL that resolves to a local file, such as http://ourstore.com/specials.doc.htm a URL mapping event will take place on the server, to convert the logical URL to a physical file path. The filter should intercept each URL mapping event, by setting the SF_NOTIFY_URL_MAP flag in the HTTP_FILTER_VERSION structure on the GetFilterVersion() call. The other flag set should be the SF_NOTIFY_ORDER_HIGH to be certain to get the notification as early as possible to make the necessary conversion before, potentially, other filters that may need to use the data that results.

As preparation for writing the HttpFilterProc call, the pseudocode for doing actual filter processing is as follows:

```
IF URL request is filename.ext.htm
        IF filename.ext EXISTS
                IF filename.ext.htm MISSING or OLDER than filename.ext
                    LOOK FOR CONVERSION PROGRAM FOR ext
```

```
                    IF FOUND
                            CONVERT filename.ext TO filename.ext.htm
```

With this information about desire functionality, we're now ready to write the ISAPI filter.

GetFilterVersion

The first function we need to write is GetFilterVersion(). This does the three steps outlined in the discussion of GetFilterVersion responsibilities for all ISAPI filters identified earlier:

- Provides version information to the server with the following:

```
pFilterVersion->dwFilterVersion = HTTP_FILTER_REVISION;

strcpy (pFilterVersion->lpszFilterDesc,

"CVTDOC - Converts document or data into HTML if HTML not present
(or older");
```

  This provides the ISAPI filter revision number back to the server, as well as a text description of CVTDOC.

- Sets the priority of the filter (determines the order it's called in for these events).

- Register what events the filter is interested in.

These are accomplished by setting flags as shown:

```
pFilterVersion->dwFlags=(SF_NOTIFY_ORDER_HIGH | // be sure to intercept!
                    SF_NOTIFY_SECURE_PORT |
                    SF_NOTIFY_NONSECURE_PORT |
                    SF_NOTIFY_URL_MAP // tell us about all URL requests
                    );
```

This sets the notification priority high, tells it that you are interested in sessions over secure and nonsecure ports, and registers the filter for all URL map events.

The entire GetFilterVersion() code is:

```
BOOL WINAPI GetFilterVersion (PHTTP_FILTER_VERSION pFilterVersion)
{
        pFilterVersion->dwFilterVersion = HTTP_FILTER_REVISION;
        strcpy (pFilterVersion->lpszFilterDesc,
```

```
"CVTDOC - Converts document or data into HTML if HTML not present
or older");
// now register for events we're interested in
pFilterVersion->dwFlags=(SF_NOTIFY_ORDER_HIGH | // be sure to
⌐intercept!
                        SF_NOTIFY_SECURE_PORT |
                        SF_NOTIFY_NONSECURE_PORT |
                        SF_NOTIFY_URL_MAP  // tell us about all URL
                        ⌐requests
                        );
hEvtLog=RegisterEventSource(NULL, "CVTDOC");// open up event log
return TRUE;
}
```

HttpFilterProc

Now you just need to write the HttpFilterProc() procedure and you're almost done.
You've already developed the pseudocode for what it needs to do. Here is the essence
of the implemented HttpFilterProc.

```
// make a copy of the supplied filename that was requested so that we can
// determine what the source file is
strcpy(szSrcFile,pURLMap->pszPhysicalPath);

// check to see if there's an extension and then save a pointer to it
if (pszExt=strrchr(szSrcFile,'.')){ // check for extension

        // is the request for a .htm or .html file
        if (!strnicmp(pszExt,".htm",3)) { // is it HTML?

                // zap the extension on the copy of the file to get the
                // source file name
                *pszExt='\0';
                // check for access() returning zero, indicating presence
                // of source file
                if (!access(szSrcFile,0)){//check for presence of file

                        // this function checks to see if the source file
                        // is newer than the requested file, or if the
```

```
                    // requested file is just not present
                    if (FileDateCompare(szSrcFile,pURLMap->pszPhysical
                    ↳Path)>0)

                            // looks for a conversion program to run
                            // based on extension then runs the
                            // conversion program
                            if (CvtToHTML(szSrcFile,pURLMap->psz
                            ↳PhysicalPath)==TRUE)

                                    // indicate that the filter
                                    // handled the request for
                                    // the URL so no other filters
                                    // process
                                    return SF_STATUS_REQ_HANDLED_
                                    ↳NOTIFICATION;
                    } // end check for presence of file

    } // end is it HTML?

    } // end check for extension
    // .
    // .
    // if we didn't attempt conversion, control is passed to next filter
    // by returning SF_STATUS_NEXT_NOTIFICATION
    return SF_STATUS_NEXT_NOTIFICATION;
```

First you parse out the source file from the full HTML file (pURLMap->pszPhysical Path), by copying the physical file path into szSrcFile and stripping off the .htm extension if it's there (if it's not then this is not a candidate URL for automatic conversion). Then you check for existence of the source file (access( ) returning 0 indicates presence). If it's there, then check to see if the source file is newer or if the HTML file is missing (with the FileDateCompare( ) function that we write elsewhere). If so, we attempt to convert the source file into HTML using the CvtToHTML( ) function. This function checks for available conversions in a registry subkey called Conversions, created just for CVTDOC, that contains extensions (e.g., .doc, .xls, .txt) and their associated conversion programs. The Conversions key is located under the HKEY_LOCAL_MACHINE\System\CurrentControlSet\Services\W3SVC\Paremeters key. Creating it and filling it with values (file extensions and corresponding conversion programs) is part of the installation process documented in this chapter. If the conversion is not attempted, then control is passed to the next filter or to the server itself by returning SF_STATUS_NEXT_NOTIFICATION. If the conversion fails or no conversion program is found, these failures are reported to the NT Event Log. In this case, the likely appearance to the Web user is a "404 Not found" error showing on their Web browser, unless the HTML file is already present on the server.

Building and Testing

These are just some tips on building ISAPI filters that may encourage you with how simple it really is. Make sure your source file contains the following headers:

```
#include <httpext.h>
#include <httpfilt.h>
```

Make sure that your INCLUDE environment variable contains the ISAPI header directory, for example, C:\INETSDK\INCLUDE, and your LIB environment variable points to the ISAPI libraries, for example, C:\INETSDK\LIB\I386. A makefile that you can model your ISAPI filter makefile on is supplied with CVTDOC, but it's worth a look to see how simple it is. ISAPI programs in general, and ISAPI filters in particular, are really very lightweight.

```
CC=cl -c
CVARS=-DWIN32 -DNDEBUG
LINK=link
LINKOPT=/DLL
LIBS=wininet.lib user32.lib
OBJS=cvtdoc.obj
LINKOUT=/OUT:cvtdoc.dll
DEFS=cvtdoc.def
.cpp.obj:
    $(CC) $(CFLAGS) $(CVARS) $*.cpp
cvtdoc.dll: $(OBJS) $(DEFS)
    $(LINK) $(LINKOPT) /DEF:$(DEFS) $(LINKOUT) $(LIBS) $(OBJS)
```

To do initial testing on the created filter, what you want to do is see that a conversion program actually gets called. Running REGEDT32.EXE, create the Conversions subkey below the W3SVC\Parameters key in the registry and add a value of .TXT with data of TXT2HTML.BAT%s. You can create a batch file TXT2HTML.BAT with one line:

```
COPY%1%1.htm
```

This batch file also shows the primary requirement of any conversion program that will be registered with CVTDOC. It needs to take the source file as its argument and create a destination HTML file that has the same name as the source file, but with a .htm appended to it. This is a characteristic of all the conversion programs supplied with CVTDOC and should be the convention followed by your own conversion programs that you register with CVTDOC. I do supply a text-to-HTML converter with the delivered CVTDOC filter. This real text-to-HTML conversion program is another TXT2HTML.BAT file that invokes a Perl script called *TXT2HTML.PL*.

Now you need to install the filter as part of the running IIS Web server. Still running REGEDT32.EXE, add the full path to CVTDOC.DLL to the Filter DLLs parameter in HKEY_LOCAL_MACHINES\System\CurrentControlSet\Services\W3Svc\Parameters.

Now create an HTML file with contents of:

```
<A HREF="test.txt.htm">Quick test"</A>
```

Create a file called test.txt with contents of:

```
<HTML><HEAD><TITLE>CVTDOC Test</TITLE></HEAD><BODY>Test
data.</BODY></HTML>
```

If you place the HTML file onto your IIS Web server, load the HTML file into your Web browser, and click on the "Quick test" link, it should result in the TXT2HTML.BAT file being invoked, and you will see the contents of test.txt on your Web browser. This means that it is calling the ISAPI filter successfully. Of course, you don't need to do any of this testing for CVTDOC, which is already complete. But this should give you some idea of the testing process for your own ISAPI filters.

Building the Conversion Programs

Now that you have a working CVTDOC ISAPI filter, you need to supply some conversion programs for it. CVTDOC ships with conversion programs for Word DOC files, Excel XLS files, and text files (with a real text-to-HTML converter written in Perl rather than the stub batch file shown previously). This is certainly an immediately useful set of conversions, and you could just use the supplied conversion programs. However, CVTDOC is primarily meant to be a tool to register any data file type and associated conversion program. So if you are planning to create conversion programs for other file types, a discussion here of how these types were created may be useful. Note that the code for these conversion programs is *not* included with the CVTDOC sample as shipped with the ActiveX development kit, which concentrates on the CVTDOC ISAPI filter code itself, and not the code for conversion programs.

Word-to-HTML Conversion—DOC2HTM.EXE

DOC2HTM.EXE is invoked with the name of the source Word document as its argument. It will create an HTML file named with the source file name and appended .htm. To install it for use by CVTDOC, create a value under the W3Svc\Parameters\ Conversions key with name of .DOC and data of (for example) C:\WWWROOT\ CGI-BIN\DOC2HTM.EXE%s.

This was an easy conversion program to create. Microsoft Word combined with Word Internet Assistant allows you to load a Word document and save it as HTML. Creating the conversion program was just a matter of automating this with Visual Basic and the WordBasic OLE automation interface. Here is the entire code for the Word-to-HTML converter supplied with CVTDOC:

```
Private Sub Form_Load()
    Dim X As Object
    Set X = CreateObject("Word.Basic")
    X.FileOpen Name:=Command
    NewFile = Command + ".htm"
    fmt = X.ConverterLookup("HTML")
    X.FileSaveAs Name:=NewFile, Format:=fmt
    Set X = Nothing
    Unload Me
End Sub
```

You must have Word 6.0 or greater *and* Word Internet Assistant installed on the IIS server machine for this code to work. Once a new conversion program is built, registering it with CVTDOC is as simple as adding a new value to the Conversions subkey of the W3Svc\Parameters key, with data of the full path to the conversion program, followed by %s.

Excel-to-HTML Conversion—XL2HTM.EXE

XL2HTM.EXE is invoked with the name of the source Excel spreadsheet. It will create an HTML file named with the source file name and an appended .htm. It will only take the data from a named range in your Excel spreadsheet entitled Export. If no Export range is available it will just export A1 through H20. To install it for use by CVTDOC, create a value under the W3Svc\Parameters\Conversions key with name of .XLS and data of (for example) C:\WWWROOT\CGI-BIN\XL2HTM.EXE%s.

Unfortunately the Excel Internet Assistant is not invokable via OLE automation as Word Internet Assistant (i.e., you cannot save as HTML within Excel). So I had to write this conversion program from scratch. The entire program handling character formatting and alignment is quite long and not that interesting for the purpose at hand (to show you how to build your own conversions). Below is a grossly oversimplified (but functional) version of the code that just shows how to get the data from the Export range into an HTML table.

```
Private Sub Form_Load()
    Dim X As Object
    Set X = CreateObject("Excel.Sheet")
    Dim App as Object
    Set App = X.Application
    App.Workbooks.Open Command
    Dim CurSheet As Object
    Set CurSheet = App.ActiveWorkbook.Worksheets("Sheet1")
    Result =CurSheet.Range("Export").Select
    If (Result <> True) Then Result =
    CurSheet.Range("A1:H20").Select

    Dim OutputFile As String
    OutputFile = Command + ".htm"
    Open OutputFile For Output As #1

    Header = "Data From " + Command
    Line = "<HTML><HEAD><TITLE>" & Header &
    "</TITLE></HEAD><BODY>"
    Print #1, Line
    Line = "<H1>" & Header & "</H1>"
```

```
        Print #1, Line
        Print #1, "<TABLE>"

        NoRows = App.Selection.Rows.Count
        NoCols = App.Selection.Columns.Count
        ' now loop through all rows and columns printing out
        contents
        For Row = 1 to NoRows
            Print #1, "<TR>"
            For Col = 1 to NoCols
                Print #1, "<TD>"
                Print #1, App.Selection.Cells(Row, Col).Text
            Next Col
        Next Row
        Print #1, "</TABLE></BODY></HTML>"

        Set X = Nothing
        Set App = Nothing
        Set CurSheet = Nothing
        Unload Me
    End Sub
```

Text-to-HTML Conversion—TXT2HTML.BAT

TXT2HTML.BAT is invoked with the name of the source Word document as its argument. It will create an HTML file named with the source file name and an appended .htm. To install it for use by CVTDOC, create a value under the W3Svc\Parameters\ Conversions key with name of .TXT and data of (for example) C:\WWWROOT\ CGI-BIN\TXT2HTML.BAT%s. You will need to have Windows NT Perl installed on your IIS machine, executable in the PATH. You can find NT Perl on the Windows NT 3.51 Resource Kit, and at http://www.perl.hip.com.

This batch file is a wrapper around TXT2HTML.PL, a Perl script for text-to-HTML conversion written by Seth Golub of the University of Washington. This script is entirely too large to present here. The batch file is as follows:

```
perl txt2html.pl < %1 > %1.htm
```

The Perl script moves through the text file placing headers around logical breakpoints, and generally attempting to "HTML-ify" the content. It won't be perfect, but the result is a bit more attractive displayed on a Web browser than a plain text file.

Creating Your Own Conversions

You can get a pretty good idea from the preceding discussion how to create your own conversion program. It should take an argument of the source file. It should generate an HTML file named with the source file name and an appended .htm. If the program in question exposes an OLE automation interface, this usually makes writing a small Visual Basic program to do the work very easy. You should be able to use the Form_Load( ) subroutines presented as a model to build another VB-based conversion program.

Using CVTDOC

As mentioned, the primary purpose of CVTDOC is to demonstrate the capabilities of ISAPI Filters. Hopefully, presenting how this filter was built has made it clear how to create your own filters. If you don't need the specific functionality offered by CVTDOC, you can stop here, fire up Developer Studio, and start hacking your own ISAPI filters.

However, based upon what you know now about the functionality available in CVT-DOC, it may have value to you in and of itself. Assuming you now would like to use CVTDOC on your own Web site, here are the instructions to do so. You can find CVT-DOC in the ActiveX SDK in the directory \INETSDK\SAMPLES\ISAPI\CVTDOC. Currently the ActiveX SDK can be downloaded from http://www.microsoft.com/intdev/sdk.

Installation
1. Copy CVTDOC.DLL to an appropriate subdirectory, such as the CGI-BIN subdirectory of your Web content directory.
2. Update the Filter DLLs parameter of IIS. Run REGEDT32.EXE.
3. Add the full path of CVTDOC.DLL to HKEY_LOCAL_MACHINE\System\ CurrentControlSet\Services\W3SVC\Parameters\FilterDLLs (the DLLs are separated by commas).
4. Create a Conversions subkey of the W3SVC\Parameters key.
5. Add each extension (e.g., .xls, .doc) as a separate value.

6. Enter the full path of the conversion program to run for each extension as the value's data.

7. List each conversion program as taking two arguments of "%s %s" unless the conversion program in question will automatically add a .htm to the source file name as its generated output file.

8. For example, a value under the Conversions key might be .doc, and the data would be c:\wwwroot\cgi-bin\doc2htm.exe %s.

9. Place the conversion programs in the directories referenced. Sample conversion programs supplied are discussed below.

Conversion Programs

There are three conversion programs supplied with this sample:

1. DOC2HTM.EXE converts Word documents (.DOC files) to HTML. It requires that Word Internet Assistant (WordIA) be installed on the IIS server machine. It has only been tested with Word 95. Usage is: DOC2HTM.EXE <Word.DOC file>. An HTML file will be generated with the filename of the original Word document, with an appended .htm, for example, SPECIALS.DOC.htm.

2. XL2HTM.EXE converts Excel spreadsheets (.XLS files) to HTML. It does not require any other software beyond Excel 5.0 or greater. Usage is: XL2HTM.EXE <Excel spreadsheet file>. Output is an HTML file with the extension .htm, for example, SAMPLE.XLS.htm. The area exported to the HTML file is the range named Export.

3. TXT2HTML.BAT converts text files (.TXT files) to HTML, attempting to mark them up with HTML tags as best as possible. It invokes Seth Golub's TXT2HTML.PL Perl script to do this. This requires that Windows NT Perl be installed on the IIS server machine. Output is an HTML file with extension .htm.

These conversion programs are intended only as samples. You can use one installation of the CVTDOC filter to convert many different data file types. In fact, CVTDOC has the most value when it has conversions installed for uncommon file types that users may not be able to handle themselves. You should be able to find HTML conversion programs for almost any data format on the Internet and the World Wide Web. However you may need to write wrapper batch files or programs that allow the conversion program to conform to the CVTDOC calling convention. This just means that the program must take two arguments, the first being the original document file, and the second being the HTML output file. Alternatively the program can take just one argument and generate HTML with the input file name and an appended .htm (as do the three supplied conversion programs).

Usage

Embed a reference in your *referring* HTML page to the document or data file name *with an appended .htm*. For example,

```
<HTML>
<HEAD><TITLE>Simple CVTDOC Example</TITLE></HEAD>
<BODY>
<H1>Welcome to the CyberStore</H1>
For maximum savings, please check out our
<A HREF="specials.doc.htm">daily specials!</A>
</BODY>
</HTML>
```

The SPECIALS.DOC file will be converted automatically by the CVTDOC ISAPI filter if either: (1) the HTML file doesn't exist yet, or (2) it's older than the updated SPECIALS.DOC file. This allows the Webmaster to keep the HTML content current with very little intervention.

The full source for CVTDOC appears in Appendix A of this book, and on the book's Web page. It is also available on the Microsoft ActiveX Software Development Kit in the SAMPLES\ISAPI\CVTDOC directory.

MFC Support for ISAPI Filters

As with ISAPI itself, there is support in Visual C++ 4.1 or greater and the Microsoft Foundation Classes for ISAPI Filters: both a wizard to assist in creating them initially and classes to assist in writing and maintaining them.

ISAPI Filter Wizard

The ISAPI filter wizard allows quick creation of the basic framework for an ISAPI filter. There is actually more to this in ISAPI Filters than there was with Internet Server Applications: both GetFilterVersion() and HttpFilterProc() have significant logic to them that can be started with the wizard. There are more upfront choices about what the filter does that can be automated with the wizard. This is reflected in the filter wizard dialogs.

The wizard is invoked just like the ISA wizard, by selecting File/New/Project Workspace from the Developer Studio menu, and then choosing the ISAPI Extension option. In the first dialog deselect the ISAPI Extension checkbox and check the ISAPI Filter checkbox. You will then see the dialog shown in Figure 6.1.

This lets you choose with what priority your filter is called. Some filters require high priority (such as the CVTDOC filter shown above). Unless this is true you should leave it at the default. The checkboxes for connection types are usually both checked on. The next six checkboxes reflect the six major types of ISAPI filters. Filters can be written that change the data coming to the server from the client, or change the data going back in the other direction. (The UPCASE sample that converts text to uppercase on the ActiveX SDK is a good example of this.) Filters can process the

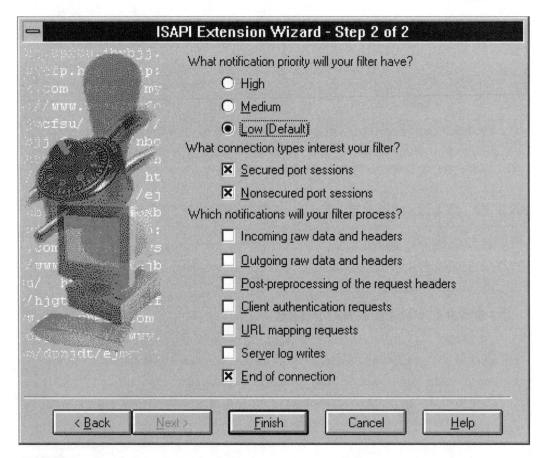

■■■■■ **Figure 6.1** ISAPI extension wizard for ISAPI filters.

HTTP headers going from client to server and back. This capability can, for example, be used to change the URL: to effect a redirection of a URL request to another logical URL address. A good example of this technique is the HOMEFILT sample on the ActiveX SDK, which redirects a request for a site's home page to instead invoke an ISAPI DLL.

Another popular server function to replace with your own ISAPI filter is a client authentication request. Instead of invoking the standard IIS authentication process, which checks the supplied name and password against the Windows NT account database, your ISAPI filter can check the name and password against your own database, perhaps a customer table stored in a SQL Server database.

Another event that can be intercepted is a URL mapping request, the logical to physical path translation that occurs any time a local resource on the Web server is requested. This is used by CVTDOC to intercept requests for particular types of files and convert those files to HTML on the fly. Note that the URL mapping request event should not (and cannot) be used to change the actual logical URL to another logical URL. This is best done with the technique of intercepting the header processing event, and changing the URL: header, as shown in the HOMEFILT example.

You can also replace the native IIS logging mechanism, which just logs TCP/IP address of the accessing browser, and what resource was accessed, with a richer set of information. For example, you might choose to log the domain name of the accessing user by performing Winsock gethostbyaddr() calls. You would do this by checking the Server log writes checkbox.

The last checkbox shown is End of connection, which can be intercepted to perform shutdown code. It doesn't hurt to leave it checked, and you can put code into that handling function generated by the wizard at your own discretion.

In general, you will not often be checking more than one of the first six notification checkboxes. That's because your filter usually has a very specific purpose. If it is intercepting more than one of those notifications, there is a good chance that what you're working with should really be decomposed into more than one ISAPI filter DLL.

Once you have selected the options for your filter, click Finish. The code for your ISAPI filter will be generated in a .CPP file, with a header .H file, a Win32 .DEF file, an .RC resource file, and a Visual C++ project .MDP file. In the example in Figure

6.2, I called the project SAMPFILT, so the wizard gave us SAMPFILT.CPP, SAMP-
FILT.H, SAMPFILT.DEF, SAMPFILT.RC files as shown.

Now the task at hand is to go into the event handling functions and do all real work.
For this example it's just the OnReadPreprocHeaders( ), unless you choose to put
some shutdown in OnEndofNetSession( ). For example, you could add some code
inside the OnReadPreprocHeader( ) function that reads the URL: header, determines
if it meets some criteria (such as being in a list of protected directories), does some
logic (such as determining privileges of the accessing user), and if so changes the URL:
header to point to a page that informs them of their lack of privileges. The access control filter presented later, called ACCSFILT, does this very thing. The point is that all
of the logic can be just written into the generated On . . . ( ) function. None of the

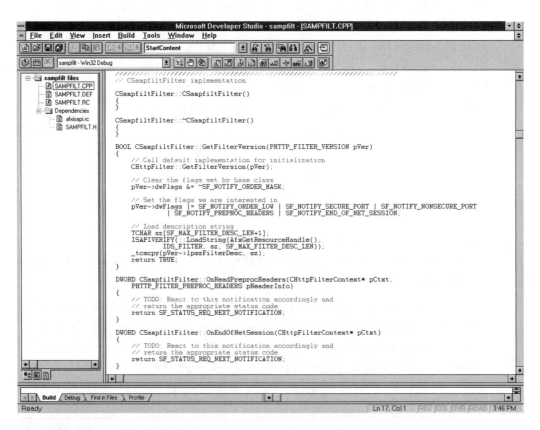

■■■■ **Figure 6.2** ISAPI filter wizard generated source files.

code to register for events with GetFilterVersion( ), or to determine what type of notification you are being called with in HttpFilterProc( ), needs to be written.

ISAPI Filter Classes

As with the Internet Server Application wizard, the ISAPI filter wizard generates code that assumes the presence of certain Microsoft Foundation Classes: specifically CHttpFilter and CHttpFilterContext. The notification handling functions (e.g., OnReadPreprocHeaders( ), OnEndofNetSession( )) are all member functions of a class for the generated ISAPI filter that is derived from CHttpFilter. A pointer to an object of the CHttpFilterContext class is supplied to each of these notification functions to allow the filter to get information about the event, such as the notification data. Note that unlike the CHttpServerContext class, there is no member that points to a CHTMLStream object. All output back to the client is performed with the WriteClient( ) and ServerSupportFunction( ) member functions of the CHttpServerContext class.

ACCSFILT: Enhanced IIS Access Control

I spent quite some time showing you how I built CVTDOC, the automatic file publishing filter. But this was built to the native ISAPI filter specification, and did not take advantage of the framework that the ISAPI filter wizard provides. I'd like to show you another example of the value of ISAPI filters, and at the same time use the ISAPI wizard skeleton code.

This utility was written in response to a dire need of a client, where the filter gave them functionality that they absolutely had to have. I hope it's another example of where this book can provide you with a capability you might not have otherwise had on your IIS Web site. If your content security needs are anything beyond the most basic, I suspect you will find some use for this filter, if only as a basis for your own efforts.

Microsoft Internet Information Server (IIS) provides a number of options for securing your Web site's content. You can protect access to any specified HTML page, file, or directory by setting the permissions to specified Windows NT users. Then, using the

Internet Service Manager, you can set IIS to use basic authentication and users will be prompted for name and password when attempting to access those pages or files. Figure 6.3 shows this option being set.

However, this requires having user accounts set up for those accessing users. This might be reasonable in an intranet situation, but for sites connected to the outside world, it may not, in fact, be a valid assumption. Fortunately, IIS, like many other Web servers has other ways of protecting access *without* requiring a user logon or account to be created. You can also grant or deny access to the entire server by IP address. That is, you can specify that all sites will be either granted or denied access, with the exception of a specified list of TCP/IP addresses or ranges. An example of this is shown in Figure 6.4.

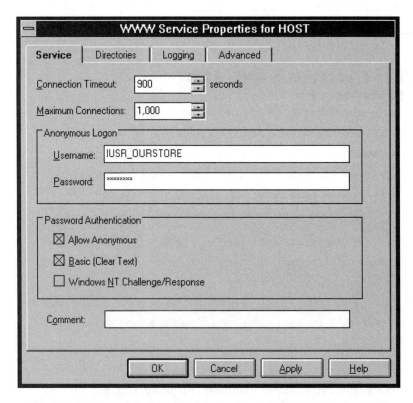

▬▬▬▬▬ **Figure 6.3** Internet Service Manager WWW service settings.

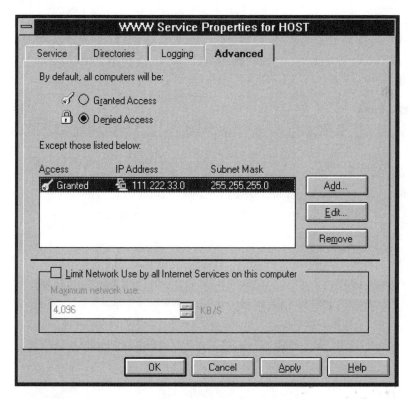

Figure 6.4 IIS access restriction by IP address.

The Problem

IIS allows restriction by:

1. User account using the native Windows NT file permission management, but requiring user accounts and logons.

2. Restriction of the entire server's access by IP address or range.

Useful as these capabilities are, they are not sufficient for many sites' needs. And in all honesty, they actually fall quite short of what some other Web servers offer.

An example of the kind of security configuration capability that is often required is the ability to restrict access by accessing domain name or domain name mask. That is, it is useful for many sites to be able to say that only users coming from *.gov or *.ourcompany.com domains can access the site. Furthermore, it is often required that only a portion of the Web site's content, a list of specific URLs or directories, needs to be restricted. In fact, the ability to have restriction of the accessing user only for specific URLs or directories would be useful for untranslated IP access restriction as well.

The Solution

Other Web servers do have this capability. Even though IIS 1.0 doesn't have it (and won't in version 2.0 either), it does have a great API for extending its capabilities, known as ISAPI filters. What I'd like to do is create an ISAPI filter that would allow Webmasters to specify some directories and URLs for special protection. They could then restrict access to those URLs to users (Web browsers) from specific domain names or domain name patterns (e.g., users from .gov sites).

This particular filter was written for a company that had a contractual requirement to limit access to portions of their content to users from .gov and .mil domains. If it weren't for this utility, they would have been forced to switch back to their brand X Web server (the horror!). As it happened, they were duly impressed with the capability of ISAPI filters to provide them with whatever security requirement they might need in the future.

The Design

So anyway, what you need is a filter that intercepts requests for URLs (by registering for the preprocess headers event), and checks to see if they are in a list of protected URLs (which can also be listed as just a directory name). If it is in the list, then it should do a domain name lookup (using the Winsock gethostbyaddr( ) call) of the accessing user's TCP/IP address (which can be retrieved with GetServerVariable( ) on the REMOTE_ADDR CGI environment variable). You then check to see if the domain name found is on a list of valid domain names or domain name suffixes that are allowed to access this protected URL (the list of protected URLs and associated domain name suffixes should be stored somewhere in the registry, like any good Win32 program). If the user is *not* a valid accessing user, then you want to redirect him or her to a special "no access allowed" HTML page. You do this by changing the URL (using the SetHeader( ) member function) to /noaccess.htm. This allows the error message that the unauthorized browser sees to be configurable by editing this file (you can make it as friendly or as hostile as you wish).

Installation and Configuration

Before I describe the actual implementation, there may be some of you that want to start using this utility. If you want to use ACCSFILT on your own site, follow these steps to set it up:

1. Download the source from the book's Web page from the ACCSFILT directory. Build ACCSFILT using the supplied makefile.

2. Copy ACCSFILT.DLL to a directory of your choice (for example C:\INETSRV\SCRIPTS).

3. Run the Registry Editor (REGEDT32.EXE) and edit the FilterDLLs parameters in the IIS WWW services Parameters subkey. This key is at HKEY_LOCAL_MACHINE\SYSTEM\CurrentControlSet\Services\W3SVC\Parameters. Edit the Filter DLLs value to add the full path to ACCSFILT.DLL, separating it from any existing DLL name with a comma. If you copied the DLL to C:\INETSRV\SCRIPTS then you would type in ,C:\INETSRV\SCRIPTS\ACCSFILT.DLL Figure 6.5 shows an example modified Filter DLLs parameter.

4. Within the Registry Editor, create a new subkey under HKEY_LOCAL_MACHINE\SYSTEM\CurrentControlSet\Services\W3SVC\Parameters. called Access (by selecting Add Key from the Registry Editor menu while positioned on the key just mentioned). Then select Add Value while positioned on the new Access key. Enter the URL of the file or directory that you wish to have protected. In Figure 6.6, I chose a top-level directory on the local Web site called /protected. Then supply one or more domain name suffixes or full domain names, separated by commas, as the value. In Figure 6.6, I restricted access to only .gov, .mil, and .ourcompany.com sites, by entering the value as

■■■■■■ **Figure 6.5** IIS filter DLLs registry value.

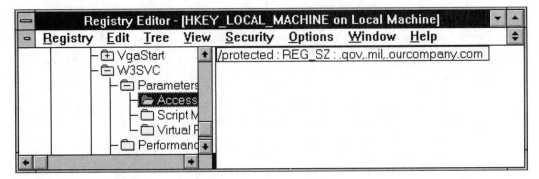

■■■■■ **Figure 6.6** Access filter registry key.

.gov,.mil,.ourcompany.com. The result of this registry setting is that only users from domain names ending in these suffixes will be able to access any URL in the /protected directory. The list of URLs can be extended beyond just this one entry by selecting Add Value again from the Access key, and the URLs can be specific HTML pages or files as well as directory names.

5. Create a file called NOACCESS.HTM and place it in your Web server root directory (e.g., C:\INETSRV\WWWROOT). The file can be as simple as the following HTML (but should be written based on the restrictions that you will use):

```
<HTML>

<HEAD><TITLE>ACCSFILT - No Access Message</TITLE></HEAD>

<BODY>Access only allowed to .gov, .mil, and .ourcompany.com
ᒪusers</BODY>

</HTML>
```

6. To load the filter, shut down the WWW Publishing Service (if it's running) from the Control Panel Services applet. Then restart the service. Check the Event Log System Log using the Event Viewer to be sure that the filter loaded. If it didn't, you will see an error that looks like Figure 6.7.

There are several factors that could cause such a problem. The most common of these are:

- The path specification is wrong: The directory name is bad or there is no ACCSFILT.DLL in the specified directory.

- One of the supplementary DLLs required for successful operation is missing on the Windows NT Server machine that IIS is running on. Common support DLLs for ISAPI filters in general include the Visual C++ 4.0 runtime library (MSVCRT40.DLL) and the MFC 4.0 runtime library (MFC40.DLL). ACCSFILT.DLL also requires that the Winsock 32 DLL (WSOCK32.DLL)

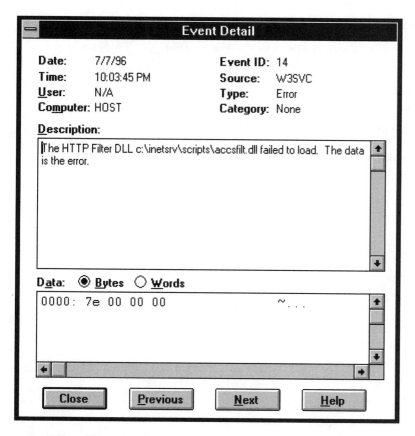

Figure 6.7 Filter load error message.

be installed on the server machine. If you get this error, check the \WINNT\
SYSTEM32 directory (or its equivalent) on the machine for these DLL files,
and supply them if they are missing.

6. Once you have verified that the DLL is being loaded, go to any Web browser
on a domain that should *not* have access to a protected URL, and attempt to
access a protected URL. The unauthorized Web browser should see the "no
access" message created in NOACCESS.HTM.

7. To check on this process, you can look in the Event Log Application Log for a
message labeled with Source of ACCSFILT. Each time a protected URL is
accessed, it is logged to the Event Log (even if accessed for the user attempting
to hit that URL). If access is denied, it will report the domain name of the denied
user in a separate Event Log message. Thus, every protected URL access will
result in either one or two log messages (one if access is granted, two if denied).

The Implementation

Here's the code for OnReadPreprocHeaders()—the function that implements the essential logic. Remember that with the ISAPI filter wizard, the GetFilterVersion() and HttpFilterProc() functions are written for you. You just need to fill in the code inside each notification handling function. For this filter, it's really just writing the code inside this one function.

```
DWORD CAccsfiltFilter::OnReadPreprocHeaders(CHttpFilterContext* pCtxr,
        PHTTP_FILTER_PREPROC_HEADERS pHeaderInfo)
{
    CHAR szUrl [2048];
    DWORD cbUrl;
    cbUrl=sizeof (szUrl);
    if ( !pHeaderInfo->GetHeader( pCtxt->m_pFC,"url",szUrl,&cbUrl)){
        return SF_STATUS_REQ_ERROR;
    }

        char szIPAddress[128],szHostname[128]="";
        DWORD dwBuffsize;
        BOOL bResult,bFoundHostname=FALSE;
        unsigned char acAddress[4];
        struct hostent *pHostent;

        dwBuffsize=sizeof szHostname;
        bResult Ctxt->m_pFC->GetServerVariable(
                pCtxt->m_pFC,"REMOTE_HOST",szHostname,&dwBuffsize);
        if (bResult!=TRUE || isdigit(szHostname[0])) {
                // no big surprise that REMOTE_HOST wasn't there
                // try to get it with REMOTE_ADDR
                dwBuffsize=sizeof szIPAddress;
                bResult Ctxt->m_pFC->GetServerVariable(
                        pCtxt->m_pFC,"REMOTE_ADDR",szIPAddress,
                        ↳&dwBuffsize);
                if (bResult==TRUE){
                        IPString2Bytes(szIPAddress,acAddress);
                        pHostent=gethostbyaddr((const char *)acAddress,4,
                        ↳PF_INET);
```

```
            if (pHostent){

                        strncpy(szHostname,pHostent->h_name,sizeof
                        ⌐szHostname);

                        bFoundHostname=TRUE;

            }

            else

                        bFoundHostname=FALSE;

        }

        else

                bFoundHostname=FALSE;

    }

    else

            bFoundHostname=TRUE;

    // now based on the hostname and directory decide whether to allow
    ⌐access

    if (!IsValidHostname(szHostname,szUrl)==TRUE)

    {

    if ( !pHeaderInfo->SetHeader( pCtxt->m_pFC,

                        "url",

                        ACCESSERRORPAGE ))

    {

        return SF_STATUS_REQ_ERROR;

    }

    }

        //

        // Pass the possibly changed header to the next filter in the
        ⌐chain

        //

    return SF_STATUS_REQ_NEXT_NOTIFICATION;

}
```

The logic of this function is fairly simple. First check to see if you have already been told the textual domain name of the accessing user, by checking the REMOTE_HOST CGI environment variable, using the GetServerVariable( ) member function. If the contents of this variable are numeric (as they will usually be unless some unusual Web browser chooses to report their domain name), then you will need to look up the domain name based on the IP address retrieved from the REMOTE_ADDR variable. Use the function IPString2Bytes( ) to convert the string returned from the variable to a form that can be used by Winsock to look up the domain name. Then make the Winsock gethostbyaddr( ) call to look up the domain name. Check this returned host name against the valid domain name suffixes stored for this URL in the Access registry key. If it matches any of the domain name suffixes, then the user is allowed access, by basically having the filter do nothing. If the user is not allowed access (there are no domain name suffix matches), then the SetHeader( ) function is used to change the URL to /NOACCESS.HTM, which reports to the user his or her lack of permission to access the requested URL. Full source code for ACCSFILT.DLL is available in Appendix A, and on the Web page for this book.

This chapter completes the coverage of server-side Web technologies: CGI programming, the ISAPI Specification, and the ISAPI Filter Specification. In the following chapters in Part II, you will explore the various client-side technologies introduced by ActiveX.

7

USING ACTIVEX

CONTROLS

ActiveX introduces a new standard for OLE Controls that makes them lightweight and efficient enough to be embedded in your Web pages. OLE Controls, also known as OCXs, have been around for some time. They were and are the traditional method of enhancing the functionality of Visual Basic applications with code that could not be done in Visual Basic. But they provide a convenient method of packaging technology into components in general. Drop the OLE control into your application, and you have then extended your application with the functionality of the control.

The new ActiveX Control standard has simplified the requirements of OLE Controls, making them easier to implement and more practical to deliver via the Web. Embedded into your Web pages, ActiveX Controls allow your static Web pages to become dynamic. You have already seen how ActiveX server-side applications (Internet Server Applications, ISAPI filters, the Internet Database Connector, etc.) make your site dynamic. But for many purposes, having client-side functionality yields a better experience for the browser user. For example, if you are trying to display graphical data to the user, a Chart control lying on the client allows you to just deliver the data points (usually a small amount of downloading) rather than the entire graphic image (usually a large amount of data). Other examples include input controls that provide validation of the input on the browser client, saving a round trip to the server if the data is erroneous.

There are now hundreds of ActiveX Controls available from Microsoft and third parties. They range from timer controls, to charting objects, to mini-spreadsheets (grid controls), to rich text editing boxes. Internet Explorer 3.0 ships with several of these controls straight out of the box, which you can begin to use in your Web content, if you can assume Internet Explorer or another browser that supports ActiveX Controls, or more specifically, acts as an ActiveX Control container. Users of Netscape browsers can download a plug-in that acts as an ActiveX container. This allows Netscape users to view content with ActiveX controls embedded. The ActiveX Control plug-in for Netscape is available from nCompass at http://www.ncompass.com.

If you can assume your user base is running either Netscape or Internet Explorer (a combination that is rapidly becoming over 95% of the installed base by most estimates), then using ActiveX Controls to deliver essential functionality becomes practical. If you can't make this assumption (for example, if you must support an installed base running Lynx on character-based DOS machines), then you can still use ActiveX Controls, but may not want to deliver the essential functionality of your Web-based application with them. For example, in a Web-based ordering system exposed to the general Internet population, it may not be practical to use ActiveX Controls to compute the sales tax and shipping on an order. This critical aspect of the system would then be denied to last-generation browsers. Far better to do the crucial system functions using Internet Server Applications, as presented in the earlier chapters. However, even in this environment, there are many features, such as graphics displays and enhanced editing controls, that non-ActiveX browsers might miss, but which will not affect their ability to use the system in some more limited form. For example, if the Lynx user misses out on the graphic display of some data, this might still be perfectly acceptable functionality.

If you are running in an intranet environment where you know exactly what your browser demographics are, you may know that all browser users are running an

ActiveX-capable browser, in which case you can be quite aggressive about incorporating central features into ActiveX Controls. I would like to first discuss how to go about embedding ActiveX Control functionality into your pages, and then go on in the next chapter to show you how to build your own ActiveX Controls.

Although this is a programming, not a webmastering or authoring, book, this technology is new enough that some background on how to integrate controls, and examples of what some controls can do, is necessary before you can get great ideas for your own control development.

ActiveX Controls can be embedded in your HTML content, using the <OBJECT> tag, which has now become part of the HTML standard. The <OBJECT> tag contains several attributes:

CODEBASE—This is the full URL of where to download the control from if it doesn't exist on the user's local machine. URLs for downloading all of the Microsoft ActiveX Web Gallery (a sample set of useful ActiveX controls) are supplied later. These URL are on the Microsoft Web site, which by default is a trusted download source by Internet Explorer. The control is digitally signed by its developer, and the certificate information is stored in the control itself. The information is displayed to the user, who can choose to proceed with the download of the control or not.

CLASSID—The unique identifier of this control as an OLE server. These are created by the developer and published along with the object.

TYPE—This is optionally specified as application/x-oleobject.

ID—You can give a name to this instance of the control.

These three attributes are the only ones unique to OBJECT. The rest of OBJECT's attributes are related to the image display of the control. They are the same as the attributes of the standard HTML <IMG> tag:

WIDTH—The width of how much space the control display takes up on the HTML page, specified in pixels.

HEIGHT—The height in pixels of the control display.

VSPACE, HSPACE—Vertical and horizontal space after control image.

ALIGN—Just as in <IMG> tag, can be "center", "bottom", "top", "left", and "right".

For example, the stock ticker OBJECT tag appears as follows:

```
<OBJECT
id=iexr2
type="application/x-oleobject"
classid="clsid:0CA4A620-8E3D-11CF-A3A9-00A0C9034920"
codebase="http://www.microsoft.com/ie/download/activex/iestock.ocx#ver
=4,70,0,1086"
width=300
height=50

>
```

ActiveX controls have properties associated with them that determine their behavior and what is displayed to the user. Properties are set with the <PARAM> tag inside an OBJECT block (everything in between the </OBJECT> tags). For example, the Stock Ticker control has a property named DataObjectName, a URL that determines where to load the ticker's data from. This property is set with the following PARAM tag:

```
<param name="DataObjectName" value="http://ourcompany.com/stockprices/
Giexrt.xrt">
```

Controls can also have events associated with them. But events are functions that are implemented by the programmer writing the control. The events supported are chosen from a set of events that a browser will send to a contained ActiveX control.

The ActiveX Component Gallery

Surveying some of the existing available ActiveX controls will give you a sense of the possibilities that already exist for integrating enhanced functionality into your pages. It may also inspire you for what controls you may be able to build (and ensure that you don't duplicate free existing software).

A free set of very useful controls is available on the Microsoft Web Site at http://www.microsoft.com/activex/controls. This set of controls (as of the Microsoft Internet Explorer 3.0 release) perform a variety of commonly needed functions. They are good examples of what is possible with controls native HTML Web pages. I'd like to show you just a few of these controls (after all this is a programming book), and how to integrate them into your pages. Check back at the URL listed for a list of currently available controls.

New Item

Let's start the survey of the Gallery controls with just about the simplest control—the New Item control. A common feature of Web sites is a **New!** graphic next to links for new content. Of course, this used to mean an automatic burden for the webmaster—removing the New graphic when the content was no longer new. The New Item control eliminates this chore, since it will allow a date to be specified after which the New indicator will no longer appear. The properties to be specified for this control are Date, which indicates when the image should stop being displayed, and optionally Image, which is a URL pointing to the image to be displayed. If Image is not specified then a New image built in to the control will be shown.

For example, the following HTML will display the New Item graphic up until October 1:

```
<html><head><title>New Item Control Test</title></head>
<body>
The New image to the right will disappear on October 1. <object
id=simplnew
type="application/x-oleobject"
classid="clsid:642B65C0-7374-11CF-A3A9-00A0C9034920"
codebase="http://www.microsoft.com/ie/download/activex/ienewitm.ocx#Ve
rsion=4, 70, 0, 1086"
width=20
height=10
>
<param name="date" value="10/1/1996">
</object>
</body>
</html>
```

This HTML and embedded control will appear as shown in Figure 7.1.

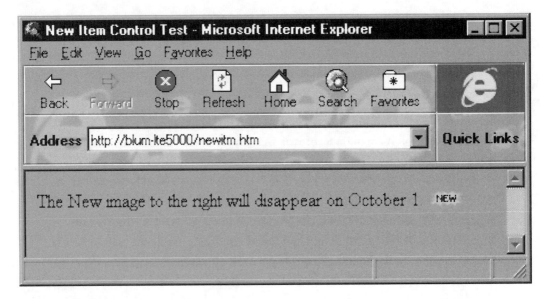

■■■■■■■ **Figure 7.1** New Item control test.

Chart

For many sites, the most useful control in the Gallery will be the Chart control. This control, embodied in the OCX file iechart.ocx, allows you to put charts of many forms into your HTML. These are Pie, Point, Line, Column, Bar, and Stock charts of various standard formats. Adding this capability to a site provides immediate value to users: They don't have to wait for their graphs to download as a huge image file. Sending GIF and JPEG images is the default way that most financial Web sites currently deliver information, and the delays can be excruciating. Using the Chart control allows you to immediately eliminate this bottleneck by allowing the user's machine to do the display, and only sending down the data used to draw the graph.

"Ah," you say, "but I don't know for certain that all users have an ActiveX-enabled browser (IE or Netscape with the nCompass plug-in)." Certainly use of these controls is more compelling if you can make this assumption. But if not, using the first part of the book's information on server-side development, you can write scripts to generate HTML on the fly that conditionally uses the Chart control: Check for the presence of a browser you know can display the control (such as Internet Explorer 3.0). If an ActiveX browser is present, then deliver the chart via the control. Otherwise generate a GIF or JPEG file with the graph, and embed it into the dynamically generated HTML page. In general, this is a technique that you may find useful in the short term while ActiveX browsers are not ubiquitous among your user community.

Anyway, the Chart control's properties are shown in Table 7.1. Note that there are some properties listed below that are not listed in the Chart documentation (on http://www.microsoft.com/ie/appdev/controls/iechart.htm), such BackColor and ForeColor, but in fact these are essential properties to set. Even more serious: the URL property is the one most often used to supply data to chart. Yet it's not listed in the property list, and the file format is undocumented. Hopefully you will find even more value in the table to clear up these undocumented aspects of this very useful control.

I have not listed some of the more rarely used properties. Examples of this are the ability to set a specific data value for a row and column on a one-at-a-time basis in the list of properties (i.e., a separate <PARAM> tag for each data point). Since you can already set entire rows of values using the Data property. For a full list of the properties, including ones you probably won't set, see the ActiveX Component Gallery page on the Chart control.

Table 7.2 shows the chart types that are available.

The specific functionality of each of these charts in many cases is obvious and implied by its name. For other chart types, you will want to look at the example invocations in the Chart demo page linked to the ActiveX Component Gallery http://www.microsoft.com/activex/controls.

The following is a full-fledged invocation of the Chart object, using the example values shown in the Property table.

```
<html>
<head><title>MSFT Price History: 12/95</title></head>
<body>
<object
codebase="http://www.microsoft.com/ie/download/activex/iechart.ocx#version=4, 70, 0, 1086"
classid="clsid:FC25B780-75BE-11CF-8B01-444553540000"
```

■■■■■■■■ **Table 7.1** Chart Control Properties

Property	Description	Example
ChartType	Specifies what type of chart. See Table 7.2. Example used is for high, low, close stock chart.	<param name="ChartType" value="17">
Rows	Number of rows in data	<param name="Rows" value="100">
Columns	Number of columns in data	<param name="Columns" value="3">
Data[n]	Note: This property is not documented but is the best method of supplying data inline if not using the URL property to read in a file. Specifies a row of data values, where n is the row number. These can be provided in a URL file as well as shown below.	<param name="data[0]" value="30 60 20 40">
ColumnNames	Specifies names of columns of data	<param name="ColumnNames" value="High Low Close">
RowNames	Specifies names of rows of data	<param name="RowNames" value="1986 1987 1988 1989 1990 1991 1992 1993 1994 1995">
URL	Note: This property is not documented on the iechart.htm page, but is used in many of the examples. Further the data format of the file is not documented. URL of data file containing values to chart. Format: First line contains a value indicating the type of chart. Second line contains the number of rows of data. Third line contains number of columns of data, and optional column headings. Subsequent lines contain rows of data. First value is row name. Subsequent values are columns of data.	<param name="url" value="www.ourcompany.com/data.txt">

■■■■■■ **Table 7.1** Continued

Property	Description	Example
BackColor	Note: This property not documented in Chart documentation. Used to control background color of the chart. The value is set as most HTML background colors are: with"#rrggbb", where rr is the hex encoded red value of the color between 0 and 255, gg the greenvalue, and bb the blue value. The example shown yields a white background.	`<param name="BackColor" value="#ffffff">`
ForeColor	Note: This property also not documented. Controls foreground color with same value setting scheme. Example shown results in blue foreground text.	`<param name="ForeColor" value="#0000ff">`
ColorScheme	Used to determine how regions are filled. Can be set to 0, 1, or 2.	`<param name="ColorScheme" value="0">`
BackStyle	Number that determines if background is transparent (0) or opaque (1).	`<param name="BackStyle" value="1">`
HGridStyle	Note: Also undocumented. Determines whether horizontal grid lines are used. Value zero (0) means no gridlines, one (1) means solid gridlines, higher values create broken (dashed) gridlines.`<param name="HGridStyle" value="1">`	
VGridStyle	Note: Also undocumented. Determines whether vertical grid lines are used. Value zero (0) means no gridlines, one (1) means solid gridlines, higher values create broken (dashed) gridlines.	`<param name="HGridStyle" value="0">`
DisplayLegend	Value zero (0) means no legend. Value one (1) means legend is created.	`<param name="DisplayLegend" value="0">`

```
        id=OurChart
        width=400
        height=200
        align=center
        hspace=0
        vspace=0
>
<param name="hgridStyle" value="1">
<param name="vgridStyle" value="0">
<param name="colorscheme" value="0">
<param name="DisplayLegend" value="0">
<param name="BackStyle" value="1">
<param name="BackColor" value="#ffffff">
<param name="ForeColor" value="#0000ff">
<param name="url" value="ms1295.txt">
</object>
</body>
</html>
```

■■■■■■■■ **Table 7.2** Chart Control Chart Types

Chart Type	Description	Chart Type	Description
0	Pie chart	11	Simple column chart
1	Pie with wedge out	12	Stacked column chart
2	Point chart	13	Full column chart
3	Stacked point chart	14	Simple bar chart
4	Full point chart	15	Stacked bar chart
5	Line chart	16	Full bar chart
6	Stacked line chart	17	HLC Stock Chart
7	Full line chart	18	HLC Stock Chart WSJ
8	Simple area chart	19	OHLC Stock Chart
9	Stacked area chart	20	OHLC Stock Chart WSJ
10	Full area chart		

The msft1295.txt file contains the following data (prices for MSFT in December 1995).

```
18
24
3          High  Low   Close
'12/29/95 88.75 86.25 87.75
12/28/95        88    86     87
12/27/95 90.625       88.375    88.875
12/26/95 91.25 89.875     90.25
12/22/95 90.875       89.125    90.5
12/21/95 90    87.375    90
12/20/95 91.375       87    87.125
12/19/95 91.0156      87.375    90.875
12/18/95 89    85.375    87
12/15/95 89.75 87.25 88.375
12/14/95 93.5  88.625    88.75
12/13/95 92.125      90.5  91.75
12/12/95 93.125      91.125    91.375
12/11/95 94.75 93    93.125
12/08/95 94.625      92.234    94.5
12/07/95 92    88.859    90.5
12/06/95 91    86    90.625
12/05/95 88.125      85.125    86
12/04/95 89.625      85.25 87.875
12/01/95 87.875      85.875    86.25
```

This will result in the graph shown in Figure 7.2.

Animated Button

The Animated Button control lets you embed images from an AVI file (i.e., a video clip) into your Web pages. You specify which the beginning and ending frame for each state of the control. There are four states of the control:

- Down: When the control receives LButton click.
- Focus: When the control gets focus.

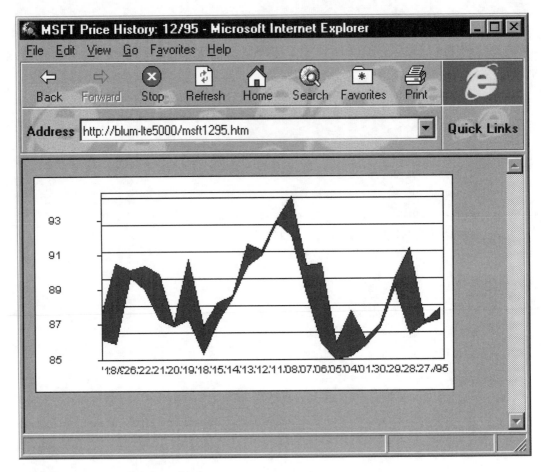

Figure 7.2 Sample chart.

- Mouseover: When mouse moves over the control.
- Default: When the mouse cursor and focus are both not on the control.

Each of these states has a start and end frame property, resulting in the following properties (set with the NAME attribute of the PARAM tag): DefaultFrStart, Default-FrEnd, MouseoverFrStart, MouseoverFrEnd, FocusFrStart, FocusFrEnd, Down-FrStart, DownFrEnd. Each of these properties should have a number of the frame set as the VALUE attribute of the PARAM tag. The only other property that needs to be set is the URL of the AVI to be used as the data source, which is done with the (you guessed it) URL property.

Here's a sample embedding of the Animated Button control. Should you wish to duplicate and test this, the CLOCK.AVI file referred to is present on any copy of Microsoft Windows NT 4.0 in the \WINNT directory. The control itself is downloaded automatically from the Microsoft Web site if it is not present on the user's machine.

```
<object
codebase="http://www.microsoft.com/ie/download/activex/ieanbtn.ocx#Version=
↳4.70.0.1086"
          id=anbtn
          classid="clsid:0482B100-739C-11CF-A3A9-00A0C9034920"
          width=300
          height=200
          align=center
          hspace=0
          vspace=0
     >
     <PARAM NAME="defaultfrstart" value="0">
     <PARAM NAME="defaultfrend" value="2">
     <PARAM NAME="mouseoverfrstart" value="3">
     <PARAM NAME="mouseoverfrend" value="5">
     <PARAM NAME="focusfrstart" value="6">
     <PARAM NAME="focusfrend" value="8">
     <PARAM NAME="downfrstart" value="9">
     <PARAM NAME="downfrend" value="11">
     <PARAM NAME="URL" value="http://ourstore.com/videos/clock.avi">
     </object>
```

Forms Controls and the HTML Layout Control

In order to support sophisticated, precise graphic design of pages, Microsoft and other vendors recognized the need for extensions to the HTML standard. The introduction of frames created was a big step, but it still did not allow exact positioning of page elements, and other advanced features from the GUI world, such as overlapping regions and transparent frames.

To address these limitations, Microsoft is working with the World Wide Web Consortium (the W3C) to define standards for 2-D layout to enable such advanced design. These extensions will eventually find their way natively into the HTML standard and browsers such as Internet Explorer and Netscape. But while the standard is being hashed out, the capabilities it provides can be accessed by incorporating the HTML Layout ActiveX Control into your pages, as you would any other ActiveX object. Remember that Netscape can host ActiveX Controls using the nCompass plug-in, so these pages can be designed for viewing by Netscape as well, during the period while the HTML tag syntax is being defined by the W3C. Until the HTML tags for this control are defined, the parameters for the HTML layout control are defined in a separate file with the extension .ALX. The following is a sample HTML page incorporating the layout control:

```
<HTML><HEAD><TITLE>Demo 2-D Layout</TITLE></HEAD>
<BODY BGCOLOR=#a01e0c>
<OBJECT CLASSID="812AE312-8B8E-11CF-93C8-00AA00C08FDF"
        ID="CyberStore" HEIGHT=400 WIDTH=600
        STYLE="LEFT:0;TOP:0;WIDTH:600;HEIGHT:400">
<PARAM NAME="URL" VALUE="http://www.cyberstore.com/sample.alx">< PARAM>
</OBJECT>
</BODY>
</HTML>
```

Note that you need to specify a HEIGHT and WIDTH, but most importantly the ALX file (in the "URL" parameter), which specifies how objects are placed onto the 2D layout. The .ALX file contains a division block, delimited by the <DIV> and </DIV> tags. These tags are anticipated to become part of the HTML standard, but in the meantime will be defined in a separate .ALX file. The syntax for an ALX file is:

```
<DIV [ID ame] STYLE = "layout-style-attributes">
   object-blocks
</DIV>
```

As indicated, the ID is an optional supplied text string that uniquely identifies the division to a client-side script. The STYLE attribute itself must have an attribute called LAYOUT set to FIXED. It also has HEIGHT and WIDTH attributes specified in number of pixels. It has an BACKGROUND attribute as a hex-encoded number specifying the background color.

The objects within a division can be placed very precisely with *x-y* coordinates, unlike objects or text within a conventional HTML page. A sample ALX file, extending the previous example, would be:

```
<OBJECT ID="Image1" STYLE="TOP:50;LEFT:50;WIDTH:100;HEIGHT:100;"
<DIV ID="CyberStore" STYLE="LAYOUT:FIXED;WIDTH:600;HEIGHT:400;">

    CLASSID="CLSID:D4A97620-8E8F-11CF-93CD-00AA00C08FDF">

    <PARAM NAME="PicturePath" VALUE="
⌐http:\\www.cyberstore.com\cyberlogo.wmf">

    <PARAM NAME="BorderStyle" VALUE="0">

    <PARAM NAME="Size" VALUE="5292;5080">

    <PARAM NAME="VariousPropertyBits" VALUE="19">

    </OBJECT>

</DIV>
```

This will display the image control at a very specific location (offset $x = 100$, $y = 100$) within the division. If this sample seems lightweight, don't worry; I give a much meatier example of a populated layout control in the next section on the ActiveX Control Pad.

The ActiveX Control Pad

I went into the previous description of how to embed the layout control directly, because it's a good example of authoring use of a complex control. However, actually writing those HTML and ALX files is not strictly necessary. There is a tool created just to create pages that incorporate the layout control and place objects on those pages. It is the ActiveX Control Pad, available at http://www.microsoft.com/workshop/author/layout. The Control Pad automates the creation of pages that incorporate ActiveX Controls and ActiveX Scripts (VB Script for now). The ActiveX Control Pad release also includes the previously discussed HTML Layout Control. Since its focus is primarily on control integration, and it introduces new controls, I would like to discuss this product here, rather than waiting until I present VBScript in a later chapter.

Once you download the ActiveX Control Pad, and run the SETUP program, it installs itself into its own program group. You can using the Control Pad to author HTML pages. It isn't particularly robust as an HTML tag editor or as an editing environment that insulates you from HTML. What it *does* do particularly well is insert ActiveX Controls or the HTML Layout Control into HTML, either new pages that you write in Control Pad or existing HTML pages. Most importantly, it allows you to create the ALX files that the HTML Layout Controls use, with a simple drag-and-drop tool palette of forms controls.

Despite the fact that Control Pad throws you into HTML first, you really should create the HTML Layout specification (the ALX file) first, since when you go to integrate the layout control into your page, you will be prompted for the ALX file. Select File/New HTML Layout, and you will be presented with a palette of forms controls and a canvas to place controls on. It is very reminiscent of Visual Basic, the Microsoft Exchange Forms Designer, and other Microsoft forms layout environments. You will then click specific forms controls and drag them to the canvas. All common form controls are available: combo boxes, list boxes, tab controls, labels, text boxes. A sample layout control populated with form controls is shown in Figure 7.3.

If you perform a Save with the image shown, the result will be the ALX file shown below. Note that each embedded control has specific x and y coordinates specified (embedded as the TOP and LEFT attributes in the STYLE attribute). Note also that a ZINDEX is specified, which allows for overlapping controls.

```
<DIV STYLE="LAYOUT:FIXED;WIDTH:261pt;HEIGHT:270pt;">
<OBJECT ID="TabStrip1"
     CLASSID="CLSID:EAE50EB0-4A62-11CE-BED6-00AA00611080"
STYLE="TOP:25pt;LEFT:17pt;WIDTH:206pt;HEIGHT:182pt;TABINDEX:1;ZINDEX:1;">
         <PARAM NAME="ListIndex" VALUE="0">
         <PARAM NAME="Size" VALUE="7276;6429">
         <PARAM NAME="Items" VALUE="Billing Information;Shipping
         ⌐Information;">
         <PARAM NAME="TipStrings" VALUE=";;">
         <PARAM NAME="Names" VALUE="Tab1;Tab2;">
         <PARAM NAME="NewVersion" VALUE="-1">
         <PARAM NAME="TabsAllocated" VALUE="2">
         <PARAM NAME="Tags" VALUE=";;">
         <PARAM NAME="TabData" VALUE="2">
         <PARAM NAME="Accelerator" VALUE=";;">
```

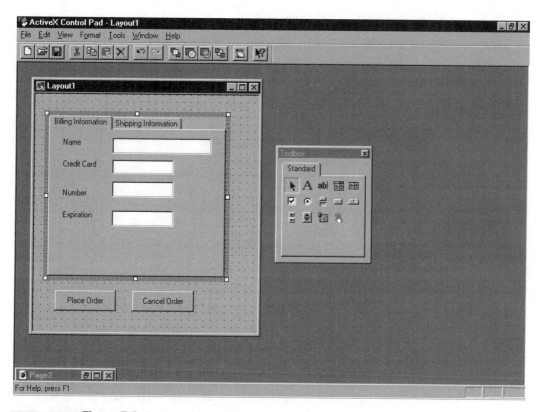

Figure 7.3 ActiveX Control Pad layout.

```
        <PARAM NAME="FontCharSet" VALUE="0">
        <PARAM NAME="FontPitchAndFamily" VALUE="2">
        <PARAM NAME="TabState" VALUE="3;3">
    </OBJECT>
<OBJECT ID="LabeL1"
    CLASSID="CLSID:978C9E23-D4B0-11CE-BF2D-00AA003F40D0"
STYLE="TOP:50pt;LEFT:33pt;WIDTH:50pt;HEIGHT:17pt;ZINDEX:3;">
        <PARAM NAME="Caption" VALUE="Name">
        <PARAM NAME="Size" VALUE="1746;583">
        <PARAM NAME="FontCharSet" VALUE="0">
        <PARAM NAME="FontPitchAndFamily" VALUE="2">
    </OBJECT>
```

```
<OBJECT ID="Label2"
    CLASSID="CLSID:978C9E23-D4B0-11CE-BF2D-00AA003F40D0"
STYLE="TOP:74pt;LEFT:33pt;WIDTH:50pt;HEIGHT:17pt;ZINDEX:5;">
        <PARAM NAME="Caption" VALUE="Credit Card">
        <PARAM NAME="Size" VALUE="1746;583">
        <PARAM NAME="FontCharSet" VALUE="0">
        <PARAM NAME="FontPitchAndFamily" VALUE="2">
    </OBJECT>

<OBJECT ID="LabeL3"
    CLASSID="CLSID:978C9E23-D4B0-11CE-BF2D-00AA003F40D0"
STYLE="TOP:107pt;LEFT:33pt;WIDTH:33pt;HEIGHT:18pt;ZINDEX:10;">
        <PARAM NAME="Caption" VALUE="Number">
        <PARAM NAME="Size" VALUE="1164;635">
        <PARAM NAME="FontCharSet" VALUE="0">
        <PARAM NAME="FontPitchAndFamily" VALUE="2">
    </OBJECT>

<OBJECT ID="Label4"
    CLASSID="CLSID:978C9E23-D4B0-11CE-BF2D-00AA003F40D0"
STYLE="TOP:132pt;LEFT:33pt;WIDTH:72pt;HEIGHT:18pt;ZINDEX:11;">
        <PARAM NAME="Caption" VALUE="Expiration">
        <PARAM NAME="Size" VALUE="2540;635">
        <PARAM NAME="FontCharSet" VALUE="0">
        <PARAM NAME="FontPitchAndFamily" VALUE="2">
    </OBJECT>

<OBJECT ID="TextBox1"
    CLASSID="CLSID:8BD21D10-EC42-11CE-9E0D-00AA006002F3"
STYLE="TOP:50pt;LEFT:91pt;WIDTH:116pt;HEIGHT:18pt;TABINDEX:4;ZINDEX:4;">
        <PARAM NAME="VariousPropertyBits" VALUE="746604571">
        <PARAM NAME="Size" VALUE="4075;635">
        <PARAM NAME="FontCharSet" VALUE="0">
        <PARAM NAME="FontPitchAndFamily" VALUE="2">
    </OBJECT>
```

```
<OBJECT ID="ListBox1"
     CLASSID="CLSID:8BD21D20-EC42-11CE-9E0D-00AA006002F3"
STYLE="TOP:74pt;LEFT:91pt;WIDTH:72pt;HEIGHT:17pt;TABINDEX:8;ZINDEX:8;">
        <PARAM NAME="ScrollBars" VALUE="3">
        <PARAM NAME="DisplayStyle" VALUE="2">
        <PARAM NAME="Size" VALUE="2540;582">
        <PARAM NAME="MatchEntry" VALUE="0">
        <PARAM NAME="FontCharSet" VALUE="0">
        <PARAM NAME="FontPitchAndFamily" VALUE="2">
    </OBJECT>

    <OBJECT ID="TextBox3"
     CLASSID="CLSID:8BD21D10-EC42-11CE-9E0D-00AA006002F3"
STYLE="TOP:99pt;LEFT:91pt;WIDTH:72pt;HEIGHT:18pt;TABINDEX:9;ZINDEX:9;">
        <PARAM NAME="VariousPropertyBits" VALUE="746604571">
        <PARAM NAME="Size" VALUE="2540;635">
        <PARAM NAME="FontCharSet" VALUE="0">
        <PARAM NAME="FontPitchAndFamily" VALUE="2">
    </OBJECT>

<OBJECT ID="TextBox4"
     CLASSID="CLSID:8BD21D10-EC42-11CE-9E0D-00AA006002F3"
STYLE="TOP:132pt;LEFT:91pt;WIDTH:72pt;HEIGHT:18pt;TABINDEX:12;ZINDEX:12;">
        <PARAM NAME="VariousPropertyBits" VALUE="746604571">
        <PARAM NAME="Size" VALUE="2540;635">
        <PARAM NAME="FontCharSet" VALUE="0">
        <PARAM NAME="FontPitchAndFamily" VALUE="2">
    </OBJECT>
<OBJECT ID="CommandButton1"
     CLASSID="CLSID:D7053240-CE69-11CD-A777-00DD01143C57"
STYLE="TOP:223pt;LEFT:25pt;WIDTH:72pt;HEIGHT:24pt;TABINDEX:6;ZINDEX:6;">
        <PARAM NAME="Caption" VALUE="Place Order">
        <PARAM NAME="Size" VALUE="2540;846">
        <PARAM NAME="FontCharSet" VALUE="0">
```

```
        <PARAM NAME="FontPitchAndFamily" VALUE="2">
        <PARAM NAME="ParagraphAlign" VALUE="3">
    </OBJECT>

  <OBJECT ID="CommandButton2"
      CLASSID="CLSID:D7053240-CE69-11CD-A777-00DD01143C57"
STYLE="TOP:223pt;LEFT:116pt;WIDTH:72pt;HEIGHT:24pt;TABINDEX:7;ZINDEX:7;">
        <PARAM NAME="Caption" VALUE="Cancel Order">
        <PARAM NAME="Size" VALUE="2540;846">
        <PARAM NAME="FontCharSet" VALUE="0">
        <PARAM NAME="FontPitchAndFamily" VALUE="2">
        <PARAM NAME="ParagraphAlign" VALUE="3">
    </OBJECT>
  </DIV>
```

Now you need to get the layout control and its corresponding ALX file integrated into your Web page. ActiveX Control Pad supports this by allowing you to invoke Insert

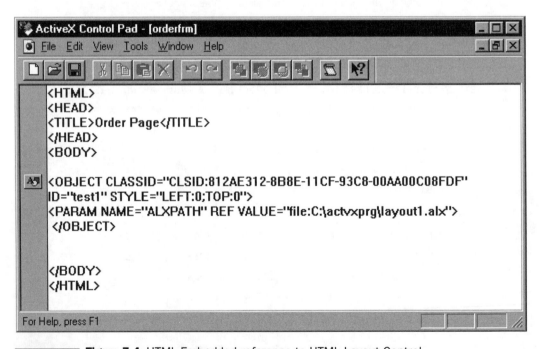

Figure 7.4 HTML Embedded reference to HTML Layout Control.

HTML Layout Control from the Edit menu. For the example just given, this will appear as shown below in Figure 7.4.

The appearance of the HTML page with the control embedded and the ALX file defined above is shown in Figure 7.5.

More information on the HTML Layout Control is available on the Microsoft Site Builder's Workshop: http://www.microsoft.com/workshop. There are some aspects of

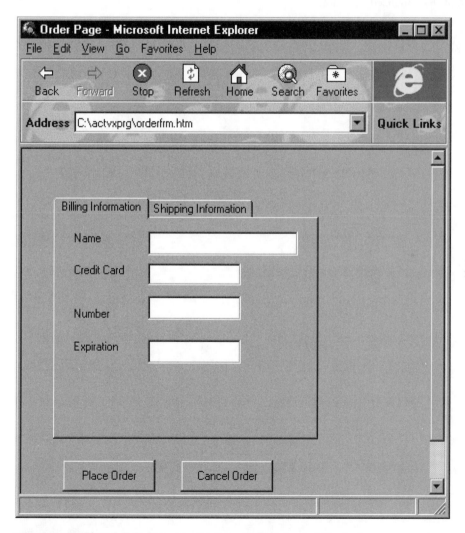

▮▮▮▮▮▮▮ **Figure 7.5** Browser display of HTML Layout Control.

incorporating the Layout Control that may change by the time you read this. At some point the separate ALX file for the HTML Layout Control will not be necessary. All of the content in there is just HTML anyway, so eventually that content will be displayed inside a <DIV> tag in the main body of the HTML. Also, the functionality of the HTML Layout Control will eventually work its way into the browser as the standards for specifying 2-D layout get adopted by the W3C. IE will probably be the first to handle the syntax natively, but Netscape and others should follow suit quickly once the W3C has finalized its syntax.

Okay, enough on how to integrate somebody else's controls. Let's go on in Chapter 8 to show you how to start writing your own controls.

8

WRITING ACTIVEX CONTROLS

You will likely get benefit from Chapter 7, "Using ActiveX Controls," whether or not you will write your own ActiveX controls. If you are authoring any Web content, or even just doing server-side Web programming, knowledge of how to integrate controls into your content is invaluable to take advantage of the capabilities of the thousands of existing ActiveX Controls in your pages. But what is necessary to go beyond that and create your own controls?

In earlier chapters on building Internet Server Applications and ISAPI filters, C programming background was sufficient. In this chapter, I will assume that you are a competent C++ programmer. If you are new to C++ and Windows programming, building an ActiveX Control should probably not be one of your earlier projects. The best starting path down this road for you may be to work through the MFC tutorial that ships with Visual C++, or work through one of the better Windows programming books, such as Kruglinski's *Inside Visual C++* (Microsoft Press, 1996).

This warning doesn't really apply to a lot of the C programming going on in earlier chapters. ISAPI development is quite approachable at the C programming level, and Windows programming experience is completely optional. There isn't much going on there that isn't present in just about any C program on any platform. Yes, I did present some C++, but just to make life easier for the programmer with some handy labor-saving classes. No creation of your own classes is necessary. For example, you can use the HTMLForm class as if it were an intrinsic data type in C, and just call the exposed member functions as you see fit. Creating objects and using objects are really two different levels of difficulty. As a recent skeptical C programmer student of mine quipped, "I used those objects but I didn't inhale." Well, creation of controls does require inhalation of C++ class creation and Windows development.

Just so you don't get too discouraged by this caveat, remember this technology is just one of the palette of options for building interactive functionality for Web sites. Most things can be done with server-side technology. And since such applications will generally not rely upon the presence of any specific Web browser, there is a powerful argument for doing as much "smart stuff" as possible on the server-side. However, some things do work better on the client, such as client-side validation of form data, and client-side display of graphics and image manipulation.

But ActiveX Controls are not even the only ActiveX client-side technology. Scripts can perform client-side data validation and simple calculations. Despite its newness, Java applets can be an easier technology to incorporate Web client functionality than writing an ActiveX Control from scratch (and Microsoft Visual JH is a great Java development tool). Java applets have some disadvantages as well, since ActiveX Controls can be integrated just about anywhere, into any OLE Container application. The important thing to remember is that if you need some specific functionality, ActiveX Controls might be a way to get it, especially if the control already exists.

If it doesn't exist, you can write it, but you should also double-check that it might not be better to implement that feature on the server. You can also evaluate whether the specific capability can be more easily built with a Java applet. However, if you wish to create controls that can be used anywhere, inside a Web page or out, you will tend to favor the ActiveX Control approach. Also, those experienced Windows C++ programmers among you will probably want to stay there. Java is frankly a more limited programming language. Yes, in a vacuum it may be easier to learn than C++, and do more to protect programmers from themselves (and users from programmers!), but in fact it is missing some of the expressiveness and power of its forebear. So if you have the appropriate Windows and C++ development experience to tackle ActiveX Control building, read on!

It also will help a great deal if you have some exposure to the concepts behind OLE and COM (the Component Object Model) programming. ActiveX Controls are just OLE controls, with much less required in the form of interfaces and methods. Thus, any OLE Control is basically already an ActiveX Control (though there are a few additional things you may wish to do to the OLE Control to make it optimal for use on Web pages, such as stamping it with a certificate indicating the author of the control).

Those of you who are already C++ and OLE programmers can take immediate heart from the last sentence. Yes, you can use your existing OLE Controls in your Web pages, and can modify them in minor ways to become even more optimal ActiveX Controls. I'm not going to emphasize this path, however. There are lots of good books on OLE programming and building OLE Controls, including Adam Denning's excellent *OLE Controls Inside and Out* (Microsoft Press, 1995), which is particularly relevant to this subject. Denning thoroughly explains how to build full-featured OLE Controls that can be placed in any compliant OLE Container, both using the wizard in the Visual C++ Control Development Kit (the CDK), and by hand in C++. These controls will work just fine in Web pages using the integration process described in Chapter 7. However, in this section we will emphasize the process of building lightweight ActiveX controls from scratch, controls that you already know you want to run great from Web pages.

There are currently three main ways to develop ActiveX Controls:

- Use Visual C++ Control Development Kit. The CDK has existed for some time, and the process of creating OCXs is little changed to use these controls in Web pages.

- Use the BaseCtl sample, also known as the ActiveX Control Framework, to build the leanest, highest performance possible controls.

- Use the ActiveX Template Library, written specifically to enable ActiveX Control development.

I will now discuss the ActiveX specific methods for building controls extensively.

The ActiveX Control Framework

One of the problems with using MFC for OLE Control development is that the browser must have MFC installed. If he or she doesn't, it's a significant download time to retrieve the file (MFC40.DLL) and install it on the system. In addition, there is some overhead in an OLE Control written with the Visual C++ Control Wizard that is not really necessary for ActiveX controls. To counter this potential disadvantage, when ActiveX Controls were first introduced, sample code was provided to create minimalist ActiveX controls. This control includes only the interfaces necessary to make effective controls that will be hosted on Web pages.

There is a basic philosophical difference between the Visual C++ Control Development Kit (the CDK) and the ActiveX Control Framework. The CDK generates lots of default code. Even the most basic control has substantial functionality. The ACF has as little code as possible, anticipating its inclusion into a Web page. Everything in ACF leans in the direction of small code size and high performance, at the acknowledged cost of less default functionality. However, it is easy enough to add code where necessary.

The ActiveX Control Framework comes with the ActiveX SDK. As of this writing, this is available at http://www.microsoft.com/intdev/controls/ctrlfmk-f.htm, which points to various download sites for this. It is currently an eight-megabyte download. The ActiveX SDK also ships with the Microsoft Developer Network CDs, and on its own CD.

The framework itself is located in the SAMPLES\BASECTL subdirectory of the installed SDK (generally \INETSDK\SAMPLES\BASECTL). BASECTL has the following subdirectories:

- Framewrk
- Ielnk
- Iemime
- Include
- Todosvr
- Webimage

The Framewrk directory contains the C++ code you will use to build your controls. The Include directory contains the C++ header (.H) files you will use. The other directories contain sample controls built with the framework. Running MAKEALL.BAT in the SAMPLES directory will build the BASECTL samples along with all of the other samples, assuming that you have Microsoft Visual C++ 4.0 or greater installed.

The classes you will be most concerned with are CInternetControl and CProperty-Page. To create your own control, you will usually derive your own class from CInternetControl. CInternetControl itself is derived from COLEControl, which is derived from CAutomationObject. This paradigm will be very familiar to users of the Microsoft Foundation Classes. CAutomationObject gives your object the characteristics of an OLE automation server. This makes sense since every OLE Control is an OLE automation server. COLEControl extends the CAutomationObject capabilities with the necessary characteristics of an OLE Control. Strictly speaking, your object can inherit directly from COLEControl, and the first BASECTL samples did just that. However, CInternetControl gives your class some additional very useful capabilities, mostly related to URL monikers for downloading of data. Your class will call method SetupDownload() with the URL where the data is loaded, and override method OnData() to process the resulting data. (The technology that allows this is something called *URL monikers,* which I will discuss later.)

In addition to inheriting from CInternetControl, your class will need to inherit from an OLE automation interface that describes your control's properties and methods. Such interfaces are defined in .IDL (Interface Description Language) files and made into type library (.TLB) files using the utility MKTYPLIB. It's not actually required that your control implement its own properties and methods, but it is required that it at least implement the pure virtual methods listed in the CAutomationObject class. Remember that any class that wants to have objects instantiated of it must implement all the pure virtual member functions of its parent classes. (For those new to this concept of *pure virtual functions,* see the note below before continuing on.)

NOTE

Pure virtual functions are functions that are declared in a class, and suffixed with =0;. The presence of a pure virtual function in a class makes the class *abstract*—objects can not be instantiated of that class. When deriving classes from abstract classes, if you want to create objects of the class it is critical that you *override* all of the pure virtual functions of the abstract base class (provide your own declarations of them). You must also implement the code for these functions (provide definitions for them). The bulk of the work in using the ActiveX Control Framework is providing implementations of all of the functions that were pure virtual in the ACF base classes.

CInternetControl has no pure virtual functions, though it has a few virtual functions that will usually be overridden by our control class, for example, OnData(). But COLEAutomation has several member functions that will need to be provided in our control's class. These are the main WindowProc() function, member functions for loading and saving the control's state (LoadBinaryState(), SaveBinaryState(), Load-TextState(), SaveTextState()), OnDraw() to display the control, and RegisterClass-Data() to assist in control installation. If you want your control to have a property page, you will have to write a class derived from CPropertyPage. Your class must implement the pure virtual DialogProc() member function.

If you are new to OLE/COM programming, then this may be an overwhelming amount of information. Don't worry. Even if you stick with the BaseCtl framework to implement your control, you can start with one of the supplied samples, such as WebImage or ToDoSvr, and modify them according to the needs of your control. You will see in the next section that the ActiveX Template Library makes the development process even easier.

The WebImage Control Example

Let's walk through an example, the WebImage control, to see how this is done. Below is the class definition for CWebImageControl (file Wimgctl.cpp in the INETSDK\SAM-PLES\BASECTL\WEBIMAGE directory). First take note of the class derivation header. The class name we are creating is CWebImageControl. It is derived from CInternet-Control, IWebImage, and ISupportErrorInfo. The essential functionality comes from CInternetControl. This has the Internet-specific functions for downloading declared. In the private section of the class two member functions are declared that you need to implement: OnData() and OnProgress() to override CInternetControl's pure virtual functions. CInternetControl inherits from COLEControl, and so our class needs to override and implement LoadBinaryState(), SaveBinaryState(), LoadTextState(), SaveTextState(), OnDraw(), WindowProc(), and RegisterClassData().

```
class CWebImageControl :
    public CInternetControl,
    public IWebImage,
    public ISupportErrorInfo
{
```

```
public:
  // IUnknown methods
    DECLARE_STANDARD_UNKNOWN();
  // IDispatch methods
    DECLARE_STANDARD_DISPATCH();
  // ISupportErrorInfo methods
    DECLARE_STANDARD_SUPPORTERRORINFO();
  // IWebImage methods
  //
  // TODO: copy over the method declarations from CWebImageInterfaces.H
  //      don't forget to remove the PURE from them.
  //
  STDMETHOD(get_ReadyState) (THIS_ long FAR* thestate ;
  STDMETHOD(get_Image) (THIS_ BSTR FAR* path) ;
  STDMETHOD(put_Image) (THIS_ BSTR path) ;
  STDMETHOD_(void, AboutBox) (THIS) ;
  STDMETHOD(Scramble) (THIS) ;

  // OLE Control stuff follows:
  //
  CWebImageControl(IUnknown *pUnkOuter);
  virtual ~CWebImageControl();

  // static creation function. all controls must have one of these!
  //
  static IUnknown *Create(IUnknown *);
private:
  // overridables that the control must implement.
    STDMETHOD(LoadBinaryState) (IStream *pStream);
  STDMETHOD(SaveBinaryState) (IStream *pStream);
  STDMETHOD(LoadTextState) (IPropertyBag *pPropertyBag, IErrorLog
  ↳*pErrorLog);
  STDMETHOD(SaveTextState) (IPropertyBag *pPropertyBag, BOOL
  ↳fWriteDefault);
  STDMETHOD(OnDraw) (DWORD dvAspect, HDC hdcDraw, LPCRECTL prcBounds,
  ↳LPCRECTL
```

```
prcWBounds, HDC hicTargetDev, BOOL fOptimize);

    virtual LRESULT WindowProc (UINT msg, WPARAM wParam, LPARAM lParam);
    virtual BOOL    RegisterClassData (void);

    virtual HRESULT InternalQueryInterface(REFIID, void **);
    virtual void    BeforeCreateWindow(void);

    virtual BOOL    AfterCreateWindow(void);
        //      Internet specific callbacks:
        //
        ///     OnData is called asynchronously as data for an object or
        property arrives...
        virtual HRESULT OnData( DISPID id, DWORD grfBSCF,IStream * bitstrm,
DWORD amount );

        //      OnProgress is called to allow you to present progress
        ⌐indication UI
        virtual HRESULT OnProgress( DISPID, ULONG progress, ULONG themax,
        ⌐ULONG,
LPCWSTR);

    // private state information.
    //

HRESULT SetBmpPath(const char *psz);
HRESULT SetBmpPath(IStream *);
HRESULT UpdateImage();
enum bmpDownloadStates
{
    bdsNoBitsYet,
    bdsGotFileHeader,
    bdsGotBitmapInfo,
    bdsGettingBits,
    bdsBitsAreDone
};

HDC              m_dc;
bmpDownloadStates m_state;
CDibFile *       m_dibFile;
CDibSection *m_dib;
```

```
// Actual properties
char *              m_bmpPath;

};
```

The class also inherits from IWebImage. This is the OLE Automation interface defined by the ODL file. You need to supply the methods and property setting and getting functions implied by this interface. Here are the essential properties and methods from the WIMG.ODL file:

```
interface IWebImage : IDispatch {

        // properties
        [id(DISPID_READYSTATE), propget]
            HRESULT ReadyState([out, retval] long * thestate);

        [id(DISPID_BMPPATH), propget]
        HRESULT Image([out, retval] BSTR * path);
        [id(DISPID_BMPATH), propput]
                        HRESULT Image([in] BSTR path);

        // methods
        [id(DISPID_ABOUTBOX)]
            void AboutBox(void);
        [id(DISPID_SCRAMBLE)]
                HRESULT Scramble(void);
    };
```

■■■■■■■ **NOTE**

> I'm not going to define and describe the ODL file syntax and purpose here. See the *OLE2 Programmer's Reference* (Microsoft Press, 1994) for more information on ODL file syntax. Also, books such as Brockschmidt's *Inside OLE, Second Edition* (Microsoft Press, 1995), and Denning's *OLE Controls Inside and Out* (Microsoft Press, 1995) do a very good job of describing the ODL file syntax. This is one of the few places in this book where I do not try to make the material self-contained—there's just too much information to present it here completely.

These two properties and two methods in the ODL file result in five pure virtual member functions in the definition of IWebImage in the WImgInterfaces.h that need to be overridden in our CWebImageControl class. These are get_ReadyState(), get_Image(), put_Image(), AboutBox(), and Scramble().

Now as to the rest of the public interface of the class, DECLARE_STANDARD_ UNKNOWN() *defines* (i.e., both declares and provides code for) the member functions of IUnknown: QueryInterface(), AddRef() and Release(). In similar fashion, DECLARE_STANDARD_DISPATCH provides definition for the standard functions of IDispatch: GetTypeInfoCount(), GetTypeInfo(), GetIDsOfNames(), and Invoke(). DECLARE_STANDARD_SUPPORTERRORINFO() implements the InterfaceSupportsErrorInfo() function. We don't need to do anything to implement any of the IUnknown, IDispatch, or ISupportErrorInfo interfaces.

The state of the object is kept in the following private data members: m_dc, m_dibFile, m_dib, m_bmpPath, and m_State. The first three of these refer to the image itself (m_dc is a handle to a device context; m_dibFile and m_dib are objects built to handle image display of BMP files via the Web, which is not normally handled natively by HTML pages). The OnDraw() member function (that overrides the COLEControl class pure virtual function) will use m_dib member function as the source of data for the image it display. m_bmpPath is the path to the BMP file. The get_Image and put_Image member functions will be used to modify this data member.

So to summarize the CWebImageControl class definition walkthrough, you need to implement a few functions that implement the basic functionality by overriding the pure virtual functions of COLEControl. These functions are associated with loading and saving the state and rendering the current state. You also can and should provide functions that override the CInternetControl functions for OnData() (to accept data being downloaded from a remote URL and place it in the m_dib structure) and from OnProgress() (to display a progress indicator during download). Implementation of these overridden functions of COLEControl and CInternetControl is really the essence of the work.

The other major piece that we need to build when using the ActiveX Control Framework is a property page. Here's the class definition for CWebImageGeneralPage.

```
class CWebImageGeneralPage : public CPropertyPage {
```

```
public:
  static IUnknown *Create(IUnknown *pUnkOuter);

  // constructor and destructor
  //
  CWebImageGeneralPage(IUnknown *pUnkOuter);
  virtual ~CWebImageGeneralPage();

private:
  virtual BOOL DialogProc(HWND, UINT, WPARAM, LPARAM);

};
```

The next step is to write the CWebImageGeneralPage::DialogProc( ) function that is referenced in the class that overrides the pure virtual CPropertyPage::DialogProc( ) function. This DialogProc( ) will be similar to other dialog procedures you've written. See the Win32 SDK for more information on DialogProc( ). Note that in the code below the procedure handles two special messages: one for a new object (PPM_NEWOBJECTS), and another one to apply current settings from a click on OK or Apply (PPM_APPLY). Here's the code for CWebImageGeneralPage::Dialog-Proc( ), which is really most of what you had to do to implement a property page on your control.

```
BOOL CWebImageGeneralPage::DialogProc
(
    HWND    hwnd,
    UINT    msg,
    WPARAM wParam,
    LPARAM lParam
)
{
    HRESULT      hr;
    IWebImage *pWebImage;
    IUnknown    *pUnk;
    DWORD        dwDummy;
    VARIANT var;

    switch (msg) {
```

```
            // we've been given some new objects, so go and re-set up the
            dialog page.
            //
            case PPM_NEWOBJECTS:
              {

              pUnk = FirstControl (&dwDummy);
              if (!pUnk) return FALSE;

              hr = pUnk->QueryInterface(IID_IWebImage, (void **)&pWebImage);

              if (FAILED(hr)) return FALSE;

                    //VariantInit(&var);
                    BSTR bstr;
              pWebImage->get_Image(&bstr);
                    //if( var.vt == VT_BSTR )
                    //{
                MAKE_ANSIPTR_FROMWIDE(psz, bstr);//var.bstrVal);
                SetDlgItemText(hwnd, IDC_URL, psz);
                SysFreeString(bstr);//var.bstrVal);
                    //    }
              pWebImage->Release();
              }
              return TRUE;

            case PPM_APPLY:
              {
              char     szTmp[120];

              // get all the controls we have to update.
              //
              for (pUnk = FirstControl(&dwDummy) ; pUnk; pUnk =
        NextControl(&dwDummy))
                   {
                   hr = pUnk->QueryInterface(IID_IWebImage, (void
        **)&pWebImage);
                   if (FAILED(hr)) continue;
```

```
        GetDlgItemText(hwnd, IDC_URL, szTmp, 128);
            //VariantInit(&var);
        //var.vt = VT_BSTR;
            BSTR bstr;
        //var.bstrVal = BSTRFROMANSI(szTmp);
        bstr = BSTRFROMANSI(szTmp);
        ASSERT(bstr, "Maggots!");
        pWebImage->put_Image(bstr);
        SysFreeString(bstr);
        pWebImage->Release();
      }
      }
    return TRUE;

  case WM_COMMAND:
    switch (LOWORD(wParam)) {
      case IDC_URL:
        if (HIWORD(wParam) == EN_CHANGE)
          MakeDirty();
      }
    break;
    }
    return(FALSE);
  }
```

That's really about it. To create your own ActiveX Control with the ActiveX Control Framework, derive and implement two classes, one from CInternetControl and another from CPropertyPage. Both of these are *abstract classes,* so to make your classes *concrete* (able to make objects from them), you just need to override and implement the pure virtual functions of those classes, and add a few functions for the properties and methods of your control. Luckily for most ActiveX Controls that will be embedded in Web pages, the number of custom properties and methods is likely to be quite small. The sample control here with two properties and two methods is likely to be representative.

You should be able to be quite productive building ActiveX Controls using the ACF and the supplied examples, adding functions for getting and setting your properties and for implementing your methods, and modifying the implementations of the pure virtual functions of the ACF base classes. However, this is still a bit more work than perhaps it could be, and admittedly more work than users of the Visual C++ Control Development Kit (the CDK) have become accustomed to. Let's go on to look at what capabilities the ActiveX Template Library provides.

The ActiveX Template Library

The ATL is a more extensive attempt, developed by the Visual C++ team, to provide a framework for building ActiveX Controls. It adds an Application Wizard to generate much of the code, and utilizes the power of C++ templates. To use the ActiveX Template Library, download it from the ActiveX Template Library page at http://www.microsoft.com/visualc/atl/default.htm. To install the Active Template Library, save the downloaded file as ATL.ZIP in your Visual C++ base directory (e.g., C:\MSDEV). Then run PKUNZIP-D ATL.ZIP. This will place all the necessary C++ header files in INCLUDE directories and an application wizard for creating ATL-based controls in the TEMPLATE subdirectory of the base directory (e.g., C:\MSDEV\TEMPLATE). Two sample controls (LABRADOR and BEEPER) are placed in subdirectories of the SAMPLES subdirectory. A whitepaper, ATLWHITE.TXT, and documentation, ATLTN001.TXT, are extracted to the DOCS directory.

To run the application wizard, invoke File/New/Project Workspace, and choose the OLE Com AppWizard that appears as the last item in the Type dialog. Choose a name for your project, and then click Create as shown in Figure 8.1.

The next step is a dialog box prompting you for various options. For the purposes of this explanation leave them at their eminently reasonable defaults. For example, one of the purposes of the template library is to allow easy creation of *dual interfaces*. These are interfaces whose methods can be discovered at runtime as in OLE automation interfaces, but whose vtable entries can be called directly at compile time as well, yielding faster execution for the programs that resolve the reference at compile time. Anyway, the default is a *dual interface* since there is little reason not to use this more advanced form of COM interface (again, a full discussion of the advantages and disadvantages of dual interfaces can be found in other books such as *Inside OLE, Second Edition*). The other options also make sense, and I won't discuss the ramifications of changing them here. The next dialog allows you to change

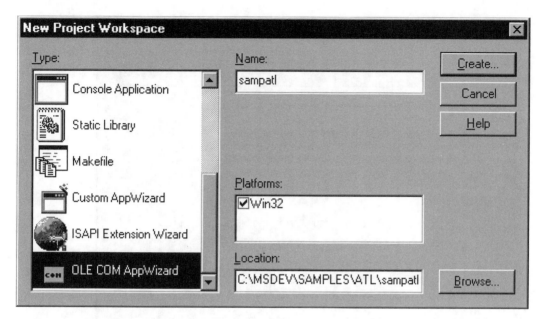

▮▮▮▮▮ **Figure 8.1** ATL AppWizard.

the names of the generated filenames, which is again not often really necessary. After clicking on Finish, you will see dialog informing you of the major files generated (Figure 8.2).

The files will be generated and you will be placed in the generated project file in Developer Studio. You aren't quite done, however. The IDL file Custom Build settings need to be set to generate the header file that you need for the main C++ file. Click on the Files button in the Project pane to display the projects file. Right-click on the IDL file and choose the Custom Build tab. Add a Build command of:

```
midl /ms_ext /c_ext <projname>1.idl
```

Then add output files of:

```
<projname>.h
<projname>.i_c
```

where <projname> is basename of the project chosen in the wizard (SAMPATL for this example). The dialog should look something like Figure 8.3.

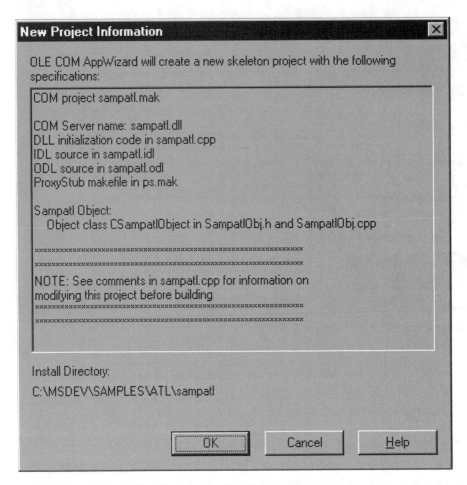

Figure 8.2 ATL generated files dialog.

Then set a custom build step on the entire project to perform the following commands:

```
regsvr32 /s /c "$(TargetPath)"
echo regsvr32 exec. time > "$(OutDir)\regsvr32.trg"
```

The output setting should be:

```
$(OutDir)\regsvr32.trg
```

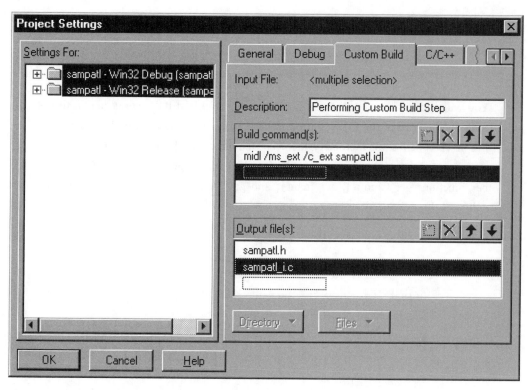

▮▮▮▮▮ **Figure 8.3** Modifying generated ATL project: entering custom build setting for IDL file.

At this point, you *could* invoke the Build process (e.g., the Build SAMPATL.DLL menu option for this project) and you would have a complete DLL, but it wouldn't do much of anything interesting. Before doing the build, let's present what's necessary to add interesting methods to your application, using the Beeper sample from the ATL distributable as the example functionality.

Adding Functionality to Your ATL Control

To add methods to your object to make it do interesting things, you should modify the IDL file generated by the AppWizard. Here is the empty generated ISampAtl interface, which you would need to populate:

```
interface ISampatl : IDispatch
{
        import "oaidl.idl";
}
```

You will add methods to this interface using the standard IDL syntax (again this is fully documented in the *OLE2 Programmer's Reference*). Here is the IDL file for the Beeper class with some methods added. The main method, Beep( ), performs the functionality of the control. The other methods (which will be generated as the C++ member functions get_Count( ), get_Item( ), and get_NewEnum( )) are there to get the values of three properties of the control.

```
interface IBeeper : IDispatch
{
        import "oaidl.idl";
        [helpstring("Play the current sound")]
                HRESULT Beep();
        [propget, helpstring("Returns number of strings in collection.")]
                HRESULT Count([out, retval] long* retval);

        [propget, id(0),
        helpstring("Given an index, returns a string in the collection")]
                HRESULT Item([in] long Index, [out, retval] BSTR* pbstr);

        [propget, restricted, id(DISPID_NEWENUM)] // Must be propget.
                HRESULT _NewEnum([out, retval] IUnknown** retval);
};
```

Once you run MIDL on the IDL file, it will generate a <projname>.h file. Inside this file, among other things, is the generated C++ interface class for the project, I<projname>. The Beeper interface generated in the Beeper.h file is shown:

```
interface IBeeper : public IDispatch
    {
    public:
        virtual /* [helpstring] */ HRESULT _stdcall Beep( void) = 0;

        virtual /* [helpstring] [propget] */ HRESULT _stdcall get_Count(
```

```
            /* [retval] [out] */ long _RPC_FAR *retval) = 0;

      virtual /* [helpstring] [id] [propget] */ HRESULT _stdcall
get_Item(
            /* [in] */ long Index,
            /* [retval] [out] */ BSTR _RPC_FAR *pbstr) = 0;

      virtual /* [id] [restricted] [propget] */ HRESULT _stdcall
get_NewEnum(
            /* [retval] [out] */ IUnknown _RPC_FAR *_RPC_FAR *retval) =
0;

   };
```

You need to provide a COM object that supports this interface. ATL has provided most of this COM object in the <projname>obj.h file. The wizard even makes the object a dual interface so that it can be used from OLE automation containers and still work efficiently when called from vtable entries. You will just need to add C++ member functions to the object that supports this interface. This will be in the <projname>obj.h file. You will add method declarations in a public section, using the STDMETHOD() macro. You will add member variables to reflect the object's state in a private section. An example of this is the Beeper sample included with ATL. This is the class definition for CBeeper located in the BeeperObj.h file in the SAMPLES\ATL\BEEPER subdirectory of your VC directory. The member functions and variables added to support the Ibeeper are indicated in bold:

```
    class CBeeper :
        public CComDualImpl<IBeeper, &IID_IBeeper, &LIBID_BeeperLib>,
        public CComObjectBase<&CLSID_Beeper>
    {
    public:
        CBeeper();
        BEGIN_COM_MAP(CBeeper)
            COM_INTERFACE_ENTRY(IDispatch)
            COM_INTERFACE_ENTRY(IBeeper)
            COM_INTERFACE_ENTRY_TEAR_OFF(IID_ISupportErrorInfo,
    CBeeper2)
```

```
        END_COM_MAP()

        DECLARE_NOT_AGGREGATABLE(CBeeper)

// IBeeper
public:
        STDMETHOD(Beep) ();

        STDMETHOD(get_Count) (long* retval);

        STDMETHOD(get_Item) (long Index, BSTR* pbstr);

        STDMETHOD(get_NewEnum) (IUnknown** retval);

private:
        int m_nCnt;

        CComVariant var[4];

};
```

The next step is to implement the newly defined member functions of your object in the <projname>obj.cpp file. For example, the implementation of the Beep() method defined previously is as follows (located in the BeepObj.h file):

```
STDMETHODIMP CBeeper::Beep()
{
    if (m_nCnt++ == 5)
    {
        m_nCnt = 0;
        return Error(L"Too many beeps");
    }
    MessageBeep(0);
    return S_OK;
}
```

The methods that defined your controls behavior are ready to build. Note that in the BEEPER example supplied, a Visual C++ .MDP file is not supplied. If you want to build the BEEPER example, you will need to run the MIDL command shown above manually. That is, run

```
midl /ms_ext /c_ext beeper.idl
```

Then you can invoke

```
nmake -f beeper.mak
```

to build the beeper control.

To summarize the steps involved in using ATL to build your control:

1. Use the OLE COM AppWizard to build the files.

2. Modify the build settings of the project to include the MIDL invocation, which builds your C++ interface definition in the <projname.h> file.

3. Modify the IDL file to add the necessary methods. Invoke MIDL to build the <projname.h> file.

4. Using the <projname>.h that describes the I<projname> interface, define C++ member functions (in the <projname>obj.h file) to the C<projname> class that supports the I<projname> interface.

5. In the <projname>.cpp file, implement those member functions. Add member variables to the C<projname> class.

6. Build the project.

7. Integrate the ActiveX Control into your Web pages.

The ActiveX Template Library is a great way to build very efficient, dual-interfaced ActiveX Controls. Controls are a great way to add client-side functionality to your Web pages. There are other ways to do this as well. Among those are ActiveX Scripting, specifically client-side VB Script, which I will cover in the next chapter.

VBSCRIPT

A lthough I spent the first half of this book describing all of the powerful things you can do with gateways and Internet Server Applications, if your user community is on an external Internet site, this is usually the best way to make your sites interactive and do interesting things. However, in some cases, it is useful to execute functionality on the client, that is, the user's Web browser. This almost always involves making assumptions about what Web browser accessing users are running, but in some cases (especially for corporate intranets) these are legitimate assumptions.

The last chapter covered one way to do this: ActiveX Controls. Writing ActiveX Controls and incorporating them into your Web pages is one way to provide client-side functionality to your Web pages. But for many tasks, this may be overkill. Sometimes, you just want to provide some logic within your Web pages and there may not be an ActiveX control available to provide the specific bit of functionality. Writing an ActiveX control to provide it may be more work than is necessary. Also, even if a control is available, for some tasks the overhead of downloading the control and executing it can't be justified.

What would be nice for small bits of functionality is to be able to embed the code directly into HTML pages, and have the browser execute it directly. This scripting level of programming could be done by many people at the HTML-authoring level, obviating the need for a developer in many cases. Visual Basic Scripting Edition, or VBScript, provides just this capability. And, even better, you can use this high-level "inside the HTML" scripting capability to execute server-side functionality as well, simply by indicating that the script should run on the server.

You do need to be aware that right now only the Microsoft Internet Explorer Web browser supports VBScript. Other browsers will simply ignore the embedded script. However, Microsoft makes VBScript available for licensing by other browsers and applications that need scripting for free. Also there is a plug-in for Netscape that will allow it to run VBScript. It is called the Ncompass ScriptActive Plug-In, and is available at http://www.ncompasslabs.com/binaries.

In this chapter, I'll introduce the capabilities syntax of VB Script for client-side applications, and then present sample client-side scripts. Then I'll show how the extended capabilities of server-side VB Script let you create server applications with much less work than the C-based CGI and ISAPI DLLs shown earlier.

VBScript Capabilities

The VBScript language is a subset of full Visual Basic, and even Visual Basic for Applications (the scripting language for Microsoft desktop applications such as Word and Excel). Thus VBScript code can be used in Visual Basic applications or VBA scripts. Perhaps the best way to understand what the VBScript subset really means is to talk about what VBScript *can't do* (the implication being that VBScript can do everything that VB does *except* the limitations described. This is essential knowledge for planning what tools to apply to your Web-based application. Note that these limitations apply to client-side VBScript only. Most of them are related to purposely limiting what the client can do for security purposes. Server-side VBScript has its own set of limitations.

Client-side VBScript does not support file operations: no reading or writing to the Web browser user's hard drive. This would be a major security hole for a scripting language. VBScript only supports the Variant data type. Variants can store arrays, object, numbers, date/time, or string data, so this is not a serious limitation. VBScript does not have access to any of the intrinsic predefined constants that normally are available in Visual Basic. VBScript only supports the Err object among the commonly used VB system objects. No debugging support is available for either client-side or server-side VBScript. Client-side VBScript does not support database access; however, server-side VBScript has very rich support for such operations. VBScript also does not allow use of the Windows Help system, but equivalent functionality can be performed by linking to HTML help pages. VBScript doesn't support control arrays, but it is easy enough to write handling scripts that take a numeric argument indicating which of a group of controls is called. No use of classes is allowed in VBScript. Internet Explorer does not implement the CreateObject function, so no use of the user's OLE automation servers, such as Word or Excel, is possible. Again this would be a security violation. However, other environments that support VBScript might choose to allow this, and this would not violate the intentions of VBScript itself.

More specifically, the following language features are not supported in VBScript:

- Any type conversion (since everything is a Variant type)
- Non-zero-based arrays (no Base command)
- No Array function to set entire arrays
- Date and Time functions, and various functions for parsing out components of system date and time
- Control flow keywords such as DoEvents, GoSub, and Return; GoTo in any form, line numbers and labels, and case statements
- Error handling capabilities such as OnError . . . Resume, Resume, and Resume Next
- Intrinsic graphics capabilities such as Cls, Circle, Line, Point, Pset, and Scale
- No named arguments in calling members
- Intrinsic (VB supplied) constants
- User-defined constants (so some naming convention for your variables that will be used as constants is recommended)
- Object handling (CreateObject, GetObject, TypeOf)
- File handling
- Financial functions
- Debugging keywords

These are fairly significant limitations that you will want to be keenly aware of as you write your code. You should load the pages containing your code in progress frequently to be certain you aren't using proscribed features. This is particularly important because various features, such as the Mid( ) function, have been described as not being part of VBScript, but in my testing have just worked anyway.

Note that I am not describing all the things that VBScript *can* do in detail because that would require presenting a good portion of the Visual Basic language, a topic worthy of a book unto itself. If you really are completely new to VB, you may want to use the VBScript tutorial on the Microsoft Web site: http://www.microsoft.com/vbscript/us/vbstutor. The actual online reference to language features is at http://www.microsoft.com/vbscript/us/vbstutor.

Integrating VBScripts into Your HTML

A new HTML tag, called <SCRIPT>, is placed in your HTML, and everything between <SCRIPT> and </SCRIPT> is executed by the script interpreter. If the <SCRIPT> tag has a parameter of LANGUAGE=VBS, then the information in the SCRIPT block will be executed by the VBScript engine. You should normally place the SCRIPT block inside the HEAD block of your HTML page (in between <HEAD> and </HEAD>). This allows your script to be available to any part of the HTML page.

Tying VBScript to HTML

There are three ways to attach VBScript functions and procedures to your HTML code:

- Write an event handling procedure for a specified control using the naming convention controlname_eventname for the procedure name.
- Provide an OnClick attribute for the control tag. Inside this attribute VBScript code can be written out directly, with statements separated by colons.
- Write the <SCRIPT> tag with a FOR attribute specifying the control that the script applies to and an EVENT attribute specifying which event the script handles.

By far the most common method is to write your event handling procedures all in the same <SCRIPT> block (as previously recommended) and just define different procedures for each event of each control that you will handle. For example, suppose you had the following button in your HTML:

```
<INPUT TYPE="BUTTON" NAME="btnCalcPressureGroup" VALUE="Compute
Pressure Group">
```

You can write the following *event procedure* to handle the click event for this button:

```
Sub btnCalcPressureGroup_OnClick()
rem put some code in here to do the work
End Sub
```

Other ways of doing this are to code the following button:

```
<INPUT TYPE="BUTTON" NAME="btnCalcPressureGroup" VALUE="Compute
Pressure Group"
OnClick='Depth=InputBox "Depth"
:Duration=InputBox "Duration":MsgBox "Pressure Group is: " &
CalcPressureGroup(Depth,Duration)'>
```

where CalcPressureGroup is a call to a procedure in the script block. Note that each statement is separated by colons. Of course, this could have just been a call to single procedure as well, more closely mirroring the first method of writing the event handler.

The last way to do this would be to write a script such as:

```
<SCRIPT LANGUAGE="VBScript" EVENT="OnClick"
FOR="btnCalcPressureGroup">
<!--
rem some code to do the work
-->
</SCRIPT
```

Note that in this case no Sub and EndSub is necessary to wrap the procedure.

Let's look at a more extensive example of this. The following VBScript computes the pressure group based on a supplied depth and duration. This might be part of an interactive dive planner for a scuba diving site. Note that this example, while demonstrating that VBScript has some compelling features and the ability to create reasonably complex functionality, also points out some of VBScript's limitations. There is no

Array( ) function, which makes it quite difficult to initialize multidimensional arrays. You can work around this problem by having a one-dimensional array of strings. Then initialize the two-dimensional array of values by parsing out the values out of the strings. Note that VBScript *does* have support for the Mid( ) function that makes this possible (early versions of VBScript said that this function was not supported). Also notice that all of the conversion between strings and numbers is done implicitly rather than through convert functions. The exception is that the pressure group label was computed as a number and then converted to a character with the Chr( ) function.

```
<HTML>
<HEAD>
<TITLE>Interactive Dive Calculator</TITLE>
<SCRIPT LANGUAGE="VBScript">
<!--
Dim intTable(25, 6)
Dim strVals(25)
strVals(0)="010,009,007,006,005,004,004"
strVals(1)="019,016,013,011,009,008,007"
strVals(2)="025,022,017,014,012,010,009"
strVals(3)="029,025,019,016,013,011,010"
strVals(4)="032,027,031,017,015,013,011"
strVals(5)="036,031,024,019,016,014,012"
strVals(6)="040,034,026,021,018,015,013"
strVals(7)="044,037,028,023,019,017,015"
strVals(8)="048,040,031,025,021,018,016"
strVals(9)="052,044,033,027,022,019,017"
strVals(10)="057,048,036,029,024,021,018"
strVals(11)="062,051,039,031,026,022,019"
strVals(12)="067,055,041,033,027,023,021"
strVals(13)="073,060,044,035,029,025,022"
strVals(14)="079,064,047,037,031,026,023"
strVals(15)="085,069,050,039,033,028,024"
strVals(16)="092,074,053,042,035,029,025"
strVals(17)="100,079,057,044,036,030,000"
```

```vbscript
strVals(18)="108,085,060,047,038,000,000"
strVals(19)="117,091,063,049,040,000,000"
strVals(20)="127,097,067,052,000,000,000"
strVals(21)="139,104,071,054,000,000,000"
strVals(22)="152,111,075,055,000,000,000"
strVals(23)="168,120,080,000,000,000,000"
strVals(24)="188,129,000,000,000,000,000"
strVals(25)="205,140,000,000,000,000,000"

for row=0 to 25
    for col=0 to 6
        intTable(row,col)=0
        intTable(row,col)  id(strVals(row) ,1+col*4,3)
        if (mid(intTable(row,col) ,1,1)="0") then
            intTable(row,col)  id(strVals(row) ,2+col*4,2)
        end if
    next
next

Function CalcPressureGroup(intDepth,intDuration)
    if (intDepth<35) then
        Col=0
    else
        Col=Int((intDepth-21)/10)
    end if
    bFoundGroup=TRUE
    for Row=0 to 25
        If intTable(Row,Col)=0 Then
            bFoundGroup=FALSE
            CalcPressureGroup=26
        end if
        If intDuration<=intTable(Row,Col) then
            CalcPressureGroup=Row
            Row=26
            bFoundGroup=TRUE
```

```
                    end if
            next
            if (bFoundGroup=FALSE) then
                    CalcPressureGroup=26
            end if
    End Function

    Sub btnCalcPressureGroup_OnClick()
            intDepth=101
            do while (intDepth>100)
                    intDepth = InputBox("How deep (in feet) will you be
    diving?","Depth")
                    if (intDepth>100) then
                            MsgBox "Too deep for me"
                    end if
            Loop
            intDuration = InputBox("How long (in minutes) will you be diving
    for?","Duration")
            intPressureGroup = CalcPressureGroup (intDepth,intDuration)
            if (intPressureGroup > 25) then
                    MsgBox "Too long at depth"
            else
                    MsgBox "Pressure Group is " & chr(intPressureGroup+65)
            end if
    End Sub

    -->
    </SCRIPT>
    </HEAD>
    <BODY>
    <H2>Web-Based Recreational Dive Planner</H2>
    You must be running Internet Explorer 3.0 to use this.<p>
    <INPUT TYPE="BUTTON" NAME="btnCalcPressureGroup" VALUE="Compute
    Pressure Group">
    </BODY>
    </HTML>
```

I don't actually anticipate that you are going to have some immediate need for this functionality in your own application. But this makes a pretty good example of client-side calculations. I will extend this example in the next section to take its arguments from Web page forms rather than Windows dialog boxes.

Using VBScript in HTML Forms

Using InputBox to get input from users works just fine, but results in dialog windows popping up from the pages when fields in a form on the page itself might work just as nicely. The other advantage to this approach is that it can be used in situations where some clients might not have VBScript support. For example, imagine an order form where a VBScript is used to validate the data before submission to a backend ISAPI DLL that stores the data in a database. In this case, clicking the Submit button on the form will work whether or not the Web browser supports VBScript. But the VBScript client (Internet Explorer for example) would have richer validation. For example, it might tell the user "invalid zip code, try again" before even attempting to submit the data to the database. Customers without Internet Explorer might not get the same handholding for invalid entries but they could still use the base functionality of the form.

Anyway, one way to tie a script to a form for validating field entries is to write an OnClick event procedure for the form's Submit button. For example, in the following HTML page for registration, you create a Submit_OnClick procedure. You can then access the form's values by setting a variable to Document.RegisterForm. For example, to retrieve the phone number, you can use the variable Document.Register-Form.Phone. In this example, the VBScript event procedure just checks that the phone number field has a number in it. Note that it does assume the presences of an Internet Database Connector (IDC) script in the /scripts directory called register.idc.

```
<HTML>
<HEAD>
<TITLE>Site Registration</TITLE>
<SCRIPT LANGUAGE="VBScript">
<!--
Sub Submit_OnClick
    Dim TheForm
    Set TheForm=Document.RegisterForm
    If IsNumeric(TheForm.Phone.Value) Then
```

```
            TheForm.Submit ' ok go ahead and submit
      Else
            MsgBox "Please enter numeric phone number"
      End If
End Sub
-->
</SCRIPT>
</HEAD>
<BODY>
<H2>Please Register Below</H2>
Enter data in all fields please.<p>
<FORM NAME="RegisterForm" ACTION="/scripts/register.idc">
First Name: <INPUT NAME="FirstName"> Last Name: <INPUT
NAME="LastName"><br>
Phone Number: <INPUT NAME="Phone"><br>
Email: <INPUT NAME="Email"><br>
<INPUT NAME="Submit" TYPE="Button" VALUE="Submit">
</FORM>
</BODY>
</HTML>
```

This client-side validation is an extremely valuable capability that was missing from the whole Web paradigm for quite some time. Only the introduction of VBScript and JavaScript has rectified this omission. Remember that the Internet Database Connector lacks robust field data validation (it basically just executes a SQL statement).

Another way to link VBScript functionality to a form is to write event procedures for individual fields on the form. In the preceding example, this is actually a more useful model of behavior. Rather than waiting until the form is filled out, you can let the user know of any problems immediately. It's somewhat strange that this use of VBScript is not as well known (for example the tutorial mentioned previously doesn't point this out). Anyway, in the example above, you can write a Phone_OnChange event procedure to handle failure to enter a numeric phone number immediately.

```
Sub Phone_OnChange
      Dim TheForm
```

```
      Set TheForm=Document.RegisterForm
      If Not IsNumeric(TheForm.Phone.Value)
            MsgBox "Please enter phone number"
      End If
   End Sub
```

Let's take the previous dive calculator example and recode it to tie it to Web-based fields for input. Here's the revised script.

```
<HTML>
<HEAD>
<TITLE>Interactive Dive Calculator</TITLE>
<SCRIPT LANGUAGE="VBScript">
<!--
Dim intTable(25,6)
Dim strVals(25)
strVals(0)="010,009,007,006,005,004,004"
strVals(1)="019,016,013,011,009,008,007"
strVals(2)="025,022,017,014,012,010,009"
strVals(3)="029,025,019,016,013,011,010"
strVals(4)="032,027,031,017,015,013,011"
strVals(5)="036,031,024,019,016,014,012"
strVals(6)="040,034,026,021,018,015,013"
strVals(7)="044,037,028,023,019,017,015"
strVals(8)="048,040,031,025,021,018,016"
strVals(9)="052,044,033,027,022,019,017"
strVals(10)="057,048,036,029,024,021,018"
strVals(11)="062,051,039,031,026,022,019"
strVals(12)="067,055,041,033,027,023,021"
strVals(13)="073,060,044,035,029,025,022"
strVals(14)="079,064,047,037,031,026,023"
strVals(15)="085,069,050,039,033,028,024"
strVals(16)="092,074,053,042,035,029,025"
strVals(17)="100,079,057,044,036,030,000"
strVals(18)="108,085,060,047,038,000,000"
```

```
strVals(19)="117,091,063,049,040,000,000"
strVals(20)="127,097,067,052,000,000,000"
strVals(21)="139,104,071,054,000,000,000"
strVals(22)="152,111,075,055,000,000,000"
strVals(23)="168,120,080,000,000,000,000"
strVals(24)="188,129,000,000,000,000,000"
strVals(25)="205,140,000,000,000,000,000"

for row=0 to 25
    for col=0 to 6
        intTable(row,col)=0
        intTable(row,col)  id(strVals(row) ,1+col*4,3)
        if (mid(intTable(row,col) ,1,1)="0") then
            intTable(row,col)  id(strVals(row) ,2+col*4,2)
        end if
    next
next

Function CalcPressureGroup(intDepth,intDuration)
    if (intDepth<35) then
        Col=0
    else
        Col=Int((intDepth-21)/10)
    end if
    bFoundGroup=TRUE
    for Row=0 to 25
        If intTable(Row,Col)=0 Then
            bFoundGroup=FALSE
            CalcPressureGroup=26
        end if
        If intDuration<=intTable(Row,Col) then
            CalcPressureGroup=Row
            Row=26
            bFoundGroup=TRUE
        end if
```

```
        next
        if (bFoundGroup=FALSE) then
            CalcPressureGroup=26
        end if
End Function

Sub Depth_OnChange
    Dim TheForm
    Set TheForm=Document.DiveCalcForm
    If Not IsNumeric(TheForm.Depth.Value) Then
        MsgBox "Please enter depth as a number"
    Else
        If TheForm.Depth.Value > 100 Then
            MsgBox "Too deep for me!"
        End If
    End If
End Sub

Sub Duration_OnChange
    Dim TheForm
    Set TheForm=Document.DiveCalcForm
    If Not IsNumeric(TheForm.Duration.Value) Then
        MsgBox "Please enter duration as a number"
    End If
End Sub

Sub Submit_OnClick()
    Dim TheForm
    Set TheForm=Document.DiveCalcForm
    intDepth = TheForm.Depth.Value
    intDuration = TheForm.Duration.Value
    intPressureGroup = CalcPressureGroup(intDepth,intDuration)
    if (intPressureGroup > 25) then
        MsgBox "Too long at depth"
    else
        MsgBox "Pressure Group is " & chr(intPressureGroup+65)
```

```
        end if
End Sub

-->
</SCRIPT>
</HEAD>
<BODY>
<H2>Web-Based Recreational Dive Planner</H2>
<FORM NAME="DiveCalcForm">
<I>You must be running Internet Explorer 3.0 or another browser that
supports VBScript to use this calculator.</I><p>
Depth (in feet) : <INPUT NAME="Depth"><BR>
Duration (in minutes) : <INPUT NAME="Duration"><BR>
<INPUT NAME="Submit" TYPE="Button" VALUE="Compute Pressure Group">
</FORM>
</BODY>
</HTML>
```

A more complete version of the Recreational Dive Planner is on the Web page for this book: http://www.jwiley.com/actvxprg.htm. The more complete version makes it clear what *pressure group* really means: It's used to determine allowable dive depths and times for successive dives.

Using VBScript with Objects

You can use VBScript to integrate ActiveX Controls such as those presented in the last chapter. With VBScript these objects become even more useful. Now their properties and methods can be set and invoked dynamically in response to user actions. Create your event procedures as just shown. Within these event procedures, you can now set the properties and invoke the methods of the objects on the page.

For example, if you want a button or fields in a form to control the chart object, you would create an event procedure for the button's OnClick event. Then invoke the appropriate method of the object. Here's a sample page that incorporates the Chart object described in Chapter 8. VBScript lets us change the display of the chart object, based upon what the user enters in the form.

```
<HEAD>
<TITLE>Dive Chart</TITLE>
<SCRIPT LANGUAGE="VBScript">
<!--
Sub ChartIt_OnClick
     Dim TheForm
     Set TheForm=Document.DiveChartForm
     intDepth = TheForm.Depth.Value
     MsgBox intDepth
     DiveChart.Data[1]= -intDepth
End Sub
-->
</SCRIPT>
</HEAD>
<BODY>
<FORM NAME="DiveChartForm">
Depth (in feet) : <INPUT NAME="Depth"><BR>
Duration (in minutes) : <INPUT NAME="Duration"><BR>
<INPUT NAME="ChartIt" TYPE="Button" VALUE="Chart Dive">
</FORM>
<H2>The Chart</H2>
<object
     id=DiveChart
     classid="clsid:FC25B780-75BE-11CF-8B01-444553540000"

     CODEBASE="/workshop/activex/gallery/ms/chart/other/iechart.ocx#Ve
rsion=4,70,0,1112"
     TYPE="application/x-oleobject"
     width=400
     height=200
>
<param name="hgridStyle" value="3">
<param name="vgridStyle" value="0">
<param name="colorscheme" value="0">
<param name="DisplayLegend" value="0">
```

```
<param name="BackStyle" value="1">
<param name="BackColor" value="#ffffff">
<param name="ForeColor" value="#0000ff">
<PARAM NAME="Scale" VALUE="100">
<param name="ChartType" value="5">
<param name="Rows" value="3">
<param name="RowNames"="Start Dive Finish">
<param name="Columns" value="1">
<param name="ColumnNames" value="Depth">
<param name="data[0]" value="0">
<param name="data[1]" value="0">
<param name="data[2]" value="0">
</object>
</BODY>
</HTML>
```

Clicking on the Button results in setting the "Data[0]" property of the Chart control. This displays a line graph depicting the depth of the dive, based on what the user entered in the form. In general, it's only when controlled by a scripting language such as VBScript that ActiveX Controls reach their full potential. A major part of the value of ActiveX Controls is the ability to set properties and call methods on the fly. If you are only statically embedding these controls in your pages, you aren't leveraging the capabilities of ActiveX to the fullest.

VBScript is very useful in providing client-side logic in your pages without the necessity of learning Java. The small but useful subset of VB that VBScript provides is easy for other browser and application vendors to implement, meaning that there will be implementations of VBScript in other browsers (Netscape already indirectly supports it via the Ncompass Plug-In) and applications. One place where having an easy-to-use, lightweight but powerful scripting method would be useful would be in controlling server-side functionality. The next chapter discusses server-side VB Script, also known as the ActiveX Server Framework.

ACTIVEX SERVER

One of the things you might have remembered from the discussion of server-side applications in Part I of this book is that there were no really satisfying ways of providing server-side functionality at a programming level higher than C++ or Perl, for example, for Visual Basic developers with little or no C or Perl background. Just what were the options for VB developers? Well, they could use the OLEISAPI sample presented earlier in discussing the ISAPI samples. This requires programmers to build their Visual Basic programs as OLE automation servers that expose methods according to a carefully defined set of arguments for each method. This is not for the faint of heart, and inappropriate for the casual VB user that we really would like to enable to build Web functionality. The second option is to use the WinCGI "standard" that was introduced by WebSite. The ActiveX SDK ships with a sample called IS2WCGI that will wrap the WinCGI program and allow it to be called from IIS. However, this is just as difficult to program to as CGI, and has even worse negative performance implications.

What I'd like is to be able to program in something as highend as Visual Basic, but with higher-level objects for grabbing information from the server, the user's client, and the forms the user may have filled out. There should be objects that allow easy access to this information without parsing it from the system environment, parsing form field data from standard input, or learning how to read and write cookies from the user's browser. An attempt was made to wrap some of these nasty details up in C++ classes earlier. For use in a higher-level language you will want explicit objects always available that have this information already parsed and available in easy-to-use form. It would also be nice if some of the other common Web tasks, such as keeping track of a user's session across multiple page hits, and accessing backened ODBC databases could all be done from high-level objects with much of the legwork underlying these chores done for you. In effect, this lets you build dynamic Web content right into your Web pages, at a level of abstraction no more difficult to use than HTML.

Server-side VBScript, also known as ActiveX Server, provides just these capabilities. ActiveX Server was codenamed Denali, and you will see references to that in the online documentation so don't be confused. The syntax of ActiveX Server is basically the same as client-side VB Script. There are just some more intrinsic objects available to make a lot of the jobs just discussed much easier. To build your ActiveX Server pages, you build Web pages as you normally would in your favorite text or HTML editor. Save your pages, however, as a .ASP file, rather than a .HTM or .HTML file.

The .ASP extension is the clue to IIS that it should run ActiveX Server. In the Script Map key under the HKEY_LOCAL_MACHINE\System\CurrentControlSet\Services\ W3SVC\Parameters registry key, you'll notice that .ASP is mapped to the DENALI.DLL (the DLL name may change by the time you read this). So any file with extension .ASP is executed by the ActiveX Server ISAPI DLL (DENALI.DLL). ActiveX Server displays any HTML found in the file, but more importantly executes the VBScript that it finds inside blocks delimited by <% and %>. These can be calculations:

```
<% total= 1 + salestaxrate * subtotal %>
```

It can be control flow:

```
<% for i = 1 to itemcount

    subtotal = subtotal + price(i)

  next

%>
```

It can also be actually generating output to the browser. Here ActiveX Server introduces a new convention, =*varname* to print out a variable (in its own script block).

```
Total is: <% total>
```

As with client-side VB Script, subroutines and functions are embedded inside a SCRIPT block, generally starting with <SCRIPT LANGUAGE=VBScript RUNAT= Server>. Note the new attribute for the SCRIPT tag, RUNAT. Every ASP file with procedures should include the SCRIPT tag with the RUNAT attribute set to Server. You can also specify JavaScript as the language in which to build your procedures (subroutines or functions).

```
<SCRIPT LANGUAGE=JavaScript RUNAT=Server>
function PrintTotal ()
{
    total=subtotal * (1 + salestaxrate)
    Response.Write(total);
}
</SCRIPT>
```

This is invoked with the code:

```
<%= PrintTotal%>
```

A set of ActiveX Server scripts (.ASP files) in a virtual directory on your server is considered an ActiveX Server *application*. This virtual directory needs to be set up in IIS with both read and execute permission—each page will potentially be both read and displayed as HTML, and executed with scripting functionality. Calling this collection an application is more than just semantics. There are application-wide files, such as the global.asp file that contains many application settings and options, that must be in this virtual directory.

ActiveX Server Objects

As mentioned, ActiveX Server provides several objects that make building Web applications much easier. At a high level these are the Request object to interpret input from the user, the Response object to send information back to the user, the Session object to keep the state of a user's progress through the application, and the Application object that allows you to convey information to all users of the ActiveX Server application.

The Request Object

The most commonly used object is the Request object. This contains *collections* for four common types of information that an application might want to interpret from the user. Request collection contents can be accessed with the syntax

```
Request.<collection> ( <variable name )
```

or just Request(<variable name>). The four collection types are Form, QueryString, ServerVariables, and Cookies.

The Form collection allows you to easily access the field values coming back from a form the user has submitted. Its value is very similar to the HTMLForm C++ class presented earlier. The field values are all accessible just by indexing the Form collection by the field name, and the values are already URL-decoded (+ signs and escape codes are translated and removed). For example to get the "AmountOrdered" field value from a form, and use it to compute a total, you might use the following ActiveX server code.

```
<!-- total.asp -->
<% total = Request.Form("Price" *
Request.Form("AmountOrdered") %>
    Your order costs <% total%>
```

This script would be embedded inside your HTML as follows:

```
<FORM ACTION="/ourstore/total.asp" METHOD=POST>
<!-- hidden so user can't edit the price -->
<!-- Price retrieved via IDC right now -->
Product: <%Description%>
<INPUT TYPE="hidden" NAME="UnitPrice" VALUE="<%Price%>">
<INPUT NAME="Quantity">
<INPUT TYPE="Submit" VALUE="Order">
</FORM>
```

Notice that the method is POST in the above example. For the Form collection to work, this *must* be specified. The Form collection has another interesting twist. If there is more than one field of the same name, it will allow you access to each of the values by indexing the Request.Form("name") variable. In the preceding example, if you had multiple products each with its own field named "Quantity", the TOTAL.ASP file might look like:

```
<% total=0
      for i=0 to Request.Form("Quantity").Count-1
      total = total + Request.Form("Quantity") (i)
      next %>
Your order costs <%=total%>
```

The QueryString collection is very similar. It should be used if the form action was invoked with the GET method. It's not clear why you would want to do that, but the GET method is the default if no METHOD attribute is specified, so it does sometimes happen. QueryString also has the contents of the arguments passed as parameters to the .ASP file (after the question mark) if the .ASP was linked to with an <A HREF> tag.

The ServerVariables collection allows you to get access to any of the CGI environment variables maintained by the server (and enumerated in detail in earlier chapters). For example, to retrieve the value of indicating the user's browser, you might use the following code:

```
<% Dim theBrowser
theBrowser=ServerVariables ("USER_AGENT")
if theBrowser ="Mozilla/2.0 (compatible; MSIE 3.0B; Windows
NT)" then%>
Congratulation on your choice of browser. The pages we show
you from here on will be optimized for Internet Explorer.
<%endif%>
```

The Cookies collection allows you to get access to cookies that you may have set for a user on a previous page access or session. The Response object lets you set these values. Cookies lets your Web application store information about the user, their actions, and their preferences on the user's machine, and access them later. This allows you to do things in your Web application such as:

- Have default fields in an order form default to entries the user made the last time he or she used the form.

- Allow the user to specify items or links he or she wants to appear on the start page for your site and have those items appear on the user's subsequent accesses of that page.

- Store a preferred page size, allowing the user to specify how many records he or she should see at a time when browsing or searching through a catalog.

Anyway, cookies are a very powerful mechanism that allows you to do a lot of more advanced functionality on your site that is very sensitive to user's needs and preferences. As we will see in a minute, there is less need for cookies in ActiveX Server due to the Session object that ActiveX Server provides. The Session object can maintain many settings and preferences across a user's entire session of using your Web application. However if the settings need to be truly persistent, then cookies are the right mechanism since the Session object goes away after the user's session.

The Response Object

Just as the Request object contained several helpful properties for getting information from the user, the Response object provides facilities that help your application to communicate back to the user. You've already seen that just including HTML does this, but sometimes it is useful to make method calls within procedures. The most common way to do this is with the Response.Write method. The previous example could be rewritten with Response.Write as follows, keeping you in scripting context during the whole block:

```
<% Dim theBrowser
theBrowser=ServerVariables("USER_AGENT")
if theBrowser ="Mozilla/2.0 (compatible; MSIE 3.0B; Windows
NT)" then
        Response.Write "Congratulation on your choice of
browser. The pages we show you from here on will be
optimized for Internet Explorer."
endif%>
```

You saw in earlier chapters on CGI and ISAPI that you could redirect to another URL with the "Location:" header (in CGI) or with the appropriate flag on ServerSupport-Function() (in ISAPI). Well ActiveX Server makes it even easier. Just call the Response.Redirect method with the URL desired.

The Response.ContentType method allows you to change the content type that is returned to the user. This is the same as the CGI header "Content-Type:" that is normally set to "text/html." This can be useful, for example, to display raw HTML to users without the normal difficult workarounds required in static HTML text. Just set the content type to "text/plain", list out the HTML you want to display in raw form, and set the content type back to "text/html".

The Response.SetCookie method lets you store named values on the user's machine. Again, the Session object you are about to see allows a similar capability with less work. So you may want to restrict your use of Response.SetCookie to situations where you need to store values persistently across multiple user sessions. The Set-Cookie method has the following syntax:

```
Response.SetCookie(name,value,[expires,domain,path,secure])
```

where the two required arguments are the name to be used later to retrieve the value, and the value to be stored.

The Session Object

This feature of ActiveX Server allows Web application builders to build state-based applications with much greater ease than was ever before possible. When writing their first Web-based application, most developers are immediately struck by the limitations of Web development's stateless nature. That is, when the user invokes a program by clicking on a link or submitting a form, the program has no idea what that user has done as recently as a couple seconds earlier.

Cookies were invented to circumvent just this problem. The gateway or server application author can store information about the user right on a user's hard drive. For example, if the user is clicking through a Web commerce site, buying product after product, you typically want to allow them to store their purchases in a virtual shopping basket. Before ActiveX Server, doing this without using cookies is difficult. It requires passing around an argument, usually one indicating a session ID between each page in the Web site. This can be done by generating all forms with hidden fields containing a session identifier, or generating all pages dynamically with session identifiers passed as arguments to each URL on the page. However, implementing this is not easy by any means.

Cookies simplify this problem enormously because the necessary information, for example a session identifier, can be stored on the user's machine. The cookie variable, for example "Session," can be queried by the server application whenever it needs to. To implement a shopping basket, each time the user selects a product for purchase, it can be stored in a shopping basket table with all of the product information in each record, but also a field labeled "Session." When the user is ready for checkout, he or she clicks on the Checkout link, and the checkout server application queries their "Session" cookie to determine which rows in the Session table should be retrieved, displayed, and totalled to allow the user to confirm his or her purchase. Of course, this isn't the only way to implement a shopping basket. With cookies available, you could actually store each product ID in a single cookie called "Ordered." When the shopper (user) checks out, records can be retrieved from the products table based on the product IDs concatenated in the cookie.

There's just one problem with this. Not all browsers support cookies. Old versions of Mosaic don't, and neither do most text-based browsers such as Lynx. For intranet applications this may not be a factor, since you often know just what your browser demographics are ahead of time. But for many sites that will be exposed to the wide wild Internet (such as a commerce site) it may not be acceptable to eliminate potential paying customers from participating.

ActiveX Server's Session object eliminates this dilemma. If cookies are available on the user's browser it uses them to implement the capability of having variables that persist for a user's whole session. Specifically, the ActiveX Server script interpreter looks for the SessionID cookie coming from the user in the HTTP headers. If it's not there and the user has a cookie-capable browser, it generates a unique ID and sets the SessionID cookie.

If cookies are *not* available on the user's browser, ActiveX Server has a bit more work to do. You just saw how this could be done with cookieless browsers. The ActiveX Server engine adds the session ID to all URLs on the page that is sent back to the user. This has one limitation that isn't quite acknowledged in the documentation. To make the Session object maintain its state throughout the application for users with cookie-less browsers, *all* pages in the application (the site) must be .ASP files. This is necessary to insure that the ActiveX Server engine modifies the URLs to include the session ID on every link made.

The Session object lets you store whatever variable name and value you want to apply to a user's whole path through your site. You can name the Session variables as you choose. For example, to store a user's number of products purchased, you might want to create a Session("ItemCount") variable. The following code grabs the item count if it's there, initializes it if not, ups the count by one, and then stores it.

```
<% If Not IsEmpty(Session("ItemCount")) Then
     iCount = Session("ItemCount")
Else
     iCount=0
End If
iCount=iCount+1
Session("ItemCount")=iCount
%>
```

You can also store user preferences in a session object. On logging in you might allow a user to choose various options of viewing the site, such as whether to see just text or full graphics-laden pages. This can be stored, for example, in a "Textonly" session variable. Subsequent pages can then contain the following IF statement surrounding their content:

```
<%If Session("Textonly")="Yes">
text only version
<%Else%>
graphics version
<IMG SRC="images/logo.gif">
<%End if%>
```

The Session object even lets you store and retrieve array values. The following code allows you to retrieve the "Basket" Session variable, and initialize it if not present:

```
<%
If Not IsEmpty(Session("Basket")) Then
     aBasket = Session("Basket")
Else
     Dim aBasket(10)
     Session("Basket") = aBasket
End If
%>
```

These arrays can of course be two-dimensional as well. But for a shopping basket, usually just the product ID is sufficient, since the rest of the product information can normally be retrieved from a database (and I'll show in a minute how ActiveX Server makes this easy). Notice that a specific size is initially created (ten items), but this can be expanded dynamically with the Visual Basic ReDim( ) statement.

By default the user's session ends when a user has not hit a page on the site in 20 minutes. This default can be overridden with by setting Session.Timeout to another value. Also, a session can be explicitly ended in your ActiveX Server script code with the Session.Abandon method.

If you want to initially set values of the session object for a user, you can create script code that is run each time a session starts. You do this by creating a special SCRIPT tag invocation with attribute FOR=Session and EVENT=OnStart and placing it in a file called GLOBAL.ASP that should be placed in the root directory of the alias (or virtual directory) for your application. For example, placing the following code in GLOBAL.ASP changes the default session timeout:

```
<SCRIPT FOR=Session EVENT=OnStart LANGUAGE=VBScript
RUNAT=Server>
rem This changes the session timeout to one hour
Session.Timeout=60
</SCRIPT>
```

The Application object operates in very similar fashion to the Session object, but is available to all users of your site. Examples of uses of the Application object would be to create messages available to all users in the site, or to track system status that is relevant for all users of the site.

ActiveX Server Components

ActiveX Server has the ability to create and utilize OLE Automation servers, now called ActiveX Server Components. There are five such components that ship with ActiveX Server. These are the Connection component for database access, the advertisement rotator, the Browser Capability component, the TextStream component, the Page Navigation component.

The Connection Component

The first and most important component is the Connection component. This allows access to any ODBC datasource from within your .ASP files. In this sense, it may sound a bit like the Internet Database Connector (the IDC). In fact, that's true. You can use ActiveX Server and the Connection component anywhere where you once used the IDC. But now you have much more control over what you do with that data. You can individually manipulate each of the returned records using all of the power of VBScript. The programmatic capabilities of the IDC were quite limited. For example, only one SQL statement could be executed per IDC, and of course the IDC itself drove display of the HTML template page. Of course, this meant that only one SQL statement could be executed per IDC page. In some applications, this was unacceptable. Indeed, in trying to overcome this particular limitation, I met many attendees of my seminars that had written their own CGI or ISAPI-based equivalents of the IDC.

More importantly, the IDC established a new connection *every time* it was invoked. The resulting performance hit was unacceptable for most externally used Internet applications. Of course you couldn't really blame the implementors of the IDC too much. Although ISAPI (the IDC is of course just an ISAPI DLL) had the capability of saving database connection handles in static memory (indeed this is a major advantage of ISAPI over CGI), there was no canonical way to allow the database state for a particular user to be saved. Maybe it could have used cookies to do so, but that would actually have been a bit advanced for the time (1995, or a decade ago in Web years). Many browsers at the time did not support cookies, and ActiveX Server was not available to provide its magic of sessions with cookieless browsers. The introduction of the Session object enables ActiveX Server to keep database connections open. This is an immediate huge performance gain. Combined with the VBScript language features for manipulating the data and introducing complex control flow to the application, use of the IDC may be restricted to only those cases where you want to force the minimum amount of programming for maintenance purposes.

You create Connection objects in your .ASP files with the Server.CreateObject ("ADO.Connection") command. Indeed all ActiveX Server Components use the Server.CreateObject( ) command with the appropriate object name. Typically you will want to create the Connection object, tie it to a datasource with the Open( ) method of the created object, and save the object for future use by storing it in a session variable. The Open( ) method of the Connection object takes the name of the datasource as its first, and only required, argument. The username and password can be optionally supplied as the second and third arguments.

As with much .ASP code, you will always have a check for whether this has been done before or not by testing the contents of a session variable, and performing the initialization if necessary. This typically looks something like this:

```
If IsObject (Session("Conn")) Then
    Set Conn=Session("Conn")
Else
    Set Conn = Server.CreateObject("ADO.Connection")
    rem Catalog should be changed to the ODBC DSN you use
    Conn.Open("Catalog")
    Session("Conn") = Conn
End If
```

Once you create your connection you can use it to execute SQL commands and interpret their results. The commands are executed with the OpenResultSet method. This command has one required argument, the SQL statement, to execute. The next optional argument is the type of cursor to use: adOpenForwardOnly (the default) and adOpenStatic, which allows movement forward and backward in the result set. There are other much less frequently used optional arguments for locking type and prepared SQL execution (appropriate if you will be frequently reexecuting the same query). Consult the ActiveX Server reference for details. To manipulate or display each row of the result set, call the MoveNext method. You can get fields from the result set records by subscripting the result set variable with an integer index or the name of the field.

The following code shows a selection of a set of products matching a given description from the database.

```
<%
Set Result=Conn.OpenResultSet (
"SELECT PARTNUM, DESCRIPTION, MANUFACTURER, CATEGORY
FROM PRODUCTS WHERE DESCRIPTION LIKE '%" & SrchStr & "%'%>
<TABLE>
<TR><TH>Part
```

```
Number<TH>Description<TH>Manufacturer<TH>Category

    <%Do Until Result.EOF

        Response.Write "<TR><TD>" & Result["PartNum"]

        Result.MoveNext

    Loop

    %>

    </TABLE>
```

MoveFirst and MovePrevious let you move backward in a result set open with the adOpenStatic flag. MoveNextPage and MovePreviousPage let you move a page at a time through the result set. The page size (or number of rows) is determined by the result set's PageSize property. The contents of these pages can then be displayed to the user using the currently *completely undocumented* AppendResultHTML( ) method of the Response object. This method takes the result set object as its argument and spews out the current page of the result set as HTML. If you wish to just run an SQL statement but aren't interested in its return (and don't want to pay the overhead to gather it together into an object), then invoke the Execute method of the Connection object with the SQL command you want to run.

There are many other methods and properties of both the ResultSet and the Connection object, all documented in the ActiveX Server Component Reference that ships with ActiveX Server. However, the summary I've given you here certainly gives you the main weapons to apply the Connection object effectively.

The Browser Capabilities Component

In my opinion, the next most important component in building most Web applications with ActiveX Server is the browser capability component. Currently most advanced Web sites that try to create content optimized for the capabilities of all browsers are a horrendous mishmash of scripts, server-side includes, and CGI programs that test the contents of HTTP_USER_AGENT and attempt to output HTML and HTML extensions that are just the right combination for the browser capabilities they think they are detecting. For example, a script that displays a site's top page might try to determine if the user's browser can support frames, and if so deliver a table of contents to the site using frames. If the script thinks the user can only see text, it can usually do a better job of delivering text-only content than relying on the ALT attribute of HTML tags such as IMG. If the script detects Internet Explorer as the browser it may include some ActiveX controls for some features.

All of this effort is legitimate and the browser capability component doesn't promise to remove the work. What it can do is rationalize the capability testing process, and provide an initial knowledge base of how different browser strings found in the HTTP headers map to browser capabilities. This knowledge base is just a text file, BROWSER.INI, and can actually be extended to accommodate new capabilities and new browser strings.

This object is created with the command CreateObject("MSWC.BrowserType"). A capability such as frames can be tested by checking to see if the object's Frames property is set to "true." For example:

```
<% Set browser = Server.CreateObject ("MSWC.BrowserType") %>
<% if browser.frames="true" then %>
<frameset cols="30%,70%">
<% end if %>
```

The other capabilities that are testable are listed in Table 10.1. Note that this is just what is available straight out of the box, and the list is actually quite extensible, as shown in the next section on the BROWSER.INI file.

■■■■■■■ **Table 10.1** Browser Type Capabilities

Capability Name	Description
Browser	Name of the browser
Version	Version of the browser
Frames	Does browser support frames? (TRUE or FALSE)
Tables	Does browser support tables?
VBScript	Does browser support VBScript?
JavaScript	Does browser support JavaScript?
Cookies	Does browser support Cookies?
Height	Vertical screen resolution (e.g., 768)
Width	Horizontal screen resolution (e.g., 1024)
BackgroundSounds	Does browser support background sounds?

■■■■■■■

The list of capabilities and what browser supports what capabilities can be maintained and extended via the BROWSER.INI file. This file lists each of the capabilities' names and their values on a separate line in a section labeled with the browser value that shows up in the HTTP header HTTP_USER_AGENT. The BROWSER.INI file must reside in the same directory as the BROWSER.DLL. In the current release of ActiveX server, this is the INETSRV\Denali\Cmpnts directory.

For example, the following section in the BROWSER.INI file details the capabilities of Microsoft Internet Explorer Version 3.0A for Windows 95:

```
[Mozilla 2.0 (compatible; MSIE 3.0A; Windows 95)]
browser=IE
Version=3.0
majorver=#3
minorver=#0
frames=TRUE
tables=TRUE
cookies=TRUE
backgroundsounds=TRUE
vbscript=TRUE
javascript=TRUE
platform=Win95
```

Note that the capability called Browser, combined with the Version capability, gets us out of the nasty business of trying to parse the HTTP_USER_AGENT header and figure out what browser it really is. It's not obvious that the header name above is Internet Explorer 3.0).

Also, you can feel free to add any capability name you wish to the BROWSER.INI file. For example, one candidate for a new capability might be "controls." You could add lines saying "controls=TRUE" to only the browsers that had the ability to easily download ActiveX Controls. For now that would mean updating most of the sections in BROWSER.INI.

Another really powerful aspect of the BROWSER.INI repository is that you can easily add new browser types. First find out what contents of HTTP_USER_AGENT are reported for the new browser. Then add a section with that name to BROWSER.INI.

If the browser is a new version of an existing browser, and has many of the same capabilities as an existing browser, you can include a parent pointer to refer the browser component to another browser's entries for values. Additional values or overridden values can be listed after the "parent=" line. For example, the following section is defined for Internet Explorer 3.0B at 1024 by 768 resolution:

```
[Mozilla/2.0 (compatible; MSIE 3.0B; Windows 95; 1024, 768]
parent=Mozilla/2.0
platform=Win95
Height=#768
Width=#1024
```

All of the values for IE 3.0B at this resolution are inherited from the section shown above for IE 3.0A at all resolutions, with the exception that there are additional capabilities listed: Height and Width. Other properties of the parent browser could be overridden. For example, if a capability was not implemented in one version of a browser but was added in a subsequent release, the newer browser would probably inherit most values with a "parent=" line and then change the value for the new capability to TRUE.

There are other existing ActiveX Server Components that I haven't really discussed here. The TextStream component adds file input and output (on the server of course!) to ActiveX Server. This is an important addition since VBScript of course has no file I/O. The methods are all fairly intuitive: CreateTextFile, OpenTextFile, ReadLine, WriteLine. The AtEnd property lets you test for end of file. The other two components can actually be implemented fairly easily by yourself once you have TextStream.

The Content Linking component lets you list a bunch of URLs and descriptions in a file and provides methods to retrieve the "n-th URL" or the "n-th description" from the file. This supposedly makes it easier to build table of contents pages and pages with links to the next document and the previous document. However, this is a very thin, almost nonexistent, layer of abstraction over what you can do with VBScript arrays combined with the TextStream component to provide file I/O, so it's difficult to see the value of this particular component.

The advertisement rotator displays a new image file each time its GetAdvertisement method is called. Of course, this has the same aspect as Content Linking. It's pretty easy to keep a Session variable called Session("AdNumber"), which should have a number between one and the number of image files referred to in a text file. Each time your script is invoked, you can just increment session variable number, and restart at 1 after the highest number is reached. The TextStream object makes it easy to load up these image names into an array, which can be indexed with this number. So again, this particular component is of somewhat dubious general value. Anyway, the Connection component, the browser capabilities component, and the TextStream component are all quite valuable tools, demonstrating the power of ActiveX Server Components.

The Shopping Basket Sample

Let's take a look at an example that ties together all of the useful technologies discussed in this chapter: ActiveX Server Components (especially the Active Data Objects component), session variables, and the Request and Response objects. It is also a good example of the capabilities of ActiveX Server in general. It's the venerable shopping basket example that's been nibbled at for most of this chapter, shown here in its entirety. You'll see that it does many things that would be quite difficult without the full capabilities of ActiveX Server. Many of you may find immediate use for this sample in your own efforts.

The shopping basket is stored persistently using a Session variable called "Basket" that contains the values of a two-dimensional array also called "Basket." In this basket you store the part numbers *and quantities* of products ordered. That's all you need to store persistently. You can reload the rest of the product information from the Products table that this runs from. This is a different approach from the "Adventure Works" sample shopping basket that ships with ActiveX Server—only the keys are stored.

In the top portion of the shopping basket are the command handlers. This shopping basket supports four major commands:

- RECALC—recomputes the subtotal based on any quantity changes the customer may have made.

- SHOP MORE—goes back to the product list that the customer was shopping from. I'll show a sample product list script following, but if you are going to use this, you would change the URL to your own "shopping area" page.

- PURCHASE—recompute the subtotal and link off to the page to finalize the purchase, usually a "ship page" where the shopper supplies billing and shipping information.

- CANCEL—empties out the shopping basket and returns the customer to the "shopping area."

Note that another feature that could be added is a checkbox to allow selection or deselection of items. If an item was deselected, subsequent displays of the basket would show the list without the deselected item.

```
[SHOPBSKT.ASP - ActiveX Server-Based Shopping Basket]

<SCRIPT LANGUAGE=VBScript RUNAT=Server>
</SCRIPT>
<%
If IsObject (Session("Conn")) Then
        Set Conn=Session("Conn")
Else
        Set Conn=Server.CreateObject("ADO.Connection")
        Ret=Conn.Open("COMMERCE","sa","")
        Session("Conn") = Conn
End If

If Not IsEmpty(Session("Items")) Then
        nItems = Session("Items")
Else
        nItems = 0
        Session("Items") Items
End If

If Not IsEmpty(Session("Basket")) Then
        Basket = Session("Basket")
Else
        Dim Basket(10,2)
        Session("Basket")=Basket
End If

If IsNull(Basket(1,1)) Then
        nItems=0
End If
```

```
If Request("partnum")<>"" Then
     nItems = nItems+1
     Session("Items") Items
     Basket(nItems,1)=Request("partnum")
     Basket(nItems,2)=1
     Session("Basket")=Basket
End If

SELECT CASE Request("Action")

CASE "RECALC"
     For i = 1 to nItems
          If IsNumeric(Request("Quantity" & CStr(i))) Then
               Basket(i,2) = Request("Quantity" & CStr(i))
          Else
               Basket(i,2) = 1
          End If
     Next
     Session("Basket") = Basket
     Session("Items") = nItems

CASE "SHOP MORE"
     For i = 1 to nItems
          If IsNumeric(Request("Quantity" & CStr(i))) Then
               Basket(i,2) = Request("Quantity" & CStr(i))
               Else
               Basket(i,2) = 1
          End If
     Next
     Session("Basket") = Basket
     Response.Redirect "/commerce/prodlist.asp"

CASE "CANCEL"
     nItems = 0
     Session("Items") = nItems
     Response.Redirect "/commerce/prodlist.asp"
```

```
CASE "PURCHASE"
     For i = 1 to nItems
          If IsNumeric(Request("Quantity" & CStr(i))) Then
               Basket(i,2) = Request("Quantity" & CStr(i))
          Else
               Basket(i,2) = 1
          End If
     Next
     Session("Basket") = Basket
     Response.Redirect "/commerce/shipping.asp"
CASE ELSE
END SELECT

%>
<HTML>
<HEAD>
<TITLE>Shopping Basket</TITLE>
</HEAD>
<BODY>
<FORM ACTION="/commerce/shopbskt.asp?" METHOD=POST>
<TABLE BORDER>
<TR><TH>Product<TH>Price<TH>Quantity
<%
iSubtotal = 0
For i = 1 to nItems
%>

<%
     Cmd="Select * From products Where partnum='" & basket(i,1) & "'"
     Set Conn=Session("Conn")
     Set RS=Conn.Execute(Cmd)
%>
<TR><%=RS("productname")%><TD><%=RS("price")%>
<TD><INPUT NAME=<%Response.Write "Quantity" & CStr(i)%>
VALUE="<%=Basket(i,2)%>">
<%
```

```
Subtotal=Subtotal+(CDbl(Basket(i,2))*CDbl(RS("Price")))
Next
%>
<!-- subtotal row -->
<TR>
<TD>------><TD>Subtotal:<TD><%=Subtotal%>
<!-- buttons row -->
<TR>
<TD>
<INPUT TYPE=SUBMIT NAME="Action" VALUE="RECALC">
<INPUT TYPE=SUBMIT NAME="Action" VALUE="SHOP MORE">
<%If nItems > 0 Then%>
<INPUT TYPE=SUBMIT NAME="Action" VALUE="PURCHASE">
<%End If%>
<INPUT TYPE=SUBMIT NAME="Action" VALUE="CANCEL">
</TABLE>
</FORM>
</BODY>
</HTML>
```

The Shopping Area

The shopping basket refers to the ActiveX Server script PRODLIST.ASP as its shopping area. In fact, that's where the shopping basket is invoked from as well. Here is a simple product list ActiveX Server program. You will probably develop your own shopping area, tailored to your own database and table definitions, but I'll present the one used in this example for completeness.

```
[PRODLIST.ASP - The "Shopping Area"]
<!-- PRODLIST.ASP -->
<HTML>
<HEAD>
<TITLE>Product List</TITLE>
</HEAD>
<BODY>
<H1>Select Products</H1>
<%
```

```
Set Conn = Server.CreateObject("ADO.Connection")
Ret=Conn.Open("COMMERCE","sa","")
Set RS=Conn.Execute("SELECT * FROM PRODUCTS")
%>
<TABLE BORDER>
<TH>Product Name<TH>Price<TH>Available<TH>Link
<% While Not RS.EOF %>
<TR><%=RS("productname")%>
<TD><%=RS("price")%>
<TD><%=RS("available")%>
<TD><A
HREF="/commerce/shopbskt.asp?partnum=<%=RS("partnum")%>">BUY!</A>
<% RS.MoveNext
Wend %>
</BODY>
</HTML>
```

Shopping Basket Operation

Let's show the shopping basket being used from some simple pages. Figure 10.1 shows a small product list built with the PRODLIST.ASP just shown.

Clicking on any of the BUY! links takes you to the shopping basket itself. From the shopping basket, you can change quantities, RECALC the subtotal of products ordered, SHOP MORE and go back to the product list. This would result in a display such as that in Figure 10.2.

When the customer is finished they can click on PURCHASE and they will be taken to a script called SHIPPING.ASP (not shown here).

The Database Definition

You may feel free to integrate this shopping basket in your own commerce Web applications or sites. You would probably integrate it into your own database definition, which requires changing the fields in PRODLIST.ASP and SHOPBSKT.ASP accordingly. If you want to use an existing database definition, and not have to change the field names, you can use the PRODUCTS table defined for this example. The PRODUCTS table used for this sample has the following definition, as shown in SQL Server

Figure 10.1 Product list.

6.5 Enterprise Manager in Figure 10.3. You will very likely change the field names used in SHOPBSKT.ASP to correspond with your own table definitions.

Also, make sure to change the statement in SHOPBSKT.ASP that does the database logon (Conn.Open("commerce","sa","")) to use a logon ID and password that is appropriate for your database server environment. Using the SA account is not recommended in a production environment, but it's common practice for many database samples. For example, all of the Internet Database Connector samples used this ID, since it's available on most SQL Server installations.

If you do choose to use sample tables in your efforts, here are a couple more files you may find useful. Following is the HTML code (ADDPROD.HTM) for a form to enter data into this table.

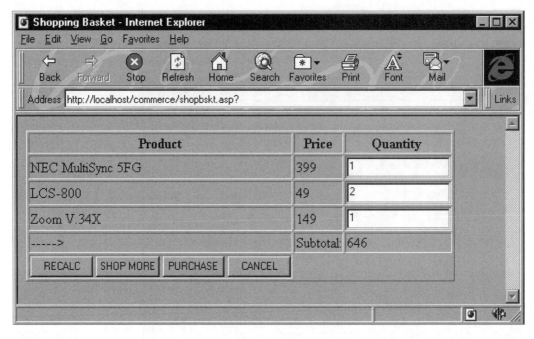

Figure 10.2 A filled shopping basket.

```
[Form to Enter Product Data]

<!-- ADDPROD.HTM -->

<HTML>

<HEAD>

<TITLE>Product Creation Page</TITLE>

</HEAD>

<BODY>

<H1>Add Product to Database</H1>

<FORM ACTION="/commerce/addprod.asp">

<TABLE>

<TR>Part Number<TD><INPUT NAME="partnum"><BR>

<TR>Name<TD><INPUT NAME="productname"><BR>

<TR>Description<TD><INPUT NAME="proddesc"><BR>

<TR>Manufacturer ID<TD><INPUT NAME="manuid"><BR>

<TR>Manu. Part Number<TD><INPUT NAME="manupn"><BR>

<TR>Price<TD><INPUT NAME="price"><BR>
```

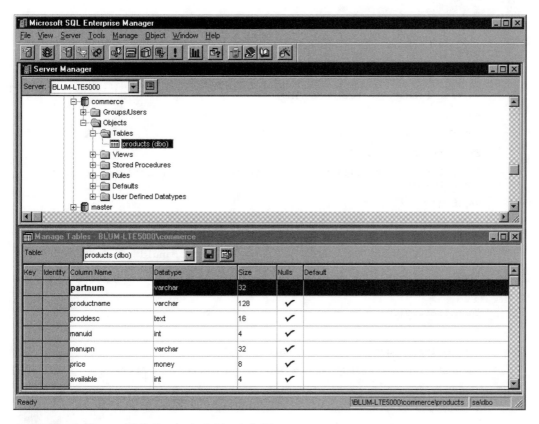

Figure 10.3 Products table definition.

```
<TR># Available<TD><INPUT NAME="available"><BR>
<TR><INPUT TYPE="Reset" VALUE="Cancel">
<TD><INPUT TYPE="Submit" VALUE="Add Product">
</FORM>
</BODY>
</HTML>
```

Next is the ActiveX Server program (.ASP file) that processes this form and inserts the record for the product into the PRODUCTS table.

```
[Script to Insert Product]
<!-- ADDPROD.ASP -->
<HTML>
```

```
<HEAD>
<TITLE>Product Add Confirmation</TITLE>
</HEAD>
<BODY>
<H1>Add Product to Database</H1>
<%
Set Conn = Server.CreateObject("ADO.Connection")
Err=Conn.Open("COMMERCE","sa","")
Cmd="INSERT products(partnum,productname,proddesc,manuid,manupn,price,
↳available)
VALUES("
Cmd=Cmd & "'" & Request("partnum") & "','" & Request("productname") &
↳"','"
        & Request("proddesc") & "'," & Request("manuid") & ",'"
        & Request("manupn") & "'," & Request("price")
        & "," & Request("Available") & ")"
Conn.Execute(Cmd)
%>
Successfully added product to database.<P>
<A HREF="/commerce/addprod.htm">Add another product</A><P>
<A HREF="/commerce/prodlist.asp">List products</P>
</BODY>
</HTML>
```

Note that this script will also let you click over to the shopping area (PRODLIST.ASP) to start filling a shopping basket.

The full source code for this sample basket implementation is listed in Appendix A of this book. A working demo of the shopping basket, running against a small test database, is available on this book's Web page (http://www.wiley.com/compbooks/). The full ActiveX Server programs (.ASP files) are also available on these pages.

11

JAVA, VISUAL J++, AND ACTIVEX

J ava has attracted lots of attention in the computer industry and the world at large. The level of publicity is unprecedented for what is after all a programming language to be interacted with directly by just a small subset of Web users—Web application developers. End users should in general be blissfully unaware of the implementation mechanism for any application they are using. This maxim should apply to Web applications and Java as well.

Nevertheless, despite all the hype, Java does fill a real and valuable niche in the pantheon of programming languages. It sports C-like syntax, a much purer (though simpler) object model than C++, and a level of learning difficulty considerably lower than C++ (especially for developers with less programming experience). It comes with a respectable library for input and output, windowing, graphics, math, and TCP/IP and Internet networking. This library has no procedural code vestiges (such as the C runtime library used by C++ programmers). Finally Java has the ability to create applets that are hosted inside HTML pages (and thus Web browsers as well). These applets are limited in ways that protected the Web browser users and their machines, making it feasible and acceptable to download and run these applications on-the-fly while perusing Web sites. Viewed narrowly, Java applets could be considered an alternative to the ActiveX Controls for client side functionality presented earlier. So a chapter on Java might not seem to belong in a book about ActiveX. However, there are several advantages that ActiveX brings to Java development. For one thing, the Java object model that centers on classes providing interfaces maps very nicely to the COM model. This has the distinct benefit that Java applets can call ActiveX Controls (which are just COM controls), and the Java language provides nice mechanisms to abstract COM functionality. Contrary to popular belief, Java and ActiveX Controls are quite complementary technologies. In addition, Microsoft tools such as Visual J++, a Java version of Visual C++ that uses the familiar Microsoft Developer Studio IDE, provide great facilities for Java development.

In this chapter, I will not attempt to present a tutorial for Java development. The dozens of books available on Java now can do a much better job of that. What I do want to show you is how several parts of the ActiveX set of technologies can be useful complements to Java. Along the way, I'll show you how Visual J++ in itself provides a great development environment for Java.

The Visual J++ Development Environment

Microsoft Visual J++ includes support for developing Java applications and applets in its Developer Studio environment. Currently this product is available in beta form for free download at http://www.microsoft.com/visualj. By the time you read this book, it should be available as a commercial shipping product.

In the following example, I will show how to create a Java applet, called OPTIONS. This is a little applet that will compute the fair price of an option using Black-Scholes Option Pricing Model. Now that many Web sites are acting as the source for stock information, this might be a useful applet for many Web applications. The real purpose is just to show an applet that does some nontrivial computation that makes sense to do on the client rather than hitting a server-based gateway to do the work. I will demonstrate building this applet throughout this chapter.

Running the Applet Wizard

To create a Java applet or application, select File/New/Project Workspace as you would to create a C++ application or DLL. Then select Java Applet Wizard or Java Workspace from the New Project menu (Figure 11.1).

In the applet wizard's first dialog you merely choose whether you want to allow it to be an application as well as an applet. In this example, let's set it to be just an applet. On the next dialog (Step 2), choose the size of the applet on the page in pixels. The other option determines whether an HTML page is generated with a sample invocation of your applet. Even if you have your own HTML page ready to embed the applet into, it can't hurt to accept this. If your applet accepts parameters and you haven't used many Java applets before, the sample applet invocation complete with parameters in the generated HTML should help.

The next dialog has several important options (Figure 11.2). It will allow you to generate applets that are multithreaded. How does it do this? If you choose to make your application multithreaded, this is performed by specifying *implements Runnable* in your Applet-derived class definition, a Thread member object is generated in the

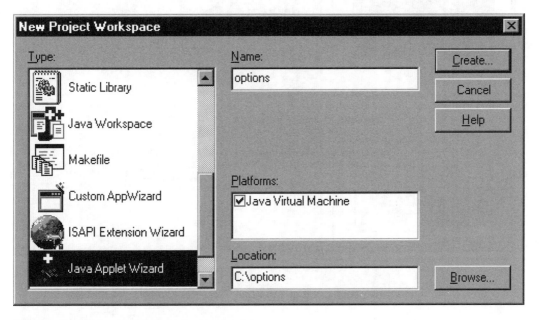

Figure 11.1 Applet wizard setup.

code, the run( ) method is created where the work of the thread will be performed, and the start( ) and stop( ) methods are filled in with thread startup and shutdown code. I will show a full example of this a bit later. In the meantime, let's not make our first applet multithreaded. The other option that appears on this page is to allow the wizard to generate support for animation. Again, for this first applet, keep it simple and do not include this feature. The last group of checkboxes generates mouse event handlers, methods that are invoked when the mouse is positioned over the applet on the Web page, when it moves off the applet, when the mouse is clicked onto the applet, and when it is released. This is a very useful set of features, but don't use it for this first applet.

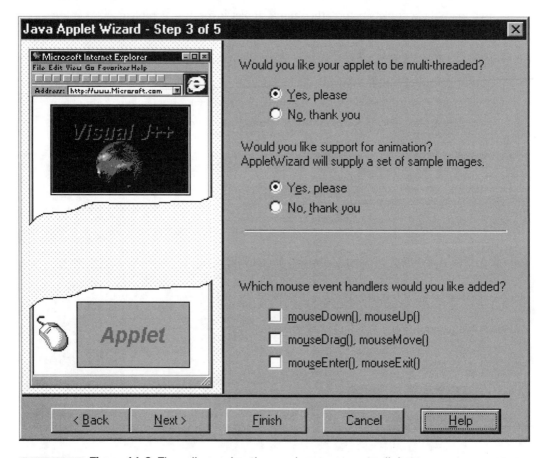

■■■■■■ **Figure 11.2** Threading, animation, and mouse events dialog.

The next dialog controls the parameters for applet (Figure 11.3). Here we have all the parameters that the Black-Scholes model needs: stock price, strike price of option, historical variance of the stock, the current "risk-free rate" (T-bill rates for the time period in question), and time interval in fraction of a year. Note that the applet itself will prompt for these options, but it's nice to be able to preset them in the calling HTML using the PARAM tag.

The wizard then generates a Java source file, an HTML file, and a project to contain them. Figure 11.4 shows the generated project and source file in Microsoft Developer Studio.

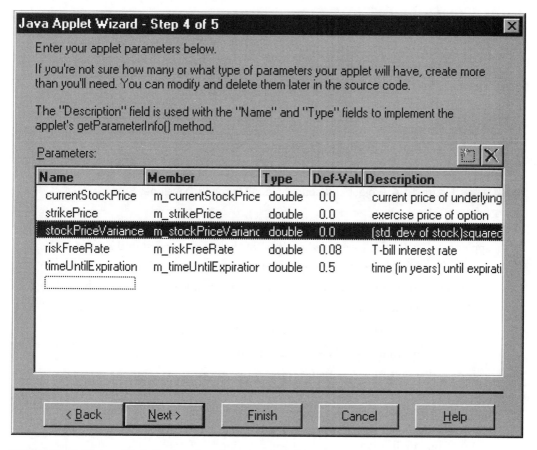

Figure 11.3 Applet wizard parameters dialog.

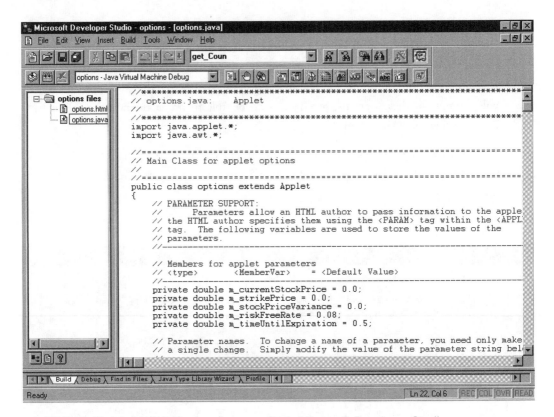

Figure 11.4 Project and source file in Microsoft Developer Studio.

The applet code is created with all of the parameters listed as private members of the applet subclass (in this case called options) of the types specified in the wizard. The names of the parameters also become private member variables. The code is generated in the getParameterInfo( ) function to retrieve the parameter values from the calling HTML. The methods generated are:

- options( )—The constructor for the applet, with no code filled in.
- getAppletInfo( )—Miscellaneous information about the applet.
- getParameterInfo( )—Returns descriptive information about the parameters of the application.
- init( )—Contains code to retrieve the values of the parameters for a given invocation. It is also where you will be putting the dialog box invocation for your application.

- destroy( )—Empty by default. Will contain cleanup code for anything that you do in init( ) that might need it.
- paint( )—Empty by default. The simplest applets often contain some code to do text or graphics output in this function.
- start( )—Empty by default if no multithreaded support. If this were a multi-threaded (MT) application, the thread initialization code would have been generated here.
- stop( )—Empty by default. Contains thread shutdown code if it's an MT application.

After these methods is a comment labeled:

```
//TODO: place additional applet code here
```

In fact, that's just what you'll do to build the OPTIONS applet: add a bunch of methods that do the real work of the application at the end of the public methods enumerated previously. Before you do that, following is the sample applet code initially generated. Due to Java's wonderful expressive simplicity, it's short enough to safely list it here, without interrupting the flow of the discussion too badly.

```
//****************************************************************************
// options.java:      Applet
//
//****************************************************************************
import java.applet.*;
import java.awt.*;

//============================================================================
// Main Class for applet options
//
//============================================================================
public class options extends Applet
{
        // PARAMETER SUPPORT:
        //Parameters allow an HTML author to pass information to the applet;
        // the HTML author specifies them using the <PARAM> tag within the <APPLET>
        // tag. The following variables are used to store the values of the
```

```
    // parameters.
//---------------------------------------------------------------------------

// Members for applet parameters
// <type>        <MemberVar>    = <Default Value>
//---------------------------------------------------------------------------
    private double m_currentStockPrice = 0.0;
    private double m_strikePrice = 0.0;
    private double m_stockPriceVariance = 0.0;
    private double m_riskFreeRate = 0.08;
    private double m_timeUntilExpiration = 0.5;

// Parameter names. To change a name of a parameter, you need only make
// a single change. Simply modify the value of the parameter string below.
//---------------------------------------------------------------------------
    private final String PARAM_currentStockPrice = "currentStockPrice";
    private final String PARAM_strikePrice = "strikePrice";
    private final String PARAM_stockPriceVariance = "stockPriceVariance";
    private final String PARAM_riskFreeRate = "riskFreeRate";
    private final String PARAM_timeUntilExpiration = "timeUntilExpiration";

    // options Class Constructor
    //-----------------------------------------------------------------------
    public options()
    {
            // TODO: Add constructor code here
    }

    // APPLET INFO SUPPORT:
    //The getAppletInfo() method returns a string describing the applet's
    // author, copyright date, or miscellaneous information.
//---------------------------------------------------------------------------
    public String getAppletInfo()
    {
            return "Name: options\r\n" +
                    "Author: Adam Blum\r\n" +
                    "Created with Microsoft Visual J++ Version 1.0";
```

```java
    }

    // PARAMETER SUPPORT
    //The getParameterInfo() method returns an array of strings describing
    // the parameters understood by this applet.
    //
// options Parameter Information:
// { "Name", "Type", "Description" },
//----------------------------------------------------------------------
    public String[] [] getParameterInfo()
    {
      String[] [] info =
      {
        { PARAM_currentStockPrice, "double", "current price of underlying" },
        { PARAM_strikePrice, "double", "exercise price of option" },
        { PARAM_stockPriceVariance, "double", "(std. dev of stock)squared" },
        { PARAM_riskFreeRate, "double", "T-bill interest rate" },
        { PARAM_timeUntilExpiration, "double", "time (in years) until
expiration" },
      };
          return info;
    }
    // The init() method is called by the AWT when an applet is first loaded or
    // reloaded. Override this method to perform whatever initialization your
    // applet needs, such as initializing data structures, loading images or
    // fonts, creating frame windows, setting the layout manager, or adding UI
    // components.
//----------------------------------------------------------------------
    public void init()
    {
            // PARAMETER SUPPORT
            //The following code retrieves the value of each parameter
            // specified with the <PARAM> tag and stores it in a member
            // variable.
            //----------------------------------------------------------
```

```
      String param;
      // currentStockPrice: current price of underlying
      //------------------------------------------------------------------
      param = getParameter(PARAM_currentStockPrice);
      if (param != null)
            m_currentStockPrice = Double.valueOf(param).doubleValue();

      // strikePrice: exercise price of option
      //------------------------------------------------------------------
      param = getParameter(PARAM_strikePrice);
      if (param != null)
            m_strikePrice = Double.valueOf(param).doubleValue();

      // stockPriceVariance: (std. dev of stock)squared
      //------------------------------------------------------------------
      param = getParameter(PARAM_stockPriceVariance);
      if (param != null)
            m_stockPriceVariance = Double.valueOf(param).doubleValue();

      // riskFreeRate: T-bill interest rate
      //------------------------------------------------------------------
      param = getParameter(PARAM_riskFreeRate);
      if (param != null)
            m_riskFreeRate = Double.valueOf(param).doubleValue();

      // timeUntilExpiration: time (in years) until expiration
      //------------------------------------------------------------------
      param = getParameter(PARAM_timeUntilExpiration);
      if (param != null)
            m_timeUntilExpiration = Double.valueOf(param).doubleValue();

// If you use a ResourceWizard-generated "control creator" class to
// arrange controls in your applet, you may want to call its
// CreateControls() method from within this method. Remove the following
// call to resize() before adding the call to CreateControls();
// CreateControls() does its own resizing.
//------------------------------------------------------------------------
      resize(320, 240);
```

```
        // TODO: Place additional initialization code here
}

// Place additional applet clean up code here. destroy() is called when
// when you applet is terminating and being unloaded.
//------------------------------------------------------------------------
public void destroy()
{
        // TODO: Place applet cleanup code here
}

// options Paint Handler
//------------------------------------------------------------------------

public void paint(Graphics g)
{
}

//The start() method is called when the page containing the applet
// first appears on the screen. The AppletWizard's initial implementation
// of this method starts execution of the applet's thread.
//------------------------------------------------------------------------

public void start()
{
        // TODO: Place additional applet start code here
}
// The stop() method is called when the page containing the applet is
// no longer on the screen. The AppletWizard's initial implementation of
// this method stops execution of the applet's thread.
//------------------------------------------------------------------------
public void stop()
{
}

// TODO: Place additional applet code here

}
```

The next step is to fill in the functionality of the applet in the appropriate places in the generated Java source code (in this case *options.java*). The main tasks you'll be performing are: designing a dialog for your applet field using the Java Resource Wizard, incorporating this dialog into the init( ) method, and then writing an event handler in a new public method called action( ).

Designing Java Applet User Interfaces Using Visual J++

In the sample OPTIONS applet it would be helpful to supply fields for each of the values needed to compute the option value. Visual J++ has several features to assist in this design process, primarily the Resource Template Wizard and the Java Resource Wizard.

Of course, you can do this manually in Java using the various components available in Java's Abstract Windowing Toolkit (AWT). For example, you can put the following code into applet's init( ) method, and you'll get a label, a text field, and a button.

```
public void init() {
     add (new Label("Current Price: "));
     curPrice = new TextField(5);
     add(curPrice);
     add(new Button("Compute"));
}
```

If you included a layout manager in the init( ) method, you could have had precise control of where the components were placed on the applet. You could have added a FlowLayout, GridLayout, GridBagLayout, BorderLayout or PanelLayout to the applet with the setLayout( ) command. This would allow you to place components on the applet flowing from left to right or in a grid of specified height and width. But it doesn't make it easy to do the kind of precise two-dimensional layout you may be used to as Windows developers.

Fortunately with Visual J++ the familiar Windows tools for doing dialog layout are available to you. The first step in doing this is to create a Resource Template. Select File/New Resource Template from the Developer Studio menu. Then invoke Save As, and save it as a named .RCT file in your project directory. For this example, it is saved as OPTIONS.RCT in the C:\OPTIONS directory.

Next, select Insert/Resource and choose Dialog. You will then see an empty Windows dialog. You should restrict yourself to the controls that have corresponding components in Java's AWT. The available controls and the corresponding Java components are shown in Table 11.1 below.

In this example, you will add several static text controls, several edit box controls, and a couple buttons. As you go along adding controls, make sure to give the edit box controls meaningful names so that you can retrieve the values later. You should also do this for button names. It's not usually necessary to name the static text controls that you won't be modifying. However, one of the static text controls below will be modified: The last line will display the option value. Name this IDC_LBLOPTIONVALUE, since the Windows dialog convention for controls is to begin their names with IDC_. Note that this means that will be the name of that component in your Java code. Java purists may not like this name, so they should feel free to rename the controls (which will become AWT component names) to something more "Javaish" (perhaps just "1" instead of "IDC_LBLOPTIONVALUE"). While renaming fields, you may want to rename the overall dialog by doubleclicking on the frame, and changing the name

▬▬▬▬ **Table 11.1** Windows Controls and Corresponding Java Components

Windows Resource	Java Component
Static Text control	Label class
Edit Box control	TextField class
Multiline edit control	TextArea class
Button control	Button class
Check Box control	CheckBox class
Radio Button control	CheckBox class
List Box control	List class
Combo Box control	Choice class
Horizontal Scrollbar control	Scrollbar class
Vertical Scrollbar control	Scrollbar class

▬▬▬▬▬

from IDD_DIALOG1 to something like IDD_OPTIONS or OptionDialog. This name will determine the name of the generated Java class from the set of controls.

You may also want to take advantage of the ability to set the field Tab Order by choosing the option from the Layout menu. Finally, you can test the created dialog by running Test from the Layout menu. The result of dropping controls onto the dialog, naming them, and setting the tab order is a dialog such as that shown in Figure 11.5.

Save your dialog to the resource template (.RCT file) you created. Now you have a Windows dialog that resembles what you want to display in your applet. But you're not done yet. All you have now is a Windows resource. What you really want is a Java class that creates AWT components with the same layout and naming as the Windows resource you just designed.

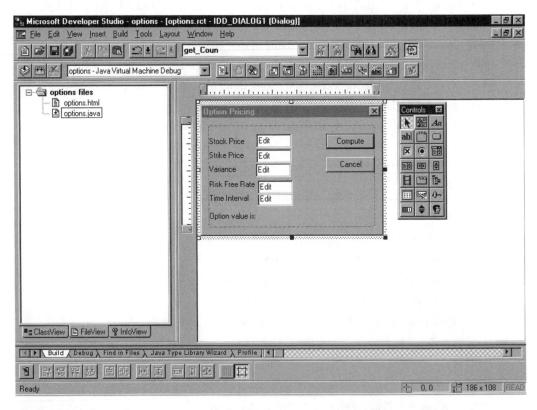

Figure 11.5 Building the layout using the Resource Editor.

To build the Java control creator class, run the Java Resource Wizard. From the Tools menu, select Java Resource Wizard (Figure 11.6). Choose the .RCT file you just created. The next dialog lets you override the class name. Leave the name of your class as IDD_OPTIONS.

After you click Finish two files will be generated. DialogLayout.java contains a layout manager class used by your generated Java class for two dimensional layout. Another Java source file is generated with the basename of your chosen control creator class name, in this case IDD_OPTIONS.java. You should add the generated files to your project. Here is the the generated Java file containing the control creator class.

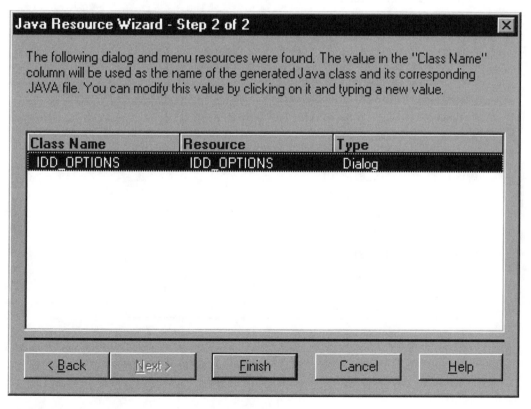

Figure 11.6 Java Resource Wizard.

```
//----------------------------------------------------------------
// IDD_OPTIONS.java:
//            Implementation of "control creator" class IDD_OPTIONS
//----------------------------------------------------------------
import java.awt.*;
import DialogLayout;

public class IDD_OPTIONS
{
       Container     m_Parent       = null;
       boolean       m_fInitialized = false;
       DialogLayout m_Layout;

       // Control definitions
       //-----------------------------------------------------------
       TextField     IDC_CURPRICE;
       TextField     IDC_STRIKEPRICE;
       TextField     IDC_STOCKPRICEVARIANCE;
       TextField     IDC_RISKFREERATE;
       TextField     IDC_TIMEUNTILEXPIRATION;
       Button        IDCOMPUTE;
       Button        IDCANCEL;
       Label         IDC_STATIC1;
       Label         IDC_STATIC2;
       Label         IDC_STATIC3;
       Label         IDC_STATIC4;
       Label         IDC_STATIC5;
       Label         IDC_LBLOPTIONVALUE;

       // Constructor
       //-----------------------------------------------------------
       public IDD_OPTIONS (Container parent)
       {
              m_Parent = parent;
       }

       // Initialization.
```

```
//------------------------------------------------------------
public boolean CreateControls()
{

        // CreateControls should be called only once
        //-----------------------------------------------------
        if (m_fInitialized || m_Parent == null)
                return false;

        // m_Parent must be extended from the Container class
        //-----------------------------------------------------
        if (!(m_Parent instanceof Container))
                return false;

        //Since a given font may not be supported across all platforms, it
        //is safe to modify only the size of the font, not the typeface.
        //-----------------------------------------------------
    Font OldFnt = m_Parent.getFont();
    if (OldFnt != null)
    {
        Font NewFnt = new Font(OldFnt.getName(), OldFnt.getStyle(), 8);
        m_Parent.setFont(NewFnt);
    }

        // All position and sizes are in dialog logical units, so we use a
        // DialogLayout as our layout manager.
        //-----------------------------------------------------
        m_Layout = new DialogLayout(m_Parent, 186, 108);
        m_Parent.setLayout(m_Layout);
        m_Parent.addNotify();

        Dimension size   = m_Layout.getDialogSize();
        Insets    insets = m_Parent.insets();

        m_Parent.resize(insets.left + size.width
                + insets.right, insets.top + size.height + insets.bottom);
```

```
// Control creation
//-----------------------------------------------
IDC_CURPRICE = new TextField ("");
m_Parent.add(IDC_CURPRICE);
m_Layout.setShape(IDC_CURPRICE, 56, 14, 38, 14);

IDC_STRIKEPRICE = new TextField ("");
m_Parent.add(IDC_STRIKEPRICE);
m_Layout.setShape(IDC_STRIKEPRICE, 56, 28, 38, 14);

IDC_STOCKPRICEVARIANCE = new TextField ("");
m_Parent.add(IDC_STOCKPRICEVARIANCE);
m_Layout.setShape(IDC_STOCKPRICEVARIANCE, 55, 41, 38, 14);

IDC_RISKFREERATE = new TextField ("");
m_Parent.add(IDC_RISKFREERATE);
m_Layout.setShape(IDC_RISKFREERATE, 57, 57, 38, 14);

IDC_TIMEUNTILEXPIRATION = new TextField ("");
m_Parent.add(IDC_TIMEUNTILEXPIRATION);
m_Layout.setShape(IDC_TIMEUNTILEXPIRATION, 57, 68, 38, 14);

IDCOMPUTE = new Button ("Compute");
m_Parent.add(IDCOMPUTE);
m_Layout.setShape(IDCOMPUTE, 129, 15, 50, 14);

IDCANCEL = new Button ("Cancel");
m_Parent.add(IDCANCEL);
m_Layout.setShape(IDCANCEL, 129, 36, 50, 14);

IDC_STATIC1 = new Label ("Stock Price", Label.LEFT);
m_Parent.add(IDC_STATIC1);
m_Layout.setShape(IDC_STATIC1, 7, 17, 38, 8);

IDC_STATIC2 = new Label ("Strike Price", Label.LEFT);
m_Parent.add(IDC_STATIC2);
m_Layout.setShape(IDC_STATIC2, 7, 30, 37, 8);

IDC_STATIC3 = new Label ("Variance", Label.LEFT);
m_Parent.add(IDC_STATIC3);
m_Layout.setShape(IDC_STATIC3, 7, 43, 37, 8);
```

```
IDC_STATIC4 = new Label ("Risk Free Rate", Label.LEFT);
m_Parent.add(IDC_STATIC4);
m_Layout.setShape(IDC_STATIC4, 7, 57, 48, 8);

IDC_STATIC5 = new Label ("Time Interval", Label.LEFT);
m_Parent.add(IDC_STATIC5);
m_Layout.setShape(IDC_STATIC5, 7, 70, 48, 8);

IDC_LBLOPTIONVALUE = new Label ("Option value is:", Label.LEFT);
m_Parent.add(IDC_LBLOPTIONVALUE);
m_Layout.setShape(IDC_LBLOPTIONVALUE, 7, 87, 50, 8);

m_fInitialized = true;
return true;
    }

}
```

Note that the code is fairly small and simple for program generated code. In fact, it would make a good primer even for handwriting AWT code, with one exception. The m_Layout.setShape( ) calls use a layout called DialogLayout that is not a standard part of the AWT toolkit. In fact it's another unique part of Visual J++. It's a layout manager like FlowLayout or GridLayout but allows precise placement of components in *dialog logical units* : x/y coordinates relative to the upper left corner of the designed dialog. The source for this class is also generated by the Java Resource Wizard and is the same for every applet.

Now you just need to add the control creator class to our applet. First add an import statement to the top of your options.java file (the file that contains the applet class), preferably just after the import statements for java.applet and java.awt.*

```
import IDD_OPTIONS;
```

Next make the control creator class a private member of your applet class. This isn't mentioned in the VJ++ documentation, but it's a good way to make sure that the values in the fields are accessible to all methods of your class. Right after the class declaration, place the following code.

```
private IDD_OPTIONS dlg;
```

Next place the initialization of this member in the init( ) method. Each applet wizard generated by the init( ) method contains the following code:

```
// If you use a ResourceWizard-generated "control creator" class to
// arrange controls in your applet, you may want to call its
// CreateControls() method from within this method. Remove the following
// call to resize() before adding the call to CreateControls();
// CreateControls() does its own resizing.
//-------------------------------------------------------------------
        resize(320, 240);
```

So in fact, heeding that advice, delete the resize( ) statement and add the following code.

```
dlg = new IDD_OPTPRICE(this);
dlg.CreateControls();
```

At this point the documentation falls silent about what else is necessary to make your applet functional. If you left the applet as it is, it would run and look nice but not do much of anything useful. You can enter numbers just fine, but the applet won't do the computation. Let's now add the functionality to make it compute the option's value.

All Java AWT components, except labels, generate actions. To handle these actions you add a public method to your applet class called action( ). Inside this method, you check what event was called and, usually, fire off an appropriate handler function for that event. In this applet, the only event you particularly care about right now is when the user clicks on the Compute button. Below is an action( ) method to handle the Compute button click.

```
public boolean action(Event evt,Object arg)
{
    if (evt.target instanceof Button){
        ComputeOptionValue();
    }
    return true;
}
```

Next, write a private method called computeOptionValue( ) to do the actual computations. Grab the values from the field names specified when you designed the dialog (IDC_CURPRICE, etc.). This is performed with the getText( ) method. Take note of the conversion process for turning the text from the field into double precision floating point numbers (type double). This may seem indirect to users of C and C++ that would do a simple atof() or strtod() call, but it's actually the canonical way of doing the conversion. It's also significantly more object-oriented, and, despite the lengthy syntax, probably easier for non-C and C++ programmers to learn.

```
private boolean computeOptionValue()
{
/* grab values from following fields
TextField      IDC_CURPRICE;
TextField      IDC_STRIKEPRICE;
TextField      IDC_STOCKPRICEVARIANCE;
TextField      IDC_RISKFREERATE;
TextField      IDC_TIMEUNTILEXPIRATION;
*/
       double currentPrice=
              (Double.valueOf(dlg.IDC_CURPRICE.getText())).doubleValue();
       double strikePrice=
              (Double.valueOf(dlg.IDC_STRIKEPRICE.getText())).doubleValue();
       double stockPriceVariance=
         (Double.valueOf(dlg.IDC_STOCKPRICEVARIANCE.getText())).doubleValue();
       double timeUntilExpiration=(
       Double.valueOf(dlg.IDC_TIMEUNTILEXPIRATION.getText())).doubleValue();
       double riskFreeRate=
              (Double.valueOf(dlg.IDC_RISKFREERATE.getText())).doubleValue();

/* compute the option's value! */
       double optionValue=doBlackScholes(currentPrice,
                                strikePrice,
                                stockPriceVariance,
                                timeUntilExpiration,
                                riskFreeRate);

/* print out the value! */
       dlg.IDC_LBLOPTIONVALUE.setText(
              "Option value is: " + String.valueOf(optionValue));
       return true;
}
```

The actual computation of the option's value is encapsulated in the doBlackScholes( ) private method. The method of computation isn't too important for this discussion of J++ features, but the code involved is presented in the full source for the applet. I chose to print the result by changing the label component's text. I didn't have to do a refresh of the screen. The Java implementation handles such details.

Once the applet is complete it's easy to test with the generated HTML. Here's the testbed for the Options applet, OPTIONS.HTML. Note that the size specified in the applet wizard is supplied as the width and height attributes of the applet tag. Also the parameter names and default values supplied during the wizard are placed into the applet tag.

```
<html>
<head>
<title>options</title>
</head>
<body>
<hr>
<applet
    code=options.class
    id=options
    width=320
    height=240 >
    <param name=currentStockPrice value=0.0>
    <param name=strikePrice value=0.0>
    <param name=stockPriceVariance value=0.0>
    <param name=riskFreeRate value=0.08>
    <param name imeUntilExpiration value=0.5>
</applet>
<hr>
<a href="options.java">The source.</a>
</body>
</html>
```

Figure 11.7 shows what the completed applet looks like running in the test bed HTML.

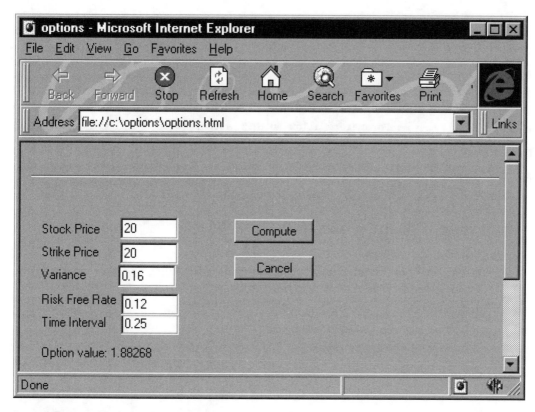

▬▬▬▬▬ **Figure 11.7** Completed applet.

Following is the listing for the completed OPTIONS applet.

```
//*****************************************************************************
// options.java:      Applet
//
//*****************************************************************************
import java.applet.*;
import java.awt.*;

import IDD_OPTIONS;
//=============================================================================
// Main Class for applet options
//
```

```
//===============================================================================
public class options extends Applet
{
     private IDD_OPTIONS dlg;

     // PARAMETER SUPPORT:
     //              Parameters allow an HTML author to pass information to the
     // applet; the HTML author specifies them using the <PARAM> tag within the
     // <APPLET> tag.  The following variables are used to store the values of
     // the parameters.
     //-----------------------------------------------------------------------

     // Members for applet parameters
     // <type>         <MemberVar>     = <Default Value>
     //-----------------------------------------------------------------------
        private double m_currentStockPrice = 0.0;
        private double m_strikePrice = 0.0;
        private double m_stockPriceVariance = 0.0;
        private double m_riskFreeRate = 0.0;
        private double m_timeUntilExpiration = 0.0;

     // Parameter names.  To change a name of a parameter, you need only make
        // a single change.  Simply modify the value of the parameter string
        // below.
     //-----------------------------------------------------------------------
        private final String PARAM_currentStockPrice = "currentStockPrice";
        private final String PARAM_strikePrice = "strikePrice";
        private final String PARAM_stockPriceVariance = "stockPriceVariance";
        private final String PARAM_riskFreeRate = "riskFreeRate";
        private final String PARAM_timeUntilExpiration = "timeUntilExpiration";
        // options Class Constructor
        //--------------------------------------------------------------------
        public options()
        {
             // TODO: Add constructor code here
        }

        // APPLET INFO SUPPORT:
```

```
    //                  The getAppletInfo() method returns a string describing the
    // applet's author, copyright date, or miscellaneous information.
//-------------------------------------------------------------------------
    public String getAppletInfo()
    {
            return "Name: options\r\n" +
                   "Author: Adam Blum\r\n" +
                   "Created with Microsoft Visual J++ Version 1.0";
    }

    // PARAMETER SUPPORT
    //                  The getParameterInfo() method returns an array of strings
describing
    // the parameters understood by this applet.
    //
    // options Parameter Information:
    // { "Name", "Type", "Description" },
    //-------------------------------------------------------------------------
    public String[] [] getParameterInfo()
    {
            String[] [] info =
            {
                        { PARAM_currentStockPrice, "double", "current price of
ᒐunderlying"},
                        { PARAM_strikePrice, "double", "exercise price of option" },
                        { PARAM_stockPriceVariance, "double", "(std. dev of
ᒐstock)squared"},
                        { PARAM_riskFreeRate, "double", "T-bill interest rate" },
                        { PARAM_timeUntilExpiration, "double", "time (in years)
ᒐuntil expiration" },
            };
            return info;
    }

    // The init() method is called by the AWT when an applet is first loaded
    // or reloaded. Override this method to perform whatever initialization
    // your applet needs, such as initializing data structures, loading images
    // or fonts, creating frame windows, setting the layout manager, or adding
    // UI components.
```

```
//--------------------------------------------------------------------------

public void init()
{
        // PARAMETER SUPPORT
        //               The following code retrieves the value of each
        // parameter specified with the <PARAM> tag and stores it in a
        // member variable.
        //----------------------------------------------------------------
        String param;

        // currentStockPrice: current price of underlying
        //----------------------------------------------------------------
        param = getParameter(PARAM_currentStockPrice);
        if (param != null)
                m_currentStockPrice = Double.valueOf(param).doubleValue();

        // strikePrice: exercise price of option
        //----------------------------------------------------------------
        param = getParameter(PARAM_strikePrice);
        if (param != null)
                m_strikePrice = Double.valueOf(param).doubleValue();

        // stockPriceVariance: (std. dev of stock)squared
        //----------------------------------------------------------------
        param = getParameter(PARAM_stockPriceVariance);
        if (param != null)
                m_stockPriceVariance = Double.valueOf(param).doubleValue();

        // riskFreeRate: T-bill interest rate
        //----------------------------------------------------------------
        param = getParameter(PARAM_riskFreeRate);
        if (param != null)
                m_riskFreeRate = Double.valueOf(param).doubleValue();

        // timeUntilExpiration: time (in years) until expiration
        //----------------------------------------------------------------
        param = getParameter(PARAM_timeUntilExpiration);
        if (param != null)
```

```
                m_timeUntilExpiration = Double.valueOf(param).doubleValue();

    // If you use a ResourceWizard-generated "control creator" class to
    // arrange controls in your applet, you may want to call its
    // CreateControls() method from within this method. Remove the following
    // call to resize() before adding the call to CreateControls();
    // CreateControls() does its own resizing.
    //-----------------------------------------------------------------------
        dlg = new IDD_OPTIONS(this);
        dlg.CreateControls();

        // TODO: Place additional initialization code here
        if (m_currentStockPrice!=0){
                dlg.IDC_CURPRICE.setText(String.valueOf(m_currentStock
⌐Price));
        }
    }

    // Place additional applet clean up code here.  destroy() is called when
    // when you applet is terminating and being unloaded.
    //------------------------------------------------------------------------
    public void destroy()
    {
        // TODO: Place applet cleanup code here
    }

    // options Paint Handler
    //------------------------------------------------------------------------
    public void paint(Graphics g)
    {
    }

    //          The start() method is called when the page containing the
    // applet first appears on the screen. The AppletWizard's initial
    // implementation of this method starts execution of the applet's thread.
    //------------------------------------------------------------------------
    public void start()
    {
        // TODO: Place additional applet start code here
```

```
        }
        //                   The stop() method is called when the page containing the
        // applet is no longer on the screen. The AppletWizard's initial
        // implementation of this method stops execution of the applet's thread.
        //------------------------------------------------------------------------
        public void stop()
        {
        }

        // TODO: Place additional applet code here
        public boolean action(Event evt,Object arg)
        {
                if (evt.target instanceof Button){
                        computeOptionValue();
                }
                return true;
        }

        private boolean computeOptionValue()
        {
//      grab values from following fields
//      TextField      IDC_CURPRICE;
//      TextField      IDC_STRIKEPRICE;
//      TextField      IDC_STOCKPRICEVARIANCE;
//      TextField      IDC_RISKFREERATE;
//      TextField      IDC_TIMEUNTILEXPIRATION;
                double
currentPrice=(Double.valueOf(dlg.IDC_CURPRICE.getText())).doubleValue();
                double
strikePrice=(Double.valueOf(dlg.IDC_STRIKEPRICE.getText())).doubleValue();
                double
stockPriceVariance=(Double.valueOf(dlg.IDC_STOCKPRICEVARIANCE.getText())).double
⌐Value();
                double
timeUntilExpiration=(Double.valueOf(dlg.IDC_TIMEUNTILEXPIRATION.getText())).
⌐doubleValue();
                double
```

```
riskFreeRate=(Double.valueOf(dlg.IDC_RISKFREERATE.getText())).doubleValue();
            double optionValue=doBlackScholes(currentPrice,
                                    strikePrice,
                                    stockPriceVariance,
                                    timeUntilExpiration,
                                    riskFreeRate);
            dlg.IDC_LBLOPTIONVALUE.setText("Option value: " +
String.valueOf(optionValue));
            return true;
        }

        /* doBlackScholes
         Compute option value based on following formula:
            V=currentPrice*[N(d1)]-strikePrice*E^(-
riskFreeRate*timeUntilExpiration)*N(d2)
                    where

        d1=ln(currentPrice/strikePrice)+(riskFreeRate+stockPriceVariance/2)*time
UntilExpiration
            d2=d1 - sqrt(stockPriceVariance*timeUntilExpiration)
        */
        private double doBlackScholes(double currentPrice,
                                    double strikePrice,
                                    double stockPriceVariance,
                                    double timeUntilExpiration, // in
fraction of year!
                                    double riskFreeRate)
        {
            double
d1=(Math.log(currentPrice/strikePrice)+(riskFreeRate+stockPriceVariance/2)*time
UntilExpiration)
                            / (Math.sqrt(stockPriceVariance)*
Math.sqrt(timeUntilExpiration));
            double d2=d1-Math.sqrt(stockPriceVariance)*Math.sqrt(timeUntil
```

```
Expiration);

        double stockPriceValue=currentPrice*probZ(d1);

        stockPriceValue=stockPriceValue - strikePrice*Math.pow(Math.E,-
riskFreeRate*timeUntilExpiration)*probZ(d2);

        return stockPriceValue;

    {

    /* factorial
        computes n! where n! = n(n-1)(n-2)...
        e.g. 0! = 1, 1! = 1, 2! = 2, 3! = 6, 4 != 24
    */
    private int factorial(int value)
    {

        if (value==0)
            return 1;
        int result=value;
        while (--value>0)
            result*=value;
        return result;

    }

    /* probZ
Computes probability that deviation less than Z value will occur in
standard normal distribution. You can get this from the appendix of
any stat book but since we didn't want to type in the whole table,
we had to get a formula for it which is:
        P(z)=1/2 + 1/sqrt(2*PI) sum(0 to infinity)[(-
1^n*x^(2n+1))/(n!*2^n*(2n+1))]
        Thanks to John D. Kettelle for providing the the series
        approximation for this summation (eliminating that unpleasant task
        of summing to infinity - always a pain on x86 class computers).
    */
    private double probZ(double Zvalue)
        {
```

```
double PI=3.1415926535897932384633895O; // or thereabouts
double result=0,term;
for (int n=0;;n++){
        term=(Math.pow(-1,n)*Math.pow(Zvalue,2*n+1));
        term = term/(factorial(n)*Math.pow(2,n)*(2*n+1));
        result = result + term;
        if (Math.abs(term) < 0.000001)
                break;
}
result = result/ Math.sqrt(2*PI);
result = result + 0.5;
return result;
    }

}
```

At this point you have an applet that does a little bit of computation but is not the most functional, impressive thing. If this was a Java book, I'd start adding features that do graphics for sensitivity analysis, use Java's built-in networking capabilities to pull data in for realtime updates of stock prices, and in general take advantage of Java's features to the make the applet much more impressive. But this is not that book. What I do want to show you is how Java can be integrated with other ActiveX technologies. First you'll take a quick look at how to control Java applets, such as the one just developed, from VBScript. Then I'll spend the rest of this chapter showing you how to use the wealth of functionality available in existing COM services from your Java applets.

Controlling Java Applets with VBScript

In the OPTIONS example, you had the applet itself handle actions from buttons, process fields, and in general act as the user interface. If you want to, you can delegate more of that responsibility to encapsulating HTML pages. You can use client-side VBScript to link the fields and buttons of the HTML page to functionality in your Java applet. The methods and properties of the Java applet in the page can be accessed, set, and invoked with the syntax document.<appletID>.<method or property>. You can invoke these in the VBScript event handling procedure for the appropriate HTML form element.

For example, suppose in the previous example that you wanted the fields that prompt for value such as the current stock price and the exercise stock price to be HTML form fields, rather than Java AWT TextFields. You can just write the HTML code to operate the applet as follows:

```
<SCRIPT LANGUAGE="VBScript">
<HTML>
<HEAD>
<TITLE>Site Registration</TITLE>
<SCRIPT LANGUAGE="VBScript">
<!--
Sub Compute_OnClick
     Set TheForm=Document.ComputeForm
     currentPrice=TheForm.CurrentPrice
     strikePrice=TheForm.StrikePrice
     stockPriceVariance=TheForm.StockPriceVariance
     riskFreeRate=TheForm.RiskFreeRate
     timeUntilExpiration=TheForm.TimeUntilExpiration
     optionValue=document.options.doBlackScholes
currentPrice,strikePrice,stockPriceVariance,riskFreeRate,
timeUntilExpiration
     MsgBox "The value of the option is: " & optionValue
End Sub
-->
</SCRIPT>
</HEAD>
<BODY>
<applet
     code=options.class
     id=options
     width=320
     height=240 >
```

```
</applet>
<FORM NAME="ComputeForm">
<INPUT NAME="CurrentPrice">
<INPUT NAME="StrikePrice">
<INPUT NAME="StockPriceVariance">
<INPUT NAME="RiskFreeRate">
<INPUT NAME="TimeUntilExpiration">
<INPUT NAME="Compute" TYPE="Button" VALUE="Compute">
</FORM>
</BODY>
</HTML>
```

Note that you are now using values from HTML form fields to get values. Then use client-side VBScript to grab the values from the form fields, and invoke the applet's doBlackScholes( ) method to compute the option value, supplying as argument all of the values retrieved from the form. Of course, if you left the original applet unmodified, this Web page is suboptimal in a couple ways. It displays the Java AWT TextField components of the applet in the page. If you were actually going to use the OPTIONS applet primarily from HTML forms, you would want to modify the init( ) method to remove the dlg.CreateControls( ) call.

Controlling COM Objects from Java

Java's fresh technology should result in a lot of unleashed creativity and new ways of thinking about writing applications. But all this novelty comes at a price: a large installed base of functionality to draw on. Most Java programmers today are writing many objects that might have been otherwise accessible as existing COM components.

Just when it seemed like the whole world was writing OLE Controls, OLE Automation Servers, and other COM objects as building blocks for constructing software, along comes this new development language that seemingly (if you read the trade press uncritically) calls this whole investment into question. Ah, but does it? One goal of Visual J++, Microsoft's Java development environment, is to wrap it into the existing Developer Studio environment—providing the same advanced, interactive, highly automated facilities for writing Java code that has been enjoyed by C++ developers over the past several releases. But the most important benefit of J++, below the surface of the attractive IDE, is to provide ways for Java developers to leverage the massive installed base of COM objects as transparently as possible.

Visual J++ provides several features that facilitate use of COM objects from your Java code. Before plowing into learning how to do this, one quick caveat. Java applets are in general not supposed to allow use of such features as file input and output and the powerful system level capabilities implied by being able to invoke COM services. To get around this, Microsoft has implemented the same code signing security mechanisms available for COM controls for Java applets as well. The Internet Explorer Java virtual machine (VM) will only allow an applet to use COM and file I/O if it's a *trusted applet:* one loaded from a digitally signed cabinet file. For more details, see the following section on Java security. If you can work with this limitation, then go ahead and see how to use COM from Java.

First, you need to convert the COM object to a Java package. Visual J++ provides a mechanism to do this with the Java Type Library Wizard (TLW). The Java TLW converts a COM type library that describes a set of classes and interfaces to a set of corresponding Java classes and interfaces. When you invoke the Java TLW from the Tools menu, you will be presented with a list of all the type libraries registered on your development system, as shown in Figure 11.8.

■■■■■■■■■ **NOTE**

If you're following along within your Visual J++ compiler, you might not see the OLE/Messaging 1.0 Object Library in your list. To get this to display, first check in your \WINDOWS\SYSTEM32 directory (or \WINNT\SYSTEM32 directory) for the file MDISP32.TLB. If you are running Windows NT 4.0 or greater or Windows 95, this file should be present. If you do have this file, you just need to get this into your Registry. Run REGEDT32.EXE. In your HKEY_CLASSES_ROOT\TypeLib key, you need a subkey that looks like Figure 11.9. You may need to create the win32 subkey as shown and place the full path to the TLB file there. Once you perform these steps, the Java Type Library Wizard should display the OLE/Messaging 1.0 Object Library in the list.

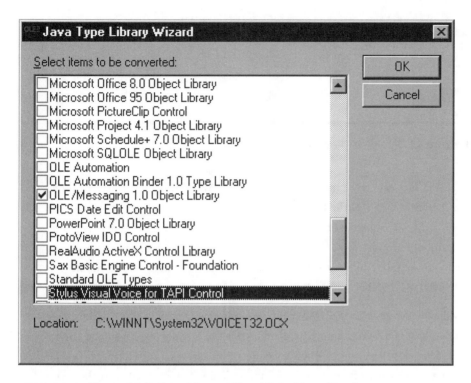

Figure 11.8 Type Library Wizard list of type libraries.

Many of the OLE automation servers that you may want to use will already have type libraries created for them. If the OLE automation server you wish to use does not have a type library, you can create one using an Object Description Language (ODL) file and the MKTYPLIB utility. See the *OLE2 Programmer's Reference* (Microsoft Press, 1994) or just the Visual C++ 4.x help system for more information on how to create type libraries. Also note that OLE Controls are by definition OLE automation servers, so Java classes can be generated for OLE controls as well (many of the type libraries listed in Figure 11.8 are for controls). Using controls requires a few more steps, and these are documented in detail below.

To demonstrate creation of a set of Java classes and interfaces, let's go ahead and run the wizard on the OLE Messaging Library. Running the wizard will generate multiple .CLASS files (compiled Java code) in a subdirectory of the C:WINDOWS\java\trustlib directory, with the subdirectory having the same name as the type library. A separate .CLASS file is generated for each COM class and each COM interface. In addition to

■■■■■ **Figure 11.9** Registry key for OLE messaging.

all the CLASS files generated, it will create a SUMMARY.TXT file in the same directory that enumerates all of the classes and interfaces generated. Note that once the CLASS files are available, the original type library files are no longer necessary. However, you still need to distribute the .OCX, .EXE, or .DLL that implements the service along with your applet. In the case of the OLE Messaging Library in this example, this is the file MDISP32.EXE.

Anyway, here's the generated SUMMARY.TXT file that describes the resulting Java package for doing OLE Messaging. Remember, this file is really just for informational purposes: a quick reference to all the generated Java classes and interfaces. Besides giving you a better sense of what the Type Library Wizard does, it will also allow you to put this particular set of classes to work, providing client-side messaging capabilities from within a Java applet.

```
public class mdisp32/_MAPIDispFolder extends java.lang.Object
{
}
public class mdisp32/_MAPIDispMessage extends java.lang.Object
{
}
public class mdisp32/_MAPIDispSession extends java.lang.Object
{
}
public interface mdisp32/AddressEntry extends com.ms.com.IUnknown
{
    public abstract com.ms.com.Variant getName();
    public abstract com.ms.com.Variant getDisplayType();
```

```java
    public abstract void putName(com.ms.com.Variant);
    public abstract com.ms.com.Variant Details(com.ms.com.Variant);
    public abstract com.ms.com.Variant getApplication();
    public abstract com.ms.com.Variant getID();
    public abstract com.ms.com.Variant gettype();
    public abstract void puttype(com.ms.com.Variant);
    public abstract com.ms.com.Variant getClass();
    public abstract com.ms.com.Variant getaddress();
    public abstract void putaddress(com.ms.com.Variant);
    public abstract com.ms.com.Variant getFields();
    public abstract com.ms.com.Variant getSession();
    public abstract void putSession(com.ms.com.Variant);
    public abstract com.ms.com.Variant getParent();
    public abstract void putParent(com.ms.com.Variant);
    public abstract com.ms.com.Variant Update(com.ms.com.Variant,
com.ms.com.Variant);
    public abstract com.ms.com.Variant Delete();
}
public interface mdisp32/Attachment extends com.ms.com.IUnknown
{
    public abstract com.ms.com.Variant getName();
    public abstract void putName(com.ms.com.Variant);
    public abstract com.ms.com.Variant getsource();
    public abstract void putsource(com.ms.com.Variant);
    public abstract com.ms.com.Variant getApplication();
    public abstract com.ms.com.Variant ReadFromFile(com.ms.com.Variant);
    public abstract com.ms.com.Variant gettype();
    public abstract void puttype(com.ms.com.Variant);
    public abstract com.ms.com.Variant getIndex();
    public abstract com.ms.com.Variant getClass();
    public abstract com.ms.com.Variant getSession();
    public abstract void putSession(com.ms.com.Variant);
    public abstract com.ms.com.Variant WriteToFile(com.ms.com.Variant);
    public abstract com.ms.com.Variant getposition();
```

```
    public abstract com.ms.com.Variant getParent();

    public abstract void putParent(com.ms.com.Variant);

    public abstract void putposition(com.ms.com.Variant);

    public abstract com.ms.com.Variant Delete();

}
public interface mdisp32/Attachments extends com.ms.com.IUnknown
{
    public abstract com.ms.com.Variant Add(com.ms.com.Variant, com.ms.
com.Variant, com.ms.com.Variant, com.ms.com.Variant);

    public abstract com.ms.com.Variant getCount();

    public abstract com.ms.com.Variant getApplication();

    public abstract com.ms.com.Variant getClass();

    public abstract com.ms.com.Variant getSession();

    public abstract void putSession(com.ms.com.Variant);

    public abstract com.ms.com.Variant getParent();

    public abstract void putParent(com.ms.com.Variant);

    public abstract com.ms.com.Variant Delete();

    public abstract com.ms.com.Variant getItem();

}
public interface mdisp32/Recipient extends com.ms.com.IUnknown
{
    public abstract com.ms.com.Variant getName();

    public abstract com.ms.com.Variant getDisplayType();

    public abstract void putName(com.ms.com.Variant);

    public abstract com.ms.com.Variant getApplication();

    public abstract com.ms.com.Variant gettype();

    public abstract com.ms.com.Variant getIndex();

    public abstract void puttype(com.ms.com.Variant);

    public abstract void putAddressEntry(com.ms.com.Variant);

    public abstract com.ms.com.Variant getAddressEntry();

    public abstract com.ms.com.Variant getClass();

    public abstract com.ms.com.Variant getaddress();

    public abstract void putaddress(com.ms.com.Variant);

    public abstract com.ms.com.Variant getSession();

    public abstract void putSession(com.ms.com.Variant);
```

```
    public abstract com.ms.com.Variant getParent();

    public abstract void putParent(com.ms.com.Variant);

    public abstract com.ms.com.Variant Delete();

    public abstract com.ms.com.Variant Resolve(com.ms.com.Variant);
}
public interface mdisp32/Recipients extends com.ms.com.IUnknown
{
    public abstract com.ms.com.Variant Add(com.ms.com.Variant, com.ms.
com.Variant, com.ms.com.Variant, com.ms.com.Variant);

    public abstract com.ms.com.Variant getCount();

    public abstract com.ms.com.Variant getResolved();

    public abstract com.ms.com.Variant getApplication();

    public abstract com.ms.com.Variant getClass();

    public abstract com.ms.com.Variant getSession();

    public abstract void putSession(com.ms.com.Variant);

    public abstract com.ms.com.Variant getParent();

    public abstract void putParent(com.ms.com.Variant);

    public abstract com.ms.com.Variant Delete();

    public abstract com.ms.com.Variant getItem();

    public abstract com.ms.com.Variant Resolve(com.ms.com.Variant);
}
public interface mdisp32/Field extends com.ms.com.IUnknown
{
    public abstract com.ms.com.Variant getName();

    public abstract com.ms.com.Variant ReadFromFile(com.ms.com.Variant);

    public abstract com.ms.com.Variant getApplication();

    public abstract com.ms.com.Variant getvalue();

    public abstract com.ms.com.Variant getID();

    public abstract void putvalue(com.ms.com.Variant);

    public abstract com.ms.com.Variant gettype();

    public abstract com.ms.com.Variant getIndex();

    public abstract com.ms.com.Variant getClass();

    public abstract com.ms.com.Variant getSession();

    public abstract com.ms.com.Variant WriteToFile(com.ms.com.Variant);

    public abstract com.ms.com.Variant getParent();
```

```
        public abstract com.ms.com.Variant Delete();
}
public interface mdisp32/Fields extends com.ms.com.IUnknown
{
        public abstract com.ms.com.Variant Add(com.ms.com.Variant, com.ms.
com.Variant, com.ms.com.Variant, com.ms.com.Variant);

        public abstract com.ms.com.Variant getCount();

        public abstract com.ms.com.Variant SetNamespace(com.ms.com.Variant);

        public abstract com.ms.com.Variant getApplication();

        public abstract com.ms.com.Variant getClass();

        public abstract com.ms.com.Variant getSession();

        public abstract void putSession(com.ms.com.Variant);

        public abstract com.ms.com.Variant getParent();

        public abstract void putParent(com.ms.com.Variant);

        public abstract com.ms.com.Variant Delete();

        public abstract com.ms.com.Variant getItem();
}
public interface mdisp32/Message extends com.ms.com.IUnknown
{
        public static final com.ms.com.Variant MAPIOBJECT;

        public abstract com.ms.com.Variant getTimeReceived();

        public abstract com.ms.com.Variant getTimeSent();

        public abstract com.ms.com.Variant Delete();

        public abstract void putTimeSent(com.ms.com.Variant);

        public abstract com.ms.com.Variant Update(com.ms.com.Variant,
com.ms.com.Variant);

        public abstract com.ms.com.Variant Send(com.ms.com.Variant,
com.ms.com.Variant, com.ms.com.Variant);

        public abstract com.ms.com.Variant Options(com.ms.com.Variant);

        public abstract void putDeliveryReceipt(com.ms.com.Variant);

        public abstract com.ms.com.Variant getEncrypted();

        public abstract void putReadReceipt(com.ms.com.Variant);

        public abstract com.ms.com.Variant getDeliveryReceipt();

        public abstract void putEncrypted(com.ms.com.Variant);
```

```
public abstract com.ms.com.Variant getID();

public abstract com.ms.com.Variant getstoreID();

public abstract com.ms.com.Variant getConversation();

public abstract com.ms.com.Variant getReadReceipt();

public abstract com.ms.com.Variant getSender();

public abstract com.ms.com.Variant gettext();

public abstract void puttext(com.ms.com.Variant);

public abstract com.ms.com.Variant getSession();

public abstract void putSession(com.ms.com.Variant);

public abstract void putimportance(com.ms.com.Variant);

public abstract void putTimeReceived(com.ms.com.Variant);

public abstract com.ms.com.Variant getConversationIndex();

public abstract com.ms.com.Variant getConversationTopic();

public abstract com.ms.com.Variant getParent();

public abstract com.ms.com.Variant getSigned();

public abstract void putSigned(com.ms.com.Variant);

public abstract void putParent(com.ms.com.Variant);

public abstract com.ms.com.Variant getAttachments();

public abstract com.ms.com.Variant getfolderID();

public abstract void putConversationIndex(com.ms.com.Variant);

public abstract void putConversationTopic(com.ms.com.Variant);

public abstract com.ms.com.Variant getSubmitted();

public abstract com.ms.com.Variant getApplication();

public abstract void putSubmitted(com.ms.com.Variant);

public abstract com.ms.com.Variant getSize();

public abstract void putConversation(com.ms.com.Variant);

public abstract com.ms.com.Variant gettype();

public abstract void puttype(com.ms.com.Variant);

public abstract com.ms.com.Variant getRecipients();

public abstract com.ms.com.Variant getClass();

public abstract com.ms.com.Variant getFields();

public abstract com.ms.com.Variant getsubject();

public abstract void putsubject(com.ms.com.Variant);

public abstract com.ms.com.Variant getSent();
```

```
        public abstract void putSent(com.ms.com.Variant);

        public abstract com.ms.com.Variant getUnread();

        public abstract void putUnread(com.ms.com.Variant);

        public abstract com.ms.com.Variant getimportance();

}
public interface mdisp32/Messages extends com.ms.com.IUnknown

{
        public abstract com.ms.com.Variant Add(com.ms.com.Variant, com.ms.
com.Variant, com.ms.com.Variant, com.ms.com.Variant);

        public abstract com.ms.com.Variant GetLast(com.ms.com.Variant);

        public abstract com.ms.com.Variant getApplication();

        public abstract com.ms.com.Variant GetPrevious();

        public abstract com.ms.com.Variant Sort(com.ms.com.Variant);

        public abstract com.ms.com.Variant GetFirst(com.ms.com.Variant);

        public abstract com.ms.com.Variant getClass();

        public abstract com.ms.com.Variant GetNext();

        public abstract com.ms.com.Variant getSession();

        public abstract void putSession(com.ms.com.Variant);

        public abstract com.ms.com.Variant getParent();

        public abstract void putParent(com.ms.com.Variant);

        public abstract com.ms.com.Variant Delete(com.ms.com.Variant);

}
public interface mdisp32/Folders extends com.ms.com.IUnknown

{
        public abstract com.ms.com.Variant GetLast();

        public abstract com.ms.com.Variant getApplication();

        public abstract com.ms.com.Variant GetPrevious();

        public abstract com.ms.com.Variant GetFirst();

        public abstract com.ms.com.Variant getClass();

        public abstract com.ms.com.Variant GetNext();

        public abstract com.ms.com.Variant getSession();

        public abstract void putSession(com.ms.com.Variant);

        public abstract com.ms.com.Variant getParent();

        public abstract void putParent(com.ms.com.Variant);

}
```

```
public interface mdisp32/Folder extends com.ms.com.IUnknown
{
    public static final com.ms.com.Variant MAPIOBJECT;

    public abstract com.ms.com.Variant getfolderID();
    public abstract com.ms.com.Variant getName();
    public abstract void putName(com.ms.com.Variant);
    public abstract com.ms.com.Variant getApplication();
    public abstract com.ms.com.Variant getID();
    public abstract com.ms.com.Variant getstoreID();
    public abstract com.ms.com.Variant getMessages();
    public abstract com.ms.com.Variant getFolders();
    public abstract com.ms.com.Variant getClass();
    public abstract com.ms.com.Variant getFields();
    public abstract com.ms.com.Variant getSession();
    public abstract void putSession(com.ms.com.Variant);
    public abstract com.ms.com.Variant getParent();
    public abstract void putParent(com.ms.com.Variant);
    public abstract com.ms.com.Variant Update(com.ms.com.Variant,
com.ms.com.Variant);
}
public interface mdisp32/InfoStore extends com.ms.com.IUnknown
{
    public abstract com.ms.com.Variant getProviderName();
    public abstract com.ms.com.Variant getName();
    public abstract com.ms.com.Variant getApplication();
    public abstract com.ms.com.Variant getID();
    public abstract com.ms.com.Variant getIndex();
    public abstract com.ms.com.Variant getClass();
    public abstract com.ms.com.Variant getSession();
    public abstract void putSession(com.ms.com.Variant);
    public abstract com.ms.com.Variant getRootFolder();
    public abstract com.ms.com.Variant getParent();
    public abstract void putParent(com.ms.com.Variant);
}
```

```
public interface mdisp32/InfoStores extends com.ms.com.IUnknown
{
    public abstract com.ms.com.Variant getCount();

    public abstract com.ms.com.Variant getApplication();

    public abstract com.ms.com.Variant getClass();

    public abstract com.ms.com.Variant getSession();

    public abstract void putSession(com.ms.com.Variant);

    public abstract com.ms.com.Variant getParent();

    public abstract void putParent(com.ms.com.Variant);

    public abstract com.ms.com.Variant getItem();
}
public interface mdisp32/Session extends com.ms.com.IUnknown
{
    public static final com.ms.com.Variant MAPIOBJECT;

    public abstract com.ms.com.Variant GetAddressEntry(com.ms.com.
⌐Variant);

    public abstract com.ms.com.Variant getName();

    public abstract com.ms.com.Variant getInfoStores();

    public abstract com.ms.com.Variant AddressBook(com.ms.com.Variant,
com.ms.com.Variant, com.ms.com.Variant, com.ms.com.Variant, com.ms.com.
⌐Variant, com.ms.com.Variant, com.ms.com.Variant, com.ms.com.Variant,
⌐com.ms.com.Variant);

    public abstract com.ms.com.Variant GetMessage(com.ms.com.Variant,
com.ms.com.Variant);

    public abstract com.ms.com.Variant Logoff();

    public abstract com.ms.com.Variant getApplication();

    public abstract com.ms.com.Variant GetFolder(com.ms.com.Variant,
com.ms.com.Variant);

    public abstract com.ms.com.Variant getClass();

    public abstract com.ms.com.Variant getOperatingSystem();

    public abstract com.ms.com.Variant getInbox();

    public abstract com.ms.com.Variant getOutbox();

    public abstract com.ms.com.Variant Logon(com.ms.com.Variant,
com.ms.com.Variant, com.ms.com.Variant, com.ms.com.Variant, com.ms.com.
⌐Variant);
```

```
    public abstract com.ms.com.Variant getSession();
    public abstract void putSession(com.ms.com.Variant);
    public abstract com.ms.com.Variant getVersion();
    public abstract com.ms.com.Variant GetInfoStore(com.ms.com.Variant);
    public abstract com.ms.com.Variant getCurrentUser();
    public abstract com.ms.com.Variant getParent();
    public abstract void putParent(com.ms.com.Variant);
}
public interface mdisp32/mapiObjectClass extends com.ms.com.IUnknown
{
    public static final int mapiUnknown;
    public static final int mapiSession;
    public static final int mapiInfoStore;
    public static final int mapiFolder;
    public static final int mapiMsg;
    public static final int mapiRecipient;
    public static final int mapiAttachment;
    public static final int mapiField;
    public static final int mapiAddressEntry;
    public static final int mapiInfoStores;
    public static final int mapiFolders;
    public static final int mapiMessages;
    public static final int mapiRecipients;
    public static final int mapiAttachments;
    public static final int mapiFields;
    public static final int mapiAddressEntries;
}
public interface mdisp32/mapiDisplayType extends com.ms.com.IUnknown
{
    public static final int mapiUser;
    public static final int mapiDistList;
    public static final int mapiForum;
    public static final int mapiAgent;
    public static final int mapiOrganization;
```

```
    public static final int mapiPrivateDistList;
    public static final int mapiRemoteUser;
}
public interface mdisp32/mapiAttachmentType extends com.ms.com.IUnknown
{
    public static final int mapiFileData;
    public static final int mapiFileLink;
    public static final int mapiOle;
}
public interface mdisp32/mapiRecipientType extends com.ms.com.IUnknown
{
    public static final int mapiTo;
    public static final int mapiCc;
    public static final int mapiBcc;
}
public interface mdisp32/mapiFieldType extends com.ms.com.IUnknown
{
    public static final int vbEmpty;
    public static final int vbNull;
    public static final int vbInteger;
    public static final int vbLong;
    public static final int vbSingle;
    public static final int vbDouble;
    public static final int vbCurrency;
    public static final int vbDate;
    public static final int vbString;
    public static final int vbBoolean;
    public static final int vbDataObject;
    public static final int vbBlob;
    public static final int vbArray;
}
public interface mdisp32/mapiSortOrder extends com.ms.com.IUnknown
{
    public static final int mapiNone;
```

```
    public static final int mapiAscending;
    public static final int mapiDescending;
}
public interface mdisp32/mapiImportance extends com.ms.com.IUnknown
{
    public static final int mapiLow;
    public static final int mapiNormal;
    public static final int mapiHigh;
}
```

Whew! That's a lot of classes. But you're going to be using them all shortly to build a Java applet with messaging capabilities. Also examining the generated code compared with the original COM library shows how COM concepts are translated to Java. The COM coclasses _MAPIDispSession, _MAPIDispFolder, and _MAPIDisp-Message becomes Java public classes. Each COM dispinterface is translated into a Java public interface. Each COM module becomes a Java public interface with public static final members.

For ODL data types that are supported natively by Java the translations are easy. Some ODL data types require special Java classes to support them. BSTR variables become objects of class java.lang.String. Other ODL data types unique to COM use classes provided by Visual J++ to support COM objects. VARIANT becomes com.ms.com.Variant. IUnknown * is converted to com.ms.com.Variant. IDispatch * becomes java.lang.Object.

Figure 11.10 shows what the original COM object for the Message dispinterface looked like in the OLE2 Object Viewer (available on the J++ Tools menu).

Here's the beginning of the Message class again. Just a few lines are sufficient to show the basic mapping. Each function listed above (Delete(), Options(), Send(), and Update()) gets its own public member function in the Java Message class. Each variable/data member gets one or two member functions depending on whether its read-only or not: one function prefixed with get and another prefixed with put.

```
        public interface mdisp32/Message extends com.ms.com.IUnknown
        {
            public static final com.ms.com.Variant MAPIOBJECT;
```

```
            public abstract com.ms.com.Variant getTimeReceived();
            public abstract com.ms.com.Variant getTimeSent();
            public abstract com.ms.com.Variant Delete();
            public abstract void putTimeSent(com.ms.com.Variant);
            public abstract com.ms.com.Variant Update(com.ms.com.Variant,
    com.ms.com.Variant);
            public abstract com.ms.com.Variant Send(com.ms.com.Variant,
        com.ms.com.Variant, com.ms.com.Variant);
            public abstract com.ms.com.Variant Options(com.ms.com.Variant);
```

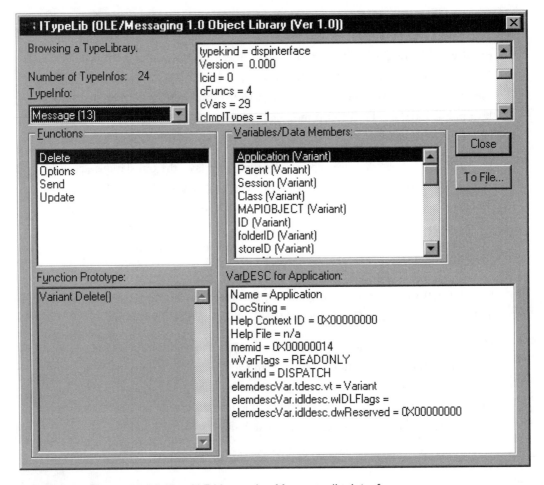

Figure 11.10 The OLE Messaging Message dispinterface.

```
public abstract void putDeliveryReceipt(com.ms.com.Variant);
public abstract com.ms.com.Variant getEncrypted();
```

Using the Type Library Wizard Generated Classes

Let's go ahead and build an application with these OLE Messaging Java classes. First a bit of background on OLE/Messaging is in order. OLE Messaging is an OLE automation server that provides a rich set of electronic mail services. These messaging facilities are more than just the capability of sending email. It means being able to look up names in the enterprise-wide directory or the user's email personal address book. It includes the ability to retrieve messages from the user's *message store*—their Inbox or other folders. These capabilities do imply the presence of the Microsoft Exchange client (usually depicted as the Inbox on the user's desktop). However, they do not need to have an Exchange server account or connection—the client can use the Internet, fax, MSMail, or other messaging systems as transports. Every Windows 95 or Windows NT 4.0 machine has the Exchange client, so building an applet that relies on an Exchange profile is reasonable for applets that already target Win32 platforms (if you're going to use COM services that already implies Win32). Also note that any applet you build that uses OLE Messaging won't actually display the Exchange client—it just requires that the client is installed on the user's machine.

This section is intended to discuss Java and COM, not be a primer on OLE Messaging, so I won't actually delve into presenting the whole OLE Messaging API. I'll just explain the calls as they are used. Despite its status as an example, you may find these Java classes for OLE Messaging to be quite useful in your own applet development efforts. Allowing messaging capabilities (email sending and receiving and directory access) from your Web applications is likely to be very handy for many applications.

For this example, I propose to build an applet that will allow Web users to fill in a recipient, a subject, and a message body. The applet will send a message with the supplied subject and message body off to the specified recipient. Again, you'll start this applet using Visual J++'s Java Applet Wizard, calling it OLEMSG, and keeping it as simple as possible (no multithreading, animation, or event support will be requested). But you will allow the applet to be called with several parameters. The result of running the wizard are the OLEMSG.java file with the applet skeleton and OLEMSG.html with the test Web page (Figure 11.11).

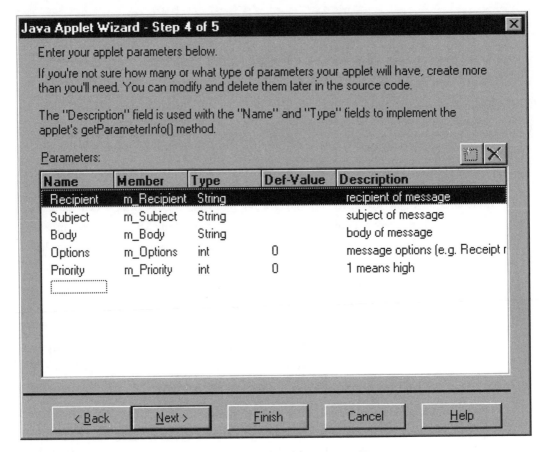

Figure 11.11 Java Applet Wizard for sample OLEMSG applet.

Now that you have an application skeleton you can start putting code into it. As a first step, put the following lines at the top of the code to allow you to refer more easily to your generated OLE Messaging classes and some other Java classes for COM programming in general.

```
import com.ms.com.*;
import mdisp32.*;
```

Note that these statements are not required. Any class can be referred to with its full name, but this import statement allows classes to be referred to with the short name, for example, Message.

Now, it will be a better applet if you use Java AWT fields to prompt for input rather than HTML form field. The preceding section showed that you can write the applet to get its value from HTML forms. But as a general practice this has a couple of disadvantages. First of all, it requires VBScript to gather up the field values from the form and call the Java applet method. You might want the applet to be usable from browsers such as Netscape that don't support VBScript. Secondly, this will require more work for HTML authors to integrate the applet, since an HTML form would have to be coded each time the applet was used.

Instead, you can prompt for the field values using a set of Java AWT fields inside the applet itself. As you did earlier, you'll create the set of fields using the the Visual J++ Java Resource Wizard. The first step is to create a Windows dialog resource to be converted by the Java Resource Wizard. First create a new resource template (.RCT) file. Then select Insert/Resource and choose Dialog as the type of resource, designing the dialog shown in Figure 11.12.

You can convert this to Windows dialog to a Java class containing all of the fields as AWT components by running the Java Resource Wizard and selecting the Resource Template (.RCT) file. Now change the init( ) method of the applet to add the creation of the Java AWT class. Remove the call of the resize( ) function and add the following code.

```
dlg = new IDD_SENDMSG(this);
dlg.CreateControls();
```

Now provide an event handling function to intercept the click on the Send button.

```
public boolean action(Event evt,Object arg)
{
    // handle button events
    if (evt.target instanceof Button) {
        if ((String)arg.equals("Send"))
            sendMsg();
    }
    return true;
}
```

The sendMsg( ) method gets the field values, calls another method to do the send with OLE Messaging, then clear the fields out.

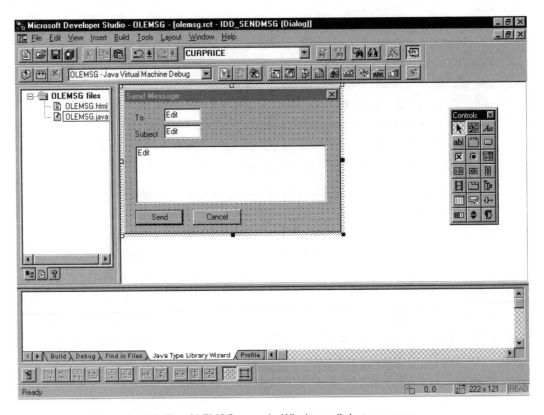

■■■■■■■■■ **Figure 11.12** The OLEMSG sample Windows dialog resource.

```java
public boolean sendMsg()
{
    String recipient=dlg.IDC_RECIPIENT.getText();
    String subject=dlg.IDC_SUBJECT.getText();
    String body=dlg.IDC_BODY.getText();
    int result=doOLEMsgSend();
    dlg.IDC_RECIPIENT.setText("");
    dlg.IDC_SUBJECT.setText("");
    dlg.IDC_BODY.setText("");
    return true;
}
```

Here's the code for the doOLEMsgSend( ) function, which encapsulates all of the OLE Messaging code. It's here that you start using the Type Library Wizard generated classes for the various OLE interfaces.

```
private boolean doOLEMsgSend(String recipient,
                             String subject,
                             String body)
{
    Session session;
    session = (Session)new _MAPIDispSession();
    session.getVersion();
    Variant opt = new Variant();
    opt.noParam();
    Variant varProfile ew Variant();
    varProfile.putString("MS Exchange Settings");
    try {
        session.Logon(varProfile,opt,opt,opt,opt);
        Folder outbox = (Folder) session.getOutbox();
        Messages messages = (Messages) outbox.getMessages();
        Variant varSubject ew Variant();
        Variant varBody ew Variant();
        varSubject.putString(subject);
        varBody.putString(body);
        Message message = (Message)
        messages.Add(varSubject,varBody,opt,opt);
        Variant varRecip ew Variant();
        Recipients recips = (Recipients) message.getRecipients();
        varRecip.putString(recipient);
        Recipient recip=(Recipient)recips.Add(varRecip,opt,opt,opt);
        recip.Resolve(opt);
        message.Update(opt,opt);
        message.Send(opt,opt,opt);
        session.Logoff();
    }
    catch (ComFailException e)
```

```
            {
                    String errMsg;
                    errMsg = e.getMessage();
                    dlg.IDC_SUBJECT.setText(errMsg);
            }
            return true;
    }
```

The logic can be summarized as follows:

- Logon to establish the session: session.Logon();
- Point an object to the session's Outbox folder: Folder outbox=session.getOutbox();
- Add a message to the outbox: message=messages.Add(varSubject,varRecipient,opt,opt);
- Add a recipient to that message: recips.Add(varRecip,opt,opt,opt)
- Send the message: message.Send(opt,opt,opt);

It's not worth delving deeper than this into the messaging functionality since I am trying to teach you use of Java, not OLE Messaging. But it's worth pointing out a couple more things about the application. Many OLE Messaging functions (and OLE automation server methods in general) have optional arguments, which revert to a default value if not specified. However, you need to give the translated Java function each argument. If you want a particular argument be a null argument, you need to give it a "null parameter." You do this by creating a Variant and invoking the noParam() method on it. This was done previously with the code:

```
Variant opt = new Variant();
opt.noParam();
```

Then any function that needs a null argument can just be passed the "opt" variable (or whatever variable you created). For example, the Logon() function took its last four arguments as "opt."

The other thing to notice about the code is the try {} catch {} clause. The specific exception that is caught is ComFailException (the full name is com.ms.com.ComFailException but the import command allows use of this shorthand). Any failure in any of the OLE Messaging calls will result in the code inside the catch clause getting invoked, and the reason for the failure being displayed in the form. If you wanted, there could be multiple try clauses for each OLE Messaging operation that you attempt to perform, which would allow the catch clause code to be more specific about the cause of the error.

Running the OLEMSG.HTML test page (shown in Figure 11.13) generated by the applet wizard will result in the message being sent to the name specified in the To field.

The full set of code for the OLEMSG sample Java applet, the IDD_SENDMSG.java dialog layout code, and the applet itself defined in OLEMSG.java, appears in the appendices.

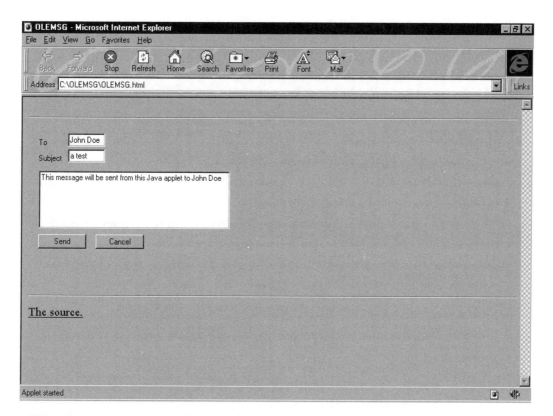

Figure 11.13 OLEMSG Java applet.

Using OLE Controls from Java

Many of the type libraries that showed up in the Java Type Library Wizard dialog box earlier were in fact OLE Controls. The Type Library Wizard will create Java classes that allow you to use these controls, but you need to perform a few more steps than you had to with a COM server such as the OLE Messaging server just demonstrated.

There are two ways to use OLE Controls in your Java applets. You can have your Java applet handle events from the control, and you can invoke methods or set properties on the control. To handle OLE Control events, you will write VBScript code to handle the event. Within your VBScript code call your Java applet methods as discussed in the earlier section "Controlling Java Applets from VBScript." In effect, VBScript acts as the glue between the OLE Control and your Java applet, intercepting OLE Control events with event handling procedures and invoking Java methods from those procedures.

To invoke methods on the control from your Java applet, you need to pass the control to your applet. Make sure that you have run the TLW on the OLE Control so you can use interfaces exposed by the control. Remember how you used the OLE automation server in the last example? You just created an object of the class type with the new command and type cast it to an available interface.

To use an OLE Control within your Java applet, you need to do something slightly different. You won't actually create the control in your Java code. You just need to provide a method to allow the control to be passed to your Java applet. This method should just take an argument of type Object. Within the method, you can typecast Object to one of the interfaces supported by the control. Often you will want to store this interface persistently by having a member of the applet class of the data type of the interface class. The list of interface classes exposed by the OLE Control will be presented in the summary.txt file generated by the Type Library Wizard.

For example, if your applet class was called Controller, and you wanted to use a control called CControl through its interface called Iinterface, the following code would do the job.

```
import control.*;//classes based on hypothetical CONTROL.TLB type library
public Controller extends Applet
{
    // IInterfaceinterface defined in package MSOUTL32
```

```
    IInterface m_interface;

    public void passCtrl(Object obj)
    {
        m_interface= (IInterface)obj;
    }
    // more code
    // ...
}
```

But you're still not done. You still need a way to pass the control to your applet in this first place (a way to call the passCtrl() method). You can do this with VBScript. The general approach is to embed the OLE Control into the Web page with the <OBJECT> tag and the techniques described at length in earlier chapters. Be sure to give the OLE Control an ID attribute that is easily referenced. You will be using this ID as the argument to our Java applet's passCtrl() method. The next step is to put your Java applet into your page. Again, give it an easily referenced ID tag. This will be used by your VBScript program to invoke the applet. Finally, add a VBScript sub window_onLoad() event handling procedure to the page. This will be invoked each time the page is loaded. Inside this script, just call your applet passCtrl() method, with the syntax document.<appletID>.passCtrl<controlID>.

For example, the entire HTML page might look something like this:

```
<HTML>
<HEAD>
<TITLE></TITLE>
<SCRIPT>
<!--
Sub window_onLoad
    document.Controller.passCtrl Chart
End Sub
-->
</SCRIPT>
</HEAD>
<BODY>
Here's an OLE Control.
```

```
<OBJECT ID=Chart
    classid="clsid:FC25B780-75BE-11CF-8B01-444553540000"
    CODEBASE="http://www.microsoft.com/workshop/activex/gallery/
ms/chart/other/iechart.ocx#Version=4,70,0,1112"
    TYPE="application/x-oleobject"
    width=400
    height=200
>
</OBJECT>
<P>
... and we're going to try to pass it to this applet.
<APPLET CODE="Controller.class" ID=Controller>
</APPLET>
</BODY>
</HTML>
```

Java Security and Use of COM

To understand the limitations of using COM within your Java applets, you need to understand the security model of Java VMs (virtual machines or browser runtime environments). Most Java applets run in a *sandbox,* which means they are not allowed to perform operations that could compromise the security of the user's machine. This is appropriate since applets are often downloaded dynamically from a Web site and run immediately without any checking or intervention by the user. One of the restrictions of the sandbox is that the applets can't do file input and output and of course they would not be able to invoke COM services, given the large security hole that would present (once the applet can run COM services it can do much more harm even than the danger represented by allowing file input and output).

If it was this simple, we would have to stop right here in our discussion of using COM from Java. However, the Internet Explorer Java VM supports the concept of a *trusted class.* Trusted classes are those loaded from a digitally signed cabinet (.CAB) file. The tools for creating such cabinet files are located on the ActiveX SDK. They are also included in Visual J++. CABDEVKIT.EXE is the toolkit to create .CAB files. CODE-SIGNKIT.EXE allows you to digitally sign the file. You will need to work with these tools if you are going to create applets distributed over the Internet that use COM services. Unpackaged Java applets downloaded directly from a Web site or off the network would do not qualify as trusted classes, which would eliminate use of COM within the applet.

If you decide that it is possible to have your applet be a trusted class, then you can use COM services (and in fact do other operations normally verboten such as reading from and writing to the user's file system). As a matter of good practice you should install your COM service libraries or classes to the directory specified in the the Java VM's TrustedLibsDirectory subkey of the Java VM in the registry (HKEY_LOCAL_MACHINE\Software\Microsoft\Java VM). In the preceding example, this was C:\WINDOWS\java\trustlib. The Java Type Library Wizard does in fact install its generated classes here. Only trusted classes have access to the directory specified here, and an untrusted applet would not even be able to get to that directory. But is the security that naive? If you copy the COM classes to, say the C:\WINNT\JAVA\CLASSES directory, would a normal applet be able to use it? No. The Internet Explorer Java VM will not allow use of forbidden operations such as COM service use of file I/O for untrusted classes.

Also, bear in mind that this behavior is currently limited only to the Internet Explorer Java VM. However, as a result of the deal between Sun and Microsoft announced midsummer 1996, the IE VM is the *reference implementation* of Java for Win32 platforms. This means that other Java VMs that wish to comply with the reference standard for Win32 endorsed by the Java standard bearers themselves (Sun) should provide this functionality as well. This doesn't solve the problem for other platforms, but currently use of COM would imply a Win32 client, so that is not a severe limitation. In summary, using COM from Java is certainly a powerful way of adding functionality to what is currently a very young language with little available code base to draw upon. However, it may be more appropriate in situations where you know exactly what your browser base of the intended application is.

SOURCE CODE

SENDFORM

This sample application demonstrates HTML form parsing and sending messages. It can be built either as a CGI application or an ISAPI.DLL. There are two main source components (SENDFORM.CPP and HTMLFORM.CPP), three header files (SEND-FORM.H, HTMLFORM.H, and ASSOCARR.H), and a MAKEFILE.

MAKEFILE

This file can be invoked on a machine with Microsoft Visual C++ installed with NMAKE-F MAKEFILE.

```
CC=cl -c
CFLAGS=
CVARS=-DWIN32 -DNDEBUG
LINK=link
LINKOPT=/DLL
LIBS=wininet.lib user32.lib mapi32.lib advapi32.lib
OBJS=sendform.obj htmlform.obj
LINKOUT=/OUT:sendform.dll
```

```
DEFS=sendform.def

all: sendform.dll
.cpp.obj:
    $(CC) $(CFLAGS) $(CVARS) $*.cpp

sendform.dll: $(OBJS) $(DEFS)
    $(LINK) $(LINKOPT) /DEF:$(DEFS) $(LINKOUT) $(LIBS) $(OBJS)
```

SENDFORM.H

```
/////////////////////////////////////////////////////////////////
// FILE:
// sendform.h
// DESCRIPTION:
//      header file for SENDFORM sample ISAPI DLL for sending messages via CMC
//      mostly CMC function call typedefs

// prototypes
void Log(char *pszText);
BOOL InitSimpleCMC (void);
void DeinitSimpleCMC();
BOOL SendMsg(char *pszTo,char *pszSubject,char *pszBody);
BOOL CMCSendMsg(char *pszTo,char *pszSubject,char *pszBody);
BOOL ExtMAPISendMsg(char *pszTo,char *pszSubject,char *pszBody);

// typedefs
typedef CMC_return_code (FAR PASCAL *LPFNCMCQUERYCONFIGURATION)
    (CMC_session_id session, CMC_enum item,CMC_buffer reference,CMC_extension FAR
↳*config_extensions);

extern LPFNCMCQUERYCONFIGURATION lpfnCMCQueryConfiguration;

#define CMCQueryConfiguration           (*lpfnCMCQueryConfiguration)

typedef CMC_return_code (FAR PASCAL *LPFNCMCLOGON)(
    CMC_string              service,
    CMC_string              user,
    CMC_string              password,
    CMC_enum                character_set,
    CMC_ui_id               ui_id,
    CMC_uint16              caller_cmc_version,
    CMC_flags               logon_flags,
    CMC_session_id FAR      *session,
    CMC_extension FAR       *logon_extensions
);

typedef CMC_return_code (FAR PASCAL *LPFNCMCLOGON)(
    CMC_string              service,
    CMC_string              user,
    CMC_string              password,
    CMC_enum                character_set,
    CMC_ui_id               ui_id,
    CMC_uint16              caller_cmc_version,
    CMC_flags               logon_flags,
    CMC_session_id FAR      *session,
```

```
    CMC_extension FAR       *logon_extensions
);

extern LPFNCMCLOGON lpfnCMCLogon;

#define CMCLogon            (*lpfnCMCLogon)

typedef CMC_return_code (FAR PASCAL *LPFNCMCLOGOFF)(
    CMC_session_id          session,
    CMC_ui_id               ui_id,
    CMC_flags               logoff_flags,
    CMC_extension FAR       *logoff_extensions
);

extern LPFNCMCLOGOFF lpfnCMCLogoff;

#define CMCLogoff           (*lpfnCMCLogoff)

typedef CMC_return_code (FAR PASCAL *LPFNCMCFREE)(
    CMC_buffer              memory
);

extern LPFNCMCFREE lpfnCMCFree;

#define CMCFree     (*lpfnCMCFree)

typedef CMC_return_code (FAR PASCAL *LPFNCMCLOOKUP)(
    CMC_session_id          session,
    CMC_recipient FAR       *recipient_in,
    CMC_flags               look_up_flags,
    CMC_ui_id               ui_id,
    CMC_uint32 FAR          *count,
    CMC_recipient FAR * FAR *recipient_out,
    CMC_extension FAR       *look_up_extensions
);

extern LPFNCMCLOOKUP lpfnCMCLookUp;

#define CMCLookUp (*lpfnCMCLookUp)

typedef CMC_return_code (FAR PASCAL *LPFNCMCSEND)(
    CMC_session_id          session,
    CMC_message FAR         *message,
    CMC_flags               send_flags,
    CMC_ui_id               ui_id,
    CMC_extension FAR       *send_extensions
);

extern LPFNCMCSEND lpfnCMCSend;

#define CMCSend (*lpfnCMCSend)

typedef CMC_return_code (FAR PASCAL *LPFNCMCREAD)(
    CMC_session_id          session,
    CMC_message_reference   *message_reference,
    CMC_flags               read_flags,
```

```
    CMC_message FAR * FAR    *message,
    CMC_ui_id                ui_id,
    CMC_extension FAR        *read_extensions
);
```

SENDFORM.CPP

```cpp
////////////////////////////////////////////////////////////////////////////
// MODULE:
//               SENDFORM.CPP
//
// DESCRIPTION:
//               ISAPI program to send contents of form to specified email address via MAPI
//
// USES:
//               ISAPI (httpext.h) - to read data from Internet Server
//               HTMLForm class (htmlform.h) - to parse form data into form fields and
// ⌐values
//
// EXPORTS:
//               DllEntryPoint
//               GetExtensionVersion
//               HttpExtensionProc
//
#include <ctype.h>
#include <iostream.h>
#include <strstrea.h>
#include <httpext.h>
#include <xcmc.h>
#include "htmlform.h"
#include "sendform.h"

HINSTANCE hlibCMC = (HINSTANCE)NULL;
LPFNCMCQUERYCONFIGURATION lpfnCMCQueryConfiguration = NULL;
LPFNCMCLOGON lpfnCMCLogon = NULL;
LPFNCMCLOGOFF lpfnCMCLogoff = NULL;
LPFNCMCFREE lpfnCMCFree = NULL;
LPFNCMCLOOKUP lpfnCMCLookUp = NULL;
LPFNCMCSEND lpfnCMCSend = NULL;

HANDLE hEvtLog;

///////////////////////////////////////
// FUNCTION:
//               DllEntryPoint
// DESCRIPTION:
//               DllEntryPoint allows potentialinitialization of state variables.
// RETURNS:
//               TRUE - only TRUE right now
BOOL WINAPI DllEntryPoint (HINSTANCE hinstDLL, DWORD dwReason, LPVOID lpv)
{
    return (TRUE);
}

///////////////////////////////////////
// FUNCTION:
```

```
//   GetExtensionVersion
// DESCRIPTION:
//              Return the version this server is built for. See <httpext.h> for
//              a prototype. This function is required by the spec.
// RETURNS:
//              TRUE - only TRUE right now
BOOL WINAPI GetExtensionVersion (HSE_VERSION_INFO *pVersionInfo)
{
    pVersionInfo->dwExtensionVersion = MAKELONG (HSE_VERSION_MINOR, HSE_VERSION_MAJOR);
    lstrcpyn ((LPTSTR) pVersionInfo->lpszExtensionDesc,
            TEXT("SENDFORM - Sends form to specified address"),
            HSE_MAX_EXT_DLL_NAME_LEN);

        hEvtLog=RegisterEventSource(NULL,"SENDFORM");

    return TRUE;
}


/////////////////////////////////////
// FUNCTION:
//   HttpExtensionProc
// DESCRIPTION:
//       Reads in form data and sends message via MAPI
//       to To:, Cc:, Bcc: specified in form
//       with Subject and Body also specified by form
// RETURNS:
//       HSE_STATUS_SUCCESS - if everything works OK
DWORD WINAPI HttpExtensionProc (EXTENSION_CONTROL_BLOCK *pECB)
{
        ISAPIForm form(pECB);
        char *lpszBody;
        // if there's a Body field, then use that for message
        if (!(lpszBody=form["Body"]))
        {// if there is no body field, then just bundle up all form field for message
                ostrstream s;
                s << form;
                lpszBody=s.str();
        }
        if (!form["To"]){ // must have recipient specified
                pECB->ServerSupportFunction(pECB->ConnID,
                                HSE_REQ_SEND_RESPONSE_HEADER,
                                (LPDWORD) "400 Bad Request",
                                NULL,
                                (LPDWORD)"\r\n");
                form.Write("<H2>No recipient specified</H2>");
                pECB->dwHttpStatusCode=400;
                return HSE_STATUS_ERROR;
        }
        form.Display();
        BOOL bResult=SendMsg(form["To"],form["Subject"]?form["Subject"]:"(no subject)",
⌐lpszBody);
        if (bResult==TRUE)
                form.Write("<H2>Message sent successfully</H2>");
        else
                form.Write("<H2>Failed to send message</H2>");
        return bResult==TRUE?HSE_STATUS_SUCCESS:HSE_STATUS_ERROR;
```

```
}

////////////////////////////////////////
// FUNCTION:
//    SendMsg
// DESCRIPTION:
//      Use Common Messaging Calls (CMC) to send message contained in Body
//      to To, from From, with subject Subject
// RETURNS:
//              TRUE - if everything works OK
//              FALSE - error
BOOL SendMsg(char *pszTo,char *pszSubject,char *pszBody)
{
      // level of indirection because some day we may want to use direct Extended MAPI
      return CMCSendMsg(pszTo,pszSubject,pszBody);
}

BOOL CMCSendMsg(char *pszTo,char *pszSubject,char *pszBody)
{
      if (!InitSimpleCMC())
            return FALSE;

      CMC_return_code Status;
      CMC_session_id Session;
      BOOL bMsgSent=FALSE;

      // Log on to system WITHOUT USING UI!
      Status = CMCLogon(
            NULL,          // Default service
            NULL,          // supply username
            NULL,          // supply password
            NULL,          // Default Character set
            (CMC_ui_id)NULL,   // Default UI ID
            CMC_VERSION,       // Version 1 CMC calls
            0,                 // don't allow use of UI!
            &Session,          // Returned session id.
            NULL);             // No extensions.
      // error handling
      if (Status==0){

            // Do CMC send
            CMC_message     Message;
            CMC_recipient   Recip;
            // Build recipient
            Recip.name       = (char *)pszTo;
            Recip.name_type  = CMC_TYPE_INDIVIDUAL;
            Recip.address    = NULL;              // Look_up address
            Recip.role       = CMC_ROLE_TO;       // a "To" recipient.
            Recip.recip_flags    = CMC_RECIP_LAST_ELEMENT; // Not the last element
            Recip.recip_extensions = NULL;                // No recipient extensions

            // Put it together in the message structure.
            Message.message_type        = NULL;    /* Interpersonal message type */
            Message.subject             = (char *)pszSubject;    /* Message subject
↳*/
            Message.text_note           = (char *)pszBody;   /* Message note          */
```

```
                  Message.recipients         = &Recip;      /* Message recipients    */
                  Message.attachments                 = NULL;
                  Message.message_flags      = 0;        /* No flags              */
                  Message.message_extensions = NULL;      /* No message extensions  */

                  // Send the message!
                  Status = CMCSend(
            Session,            /* Session ID. - set with logon call */
            &Message,                 /* Message structure          */
            0,                   /* No flags                   */
            0,          /* No UI will be used.            */
            NULL);                   /* No extensions              */
              if (Status==0){
                     bMsgSent=TRUE;
              }
              else
                     Log("Failed to send");
              // Log off from the session
                  Status = CMCLogoff(
            Session,            /* Session ID                 */
            (CMC_ui_id)NULL,     /* No UI will be used.         */
            0,                   /* No flags                   */
            NULL);                   /* No extensions              */
              if (Status!=0)
                     Log("Failed to log off");
       }
       else {
              char szMsg[256];
              wsprintf(szMsg,"Failed to logon with status %d.",Status);
              Log(szMsg);
       }
    /* error handling */
       DeinitSimpleCMC();

       return bMsgSent;
}

////////////////////////////////////
// FUNCTION:
//          InitSimpleCMC
// DESCRIPTION:
//    Loads the DLL containing the simple CMC functions and sets
//    up a pointer to each. Wrappers for the function pointers
//    are declared in CLIENT.H.
// RETURNS:
//    TRUE if sucessful, else FALSE
BOOL InitSimpleCMC (void)
{
    char    szMsgBuf[512]="";
    char    szLibName[32]="MAPI32.dll";
    // Get INI directives for alternate DLL PATH
    GetProfileString( "Mail", "CMCDLLNAME32", szLibName, szLibName,
            sizeof(szLibName) - 1 );

    if ((hlibCMC = LoadLibrary (szLibName)) < (HINSTANCE) 32)
    {
```

```
                wsprintf(szMsgBuf,"Cannot Load %s. Check to see that you have %s in your
⌐path or
'~SystemRoot~\\System' "
                                "directory. You may change the CMC dll path by adding a [MAIL]
⌐section to
your "
                                "WIN.INI file wtih the following entry:
CMCDLLNAME=\\MAPI.REL\\MAPI.DLL",
                                szLibName,szLibName);
                Log(szMsgBuf);
                return FALSE;
    }

    if (!(lpfnCMCQueryConfiguration = (LPFNCMCQUERYCONFIGURATION)GetProcAddress (hlibCMC,
"cmc_query_configuration") ))
    {
                Log("Cannot Load cmc_query_configuration process address.");
                return FALSE;
    }

    if (!(lpfnCMCLogon = (LPFNCMCLOGON)GetProcAddress (hlibCMC, "cmc_logon") ))
    {
                Log("Cannot Load cmc_logon process address.");
                return FALSE;
    }

    if (!(lpfnCMCLogoff = (LPFNCMCLOGOFF)GetProcAddress (hlibCMC, "cmc_logoff") ))
    {
                Log("Cannot Load cmc_logoff process address.");
                return FALSE;
    }

    if (!(lpfnCMCSend = (LPFNCMCSEND)GetProcAddress (hlibCMC, "cmc_send") ))
    {
                Log("Cannot Load cmc_send process address.");
                return FALSE;
    }
    return (TRUE);

}

/////////////////////////////////////
// FUNCTION:
//          DeinitSimpleCMC
// DESCRIPTION:
// RETURNS:
//     none
void DeinitSimpleCMC ()
{
    if (hlibCMC)
    {
        FreeLibrary (hlibCMC);
        hlibCMC = (HINSTANCE) NULL;
    }
}
void Log(char *pszText)
```

```
{
        LPSTR aszMsg[]={
"..........................................................................",
                };
        strncpy(aszMsg[0],pszText,strlen(aszMsg[0]));
        ReportEvent(hEvtLog,EVENTLOG_WARNING_TYPE,0,
                                1,          // event identifier
                                NULL,1,0,
                                (const char **)aszMsg,NULL);
}

// exe to test program from main for debugging
#ifdef CGIFORM
void main()
{
        hEvtLog=RegisterEventSource(NULL,"SENDFORM");
        CGIForm form;
        char *lpszBody;
        // if there's a Body field, then use that for message
        if (!(lpszBody=form["Body"]))
        {// if there is no body field, then just bundle up all form field for message
                ostrstream s;
                s << form;
                lpszBody=s.str();
        }
        BOOL bResult=SendMsg(form["To"],form["Subject"]?form["Subject"]:"(no subject)",
ᒑlpszBody);
        form.Display();
        if (hResult==0)
                cout <<"<H2>Message sent successfully</H2>";
        else
                cout <<"<H2>Failed to send message: " << hResult << "</H2>";
}
#endif
```

HTMLFORM.H

```
/*
  HTMLFORM.H
  class definition for HTMLFORM class
  and derived classes CGIForm and ISAPIForm
  This class hierarchy provide methods for both HTML form display
  and for retrieving values from HTTP transmitted forms
  via CGI or ISAPI interface.

*/

#include <stdio.h>
#include <string.h>
#include <iostream.h>
#include <fstream.h>
#include <httpext.h> // http extensions

#include "assocarr.h"

// nonmember helper functions
```

```
void UrlDecode(char *p) ;
char *GetField(char *p) ;

// tiny string class implementation
class String{
friend ostream& operator<<(ostream& os,String& s) ;
                             char *rep;
public:
                  String(const char *s){
                          if (!s)
                                  rep=NULL;
                          else {
                                  rep=new char[strlen(s)+1];
                                  strcpy(rep,s);
                          }
                  }
                  String(){}
                  String(int n){if (!n)rep=NULL;}
                  String& operator=(const char *s){
                          delete []rep;
                          rep ew char[strlen(s)+1];
                          strcpy(rep,s);
                          return *this;
                  }
                  ~String(){}
                  int operator==(const String& s)
                  {
                          return !strcmp(s.rep,rep);
                  }
                  operator char*(){return rep?rep:"~";}
} ;

class HTMLForm {
protected:
                  AssocArray<String,String> aFields;
                  friend ostream& operator<<(ostream& os,HTMLForm& form);
                  int Size(){return aFields.Size();}
                  int nError;
                  int Parse(char *pszData);
public:
                  HTMLForm();
                  HTMLForm(AssocArray<String,String> init);
                  HTMLForm(const HTMLForm& form);
                  operator=(const HTMLForm& form);
                  virtual HTMLForm::~HTMLForm(){}
                  String operator[](const String& sFieldName);
                  char *operator[](const char *pszFieldName);
                  void AddField(char *pszFieldName,char *pszFieldValue);
                  void AddField(const String& sFieldName,const String&
ꞁsFieldValue);

                  int Display(); // displays form contents on HTML page
                  virtual void Header();
                  virtual void Write(LPCSTR pszText) = 0;
                  int Store(char *pszCSVFileName); // appends field values
ꞁto specified CSV
file
```

```
};

class CGIForm: public HTMLForm {
public:
                           void Header()
                           {
                               cout << "Content-type: text/html\r\n";
                                   cout <<"Status: 200 OK\r\n";
                               cout <<"\r\n"; // finished sending headers
                           }
                           int Display()
                           {
                                   Header();
                                   cout << "<H1>Form Data</H1>\n";
                                   aFields.First();
                                   while (aFields.Current()){
                                           cout << aFields.Current()->Key() << ": "
<<
(aFields.Current())->Value() << "<p>\n";

                                           ++aFields;
                                   }
                                   return 1;
                           }
                           void Write(LPCSTR pszText)
                           {
                                   cout << pszText;
                           }
                           CGIForm();
                           virtual ~CGIForm(){}
};

class ISAPIForm: public HTMLForm {
                           EXTENSION_CONTROL_BLOCK *pECB;
public:

                           ISAPIForm(const EXTENSION_CONTROL_BLOCK *pECB);
                           ~ISAPIForm(){}
                           void Write(LPCSTR lpsz)
                           {
                               DWORD dwBytesWritten;
                                   dwBytesWritten = lstrlen (lpsz);
                               pECB->WriteClient (pECB->ConnID, (PVOID) lpsz,
&dwBytesWritten, 0);
                           }
                           virtual void Header(){
                               pECB->ServerSupportFunction(pECB->ConnID,
                                       HSE_REQ_SEND_RESPONSE_HEADER, "200 OK",
NULL,(LPDWORD)"Content-type: text/html\r\n\r\n");
                           }
                           int Display()
                           {
                                   Header();
                                   Write(TEXT("<H1>Form Data</H1>\n"));
                                   aFields.First();
                                   char szText[256];
                                   while (aFields.Current()){
                                   sprintf(szText,"%s: %s<br>\n",(char *)aFields.
```

```
⌐Current()->Key(),(char *)(aFields.Current()->Value() ));
                                           Write(TEXT(szText));
                                           ++aFields;
                              }
                       return 1;
             }
};
```

HTMLFORM.CPP

```
//
//      HTMLForm.cpp
//
// Implementation of methods for HTMLForm class
// and derived ISAPIForm and CGIForm classes
//
#include "htmlform.h"

//
// FUNCTION:
//              HTMLForm::HTMLForm
//
// DESCRIPTION:
//              constructor for HTML base class
//
// RETURNS:
//              NONE
HTMLForm::HTMLForm()
{
       nError=0;
}


//
// FUNCTION:
//              HTMLForm::AddField
//
// DESCRIPTION:
//              Add field and value to associative array
//
// RETURNS:
//              NONE
void HTMLForm::AddField(char *pszFieldName,char *pszFieldValue)
{
       aFields.Add((String&)pszFieldName,(String&)pszFieldValue);
}
void HTMLForm::AddField(const String& sFieldName,const String& sFieldValue)
{
       aFields.Add(sFieldName,sFieldValue);
}

String HTMLForm::operator[](const String& sFieldName)
{
       return aFields[sFieldName]?aFields[sFieldName]:"~";
}

void HTMLForm::Header()
{
```

```
        cout << "Content-type: text/html\n";
        cout <<"\n"; // finished sending headers
}

char *HTMLForm::operator[](const char *pszFieldName){
        if (!strlen(aFields[String(pszFieldName)]))
                return NULL;
        else
                return (char *)(aFields[String(pszFieldName)]);
}


//
// FUNCTION:
//              HTMLForm::Parse
//
// DESCRIPTION:
//              parse out URL-encode form data
//
// RETURNS:
//              1 - everything's OK
//              0 - problem
int HTMLForm::Parse(char *pszData)
{// create form from URL encoded string of characters
        char *pszValue, *p;
        p = strtok(pszData,"&");
        while (p!=NULL) {
                pszValue=GetField(p);
                aFields.Add(p,pszValue);
                p=strtok(NULL,"&");
        }
        return 1;
}


//
// FUNCTION:
//              HTMLForm::Parse
//
// DESCRIPTION:
//              display contents of an HTML form
//
// RETURNS:
//              1 - everything's OK
//              0 - problem
int HTMLForm::Display()
{
        this->Header();
        aFields.First();
        while (aFields.Current()){
                cout << aFields.Current()->Key() << ": " << (aFields.Current()) ->Value()
 << "<p>\n";
                ++aFields;
        }
        return 1;
}

int HTMLForm::Store(char *pszFname)
{
```

```
            ofstream os(pszFname,ios::app);
            aFields.First();
            while (aFields.Current()){
                    os << (aFields.Current())->Value() << ",";
                    ++aFields;
            }
            os << "\n";
            return 1;
}
//
// FUNCTION:
//              CGIForm::CGIForm
//
// DESCRIPTION:
//              Constructor for CGI form class
//
// RETURNS:
//              Indirectly via "nError" member
//              0  - everything's OK
//              -1 - POST method specified but no CONTENT_LENGTH env. variable
//              -2 - POST method, no CONTENT_TYPE specified
//              -3 - POST method, unrecognized CONTENT_TYPE
//              -4 - POST method, CONTENT_LENGTH of zero
//              -5 - GET method, no QUERY_STRING env. variable
//              -6 - neither GET method or POST method specified
//              -7 - either method, failed to Parse data
CGIForm::CGIForm()
{
        char *p,*pszData,*pszRequestMethod;
        nError=0;

    pszRequestMethod = getenv("REQUEST_METHOD");
    if (pszRequestMethod && !stricmp(pszRequestMethod,"POST")) {
                int nContentLength=0;
                if ((p=getenv("CONTENT_LENGTH"))!=NULL)
                        nContentLength = atoi(p);
                else
                        nError=-1; // no CONTENT_LENGTH
                if (nContentLength){
                        pszData ew char[nContentLength};
                        for(int i=0;i<nContentLength;i++){
                                if ((pszData[i]=fgetc(stdin))==EOF){
                                        break;
                                }
                        }
                    pszData[i]='\0';
                        nContentLength = i;
                        p=getenv("CONTENT_TYPE");
                        if (!p){
                                nError=-2; // no CONTENT_TYPE!
                        }
                        else if (stricmp(p,"application/x-www-form-urlencoded")){
                                nError=-3; // unsupported CONTENT_TYPE
                        }
                }
                else
```

```
                                nError=-4; // CONTENT_LENGTH of zero specified!!
}
else { // default to GET method
            pszData=getenv("QUERY_STRING");
            if (!pszData)
                    nError=-5; // get method and empty QUERY_STRING!
    }

    if (!nError) // everything ok so far
            if (!this->Parse(pszData))
                    nError=-7;
    return;
}

/////////////////////////////////////////
// FUNCTION:
//                 ISAPIForm::ISAPIForm
//
// DESCRIPTION:
//                 Build ISAPIForm from EXTENSION_CONTROL_BLOCK
//
// RETURNS:
//                 indirectly via nError variable
//                 0 - everything's OK
ISAPIForm::ISAPIForm(const EXTENSION_CONTROL_BLOCK *pECBArg)
{
            pECB=(EXTENSION_CONTROL_BLOCK *) pECBArg; // set member pECB
            char *pszData;
        // GET method
            if (!stricmp(pECB->lpszMethod,"GET"))
                pszData = pECB->lpszQueryString;
            else {
                // POST method
                if ( pECB -> cbTotalBytes == 0){
            // No data at all
                    nError=-1;
                        return;
                }
                else {
                    // Start processing of input information here.
                    if(!(pszData=(char *)LocalAlloc (LPTR,pECB->cbTotalBytes))) {
                            nError= -2;
                            return;
                    }
                        strcpy(pszData, ( CHAR * ) pECB -> lpbData );
                        DWORD cbQuery;
                        if ((cbQuery ECB->cbTotalBytes-pECB->cbAvailable) > 0 )
                                pECB->ReadClient(pECB->ConnID,
                                        (LPVOID)(pszData+pECB->cbAvailable),
                                        &cbQuery );
                        // For POST requests, two terminating characters are added to the
                    // end of the data. Ignore them by placing a null in the string.
                        *(pszData+pECB->cbTotalBytes-2)='\0';
                }
            } // end POST method data
            this->Parse(pszData);
```

```
            return;
}

////////////////////////////////////////////////////////////////
//                        NON-MEMBER HELPER FUNCTIONS

//////////////////////////////////////
// FUNCTION:
//            UrlDecode
// DESCRIPTION:
//            Turns '+'s to spaces, and escape code (%nn) to characters
// RETURNS:
//            indirectly via nError variable
//            0 - everything's OK
void UrlDecode(char *p)
{
    char *pD = p;
    while (*p) {
                if (*p=='%') {
                    /* Escape: next 2 chars are hex representation of the actual character
⌐*/
                    p++;
                        if (isxdigit(p[0]) && isxdigit(p[1])) {
                                char hold = p[2];
                                p[2]='\0';
                                *pD++=char (strtoul(p,0,16));
                                p[2]=hold;
                                p += 2;
                            }
                } // end processing escape
                else if (*p=='+') { // convert to space
                        *pD++=' ';
                        ++p;
                }
                else // just an ordinary character
                        *pD++=*p++;
    } // while *p
    *pD='\0';
    return;
}

//////////////////////////////////////
// FUNCTION:
//            GetField
// DESCRIPTION:
//            Parses out field value from "key=value" string.
//            Decodes field value at the same time.
// RETURNS:
//      The parsed out field value
char *GetField(char *pszField)
{
        char *pszValue=strchr(pszField,'=');
        if (!pszValue)
                return 0;
        *pszValue++='\0'; // terminate field name and point to value
        UrlDecode(pszValue);
```

```
            return pszValue;
}


//////////////////////////////////////
// FUNCTION:
//          ostream& operator<<(ostream& os,String& s)
// DESCRIPTION:
//              Simple stream output function for our tiny String class implementation
// RETURNS:
//      the new ostream
ostream& operator<<(ostream& os,String& s)
{
            return os << s.rep;
}


//////////////////////////////////////
// FUNCTION:
//          ostream& operator<<(ostream& os,Form& f)
// DESCRIPTION:
//              writes out form contents to stream
// RETURNS:
//      the new ostream
ostream& operator<<(ostream& os,HTMLForm& form)
{
            form.aFields.First();
            while (form.aFields.Current()){
                    os << form.aFields.Current()->Key() << ": " << form.aFields.Current()
└→Value() << "\n";
                    ++(form.aFields); // go the next field
            }
            return os;
}


// these stub functions can be enabled by compiling
// with -DTESTISAPI to test HTMLForm components on their own
#if defined(TESTISAPI)
BOOL WINAPI DllEntryPoint (HINSTANCE hinstDLL, DWORD dwReason, LPVOID lpv)
    {
    // Nothing to do here
    return (TRUE);
    }
BOOL WINAPI GetExtensionVersion (HSE_VERSION_INFO *pVer)
{
    pVer->dwExtensionVersion = MAKELONG(HSE_VERSION_MINOR, HSE_VERSION_MAJOR);
    lstrcpyn(pVer->lpszExtensionDesc,
                "Test of HTMLForm class for CGI and ISAPI form data retrieval",
                HSE_MAX_EXT_DLL_NAME_LEN );
    return TRUE;
} // GetExtensionVersion()

DWORD WINAPI HttpExtensionProc (EXTENSION_CONTROL_BLOCK *pECB)
{
            ISAPIForm form(pECB);
            form.Display();
            return HSE_STATUS_SUCCESS;
}
```

```
// this main function can be enabled by compiling
// with -DTESTCGI to test HTMLForm components on their own
#elif defined (TESTCGI) // CGI
void main(int argc,char **argv)
{
        CGIForm form;
        form.Display();
}
#endif
```

ASSOCARR.H

```
/////////////////////////////////////
// assocarray.h
// template associative array
template <class K,class V> class ArrayItem;

template <class KeyType, class ValType>
class AssocArray {
private:
        ArrayItem<KeyType,ValType> *head,*current;
        int size;
public:
        AssocArray(){current=head=0;size=0;}
        ~AssocArray(){
                ArrayItem<KeyType,ValType> *prev;
                current rev=head;
                while(prev){
                        current rev->next;
                        delete prev;
                        prev=current;
                 }
        }
        void Add(const KeyType& key, const ValType& val){
                ArrayItem<KeyType,ValType> *entry ew ArrayItem<KeyType,ValType>(key,val);
                if (!head)
                        head=entry;
                else {
                        current=head;
                        while (current->next)
                                current=current->next; // loop until end of list
                        current->next=entry;
                        current=entry;
                }
                size++;
        }
        ValType operator[](const KeyType& srchkey){
                current=head;
                while (current) {
                        if (current->key==srchkey)
                                return current->value;
                        current=current->next;
                }
                return (ValType)((const char *)NULL);
        }
        ArrayItem<KeyType,ValType> *First(){return current=head;}
        ArrayItem<KeyType,ValType> *operator++(){return current=current->next;}
```

```
        ArrayItem<KeyType,ValType> *Current(){return current;}
        int Size(){return size;}
};

template <class KeyType,class ValType>
class ArrayItem {
friend class AssocArray<KeyType,ValType>;
public:
        ArrayItem(const KeyType& k,const ValType& v):key(k),value(v){
                next=0;
        }
        KeyType& Key(){return key;}
        ValType& Value(){return value;}
private:
        KeyType key;
        ValType value;
        ArrayItem *next;
};
```

CVTDOC

MAKEFILE

```
# makefile for CVTDOC ISAPI filter
CC=cl -c
CFLAGS=
CVARS=-DWIN32 -DNDEBUG
LINK=link
LINKOPT=/DLL
LIBS=wininet.lib user32.lib mapi32.lib advapi32.lib
OBJS=cvtdoc.obj
LINKOUT=/OUT:cvtdoc.dll
DEFS=cvtdoc.def

all: cvtdoc.dll

.cpp.obj:
    $ (CC) $ (CFLAGS) $ (CVARS) $*.cpp

cvtdoc.dll: $ (OBJS) $ (DEFS)
    $ (LINK) $ (LINKOPT) /DEF:$(DEFS) $ (LINKOUT) $ (LIBS) $ (OBJS)
```

CVTDOC.DEF

```
LIBRARY CVTDOC
EXPORTS DllEntryPoint
        GetFilterVersion
        HttpFilterProc
```

CVTDOC.CPP

```
//////////////////////////////////////////////////////////////////////////
// MODULE:
//              CVTDOC.CPP
```

```
//
// DESCRIPTION:

  CVTDOC - ISAPI Filter for Dynamic Document Conversion
  -----------------------------------------------------
Web content creators and webmasters often want to "publish" a document
or data file to the Web. However, it can be very inconvenient to constantly
run a conversion program to generate new HTML each time the document
or data file is updated. Relying on the webmaster to run the conversion
program for data that is often updated is also prone to error.

CVTDOC is an ISAPI filter that converts documents to HTML dynamically
as needed when the HTML file is accessed. If the HTML file is missing
it will be generated from a source document found with the same basename.
If the HTML file is older than a source document, it will be regenerated
from the conversion program.

SETUP
-----
1. Copy CVTDOC.DLL to an appropriate subdirectory, such as the CGI-BIN
subdirectory of your Web content directory.
2. Update the Filter DLLs parameter of IIS. Run REGEDT32.EXE.
3. Add the full path of CVTDOC.DLL to
HKEY_LOCAL_MACHINE\System\CurrentControlSet\Services\W3SVC\Parameters\Filter DLLs
(the DLLs are separated by commas)
4. Create a Conversion subkey of the W3SVC\Parameters key.
5. Add each extension (e.g. .xls, .doc) as a separate value.
6. Enter the full path of the conversion program to run for each extension.
7. List each conversion program as taking two arguments of "%s %s".
8. Place the conversion program called in the directories referenced.
9. The conversion program needs to be able to be executed from the command
line with two arguments: the source file name and the generated HTML file.
You can find conversion programs for almost any data format on the Web, but
you may need to write "wrapper" batch files or programs that allow the
conversion program to conform to this format.

// USES:
//
// EXPORTS:
//           GetFilterVersion
//           HttpFilterProc
//
*/

#include <ctype.h>
#include <stdio.h>
#include <sys/types.h>
#include <sys/stat.h>
#include <io.h>
#include <iostream.h>
#include <strstrea.h>
#include <fstream.h>
#include <httpext.h>
#include <httpfilt.h>

#define W3SVCKEY "System\\CurrentControlSet\\Services\\W3SVC"
```

```
HANDLE hEvtLog;

//////////////////////////////////////
// FUNCTION:
//              DllEntryPoint
// DESCRIPTION:
//              DllEntryPoint allows potential initialization of state variables.
// RETURNS:
//              TRUE - only TRUE right now
BOOL WINAPI DllEntryPoint (HINSTANCE hinstDLL, DWORD dwReason, LPVOID lpv)
{
    return (TRUE);
}


//////////////////////////////////////
// FUNCTION:
//    GetFilterVersion
// DESCRIPTION:
//    Return the version this server is built for. See <httpext.h> for
//    a prototype. This function is required by the spec.
// RETURNS:
//        TRUE
BOOL WINAPI GetFilterVersion (PHTTP_FILTER_VERSION pFilterVersion)
{
   pFilterVersion->dwFilterVersion = HTTP_FILTER_REVISION;
   strcpy (pFilterVersion->lpszFilterDesc,
           "CVTDOC - Converts document or data into HTML if HTML not present or
ᑌolder");

        // now register for events we're interested in
        pFilterVersion->dwFlags= (      SF_NOTIFY_ORDER_HIGH | // high so we can be sure
ᑌto intercept!
                                                      SF_NOTIFY_SECURE_PORT |
                                                   SF_NOTIFY_NONSECURE_PORT |
// tell us about all URL requests
                                                      SF_NOTIFY_URL_MAP
                                                      );

        hEvtLog=RegisterEventSource(NULL,"CVTDOC");

        LPSTR aszMsg[]={
                "Loading CVTDOC filter"
        };
        ReportEvent(hEvtLog,EVENTLOG_WARNING_TYPE,0,
                            1.      // event identifier
                            NULL,1,0,
                            (const char **)aszMsg,NULL);

        return TRUE;
}

//////////////////////////////////////
//      FUNCTION:
//              Win32Exec
//      DESCRIPTION:
//              alternative to WinExec() function
```

```
//              (which should not be called in Win32 programs)
//              calls Create Process and waits for termination
// INPUTS
//              szCommand - the command line to run:
//              full path and all command line arguments
// RETURNS
//              0 - if CreateProcess fails
//              dwExitCode - if CreateProcess succeeds
//
int Win32Exec(char *szCommand)
{
        STARTUPINFO si;
        PROCESS_INFORMATION piProcess;
        ZeroMemory(&si,sizeof si);
        si.cb=sizeof si;
        BOOL result;
        result=CreateProcess(NULL,szCommand,NULL,NULL,FALSE,
                                          CREATE_DEFAULT_ERROR_MODE|
ᘪDETACHED_PROCESS,
                                               NULL,NULL,&si,&piProcess);

        DWORD dwExitCode;
        if (result==TRUE)
        {
                CloseHandle(piProcess.hThread);

                if (WaitForSingleObject(piProcess.hProcess,INFINITE)!=WAIT_FAILED)
                        GetExitCodeProcess(piProcess.hProcess,&dwExitCode);
                CloseHandle(piProcess.hProcess);

        }
        return result==TRUE? dwExitCode: 0;
}


/////////////////////////////////////////
// FUNCTION:
//              CvtToHTML
// DESCRIPTION:
//              Converts file name to HTML if:
//                      1) the file name extension is registered and associated with
ᘪconversion program
//                      2) if it's a structured storage file, and then launch the
ᘪconversion program based on the GUID instead of the extension.
// RETURNS:
//              TRUE - if we could convert it
BOOL CvtToHTML(char *pszSrcFile,char *pszHTMLFname)
{
        BOOL bConverted=FALSE;
        // check to see if we have conversion registered for this file
        char *pszExt=strrchr(pszSrcFile,'.');
        if (pszExt){
                char szKey[1024];
                strcpy(szKey,W3SVCKEY);
                strcat(szKey,"\\Parameters\\Conversions");
                HKEY hkey;
                LONG lResult=RegOpenKeyEx(HKEY_LOCAL_MACHINE,szKey,0,KEY_READ,
ᘪ&hkey);
```

```
                    char szValue[16],szData[256];
                    DWORD iValue,nLenValue=sizeof szValue,dwType,nLenData=sizeof
 szData;
                    if (1Result==ERROR_SUCCESS){
                            // look for a conversion to run
                            for (iValue=0;

             (1Result=RegEnumValue(hkey,iValue,(LPTSTR)szValue,&nLenValue,0,&dwType,
 (LPBYTE)szData,&nLenData))==ERROR_SUCCESS;

                                    iValue++)
                    {
                                    if (!_stricmp(szValue,pszExt)) // found
 conversion!

                                    {
                                            char szCmd[_MAX_PATH*2];
                                            wsprintf(szCmd,szData,
 pszSrcFile,pszHTMLFname);

                                            if (Win32Exec(szCmd)){
                                                    bConverted=TRUE;
                                            }
                                            break;
                                    }
                                    nLenValue=sizeof szValue;
                                    nLenData=sizeof szData;
                    }
            }

            LPSTR aszMsg[]={
                    "Failed to find conversion",
            };
            if (bConverted!=TRUE){
                    ReportEvent(hEvtLog,EVENTLOG_WARNING_TYPE,0,
                            1.      // event identifier
                            NULL,1,0,
                            (const char **)aszMsg,NULL);
            }
    }
    return bConverted;
}

/////////////////////////////////////
// FUNCTION:
//          FileDateCompare
// DESCRIPTION:
//          compares two file modification dates
//
// RETURNS:
//          1 - if first file is newer
//                  0 - same date
//                  -1 - first file older

int FileDateCompare(char *pszFname1,char *pszFname2)
{
        struct _stat buf1,buf2;
        if (_stat(pszFname1,&buf1))
                return -1;
```

```
            if (_stat(pszFname2,&buf2)) // 1 if file 2 not there
                    return 1;
            return buf1.st_mtime>buf2.st_mtime?1:(buf1.st_mtime<buf2.st_mtime?-1:0);
}

/////////////////////////////////////
// FUNCTION:
//              HttpExtensionProc
// DESCRIPTION:
//      Reads in form data and sends message via MAPI
//      to To:, Cc:, Bcc: specified in form
//      with Subject and Body also specified by form
// RETURNS:
//              HSE_STATUS_SUCCESS - if everything works OK
DWORD WINAPI HttpFilterProc (PHTTP_FILTER_CONTEXT pFC,DWORD dwNotificationType,LPVOID
⌐pvNotification)
{
            // look at SF_NOTIFY_URL_MAPs only!
            if (dwNotificationType==SF_NOTIFY_URL_MAP){
                    HTTP_FILTER_URL_MAP *pURLMap=(HTTP_FILTER_URL_MAP *)pvNotification;
                    char szSrcFile[_MAX_PATH];
                    char *pszExt;
                    strcpy(szSrcFile,pURLMap->pszPhysicalPath);
                    if (pszExt=strrchr(szSrcFile,'.')){ // check for extension
                                    if (!strnicmp(pszExt, ".htm",3)){ // is it HTML?
                                            *pszExt='\0';
                                            if (!access(szSrcFile,0)){//check for
⌐presence of source file
                                                            if (FileDateCompare(szSrcFile,
⌐pURLMap->pszPhysicalPath)>0) // source file newer
                                                                    if (CvtToHTML
⌐(szSrcFile,pURLMap->pszPhysicalPath)==TRUE) // convert file if possible
                                                                            return
⌐SF_STATUS_REQ_HANDLED_NOTIFICATION;
                                            }
                                    }
                            }
            }
            // can't convert it
            return SF_STATUS_REQ_NEXT_NOTIFICATION;
}
```

ACCSFILT

MAKEFILE

```
USE_ISAPI = 1
dll = 1
Proj = accsfilt
!include <inetsdk.mak>

all: $(ObjDir)\$(Proj).Dll

$(ObjDir)\$(Proj) .Dll: $* .Obj $* .Exp wsock32.lib

$(ObjDir)\$(Proj).Exp: $*.Obj
```

ACCSFILT.DEF

```
; ACCSFILT.def : declares the module parameters for the DLL.

LIBRARY          "ACCSFILT"

EXPORTS
    HttpFilterProc
    GetFilterVersion
```

ACCSFILT.H

```
/*++

Module Name:
    accsfilt.cpp

Abstract:

            This filter provides access control by accessing hostname to specified URLs and
↳directories
--*/

#include <windows.h>
#include <httpfilt.h>

#include <stdio.h>
#include <stdarg.h>

#include "resource.h"
#include "winsock.h" // necessary for gethostbyaddr() calls

#define W3SVCKEY "System\\CurrentControlSet\\Services\\W3SVC"
#define ACCESSERRORPAGE "/noaccess.htm"

HANDLE hEvtLog;

DWORD
OnPreprocHeaders(
    HTTP_FILTER_CONTEXT *          pfc,
    HTTP_FILTER_PREPROC_HEADERS * pvData
    );

BOOL
WINAPI
GetFilterVersion(
    HTTP_FILTER_VERSION * pVer
    )
{

    pVer->dwFilterVersion = MAKELONG( 0, 1 ); // Version 1.0

    //
    // Specify the types and order of notification
    //

    pVer->dwFlags = (SF_NOTIFY_SECURE_PORT          |
                            SF_NOTIFY_NONSECURE_PORT      |
```

```
                                  SF_NOTIFY_PREPROC_HEADERS     |
                                  SF_NOTIFY_ORDER_DEFAULT);

     strcpy( pVer->lpszFilterDesc, "Access control, v1.0" );

            hEvtLog=RegisterEventSource(NULL,"ACCSFILT");
     return TRUE;
}

DWORD
WINAPI
HttpFilterProc(
     HTTP_FILTER_CONTEXT *    pfc,
     DWORD                    NotificationType,
     VOID *                   pvData
     )
{
     DWORD dwRet;

     //
     // Indicate this notification to the appropriate routine
     //

     switch ( NotificationType )
     {
     case SF_NOTIFY_PREPROC_HEADERS:

            dwRet = OnPreprocHeaders( pfc,

                                        (PHTTP_FILTER_PREPROC_HEADERS) pvData );

            break;

     default:

            dwRet = SF_STATUS_REQ_NEXT_NOTIFICATION;
            break;
     }

     return dwRet;
}

/////////////////////////////////////////////////////
// FUNCTION:
//            IPString2Bytes
//
// DESCRIPTION:
//            convert TCP/IP address, e.g. 204.192.34.5 to hostname, e.g. foobar.com
//
// INPUTS:
//            szIPString - the IP address

BOOL IPString2Bytes(char *szIPString,unsigned char *aIPBytes)
{
            char *p;
            aIPBytes[0]=(BYTE)atoi(szIPString);
            p=strchr(szIPString,'.');
```

```
            if(p){
                        aIPBytes[1]=(BYTE)atoi(++p);
                        if (p=strchr(p,'.')){
                                    aIPBytes[2]=(BYTE)atoi(++p);
                                    if (p=strchr(p,'.')){
                                                aIPBytes[3]=(BYTE)atoi(++p);
                                                return TRUE;
                                    }
                                    else
                                                return FALSE;
                        }
                        else
                                    return FALSE;
            }
            else
                        return FALSE;
}

BOOL IsValidHostname(const char *pszHostname,char *pszIPAddress,const char *pszURL)
{
            BOOL bValidHostname=TRUE;
            char szKey[1024];
            strcpy(szKey,W3SVCKEY);
            strcat(szKey,"\\Parameters\\Access");
            HKEY hkey;
            LONG lResult=RegOpenKeyEx(HKEY_LOCAL_MACHINE,szKey,0,KEY_READ,&hkey);
            char szValue[16],szData[256];
            DWORD iValue,nLenValue=sizeof szValue,dwType,nLenData=sizeof szData;
            if (lResult==ERROR_SUCCESS){
                        // look for requested directory to check on permissions
                        for (iValue=0;
                                    (lResult=RegEnumValue(hkey,iValue,(LPTSTR)szValue,
 &nLenValue,0,&dwType,(LPBYTE)szData,&nLenData))==ERROR_SUCCESS;
                                    iValue++)
                        {
                                    if (!strnicmp(szValue,pszURL,strlen(szValue))) // found
 directory or URL match
                                    {
                                                LPSTR aszMsg2[]={(char *)szValue,"
 directory is protected "};
                                                ReportEvent(hEvtLog,EVENTLOG_WARNING_
 TYPE,0,
                                                            1.      // event identifier
                                                            NULL,2,0,(const char
 **)aszMsg2,NULL);

                                                bValidHostname=FALSE;
                                                char *p=szData,*p2;
                                                for(;;){
                                                            p2=strchr(p,',');
                                                            if (p2)
                                                                        *p2='\0';

                                                            //if it begins with digit its
 an IP address
                                                            if (isdigit(*p)){
```

```
                                                             if (!strnicmp
(pszIPAddress,p,strlen(p)))
                                                                     bValid
Hostname=TRUE;
                                                    }
                                                    else if (isalpha(*p)) {
                                                             if (!strnicmp
(pszHostname+strlen(pszHostname)-strlen(p),p,strlen(p)))
                                                                     bValid
Hostname=TRUE;
                                                    }
                                                    else if (*p=='-'){
                                                             if (!strnicmp
(pszHostname+strlen(pszHostname)-strlen(p+1),p+1,strlen(p+1))){
                                                                     bValid
Hostname=FALSE;
                                                                     break;
                                                             }
                                                    }
                                                    else if (*p=='*' && !*(p+1)) {
                                                             bValid
Hostname=TRUE;
                                                             break;
                                                    }

                                                    if (!p2)
                                                             break;
                                                    p 2+1;
                                          }
                                }
                                nLenValue=sizeof szValue;
                                nLenData=sizeof szData;
                      }
          }

          LPSTR aszMsg[]={
                    (char *)pszHostname,
                    " is invalid hostname for access to ",
                    (char *)pszURL
          };
          if  (bValidHostname==FALSE)
                    ReportEvent(hEvtLog,EVENTLOG_WARNING_TYPE,0,
                              1.        // event identifier
                              NULL,3,0,
                              (const char **)aszMsg,NULL);

          return bValidHostname;
}

DWORD
OnPreprocHeaders(
    HTTP_FILTER_CONTEXT *           pfc,
    HTTP_FILTER_PREPROC_HEADERS * pvData
    )
{
    CHAR  achUrl[2048];
```

```
       DWORD cb;

       cb = sizeof( achUrl );

       if ( !pvData->GetHeader( pfc,
                                 "url",
                                 achUrl,
                                 &cb ))
       {
              return SF_STATUS_REQ_ERROR;
       }

              char szIPAddress[128],szHostname[128]="";
              DWORD dwBuffsize;
              BOOL bResult,bFoundHostname=FALSE;
              unsigned char acAddress[4];
              struct hostent *pHostent;

              dwBuffsize=sizeof szIPAddress;
              bResult fc->GetServerVariable(pfc,"REMOTE_ADDR",szIPAddress,&dwBuffsize);

              dwBuffsize=sizeof szHostname;
              bResult fc->GetServerVariable(pfc,"REMOTE_HOST",szHostname,&dwBuffsize);
              if (bResult!=TRUE || isdigit(szHostname[0])) { // no big surprise that
 REMOTE_HOST wasn't there
                            // try to get it with REMOTE_ADDR
                            if (bResult==TRUE){
                                   IPString2Bytes(szIPAddress,acAddress);
                                   pHostent=gethostbyaddr((const char *)acAddress,4,
 PF_INET);
                                   if (pHostent){
                                           strncpy(szHostname,pHostent->h_name,sizeof
 szHostname);
                                           bFoundHostname=TRUE;
                                   }
                                   else
                                           bFoundHostname=FALSE;
                            }
                            else
                                   bFoundHostname=FALSE;
              }
              else
                     bFoundHostname=TRUE;

              // now based on the hostname and directory decide whether to allow access
              if (!IsValidHostname(szHostname,szIPAddress,achUrl)==TRUE)
              {
                     if ( !pvData->SetHeader( pfc,
                                   "url",
                                   ACCESSERRORPAGE ))
                     {
                         return SF_STATUS_REQ_ERROR;
                     }
              }
              //
              // Pass the possibly changed header to the next filter in the chain
```

```
            //

    return SF_STATUS_REQ_NEXT_NOTIFICATION;
}
```

DIVECALC

```
<!-- DIVECALC.HTM -->
<HTML>
<HEAD>
<TITLE>Interactive Dive Calculator</TITLE>
<SCRIPT LANGUAGE="VBScript">
<!--
Dim intTable(25,6)
Dim strVals(25)
strVals(0)="010,009,007,006,005,004,004"
strVals(1)="019,016,013,011,009,008,007"
strVals(2)="025,022,017,014,012,010,009"
strVals(3)="029,025,019,016,013,011,010"
strVals(4)="032,027,031,017,015,013,011"
strVals(5)="036,031,024,019,016,014,012"
strVals(6)="040,034,026,021,018,015,013"
strVals(7)="044,037,028,023,019,017,015"
strVals(8)="048,040,031,025,021,018,016"
strVals(9)="052,044,033,027,022,019,017"
strVals(10)="057,048,036,029,024,021,018"
strVals(11)="062,051,039,031,026,022,019"
strVals(12)="067,055,041,033,027,023,021"
strVals(13)="073,060,044,035,029,025,022"
strVals(14)="079,064,047,037,031,026,023"
strVals(15)="085,069,050,039,033,028,024"
strVals(16)="092,074,053,042,035,029,025"
strVals(17)="100,079,057,044,036,030,000"
strVals(18)="108,085,060,047,038,000,000"
strVals(19)="117,091,063,049,040,000,000"
strVals(20)="127,097,067,052,000,000,000"
strVals(21)="139,104,071,054,000,000,000"
strVals(22)="152,111,075,055,000,000,000"
strVals(23)="168,120,080,000,000,000,000"
strVals(24)="188,129,000,000,000,000,000"
strVals(25)="205,140,000,000,000,000,000"

for row=0 to 25
        for col=0 to 6
                intTable(row,col)=0
                intTable(row,col)  id(strVals(row),1+col*4,3)
                if (mid(intTable(row,col),1,1)="0") then
                        intTable(row,col)  id(strVals(row),2+col*4,2)
                end if
        next
next

Function CalcPressureGroup(intDepth,intDuration)
        if (intDepth<35) then
                Col=0
        else
```

```
                Col=Int((intDepth-21)/10)
        end if
        bFoundGroup=TRUE
        for Row=0 to 25
                If intTable(Row,Col)=0 Then
                        bFoundGroup=FALSE
                        CalcPressureGroup=26
                end if
                If intDuration<=intTable(Row,Col) then
                        CalcPressureGroup=Row
                        Row=26
                        bFoundGroup=TRUE
                end if
        next
        if (bFoundGroup=FALSE) then
                CalcPressureGroup=26
        end if
End Function

Sub Depth_OnChange
        Dim TheForm
        Set TheForm=Document.DiveCalcForm
        If Not IsNumeric(TheForm.Depth.Value) Then
                MsgBox "Please enter depth as a number"
        Else
                If TheForm.Depth.Value > 100 Then
                        MsgBox "Too deep for me!"
                End If
        End If
End Sub

Sub Duration_OnChange
        Dim TheForm
        Set TheForm=Document.DiveCalcForm
        If Not IsNumeric(TheForm.Duration.Value) Then
                MsgBox "Please enter duration as a number"
        End If
End Sub

Sub Submit_OnClick()
        Dim TheForm
        Set TheForm=Document.DiveCalcForm
        intDepth = TheForm.Depth.Value
        intDuration = TheForm.Duration.Value
        intPressureGroup = CalcPressureGroup(intDepth,intDuration)
        if (intPressureGroup > 25) then
                MsgBox "Too long at depth"
        else
                MsgBox "Pressure Group is " & chr(intPressureGroup+65)
        end if
End Sub

-->
</SCRIPT>
</HEAD>
<BODY>
```

```
<H2>Web-Based Recreational Dive Planner</H2>
<FORM NAME="DiveCalcForm">
<I>You must be running Internet Explorer 3.0 or another browser that supports
VBScriptto use this calculator.</I><p>
depth (in feet): <INPUT NAME="Depth"><BR>
duration (in minutes): <INPUT NAME="Duration"><BR>
<INPUT NAME="Submit" TYPE="Button" VALUE="Compute Pressure Group">
</FORM>
</BODY>
</HTML>
```

OPLIONS

This is the Java source and embedding HTML page for the options value calculator example presented in chapter 11.

OPTIONS.JAVA

```
//****************************************************************************
// options.java:    Applet
//
//****************************************************************************
import java.applet.*;
import java.awt.*;

import IDD_OPTIONS;

//============================================================================
// Main Class for applet options
//
//============================================================================
public class options extends Applet
{

        private IDD_OPTIONS dlg;

        // PARAMETER SUPPORT:
        //                    Parameters allow an HTML author to pass information to the
Lapplet;
        // the HTML author specifies them using the <PARAM> tag within the <APPLET>
        // tag.  The following variables are used to store the values of the
        // parameters.
    //------------------------------------------------------------------------

    // Members for applet parameters
    // <type>        <memberVar>    = <Default Value>
    //------------------------------------------------------------------------
        private double m_currentStockPrice = 0.0;
        private double m_strikePrice = 0.0;
        private double m_stockPriceVariance = 0.0;
        private double m_riskFreeRate = 0.0;
        private double m_timeUntilExpiration = 0.0;
```

```
        // Parameter names.  To change a name of a parameter, you need only make
        //      a single change.  Simply modify the value of the parameter string below.
        //-------------------------------------------------------------------------
        private final String PARAM_currentStockPrice = "currentStockPrice";
        private final String PARAM_strikePrice = "strikePrice";
        private final String PARAM_stockPriceVariance = "stockPriceVariance";
        private final String PARAM_riskFreeRate = "riskFreeRate";
        private final String PARAM_timeUntilExpiration = "timeUntilExpiration";

        // options Class Constructor
        //-------------------------------------------------------------------------
        public options()
        {
                // TODO: Add constructor code here
        }

        // APPLET INFO SUPPORT:
        //              The getAppletInfo() method returns a string describing the
applet's
        // author, copyright date, or miscellaneous information.
        //-------------------------------------------------------------------------
        public String getAppletInfo()
        {
            return "Name: options\r\n" +
                "Author: Adam Blum\r\n" +
                "Created with Microsoft Visual J++ Version 1.0";
        }

        // PARAMETER SUPPORT
        //              The getParameterInfo() method returns an array of strings
describing
        // the parameters understood by this applet.
        //
    // options Parameter Information:
    //  { "Name", "Type", "Description" },
    //-------------------------------------------------------------------------
        public String[][] getParameterInfo()
        {
                String[][] info =
                {
                        { PARAM_currentStockPrice, "double", "current price of
underlying" },
                        { PARAM_strikePrice, "double", "exercise price of option" },
                        { PARAM_stockPriceVariance, "double", "(std. dev of
stock)squared" },
                        { PARAM_riskFreeRate, "double", "T-bill interest rate" },
                        { PARAM_timeUntilExpiration, "double", "time (in years) until
expiration" },
                };
                return info;
        }

        // The init() method is called by the AWT when an applet is first loaded or
        // reloaded. Override this method to perform whatever initialization your
        // applet needs, such as initializing data structures, loading images or
        // fonts, creating frame windows, setting the layout manager, or adding UI
```

```
        // components.
  //----------------------------------------------------------------------
      public void init()
      {

            // PARAMETER SUPPORT
            //                      The following code retrieves the value of each
└parameter
            // specified with the <PARAM> tag and stores it in a member
            // variable.
            //------------------------------------------------------------------
            String param;

            // currentStockPrice: current price of underlying
            //------------------------------------------------------------------
            param = getParameter(PARAM_currentStockPrice);
            if (param != null)
                    m_currentStockPrice = Double.valueOf(param).doubleValue();

            // strikePrice: exercise price of option
            //------------------------------------------------------------------
            param = getParameter(PARAM_strikePrice);
            if (param != null)
                    m_strikePrice = Double.valueOf(param).doubleValue();

            // stockPriceVariance: (std. dev of stock)squared
            //------------------------------------------------------------------
            param = getParameter(PARAM_stockPriceVariance);
            if (param != null)
                    m_stockPriceVariance = Double.valueOf(param).doubleValue();

            // riskFreeRate: T-bill interest rate
            //------------------------------------------------------------------
            param = getParameter(PARAM_riskFreeRate);
            if (param != null)
                    m_riskFreeRate = Double.valueOf(param).doubleValue();

            // timeUntilExpiration: time (in years) until expiration
            //------------------------------------------------------------------
            param = getParameter(PARAM_timeUntilExpiration);
            if (param != null)
                    m_timeUntilExpiration = Double.valueOf(param).doubleValue();

    // If you use a ResourceWizard-generated "control creator" class to
    // arrange controls in your applet, you may want to call its
    // CreateControls() method from within this method. Remove the following
    // call to resize() before adding the call to CreateControls().
    // CreateControls() does its own resizing.
    //------------------------------------------------------------------
                dlg = new IDD_OPTIONS(this);
                dlg.CreateControls();

                // TODO: Place additional initialization code here
                if (m_currentStockPrice!=0){
                        dlg.IDC_CURPRICE.setText(String.valueOf(m_currentStockPrice));
```

```
                    }

          }

          // Place additional applet clean up code here. destroy() is called when
          // when you applet is terminating and being unloaded.
          //----------------------------------------------------------------------
          public void destroy()
          {
                    // TODO: Place applet cleanup code here
          }

          // options Paint Handler
          //----------------------------------------------------------------------
          public void paint(Graphics g)
          {
          }

          //                    The start() method is called when the page containing the
applet
          // first appears on the screen. The AppletWizard's initial implementation
          // of this method starts execution of the applet's thread.
          //----------------------------------------------------------------------
          public void start()
          {
                    // TODO: Place additional applet start code here
          }

          //                    The stop() method is called when the page containing the
applet is
          // no longer on the screen. The AppletWizard's initial implementation of
          // this method stops execution of the applet's thread.
          //----------------------------------------------------------------------
          public void stop()
          {
          }

          // TODO: Place additional applet code here
          public boolean action(Event evt,Object arg)
          {
                    if (evt.target instanceof Button){
                              computeOptionValue();
                    }
                    return true;
          }

          public boolean computeOptionValue()
          {
//         grab values from following fields
//         TextField    IDC_CURPRICE;
//         TextField    IDC_STRIKEPRICE;
//         TextField    IDC_STOCKPRICEVARIANCE;
//         TextField    IDC_RISKFREERATE;
//         TextField    IDC_TIMEUNTILEXPIRATION;
                    double currentPrice=(Double.valueOf(dlg.IDC_CURPRICE.getText())).
doubleValue();
```

```
                double strikePrice=(Double.valueOf(dlg.IDC_STRIKEPRICE.getText())).
↳doubleValue();
                double stockPriceVariance=(Double.valueOf(dlg.IDC_STOCKPRICEVARIANCE.
↳getText())).doubleValue();
                double timeUntilExpiration=(Double.valueOf(dlg.IDC_TIMEUNTILEXPIRATION.
↳getText())).doubleValue();
                double riskFreeRate=(Double.valueOf(dlg.IDC_RISKFREERATE.getText())).
↳doubleValue();
                double optionValue=doBlackScholes(currentPrice,
                                        strikePrice,
                                        stockPriceVariance,
                                        timeUntilExpiration,
                                        riskFreeRate);
                dlg.IDC_LBLOPTIONVALUE.setText("Option value: " + String.valueOf
↳(optionValue));
                return true;
        }

        /* doBlackScholes
         Compute option value based on following formula:
                V=currentPrice*^[N(d1)]-strikePrice*E^(-riskFreeRate*timeUntil
↳Expiration)*N(d2)
                        where
                d1=1n(currentPrice/strikePrice)+(riskFreeRate+stockPriceVariance/2)
↳*timeUntilExpiration
                d2=d1 - sqrt(stockPriceVariance*timeUntilExpiration)
        */
        public double doBlackScholes(double currentPrice,
                                        double strikePrice,
                                        double stockPriceVariance,
                                        double timeUntilExpiration, //
↳in fraction of year!
                                        double riskFreeRate)
        {
                double d1=(Math.log(currentPrice/strikePrice)+(riskFreeRate+stockPrice
↳Variance/2)*timeUntilExpiration)
                                / (Math.sqrt(stockPriceVariance)* Math.sqrt
↳(timeUntilExpiration));

                double d2=d1-Math.sqrt(stockPriceVariance)*Math.sqrt
↳(timeUntilExpiration);
                double stockPriceValue=currentPrice*probZ(d1);
                stockPriceValue=stockPriceValue - strikePrice*Math.pow
↳(Math.E,-riskFreeRate*timeUntilExpiration)*probZ(d2);
                return stockPriceValue;
        }

        /* factorial
                computes n! where n! = n(n-1)(n-2)...
                e.g. 0! = 1, 1! = 1, 2! = 2, 3! = 6, 4 != 24
        */
        private int factorial(int value)
        {
                if (value==0)
                        return 1;
                int result=value;
```

```
                        while (--value>0)
                                result*=value;
                return result;
        }

        /* probZ
        Computes probability that deviation less than Z value will occur in standard
⌞normal
        distribution. You can get this from the appendix of any stat book
        but since we didn't want to type in the whole table, we had to get a formula
        for it which is:
                        P(z)=1/2 + 1/sqrt(2*PI) sum(0 to infinity)[(-1^n*x^(2n+1))/
⌞(n!*2^n*(2n+1))]
        Thanks to John D. Kettelle for providing the the series approximation
        for this summation (eliminating that unpleasant task of summing to infinity -
        always a pain on x86 class computers).
        */

        private double probZ(double Zvalue)
        {
                double PI=3.14159265358979323846338950; // or thereabouts
                double result=0,term;
                for (int n=0;;n++){
                        term=(Math.pow(-1,n)*Math.pow(Zvalue,2*n+1));
                        term = term/(factorial(n)*Math.pow(2,n)*(2*n+1));
                        result = result + term;
                        if (Math.abs(term) < 0.000001)
                                break;
                }
                result = result/ Math.sqrt(2*PI);
                result = result + 0.5;
                return result;
        }

}
```

IDD_OPTIONS.JAVA

```
//-----------------------------------------------------------------------------
// IDD_OPTIONS.java:
//              Implementation of "control creator" class IDD_OPTIONS
//-----------------------------------------------------------------------------
import java.awt.*;
import DialogLayout;

public class IDD_OPTIONS
{
        Container       m_Parent        = null;
        boolean         m_fInitialized = false;
        DialogLayout m_Layout;

        // Control definitions
        //---------------------------------------------------------------------
        TextField       IDC_CURPRICE;
        TextField       IDC_STRIKEPRICE;
        TextField       IDC_STOCKPRICEVARIANCE;
```

```
TextField      IDC_RISKFREERATE;
TextField      IDC_TIMEUNTILEXPIRATION;
Button         IDCOMPUTE;
Button         IDCANCEL;
Label          IDC_STATIC1;
Label          IDC_STATIC2;
Label          IDC_STATIC3;
Label          IDC_STATIC4;
Label          IDC_STATIC5;
Label          IDC_LBLOPTIONVALUE;

// Constructor
//---------------------------------------------------------------------
public IDD_OPTIONS (Container parent)
{
      m_Parent = parent;
}

// Initialization.
//---------------------------------------------------------------------
public boolean CreateControls()
{
      // CreateControls should be called only once
      //-------------------------------------------------------------
      if (m_fInitialized || m_Parent == null)
            return false;

      // m_Parent must be extended from the Container class
      //-------------------------------------------------------------
      if (!(m_Parent instanceof Container))
            return false;

      // Since a given font may not be supported across all platforms, it
      // is safe to modify only the size of the font, not the typeface.
      //-------------------------------------------------------------
   Font OldFnt = m_Parent.getFont();
   if (OldFnt != null)
   {
            Font NewFnt = new Font(OldFnt.getName(), OldFnt.getStyle(), 8);

      m_Parent.setFont(NewFnt);
   }

      // All position and sizes are in dialog logical units, so we use a
      // DialogLayout as our layout manager.
      //-------------------------------------------------------------
      m_Layout = new DialogLayout(m_Parent, 186, 108);
      m_Parent.setLayout(m_Layout);
      m_Parent.addNotify();

      Dimension size   = m_Layout.getDialogSize();
      Insets    insets = m_Parent.insets();

      m_Parent.resize(insets.left + size.width + insets.right,
            insets.top + size.height + insets.bottom);

      // Control creation
```

```
    //---------------------------------------------------------------------
    IDC_CURPRICE = new TextField ("");
    m_Parent.add(IDC_CURPRICE);
    m_Layout.setShape(IDC_CURPRICE, 56, 14, 38, 14);

    IDC_STRIKEPRICE = new TextField ("");
    m_Parent.add(IDC_STRIKEPRICE);
    m_Layout.setShape(IDC_STRIKEPRICE, 56, 28, 38, 14);

    IDC_STOCKPRICEVARIANCE = new TextField ("");
    m_Parent.add(IDC_STOCKPRICEVARIANCE);
    m_Layout.setShape(IDC_STOCKPRICEVARIANCE, 55, 41, 38, 14);

    IDC_RISKFREERATE = new TextField ("");
    m_Parent.add(IDC_RISKFREERATE);
    m_Layout.setShape(IDC_RISKFREERATE, 57, 57, 38, 14);

    IDC_TIMEUNTILEXPIRATION = new TextField ("");
    m_Parent.add(IDC_TIMEUNTILEXPIRATION);
    m_Layout.setShape(IDC_TIMEUNTILEXPIRATION, 57, 68, 38, 14);

    IDCOMPUTE = new Button ("Compute");
    m_Parent.add(IDCOMPUTE);
    m_Layout.setShape(IDCOMPUTE, 129, 15, 50, 14);

    IDCANCEL = new Button ("Cancel");
    m_Parent.add(IDCANCEL);
    m_Layout.setShape(IDCANCEL, 129, 36, 50, 14);

    IDC_STATIC1 = new Label ("Stock Price", Label.LEFT);
    m_Parent.add(IDC_STATIC1);
    m_Layout.setShape(IDC_STATIC1, 7, 17, 38, 8);

    IDC_STATIC2 = new Label ("Strike Price", Label.LEFT);
    m_Parent.add(IDC_STATIC2);
    m_Layout.setShape(IDC_STATIC2, 7, 30, 37, 8);

    IDC_STATIC3 = new Label ("Variance", Label.LEFT);
    m_Parent.add(IDC_STATIC3);
    m_Layout.setShape(IDC_STATIC3, 7, 43, 37, 8);

    IDC_STATIC4 = new Label ("Risk Free Rate", Label.LEFT);
    m_Parent.add(IDC_STATIC4);
    m_Layout.setShape(IDC_STATIC4, 7, 57, 48, 8);

    IDC_STATIC5 = new Label ("Time Interval", Label.LEFT);
    m_Parent.add(IDC_STATIC5);
    m_Layout.setShape(IDC_STATIC5, 7, 70, 48, 8);

    IDC_LBLOPTIONVALUE = new Label ("", Label.LEFT);
    m_Parent.add(IDC_LBLOPTIONVALUE);
    m_Layout.setShape(IDC_LBLOPTIONVALUE, 7, 87, 120, 8);

    m_fInitialized = true;
    return true;
    }
}
```

DIALOGLAYOUT.JAVA

```java
// This is a part of the Microsoft Visual J++ library.
// Copyright (C) 1996 Microsoft Corporation
// All rights reserved.

//package java.awt;

import java.util.Hashtable;
import java.awt.LayoutManager;
import java.awt.Component;
import java.awt.Container;
import java.awt.Dimension;
import java.awt.Rectangle;
import java.awt.FontMetrics;
import java.awt.Insets;
import java.awt.Label;
//
// class DialogLayout
//
// DialogLayout is a simple layout manager which works with what the Win32
// API calls "dialog logical units" (DLUs). DLUs are resolution independent
// coordinates which work well for laying out controls on a dialog box. The
// mapping from DLUs to pixels is based on the font in use in the dialog box.
// An x-coordinate DLU is described as 1/4 (.25) of the of the average character
// width of the font used in the dialog. A y-coordinate DLU is described as
// 1/8 (.125) of the character height used in the dialog. One tricky issue to
// note: The average character width is not the average of all characters --
// rather it is the average of all alpha characters both uppercase and
// lowercase. That is, it is the extent of the string "a...zA...Z" divided
// by 52.
//
// This class allows you to associate a Rectangle (x, y, width, height) with a
// Component in a Container. If called upon to layout the container, this
// layout manager will layout based on the translation of dialog units to
// pixels.
//

public class DialogLayout
       implements LayoutManager
{
       protected Hashtable m_map = new Hashtable();
       protected int m_width;
       protected int m_height;

       // DialogLayout methods
       public DialogLayout(Container parent, int width, int height)
       {
              Construct(parent, width, height);
       }

       public DialogLayout(Container parent, Dimension d)
       {
              Construct(parent, d.width, d.height);
       }

       public void setShape(Component comp, int x, int y, int width, int height)
```

```
    {
            m_map.put(comp, new Rectangle(x, y, width, height));
    }

    public void setShape(Component comp, Rectangle rect)
    {
            m_map.put(comp, new Rectangle(rect.x, rect.y, rect.width, rect.height));
    }

    public Rectangle getShape(Component comp)
    {
            Rectangle rect = (Rectangle)m_map.get(comp);
            return new Rectangle(rect.x, rect.y, rect.width, rect.height);
    }

    public Dimension getDialogSize()
    {
            return new Dimension(m_width, m_height);
    }
    // LayoutManager Methods

    public void addLayoutComponent(String name, Component comp) { }
    public void removeLayout Component(Component comp) { }

    public Dimension preferredLayoutSize(Container parent)
    {
            return new Dimension(m_width, m_height);
    }

    public Dimension minimumLayoutSize(Container parent)
    {
            return new Dimension(m_width, m_height);
    }

    public void layoutContainer(Container parent)
    {
            int count = parent.countComponents();
            Rectangle rect = new Rectangle();
            int charHeight = getCharHeight(parent);
            int charWidth = getCharWidth(parent);
            Insets insets = parent.insets();
            FontMetrics m = parent.getFontMetrics(parent.getFont());

            for (int i = 0; i < count; i++)
            {
                    Component c = parent.getComponent(i);
                    Rectangle r = (Rectangle)m_map.get(c);
                    if (r != null)
                    {
                            rect.x = r.x;
                            rect.y = r.y;
                            rect.height = r.height;
                            rect.width = r.width;
                            mapRectangle(rect, charWidth, charHeight);
                            if (c instanceof Label)
                            {
```

```
                                    // Adjusts for space at left of Java labels.
                                    rect.x      -= 12;
                                    rect.width += 12;
                             }

                      rect.x += insets.left;
                      rect.y += insets.top;
                      c.reshape(rect.x, rect.y, rect.width, rect.height);
              }
       }
}

// Implementation Helpers

protected void Construct(Container parent, int width, int height)
{
       Rectangle rect = new Rectangle(0, 0, width, height);
       mapRectangle(rect, getCharWidth(parent), getCharHeight(parent));
       m_width = rect.width;
       m_height = rect.height;
}
protected int getCharWidth(Container parent)
{
       FontMetrics m = parent.getFontMetrics(parent.getFont());
       String s      = "abcdefghijklmnopqrstuvwxyzABCDEFGHIJKLMNOPQRSTUVWXYZ";
       int    width = m.stringWidth(s) / s.length();

       if (width <= 0)
              width = 1;
       return width;
}

protected int getCharHeight(Container parent)
{
       FontMetrics m = parent.getFontMetrics(parent.getFont());
       int height = m.getHeight();
       return height;
}

protected void mapRectangle(Rectangle rect, int charWidth, int charHeight)
{
       rect.x      = (rect.x      * charWidth)  / 4;
       rect.y      = (rect.y      * charHeight) / 8;
       rect.width  = (rect.width  * charWidth)  / 4;
       rect.height = (rect.height * charHeight) / 8;
}
}
```

OPTIONS.HTML

```
<html>
<head>
<title>options</title>
</head>
<body>
<hr>
```

```
<applet
    code=options.class
    id=options
    width=320
    height=240 >
    <param name=currentStockPrice value=0.0>
    <param name=strikePrice value=0.0>
    <param name=stockPriceVariance value=0.0>
    <param name=riskFreeRate value=0.08>
    <param name imeUntilExpiration value=0.5>
</applet>
<hr>
<a href="options.java">The source.</a>
</body>
</html>
```

OLEMSG

OLEMSG.JAVA

```java
//****************************************************************************
// OLEMSG.java:        Applet
//
//****************************************************************************
import java.applet.*;
import java.awt.*;

import com.ms.com.*;
import mdisp32.*;

//============================================================================
// Main Class for applet OLEMSG
//
//============================================================================
public class OLEMSG extends Applet
{
        private IDD_SENDMSG dlg;

        // PARAMETER SUPPORT:
        //                Parameters allow an HTML author to pass information to the applet;
        // the HTML author specifies them using the <PARAM> tag within the <APPLET>
        // tag. The following variables are used to store the values of the
        // parameters.
    //------------------------------------------------------------------------

        // Members for applet parameters
        // <type>          <MemberVar>     = <Default Value>
        //------------------------------------------------------------------------
        private String m_Recipient = "";
        private String m_Subject = "";
        private String m_Body = "";
        private int m_Options = 0;
        private int m_Priority = 0;
```

```
// Parameter names. To change a name of a parameter, you need only make
// a single change. Simply modify the value of the parameter string below.
//------------------------------------------------------------------------
    private final String PARAM_Recipient = "Recipient";
    private final String PARAM_Subject   = "Subject";
    private final String PARAM_Body          = "Body";
    private final String PARAM_Options   = "Options";
    private final String PARAM_Priority = "Priority";

    // OLEMSG Class Constructor
    //--------------------------------------------------------------------
    public OLEMSG()
    {
          // TODO: Add constructor code here
    }

    // APPLET INFO SUPPORT:
    //          The getAppletInfo() method returns a string describing the applet's
    // author, copyright date, or miscellaneous information.
//------------------------------------------------------------------------
    public String getAppletInfo()
    {
          return "Name: OLEMSG\r\n" +
                 "Author: Adam Blum\r\n" +
                 "Created with Microsoft Visual J++ Version 1.0";
    }
    // PARAMETER SUPPORT
    //             The getParameterInfo() method returns an array of strings describing
    // the parameters understood by this applet.
    //
// OLEMSG Parameter Information:
//  { "Name", "Type", "Description" },
    //--------------------------------------------------------------------
    public String[][] getParameterInfo()
    {
          String[][] info =
          {
                { PARAM_Recipient, "String", "recipient of message" },
                { PARAM_Subject, "String", "subject of message" },
                { PARAM_Body, "String", "body of message" },
                { PARAM_Options, "int", "message options (e.g. Receipt report)" },
                { PARAM_Priority, "int", "1 means high" },
          };
          return info;
    }

    // The init() method is called by the AWT when an applet is first loaded or
    // reloaded.  Override this method to perform whatever initialization your
    // applet needs, such as initializing data structures, loading images or
    // fonts, creating frame windows, setting the layout manager, or adding UI
    // components.
//------------------------------------------------------------------------
    public void init()
    {
          // PARAMETER SUPPORT
          //                 The following code retrieves the value of each parameter
```

```java
        // specified with the <PARAM> tag and stores it in a member
        // variable.
        //----------------------------------------------------------------------
        String param;

        // Recipient: recipient of message
        //----------------------------------------------------------------------
        param = getParameter(PARAM_Recipient);
        if (param != null)
              m_Recipient = param;

        // Subject: subject of message
        //----------------------------------------------------------------------
        param = getParameter(PARAM_Subject);
        if (param != null)
              m_Subject = param;

        // Body: body of message
        //----------------------------------------------------------------------
        param = getParameter(PARAM_Body);
        if (param != null)
              m_Body = param;

        // Options: message options (e.g. Receipt report)
        //----------------------------------------------------------------------
        param = getParameter(PARAM_Options);
        if (param != null)
              m_Options = Integer.parseInt(param);

        // Priority: 1 means high
        //----------------------------------------------------------------------
        param = getParameter(PARAM_Priority);
        if (param != null)
              m_Priority = Integer.parseInt(param);

    // If you use a ResourceWizard-generated "control creator" class to
    // arrange controls in your applet, you may want to call its
    // CreateControls() method from within this method. Remove the following
    // call to resize() before adding the call to CreateControls();
    // CreateControls() does its own resizing.
    //----------------------------------------------------------------------
        dlg = new IDD_SENDMSG(this);
        dlg.CreateControls();

        // TODO: Place additional initialization code here
}

// Place additional applet clean up code here.  destroy() is called when
// when you applet is terminating and being unloaded.
//----------------------------------------------------------------------
public void destroy()
{
        // TODO: Place applet cleanup code here
}

// OLEMSG Paint Handler
```

```
        //-------------------------------------------------------------------------
        public void paint(Graphics g)
        {
//              g.drawString("Created with Microsoft Visual J++ Version 1.0", 10, 20);
        }

        //              The start() method is called when the page containing the applet
        // first appears on the screen. The AppletWizard's initial implementation
        // of this method starts execution of the applet's thread.
        //-------------------------------------------------------------------------
        public void start()
        {
                // TODO: Place additional applet start code here
        }

        //              The stop() method is called when the page containing the applet is
        // no longer on the screen. The AppletWizard's initial implementation of
        // this method stops execution of the applet's thread.
        //-------------------------------------------------------------------------
        public void stop()
        {
        }

        // TODO: Place additional applet code here
        public boolean action(Event evt,Object arg)
        {
                // handle button events
                if (evt.target instanceof Button) {
                        if (((String)arg).equals("Send"))
                                sendMsg();
                }
                return true;
        }

        public boolean sendMsg()
        {
                String recipient=dlg.IDC_RECIPIENT.getText();
                String subject=dlg.IDC_SUBJECT.getText();
                String body=dlg.IDC_BODY.getText();
                boolean result=doOLEMsgSend(recipient,subject,body);
                dlg.IDC_RECIPIENT.setText("");
                dlg.IDC_SUBJECT.setText("");
                dlg.IDC_BODY.setText("");
                return true;
        }
        private boolean doOLEMsgSend(String recipient,String subject,String body)
        {
                Session session;
                session = (Session)new _MAPIDispSession();
                session.getVersion();
                Variant opt = new Variant();
                opt.noParam();
                Variant varProfile=new Variant();
                varProfile.putString("MS Exchange Settings");
                try {
                        session.Logon(varProfile,opt,opt,opt,opt);
```

```
                    Folder outbox = (Folder) session.getOutbox();
                    Messages messages = (Messages) outbox.getMessages();
                    Variant varSubject=new Variant();
                    Variant varBody=new Variant();
                    varSubject.putString(subject);
                    varBody.putString(body);
                    Message message = (Message) messages.Add(varSubject,varBody,opt,opt);
                    Variant varRecip=new Variant();
                    Recipients recips = (Recipients) message.getRecipients();
                    varRecip.putString(recipient);
                    Recipient recip=(Recipient)recips.Add(varRecip,opt,opt,opt);
                    recip.Resolve(opt);
                    message.Update(opt,opt);
                    message.Send(opt,opt,opt);
                    session.Logoff();
            }
            catch (com.ms.com.ComFailException e)
            {
                    String errMsg;
                    errMsg = e.getMessage();
                    dlg.IDC_SUBJECT.setText(errMsg);
            }
            return true;
        }

}
```

IDD_SENDMSG.JAVA

```java
//-----------------------------------------------------------------------------
// IDD_SENDMSG.java:
//          Implementation of "control creator" class IDD_SENDMSG
//-----------------------------------------------------------------------------
import java.awt.*;
import DialogLayout;

public class IDD_SENDMSG
{
        Container     m_Parent       = null;
        boolean       m_fInitialized = false;
        DialogLayout m_Layout;

        // Control definitions
        //-----------------------------------------------------------------------
        Button        IDSEND;
        Button        IDCANCEL;
        TextField     IDC_RECIPIENT;
        TextField     IDC_SUBJECT;
        TextField     IDC_BODY;
        Label          IDC_LBLTO;
        Label          IDC_LBLSUBJECT;
// Constructor
//-----------------------------------------------------------------------
public IDD_SENDMSG (Container parent)
{
        m_Parent = parent;
```

```
}

// Initialization.
//-------------------------------------------------------------------------
public boolean CreateControls()
{
        // CreateControls should be called only once
        //-----------------------------------------------------------------
        if (m_fInitialized || m_Parent == null)
                return false;

        // m_Parent must be extended from the Container class
        //-----------------------------------------------------------------
        if (!(m_Parent instanceof Container))
                return false;

        // Since a given font may not be supported across all platforms, it
        // is safe to modify only the size of the font, not the typeface.
        //-----------------------------------------------------------------
    Font OldFnt = m_Parent.getFont();
    if (OldFnt != null)
    {
            Font NewFnt = new Font(OldFnt.getName(), OldFnt.getStyle(), 8);
        m_Parent.setFont(NewFnt);
    }

        // All position and sizes are in dialog logical units, so we use a
        // DialogLayout as our layout manager.
        //-----------------------------------------------------------------
        m_Layout = new DialogLayout(m_Parent, 222, 121);
        m_Parent.setLayout(m_Layout);
        m_Parent.addNotify();

        Dimension size   = m_Layout.getDialogSize();
        Insets    insets = m_Parent.insets();

        m_Parent.resize(insets.left + size.width + insets.right,
                    insets.top + size.height + insets.bottom);

        // Control creation
        //-----------------------------------------------------------------
        IDSEND = new Button ("Send");
        m_Parent.add(IDSEND);
        m_Layout.setShape(IDSEND, 10, 100, 50, 14);

        IDCANCEL = new Button ("Cancel");
        m_Parent.add(IDCANCEL);
        m_Layout.setShape(IDCANCEL, 70, 100, 50, 14);

        IDC_RECIPIENT = new TextField ("");
        m_Parent.add(IDC_RECIPIENT);
        m_Layout.setShape(IDC_RECIPIENT, 40, 5, 40, 14);

                IDC_LBLTO = new Label ("To", Label.LEFT);
                m_Parent.add(IDC_LBLTO);
                m_Layout.setShape(IDC_LBLTO, 10, 10, 10, 8);
```

```
                IDC_LBLSUBJECT = new Label ("Subject", Label.LEFT);
                m_Parent.add(IDC_LBLSUBJECT);
                m_Layout.setShape(IDC_LBLSUBJECT, 10, 25, 25, 8);

                IDC_SUBJECT = new TextField ("");
                m_Parent.add(IDC_SUBJECT);
                m_Layout.setShape(IDC_SUBJECT, 40, 20, 40, 14);

                IDC_BODY = new TextField ("");
                m_Parent.add(IDC_BODY);
                m_Layout.setShape(IDC_BODY, 10, 40, 200, 55);

                m_fInitialized = true;
                return true;
        }
}
```

OLEMSG.HTML

```html
<html>
<head>
<title>OLEMSG</title>
</head>
<body>
<hr>
<applet
    code=OLEMSG.class
    id=OLEMSG
    width=320
    height=240 >
    <param name=Recipient value="">
    <param name=Subject value="">
    <param name=Body value="">
    <param name=Options value=0>
    <param name=Priority value=0>
</applet>
<hr>
<a href="OLEMSG.java">The source.</a>
</body>
</html>
```

SHOPBSKT

```asp
<SCRIPT LANGUAGE=VBScript RUNAT=Server>
</SCRIPT>
<%
If IsObject(Session("Conn")) Then
      Set Conn=Session("Conn")
Else
      Set Conn=Server.CreateObject("ADO.Connection")
      Ret=Conn.Open("COMMERCE","sa","")
      Session("Conn") = Conn
```

```
End If

If Not IsEmpty(Session("Items")) Then
     nItems = Session("Items")
Else
     nItems = 0
     Session("Items") Items
End If

If Not IsEmpty(Session("Basket")) Then
     Basket = Session("Basket")
Else
     Dim Basket(10,2)
     Session("Basket")=Basket
End If

If IsNull(Basket(1,1)) Then

     nItems=0
End If

If Request("partnum")<>"" Then
     nItems = nItems+1
     Session("Items") Items
     Basket(nItems,1)=Request("partnum")
     Basket(nItems,2)=1
     Session("Basket")=Basket
End If

SELECT CASE Request("Action")

CASE "RECALC"
     For i = 1 to nItems
          If IsNumeric(Request("Quantity" & CStr(i))) Then
               Basket(i,2) = Request("Quantity" & CStr(i))
          Else
               Basket(i,2) = 1
          End If
     Next
     Session("Basket") = Basket
     Session("Items") = nItems

CASE "SHOP MORE"
     For i = 1 to nItems
          If IsNumeric(Request("Quantity" & CStr(i))) Then
               Basket(i,2) = Request("Quantity" & CStr(i))
               Else
               Basket(i,2) = 1
          End If
     Next
     Session("Basket") = Basket
     Response.Redirect "/commerce/prodlist.asp"

CASE "CANCEL"
     nItems = 0
     Session("Items") = nItems
     Response.Redirect "/commerce/prodlist.asp"
```

```
CASE "PURCHASE"
      For i = 1 to nItems
            If IsNumeric(Request("Quantity" & CStr(i))) Then
                  Basket(i,2) = Request("Quantity" & CStr(i))
            Else
                  Basket(i,2) = 1
            End If
      Next
      Session("Basket") = Basket
      Response.Redirect "/commerce/shipping.asp"
CASE ELSE

END SELECT

%>
<HTML>
<HEAD>
<TITLE>Shopping Basket</TITLE>
</HEAD>
<BODY>
<FORM ACTION="/commerce/shopbskt.asp?" METHOD=POST>
<TABLE BORDER>
<TR><TH>Product<TH>Price<TH>Quantity
<%
iSubtotal = 0
For i = 1 to nItems
%>

<%
      Cmd="Select * From products Where partnum='" & basket(i,1) & "'"
      Set Conn=Session("Conn")
      Set RS=Conn.Execute(Cmd)
%>
<TR><%=RS("productname")%><TD><%=RS("price")%>
<TD><INPUT NAME=<%Response.Write "Quantity" & CStr(i)%>
VALUE="<%=Basket(i,2)%>">
<%
Subtotal=Subtotal+(CDbl(Basket(i,2))*CDbl(RS("Price")))
Next
%>
<!-- subtotal row -->
<TR>
<TD>-----><TD>Subtotal:<TD><%=Subtotal%>
<!-- buttons row -->
<TR>
<TD>
<INPUT TYPE=SUBMIT NAME="Action" VALUE="RECALC">
<INPUT TYPE=SUBMIT NAME="Action" VALUE="SHOP MORE">
<%If nItems > 0 Then%>
<INPUT TYPE=SUBMIT NAME="Action" VALUE="PURCHASE">
<%End If%>
<INPUT TYPE=SUBMIT NAME="Action" VALUE="CANCEL">
</TABLE>
</FORM>
</BODY>
</HTML>
```

PRODLIST.ASP

```
<!-- PRODLIST.ASP -->
<HTML>
<HEAD>
<TITLE>Product List</TITLE>
</HEAD>
<BODY>
<H1>Select Products</H1>
<%
Set Conn = Server.CreateObject("ADO.Connection")
Ret=Conn.Open("COMMERCE","sa","")
Set RS=Conn.Execute("SELECT * FROM PRODUCTS")
%>
<TABLE BORDER>
<TH>Product Name<TH>Price<TH>Available<TH>Link
<% While Not RS.EOF %>
<TR><%=RS("productname")%>
<TD><%=RS("price")%>
<TD><%=RS("available")%>
<TD><A HREF="/commerce/shopbskt.asp?partnum=<%=RS("partnum")%>">BUY!</A>
<% RS.MoveNext
Wend %>
</BODY>
</HTML>
```

ADDPROD.HTM

```
<!-- ADDPROD.HTM -->
<HTML>
<HEAD>
<TITLE>Product Creation Page</TITLE>
</HEAD>
<BODY>
<H1>Add Product to Database</H1>
<FORM ACTION="/commerce/addprod.asp">
<TABLE>
<TR>Part Number<TD><INPUT NAME="partnum"><BR>
<TR>Name<TD><INPUT NAME="productname"><BR>
<TR>Description<TD><INPUT NAME="proddesc"><BR>
<TR>Manufacturer ID<TD><INPUT NAME="manuid"><BR>
<TR>Manu. Part Number<TD><INPUT NAME="manupn"><BR>
<TR>Price<TD><INPUT NAME="price"><BR>
<TR># Available<TD><INPUT NAME="available"><BR>
<TR><INPUT TYPE="Reset" VALUE="Cancel">
<TD><INPUT TYPE="Submit" VALUE="Add Product">
</FORM>
</BODY>
</HTML>
```

ADDPROD.ASP

```
<!-- ADDPROD.ASP -->
<HTML>
<HEAD>
<TITLE>Product Add Confirmation</TITLE>
</HEAD>
```

```
<BODY>
<H1>Add Product to Database</H1>
<%
Set Conn = Server.CreateObject("ADO.Connection")
Err=Conn.Open("COMMERCE","sa","")
Cmd="INSERT products(partnum,productname,proddesc,manuid,manupn,price,available)
VALUES("
Cmd=Cmd & "'" & Request("partnum") & "','" & Request("productname") & "','"
        & Request("proddesc") & "'," & Request("manuid") & ",'"
        & Request("manupn") & "'," & Request("price")
        & "," & Request("Available") & ")"
Conn.Execute(Cmd)
%>
Successfully added product to database.<P>
<A HREF="/commerce/addprod.htm">Add another product</A><P>
<A HREF="/commerce/prodlist.asp">List products</P>
</BODY>
</HTML>
```

THE ISAPI

SPECIFICATION

AND HEADER FILES

I have been asked on several occasions, when giving seminars on this subject, where people can find the native ISAPI specification and the header files for ISAPI itself. Often this question is from people who are not using Microsoft Visual C++ or are using a version older than Visual C++ 4.1. Another reason is that ISAPI itself has recently been removed from the ActiveX SDK and is now only shipped with the Win32 SDK and with Visual C++ 4.1 or greater. For readers that don't have access to either, the header files are listed here. They are available in electronic form on the Web page for this book: **http://www.wiley.com/compbooks/**.

HTTPEXT.H

```
/********
*
* Copyright (c) 1995 Process Software Corporation
*
* Copyright (c) 1995 Microsoft Corporation
*
```

```
*
* Module Name : HttpExt.h
*
* Abstract :
*
*    This module contains the structure definitions and prototypes for the
*    version 1.0 HTTP Server Extension interface.
*
*****************/

#ifndef _HTTPEXT_H_
#define _HTTPEXT_H_

#include <windows.h>

#ifdef _cplusplus
extern "C" {
#endif
#define    HSE_VERSION_MAJOR            1       // major version of this spec
#define    HSE_VERSION_MINOR            0       // minor version of this spec
#define    HSE_LOG_BUFFER_LEN          80
#define    HSE_MAX_EXT_DLL_NAME_LEN   256

typedef    LPVOID HCONN;

// the following are the status codes returned by the Extension DLL
#define    HSE_STATUS_SUCCESS                    1
#define    HSE_STATUS_SUCCESS_AND_KEEP_CONN      2
#define    HSE_STATUS_PENDING                    3
#define    HSE_STATUS_ERROR                      4

// The following are the values to request services with the ServerSupportFunction.
// Values from 0 to 1000 are reserved for future versions of the interface

#define    HSE_REQ_BASE                          0
#define    HSE_REQ_SEND_URL_REDIRECT_RESP        ( HSE_REQ_BASE + 1 )
#define    HSE_REQ_SEND_URL                      ( HSE_REQ_BASE + 2 )
#define    HSE_REQ_SEND_RESPONSE_HEADER          {HSE_REQ_BASE + 3 )
#define    HSE_REQ_DONE_WITH_SESSION             ( HSE_REQ_BASE + 4 )
#define    HSE_REQ_END_RESERVED                  1000

//
// These are Microsoft specific extensions
//

#define    HSE_REQ_MAP_URL_TO_PATH               (HSE_REQ_END_RESERVED+1)
#define    HSE_REQ_GET_SSPI_INFO                 (HSE_REQ_END_RESERVED+2)

//
// passed to GetExtensionVersion
//

typedef struct    _HSE_VERSION_INFO {

    DWORD dwExtensionVersion;
    CHAR  lpszExtensionDesc[HSE_MAX_EXT_DLL_NAME_LEN];
```

```
} HSE_VERSION_INFO, *LPHSE_VERSION_INFO;

//
// passed to extension procedure on a new request
//
typedef struct _EXTENSION_CONTROL_BLOCK {

    DWORD      cbSize;                  // size of this struct.
    DWORD      dwVersion;              // version info of this spec
    HCONN      ConnID;                 // Context number not to be modified!
    DWORD      dwHttpStatusCode;       // HTTP Status code
    CHAR       lpszLogData[HSE_LOG_BUFFER_LEN];// null terminated log info specific to this
˪Extension DLL

    LPSTR      lpszMethod;             // REQUEST_METHOD
    LPSTR      lpszQueryString;        // QUERY_STRING
    LPSTR      lpszPathInfo;           // PATH_INFO
    LPSTR      lpszPathTranslated;     // PATH_TRANSLATED

    DWORD      cbTotalBytes;           // Total bytes indicated from client
    DWORD      cbAvailable;            // Available number of bytes
    LPBYTE     lpbData;                // pointer to cbAvailable bytes

    LPSTR      lpszContentType;        // Content type of client data

    BOOL (WINAPI * GetServerVariable) ( HCONN      hConn,
                                        LPSTR      lpszVariableName,

                                                              LPVOID        lpvBuffer,
                                        LPDWORD    lpdwSize );

    BOOL (WINAPI * WriteClient) ( HCONN      ConnID,
                                  LPVOID     Buffer,
                                  LPDWORD    lpdwBytes,
                                  DWORD      dwReserved );

    BOOL (WINAPI * ReadClient)  ( HCONN      ConnID,
                                  LPVOID     lpvBuffer,
                                  LPDWORD    lpdwSize );

    BOOL (WINAPI * ServerSupportFunction) ( HCONN      hConn,
                                            DWORD      dwHSERRequest,
                                            LPVOID     lpvBuffer,
                                            LPDWORD    lpdwSize,
                                            LPDWORD    lpdwDataType );

} EXTENSION_CONTROL_BLOCK, *LPEXTENSION_CONTROL_BLOCK;
//
// these are the prototypes that must be exported from the extension DLL
//

BOOL  WINAPI   GetExtensionVersion( HSE_VERSION_INFO *pVer );
DWORD WINAPI   HttpExtensionProc( EXTENSION_CONTROL_BLOCK *pECB );

// the following type declarations is for the server side

typedef BOOL  (WINAPI * PFN_GETEXTENSIONVERSION)( HSE_VERSION_INFO *pVer );
typedef DWORD (WINAPI * PFN_HTTPEXTENSIONPROC )( EXTENSION_CONTROL_BLOCK *pECB );
```

```
#ifdef _cplusplus
}
#endif

#endif // end definition _HTTPEXT_H_
```

HTTPFILT.H

```
/*++
Copyright (c) 1995 Microsoft Corporation
Module Name:
    httpfilt.h
Abstract:
    This module contains the Microsoft HTTP filter extension info
Revision History:
--*/
#ifndef _HTTPFILT_H_
#define _HTTPFILT_H_

#ifdef _cplusplus
extern "C" {
#endif

//
// Current version of the filter spec is 1.0
//

#define HTTP_FILTER_REVISION    MAKELONG( 0, 1);

#define SF_MAX_USERNAME         (256+1)
#define SF_MAX_PASSWORD         (256+1)

#define SF_MAX_FILTER_DESC_LEN  (256+1)

//
// These values can be used with the pfnSFCallback function supplied in
// the filter context structure
//

enum SF_REQ_TYPE
{
    //
    // Sends a complete HTTP server response header including
    // the status, server version,message time and MIME version.
    //
    // Server extensions should append other information at the end,
    // such as Content-type, Content-length etc followed by an extra
    // // '\r\n'.
    // pData - Zero terminated string pointing to optional
    // status string (i.e., "401 Access Denied") or NULL for
    // the default response of "200 OK".
    //
    // ul1 - Zero terminated string pointing to optional data to be
    // appended and set with the header. If NULL, the header will
    // be terminated with an empty line.
```

```
    //

    SF_REQ_SEND_RESPONSE_HEADER,

    //
    // If the server denies the HTTP request, add the specified headers
    // to the server error response.
    //
    // This allows an authentication filter to advertise its services
    // w/o filtering every request. Generally the headers will be
    // WWW-Authenticate headers with custom authentication schemes but
    // no restriction is placed on what headers may be specified.
    //
    // pData - Zero terminated string pointing to one or more header lines
    // with terminating '\r\n'.
    //

    SF_REQ_ADD_HEADERS_ON_DENIAL,
    //
    // Only used by raw data filters that return SF_STATUS_READ_NEXT
    //
    // ul1 - size in bytes for the next read
    //

    SF_REQ_SET_NEXT_READ_SIZE
};

//
// These values are returned by the filter entry point when a new request is
// received indicating their interest in this particular request
//

enum SF_STATUS_TYPE
{
    //
    // The filter has handled the HTTP request. The server should disconnect
    // the session.
    //

    SF_STATUS_REQ_FINISHED = 0x8000000,

    //
    // Same as SF_STATUS_FINISHED except the server should keep the TCP
    // session open if the option was negotiated
    //

    SF_STATUS_REQ_FINISHED_KEEP_CONN,
    //
    // The next filter in the notification chain should be called
    //

    SF_STATUS_REQ_NEXT_NOTIFICATION,

    //
    // This filter handled the notification. No other handles should be
    // called for this particular notification type
    //
```

```
    SF_STATUS_REQ_HANDLED_NOTIFICATION,

    //
    // An error occurred. The server should use GetLastError() and indicate
    // the error to the client
    //

    SF_STATUS_REQ_ERROR,

    //
    // The filter is an opaque stream filter and we're negotiating the
    // session parameters. Only valid for raw read notification.
    //

    SF_STATUS_REQ_READ_NEXT
};

//

// pvNotification points to this structure for all request notification types

//

typedef struct _HTTP_FILTER_CONTEXT
{
    DWORD           cbSize;

    //
    // This is the structure revision level.
    //
    DWORD           Revision;

    //
    // Private context information for the server.
    //

    PVOID           ServerContext;
    DWORD           ulReserved;

    //
    // TRUE if this request is coming over a secure port
    //

    BOOL            fIsSecurePort;

    //
    // A context that can be used by the filter
    //
    PVOID           pFilterContext;

    //
    // Server callbacks
    //

    BOOL (WINAPI * GetServerVariable) (
        struct _HTTP_FILTER_CONTEXT * pfc,
        LPSTR                         lpszVariableName,
```

```
            LPVOID                  lpvBuffer,
            LPDWORD                 lpdwSize
            );

    BOOL (WINAPI * AddResponseHeaders) (
        struct _HTTP_FILTER_CONTEXT * pfc,
        LPSTR                   lpszHeaders,
        DWORD                   dwReserved
        );

    BOOL (WINAPI * WriteClient) (
        struct _HTTP_FILTER_CONTEXT * pfc,
        LPVOID                  Buffer,
        LPDWORD                 lpdwBytes,
        DWORD                   dwReserved
        );

    VOID * (WINAPI * AllocMem) (
        struct _HTTP_FILTER_CONTEXT * pfc,
        DWORD                   cbSize,
        DWORD                   dwReserved
        );

    BOOL (WINAPI * ServerSupportFunction) (
        struct _HTTP_FILTER_CONTEXT * pfc,
        enum SF_REQ_TYPE        sfReq,
        PVOID                   pData,
        DWORD                   ul1,
        DWORD                   ul2
        );

} HTTP_FILTER_CONTEXT, *PHTTP_FILTER_CONTEXT;

//
// This structure is the notification info for the read and send raw data
// notification types
//

typedef struct _HTTP_FILTER_RAW_DATA
{
    //
    // This is a pointer to the data for the filter to process.
    //

    PVOID       pvInData;
    DWORD       cbInData;       // Number of valid data bytes
    DWORD       cbInBuffer;     // Total size of buffer

    DWORD       dwReserved;

} HTTP_FILTER_RAW_DATA, *PHTTP_FILTER_RAW_DATA;
//
// This structure is the notification info for when the server is about to
// process the client headers
//

typedef struct _HTTP_FILTER_PREPROC_HEADERS
```

```
{
    //
    // Retrieves the specified header value. Header names should include
    // the trailing ':'. The special values 'method', 'url' and 'version'
    // can be used to retrieve the individual portions of the request line
    //

    BOOL (WINAPI * GetHeader) (
        struct _HTTP_FILTER_CONTEXT * pfc,
        LPSTR                        lpszName,
        LPVOID                       lpvBuffer,
        LPDWORD                      lpdwSize
        );

    //
    // Replaces this header value to the specified value. To delete a header,
    // specified a value of '\0'.
    //

    BOOL (WINAPI * SetHeader) (
        struct _HTTP_FILTER_CONTEXT * pfc,
        LPSTR                        lpszName,
        LPSTR                        lpszValue
        );

    //
    // Adds the specified header and value
    //

    BOOL (WINAPI * AddHeader) (
        struct _HTTP_FILTER_CONTEXT * pfc,
        LPSTR                        lpszName,
        LPSTR                        lpszValue
        );

    DWORD dwReserved;
} HTTP_FILTER_PREPROC_HEADERS, *PHTTP_FILTER_PREPROC_HEADERS;

//
// Authentication information for this request.
//

typedef struct _HTTP_FILTER_AUTHENT
{
    //
    // Pointer to username and password, empty strings for the anonymous user
    //
    // Client's can overwrite these buffers which are guaranteed to be at
    // least SF_MAX_USERNAME and SF_MAX_PASSWORD bytes large.
    //

    CHAR * pszUser;
    DWORD  cbUserBuff;
    CHAR * pszPassword;
    DWORD  cbPasswordBuff;

} HTTP_FILTER_AUTHENT, *PHTTP_FILTER_AUTHENT;
```

```
//
// Indicates the server is going to use the specific physical mapping for the
// specified URL. Filters can modify the physical path in place.
//

typedef struct _HTTP_FILTER_URL_MAP
{
    const CHAR * pszURL;

    CHAR *      pszPhysicalPath;
    DWORD       cbPathBuff;

} HTTP_FILTER_URL_MAP, *PHTTP_FILTER_URL_MAP;

//
// The log information about to be written to the server log file. The
// string pointers can be replaced but the memory must remain valid until
// the next notification
//

typedef struct _HTTP_FILTER_LOG
{
    const CHAR * pszClientHostName;
    const CHAR * pszClientUserName;
    const CHAR * pszServerName;
    const CHAR * pszOperation;
    const CHAR * pszTarget;
    const CHAR * pszParameters;

    DWORD dwHttpStatus;
    DWORD dwWin32Status;

} HTTP_FILTER_LOG, *PHTTP_FILTER_LOG;

//
// Notification Flags
//
// SF_NOTIFY_SECURE_PORT
// SF_NOTIFY_NONSECURE_PORT
//
//      Indicates whether the application wants to be notified for transactions
//      that are happening on the server port(s) that support data encryption
//      (such as PCT and SSL), on only the non-secure port(s) or both.
//
// SF_NOTIFY_READ_RAW_DATA
//
//      Applications are notified after the server reads a block of memory
//      from the client but before the server does any processing on the
//      block. The data block may contain HTTP headers and entity data.
//
//
//

#define SF_NOTIFY_SECURE_PORT                   0x00000001
#define SF_NOTIFY_NONSECURE_PORT                0x00000002

#define SF_NOTIFY_READ_RAW_DATA                 0x00008000
#define SF_NOTIFY_PREPROC_HEADERS               0x00004000
```

```
#define SF_NOTIFY_AUTHENTICATION              0x00002000
#define SF_NOTIFY_URL_MAP                     0x00001000
#define SF_NOTIFY_SEND_RAW_DATA               0x00000400
#define SF_NOTIFY_LOG                         0x00000200
#define SF_NOTIFY_END_OF_NET_SESSION          0x00000100

//
// Filter ordering flags
//
// Filters will tend to be notified by their specified
// ordering. For ties, notification order is determined by load order.
//
// SF_NOTIFY_ORDER_HIGH - Authentication or data transformation filters
// SF_NOTIFY_ORDER_MEDIUM
// SF_NOTIFY_ORDER_LOW - Logging filters that want the results of any other
// filters might specify this order.
//

#define SF_NOTIFY_ORDER_HIGH                  0x00080000
#define SF_NOTIFY_ORDER_MEDIUM                0x00040000
#define SF_NOTIFY_ORDER_LOW                   0x00020000
#define SF_NOTIFY_ORDER_DEFAULT               SF_NOTIFY_ORDER_LOW

#define SF_NOTIFY_ORDER_MASK                  (SF_NOTIFY_ORDER_HIGH   |  \
                                               SF_NOTIFY_ORDER_MEDIUM |  \
                                               SF_NOTIFY_ORDER_LOW)
//
// Filter version information, passed to GetFilterVersion
//

typedef struct _HTTP_FILTER_VERSION
{
    //
    // Version of the spec the server is using
    //

    DWORD dwServerFilterVersion;

    //
    // Fields specified by the client
    //

    DWORD dwFilterVersion;
    CHAR lpszFilterDesc[SF_MAX_FILTER_DESC_LEN];
    DWORD dwFlags;

} HTTP_FILTER_VERSION, *PHTTP_FILTER_VERSION;

//
// A filter DLL's entry point looks like this. The return code should be
// an SF_STATUS_TYPE
//
// NotificationType - Type of notification
// pvNotification - Pointer to notification specific data
//

DWORD
WINAPI
```

```
HttpFilterProc(
    HTTP_FILTER_CONTEXT *          pfc,
    DWORD                          NotificationType,
    VOID *                         pvNotification
    );

BOOL
WINAPI
GetFilterVersion(
    HTTP_FILTER_VERSION * pVer
    );
#ifdef _cplusplus
}
#endif
#endif //_HTTPFILT_H_
```

AFXISAPI.H

This is the MFC wrapper for ISAPI, also referenced often in the text.

```
// This is a part of the Microsoft Foundation Classes C++ library.
// Copyright (C) 1992-1995 Microsoft Corporation
// All rights reserved.

// This source code is only intended as a supplement to the
// Microsoft Foundation Classes Reference and related
// electronic documentation provided with the library.
// See these sources for detailed information regarding the
// Microsoft Foundation Classes product.

#ifndef _AFXISAPI_H_
#define _AFXISAPI_H_

#ifdef _UNICODE
#error ERROR: ISAPI does not yet support Unicode.
#endif

///////////////////////////////////////////////////////////////////////
// Turn off warnings for /W4
// To resume any of these warning: #pragma warning(default: 4xxx)
// which should be placed after the AFX include files
#ifndef ALL_WARNINGS
// warnings generated with common MFC/Windows code
#pragma warning(disable: 4127) // constant expression for TRACE/ASSERT
#pragma warning(disable: 4134) // message map member fxn casts
#pragma warning(disable: 4201) // nameless unions are part of C++
#pragma warning(disable: 4511) // private copy constructors are good to have
#pragma warning(disable: 4512) // private operator= are good to have
#pragma warning(disable: 4514) // unreferenced inlines are common
#pragma warning(disable: 4710) // private constructors are disallowed
#pragma warning(disable: 4705) // statement has no effect in optimized code
// warnings caused by normal optimizations
#ifndef _DEBUG
```

```
#pragma warning(disable: 4701) // local variable *may* be used without init
#pragma warning(disable: 4702) // unreachable code caused by optimizations
#pragma warning(disable: 4791) // loss of debugging info in retail version
#endif
// warnings specific to _AFXDLL version
#ifdef _AFXDLL
#pragma warning(disable: 4204) // non-constant aggregate initializer
#endif
#ifdef _AFXDLL
#pragma warning(disable: 4275) // deriving exported class from non-exported
#pragma warning(disable: 4251) // using non-exported as public in exported
#endif
#endif //!ALL_WARNINGS

#define STRICT 1

#include <httpext.h>
#include <httpfilt.h>

#ifndef _INC_STDLIB
        #include <stdlib.h>
#endif
#ifndef _INC_TCHAR
        #include <tchar.h>
#endif

#ifndef UNUSED
#ifdef _DEBUG
#define UNUSED(x)
#else
#define UNUSED(x) x
#endif
#endif

#define AFXISAPI _stdcall
#define AFXIS_DATADEF

/////////////////////////////////////////////////////////////////////////
// Internet Server API Library

#ifndef _AFX_NOFORCE_LIBS
#ifndef _MAC

#ifdef _AFXDLL
#ifdef _DEBUG
        #ifdef _UNICODE
                #pragma comment(lib, "MFCISUD.lib")
        #else
                #pragma comment(lib, "EAFXISD.lib")
        #endif
#else
        #ifdef _UNICODE
                #pragma comment(lib, "MFCISU.lib")
        #else
                #pragma comment(lib, "EAFXIS.lib")
        #endif // _UNICODE
```

```
#endif // _DEBUG
#else
#ifdef _DEBUG
        #ifdef _UNICODE
                #pragma comment(lib, "UAFXISD.lib")
        #else
                #pragma comment(lib, "NAFXISD.lib")
        #endif
#else
        #ifdef _UNICODE
                #pragma comment(lib, "UAFXIS.lib")
        #else
                #pragma comment(lib, "NAFXIS.lib")
        #endif // _UNICODE
#endif // _DEBUG
#endif // _AFXDLL

#pragma comment(lib, "kernel32.lib")
#pragma comment(lib, "user32.lib")
#pragma comment(lib, "winspool.lib")
#pragma comment(lib, "advapi32.lib")

#endif // _MAC
#endif // _AFX_NOFORCE_LIBS

extern HINSTANCE AFXISAPI AfxGetResourceHandle();

///////////////////////////////////////////////////////////////////////
// AFXIASPI - MFC Internet Server API support

// Classes declared in this file

class CHtmlStream;
class CHttpServerContext;
class CHttpServer;
class CHttpFilterContext;
class CHttpFilter;

///////////////////////////////////////////////////////////////////
// CHtmlStream -- manages in-memory HTML

class CHtmlStream
{
public:
// Constructors
        CHtmlStream(UINT nGrowBytes = 4096);
        CHtmlStream(BYTE* lpBuffer, UINT nBufferSize, UINT nGrowBytes = 0);

// Operations
        void Attach(BYTE* lpBuffer, UINT nBufferSize, UINT nGrowBytes = 0);
        BYTE* Detach();
        DWORD GetStreamSize() const;
        virtual void Abort();
        virtual void Close();
        virtual void InitStream();
        virtual void Reset();
```

```
            CHtmlStream& operator<<(LPCTSTR psz);
            CHtmlStream& operator<<(short int w);
            CHtmlStream& operator<<(long int dw);
            CHtmlStream& operator<<(CHtmlStream& stream);
            CHtmlStream& operator<<(double d);
            CHtmlStream& operator<<(float f);

// Advanced Overridables
protected:
            virtual BYTE* Alloc(DWORD nBytes);
            virtual BYTE* Realloc(BYTE* lpMem, DWORD nBytes);
            virtual BYTE* Memcpy(BYTE* lpMemTarget, const BYTE* lpMemSource, UINT nBytes);
            virtual void GrowStream(DWORD dwNewLen);
            virtual void Write(const void* lpBuf, UINT nCount);

            DWORD m_nStreamSize;

public:
             virtual void Free(BYTE* lpMem);

// Implementation
protected:
            UINT     m_nGrowBytes;
            DWORD    m_nPosition;
            DWORD    m_nBufferSize;
            BYTE*    m_lpBuffer;
            BOOL     m_bAutoDelete;

public:
            virtual -CHtmlStream();
};

//////////////////////////////////////////////////////////////////
// Status codes for HTTP transactions

#define HTTP_STATUS_OK                                  200              // OK
#define HTTP_STATUS_CREATED                   201              // created
#define HTTP_STATUS_ACCEPTED        202         // accepted
#define HTTP_STATUS_NO_CONTENT                204              // no content
#define HTTP_STATUS_REDIRECT        301         // moved permanently
#define HTTP_STATUS_TEMP_REDIRECT   302         // moved temporarily
#define HTTP_STATUS_NOT_MODIFIED    304         // not modified
#define HTTP_STATUS_BAD_REQUEST               400              // bad request
#define HTTP_STATUS_AUTH_REQUIRED   401         // unauthorized
#define HTTP_STATUS_FORBIDDEN       403         // forbidden
#define HTTP_STATUS_NOT_FOUND       404         // not found
#define HTTP_STATUS_SERVER_ERROR    500         // internal server error
#define HTTP_STATUS_NOT_IMPLEMENTED 501         // not implemented
#define HTTP_STATUS_BAD_GATEWAY               502              // bad gateway
#define HTTP_STATUS_SERVICE_NA                503              // service
unavailable

//////////////////////////////////////////////////////////////////
// Parse Map macros

#ifndef AFX_PARSE_CALL
```

```
#define AFX_PARSE_CALL
#endif

typedef void (AFX_PARSE_CALL CHttpServer::*AFX_PISAPICMD) (CHttpServerContext* pCtxt);

struct AFX_PARSEMAP_ENTRY;    // declared after CHttpServer, below

struct AFX_PARSEMAP
{
        UINT (PASCAL* pfnGetNumMapEntries) ();
#ifdef _AFXDLL
        const AFX_PARSEMAP* (PASCAL* pfnGetBaseMap) ();
#else
        const AFX_PARSEMAP* pBaseMap;
#endif
        const AFX_PARSEMAP_ENTRY* lpEntries,
        -AFX_PARSEMAP();
};

struct AFX_PARSEMAP_ENTRY_PARAMS
{
        int     nParams;                        // number of parameters
        int nRequired;                          // number of parameters without defaults
        // all of these are arrays!
        LPTSTR* ppszInfo;           // pointers to name[2n], pointer to default[2n+1]
        BYTE*   ppszDefaults;       // pointers to coerced default values
        BYTE*   ppszValues;                     // pointers to coerced actual values
        -AFX_PARSEMAP_ENTRY_PARAMS();
};

#ifdef _AFXDLL
#define DECLARE_PARSE_MAP() \
private: \
        static AFX_PARSEMAP_ENTRY _parseEntries[]; \
public: \
        static const AFX_PARSEMAP parseMap; \
        static const AFX_PARSEMAP* PASCAL _GetBaseParseMap(); \
        static UINT PASCAL GetNumMapEntries(); \
        virtual const AFX_PARSEMAP* GetParseMap() const; \

#else
#define DECLARE_PARSE_MAP() \
private: \
        static AFX_PARSEMAP_ENTRY _parseEntries[]; \
public: \
        static const AFX_PARSEMAP parseMap; \
        static UINT PASCAL GetNumMapEntries(); \
        virtual const AFX_PARSEMAP* GetParseMap() const; \

#endif // _AFXDLL

#ifdef _AFXDLL
#define BEGIN_PARSE_MAP(theClass, baseClass) \
        const AFX_PARSEMAP* PASCAL theClass::_GetBaseParseMap() \
                { return &baseClass::parseMap; } \
```

```
            typedef void (AFX_PARSE_CALL theClass::*theClass##CALL) (CHttpServerContext*); \
            const AFX_PARSEMAP* theClass::GetParseMap() const \
                    { return &theClass::parseMap; } \
            AFXIS_DATADEF const AFX_PARSEMAP theClass::parseMap = \
                    { &theClass::GetNumMapEntries, &theClass::_GetBaseParseMap,
 &theClass::_parseEntries[0] }; \
            AFX_PARSEMAP_ENTRY theClass::_parseEntries[] = \
            { \

#else
#define BEGIN_PARSE_MAP(theClass, baseClass) \
            typedef void (AFX_PARSE_CALL theClass::*theClass##CALL) (CHttpServerContext*); \
            const AFX_PARSEMAP* theClass::GetParseMap() const \
                    { return &theClass::parseMap; } \
            AFXIS_DATADEF const AFX_PARSEMAP theClass::parseMap = \
                    { &theClass::GetNumMapEntries, &baseClass::parseMap,
 &theClass::_parseEntries[0] }; \
            AFX_PARSEMAP_ENTRY theClass::_parseEntries[] = \
            { \
#endif

#define ON_PARSE_COMMAND(FnName, mapClass, Args) \
            { _T(#FnName), (AFX_PISAPICMD) (mapClass##CALL)mapClass::FnName, Args },

#define ON_PARSE_COMMAND_PARAMS(Params) \
    { NULL, (AFX_PISAPICMD) NULL, Params },

#define DEFAULT_PARSE_COMMAND(FnName, mapClass) \
            { _T(#FnName), (AFX_PISAPICMD) (mapClass##CALL)mapClass::FnName, NULL },

#define END_PARSE_MAP(theClass) \
            }; \
            UINT PASCAL theClass::GetNumMapEntries() { \
                    return sizeof(theClass::_parseEntries) /\
                    sizeof(AFX_PARSEMAP_ENTRY); } \

//////////////////////////////////////////////////////////////////////
//

class CHttpServerContext
{
public:
            CHttpServerContext(EXTENSION_CONTROL_BLOCK* pECB);
            virtual ~CHttpServerContext();

// Operations
    BOOL GetServerVariable(LPTSTR lpszVariableName,
                    LPVOID lpvBuffer, LPDWORD lpdwSize);
    BOOL WriteClient(LPVOID lpvBuffer, LPDWORD lpdwBytes, DWORD dwReserved = 0);
    BOOL ReadClient(LPVOID lpvBuffer, LPDWORD lpdwSize);
    BOOL ServerSupportFunction(DWORD dwHSERRequest,
                    LPVOID lpvBuffer, LPDWORD lpdwSize, LPDWORD lpdwDataType);

            CHttpServerContext& operator<<(LPCTSTR psz);
            CHttpServerContext& operator<<(long int dw);
```

```
            CHttpServerContext& operator<<(short int w);
            CHttpServerContext& operator<<(CHtmlStream& stream);
            CHttpServerContext& operator<<(double d);
            CHttpServerContext& operator<<(float f);

            void Reset();

// Attributes
            EXTENSION_CONTROL_BLOCK* const m_pECB;
            CHtmlStream* m_pStream;
            DWORD m_dwEndOfHeaders;
#ifdef _DEBUG
            DWORD m_dwOldEndOfHeaders;
#endif
};

////////////////////////////////////////////////////////////////////
// Internet Information Server Extension Support

class CHttpServer
{
public:
            CHttpServer(TCHAR cDelimiter = '&');
            virtual ~CHttpServer();

            enum errors {
                    callOK = 0,                             // everything is fine
                    callParamRequired,  // a required parameter was missing
                    callBadParamCount,  // there were too many or too few parameters
                    callBadCommand,               // the command name was not found
                    callNoStackSpace,   // no stack space was available
                    callNoStream,                 // no CHtmlStream was available
                    callMissingQuote,   // a parameter had a bad format
                    callMissingParams,  // no parameters were available
                    callBadParam,                 // a parameter had a bad format (ie, only
one quote)
            };

// overridables
            virtual int CallFunction(CHttpServerContext* pCtxt,
                    LPTSTR pszQuery, LPTSTR pszCommand);
            virtual BOOL OnParseError(CHttpServerContext* pCtxt, int nCause);

// operations
            virtual void EndContent(CHttpServerContext* pCtxt) const;
            virtual void StartContent(CHttpServerContext* pCtxt) const;
            virtual void WriteTitle(CHttpServerContext* pCtxt) const;
            virtual LPCTSTR GetTitle() const;
            void AddHeader(CHttpServerContext* pCtxt, LPCTSTR pszString) const;

            virtual DWORD HttpExtensionProc(EXTENSION_CONTROL_BLOCK *pECB);
            virtual BOOL GetExtensionVersion(HSE_VERSION_INFO *pVer);
            virtual CHtmlStream* ConstructStream();
            virtual BOOL InitInstance(CHttpServerContext* pCtxt);

// implementation
```

```
protected:
        UINT PASCAL GetStackSize(const BYTE* pbParams);
        int CallMemberFunc(CHttpServerContext* pCtxt,
                const AFX_PARSEMAP_ENTRY* pEntry,
                AFX_PARSEMAP_ENTRY* pParams, LPTSTR szParams);
        LPTSTR GetQuery(CHttpServerContext* pCtxt,
                LPTSTR lpszQuery, DWORD cbQuery);
    const AFX_PARSEMAP_ENTRY* LookUp(LPCTSTR szMethod,
                const AFX_PARSEMAP*& pMap, AFX_PARSEMAP_ENTRY*& pParams,
                AFX_PISAPICMD pCmdDefault = NULL);
        int CountParams(LPCTSTR pszCommandLine, int& nCount);
        int ParseDefaultParams(AFX_PARSEMAP_ENTRY* pParams,
                int nParams, AFX_PARSEMAP_ENTRY_PARAMS*& pBlock,
                const BYTE* pbTypes);
        LPVOID PreprocessString(LPTSTR psz);
        void BuildStatusCode(LPTSTR szResponse, DWORD dwCode);

#if defined(_PPC_) || defined(_MPPC_)
        int PushDefaultStackArgs(BYTE* pStack,
                CHttpServerContext* pCtxt, const BYTE* pbParams,
                LPTSTR lpszParams, AFX_PARSEMAP_ENTRY_PARAMS* pDefParams,
                int nSizeArgs);
        int PushStackArgs(BYTE* pStack, CHttpServerContext* pCtxt,
                const BYTE* pbParams, LPTSTR lpszParams, UINT nSizeArgs);
        BYTE* StoreStackParameter(BYTE* pStack, BYTE nType,
                LPTSTR pszCurParam, UINT nSizeArgs, BOOL bDoShadow);
        BYTE* StoreRawStackParameter(BYTE* pStack, BYTE nType,
                BYTE* pRawParam, int nSizeArgs);
#else
        int PushDefaultStackArgs(BYTE* pStack,
                CHttpServerContext* pCtxt, const BYTE* pbParams,
                LPTSTR lpszParams, AFX_PARSEMAP_ENTRY_PARAMS* pDefParams);
        int PushStackArgs(BYTE* pStack, CHttpServerContext* pCtxt,
                const BYTE* pbParams, LPTSTR lpszParams);
        BYTE* StoreStackParameter(BYTE* pStack, BYTE nType, LPTSTR pszParam);
        BYTE* StoreRawStackParameter(BYTE* pStack, BYTE nType, BYTE* pRawParam);
#endif

        LPCRITICAL_SECTION m_pCritSec;
        const TCHAR m_cTokenDelimiter;  // can't EVER change
        DECLARE_PARSE_MAP()
};

extern "C" BOOL WINAPI GetExtensionVersion(HSE_VERSION_INFO *pVer);
extern "C" DWORD WINAPI HttpExtensionProc(EXTENSION_CONTROL_BLOCK *pECB);

struct AFX_PARSEMAP_ENTRY
{
        LPTSTR                          pszFnName;                  // if default param
Ụentry, ptr to
AFX_PARSEMAP_ENTRY_PARAMS
        AFX_PISAPICMD    pfn;                                // NULL if default param entry
        LPSTR                           pszArgs;        // NULL if default function
Ụentry
};
```

```
///////////////////////////////////////////////////////////////////
// Constants to describe parameter types

#define ITS_EMPTY                    "\x06"              // no parameters
#define ITS_I2          "\x01"       // a 'short'
#define ITS_I4          "\x02"       // a 'long'
#define ITS_R4          "\x03"       // a 'float'
#define ITS_R8          "\x04"       // a 'double'
#define ITS_PSTR                     "\x05"              // a 'LPCTSTR'

enum INETVARENUM
{
        IT_I2           = 1,
        IT_I4           = 2,
        IT_R4           = 3,
        IT_R8           = 4,
        IT_PSTR         = 5,
        IT_EMPTY = 6,
};

///////////////////////////////////////////////////////////////////
// Internet Information Server Entry Points

extern "C" DWORD WINAPI HttpFilterProc(PHTTP_FILTER_CONTEXT pfc,
    DWORD dwNotificationType, LPVOID pvNotification);

extern "C" BOOL WINAPI GetFilterVersion(PHTTP_FILTER_VERSION pVer);

///////////////////////////////////////////////////////////////////
// Internet Information Server Filter Support

class CHttpFilterContext
{
public:
        CHttpFilterContext(PHTTP_FILTER_CONTEXT pfc);
    ~CHttpFilterContext() { }

        BOOL GetServerVariable(LPTSTR lpszVariableName, LPVOID lpvBuffer,
                LPDWORD lpdwSize);
        BOOL AddResponseHeaders(LPTSTR lpszHeaders, DWORD dwReserved = 0);
        BOOL WriteClient(LPVOID lpvBuffer, LPDWORD lpdwBytes,
                DWORD dwReserved = 0);
        LPVOID AllocMem(DWORD cbSize, DWORD dwReserved = 0);
        BOOL ServerSupportFunction(enum SF_REQ_TYPE sfReq,
                LPVOID lpvBuffer, LPDWORD lpdwSize, LPDWORD lpdwDataType);

        PHTTP_FILTER_CONTEXT const m_pFC;
};

///////////////////////////////////////////////////////////////////
//

class CHttpFilter
{
public:
        CHttpFilter();
```

```
        ~CHttpFilter();

protected:

public:
        virtual DWORD HttpFilterProc(PHTTP_FILTER_CONTEXT pfc,
            DWORD dwNotificationType, LPVOID pvNotification);
        virtual BOOL GetFilterVersion(PHTTP_FILTER_VERSION pVer);

        virtual DWORD OnReadRawData(CHttpFilterContext* pfc, PHTTP_FILTER_RAW_DATA
pRawData);
        virtual DWORD OnPreprocHeaders(CHttpFilterContext* pfc,
PHTTP_FILTER_PREPROC_HEADERS pHeaders);
        virtual DWORD OnAuthentication(CHttpFilterContext* pfc, PHTTP_FILTER_AUTHENT
pAuthent);
        virtual DWORD OnUrlMap(CHttpFilterContext* pfc, PHTTP_FILTER_URL_MAP pUrlMap);
        virtual DWORD OnSendRawData(CHttpFilterContext* pfc, PHTTP_FILTER_RAW_DATA
pRawData);
        virtual DWORD OnLog(CHttpFilterContext* pfc, PHTTP_FILTER_LOG pLog);
        virtual DWORD OnEndOfNetSession(CHttpFilterContext* pfc);
};

/////////////////////////////////////////////////////////////////////////////
// Alternate debugging suppot

#include <crtdbg.h>

#ifdef _AFX
#define ISAPIASSERT(expr)                                   ASSERT(expr)
#define ISAPITRACE(str)                                       TRACE(str)
#define ISAPITRACE0(str)                                    TRACE0(str)
#define ISAPITRACE1(str, arg1)                            TRACE1(str, arg1)
#define ISAPITRACE2(str, arg1, arg2)            TRACE2(str, arg1, arg2)
#define ISAPITRACE3(str, arg1, arg2, arg3)      TRACE3(str, arg1, arg2, arg3)
#define ISAPIVERIFY(f)                                       ASSERT(f)
#else
#define ISAPIASSERT(expr)                                   _ASSERTE(expr)
#define ISAPITRACE(str)
_RPT0(_CRT_WARN, str)
#define ISAPITRACE0(str)                                    _RPT0(_CRT_WARN,
str)
#define ISAPITRACE1(str, arg1)                            _RPT1(_CRT_WARN,
str, arg1)
#define ISAPITRACE2(str, arg1, arg2)            _RPT2(_CRT_WARN, str, arg1, arg2)
#define ISAPITRACE3(str, arg1, arg2, arg3)      _RPT3(_CRT_WARN, arg1, arg2, arg3)
#ifdef _DEBUG
#define ISAPIVERIFY(expr)                                   _ASSERTE(expr)
#else
#define ISAPIVERIFY(expr)                                   ((void)(expr))
#endif
#endif

/////////////////////////////////////////////////////////////////////////////
// Inline function declarations

#ifdef _AFX_ENABLE_INLINES
```

```
#define _AFXISAPI_INLINE inline
#include <afxisapi.inl>
#endif

#undef AFX_DATA
#define AFX_DATA

#ifdef _AFX_MINREBUILD
#pragma component(minrebuild, on)
#endif
#ifndef _AFX_FULLTYPEINFO
#pragma component(mintypeinfo, off)
#endif

#endif // the whole file
```

ACTIVEX SERVER

OBJECT REFERENCE

I have found when doing Denali development that having a quick reference to the available objects is very useful, and much easier than browsing the documentation Web pages. So here's the reference table I created for your own use.

Object	Property/ Method/ Collection	Method/Property	Description	Parameters
Application	**Methods**	**Lock( )**	Prevents other clients from accessing Application objects	
		Unlock( )		
Request	**Collections**	**Cookies**	Collection of all Cookies held by the client	
		Form	Collection of all form fields submitted by the client, if using POST method	

Object	Property/ Method/ Collection	Method/Property	Description	Parameters
		QueryString	Arguments submitted to URL or form fields, if using POST method	
		ServerVariables	Values of server environment variables	
Response	Collections	Cookies	Specifies cookie values. Using this collection, you can set cookie values.	Value
	Properties	Buffer	Whether or not to buffer page output	flag = TRUE or FALSE
		ContentType	Content type for responses	string = optional string to set content type
		Expires	Length of time before page cached on browser expires	
		ExpiresAbsolute	Date and time at which page cached on browser expires	
		Status	Value of status line returned by server	
	Methods	AddHeader	Sets HTML header name to value	name,value
		AppendToLog	Adds string to end of log	string
		BinaryWrite	Writes binary information to HTTPoutput	data
		Clear	Clears any buffered output	
		End	Stops processing ASP file	

Object	Property/ Method/ Collection	Method/Property	Description	Parameters
		Flush	Sends buffered output immediately	
		Redirect	Causes browser to attempt connection to different URL	URL
		Write	Writes string to current HTTP output	string
Server	Methods	CreateObject	Creates instance of server component	progID - the name of the component to create
		HTMLEncode	Applies HTML encoding to specified string	string
		MapPath	Returns physical path for specified relative path	relativepath
		URLEncode	URL-encodes string	string
Session	Properties	SessionID	Returns session ID of current session	
		Timeout	Returns or set number of minutes determining when session is abandoned	nMinutes - if specified will change property
	Methods	Abandon	Force an abandon of a session	

MICROSOFT COM

JAVA CLASSES

As discussed in the text, Visual J++ introduces several Java classes for COM support. The user interface related class implementations (the applet and awt categories) are presented here, for ease of reference in your development efforts. These classes are also the most likely of the COM classes that you may choose to subclass to provide enhanced functionality.

applet

This class (BrowserAppletFrame) provides a more functional applet that incorporates several of the Microsoft COM extensions.

```
//
//   BrowserAppletFrame.java
//
//   Copyright (c) 1996, Microsoft Corporation
//

package com.ms.applet;

import java.util.*;
```

```
import java.io.*;
import java.awt.*;
import java.awt.image.ImageProducer;
import java.applet.*;
import java.net.*;
import com.ms.net.wininet.WininetStreamHandlerFactory;
import com.ms.applet.AppletAudioClip;
import com.ms.awt.image.ByteArrayImageSource;
import com.ms.net.wininet.URLUtils;
import sun.awt.image.URLImageSource;

class ClassLoaderEntry {
    int countRefs;
    URL codebase;
    AppletBaseClassLoader loader;

    ClassLoaderEntry(URL codebase, AppletBaseClassLoader loader)
    {
        this.countRefs = 1;
        this.codebase = codebase;
        this.loader = loader;
    }
}

public
class BrowserAppletFrame extends Frame
                    implements AppletStub, Runnable, IJavaObjectLoader
{
    /**
     * Parent window to show this applet in. AWT looks at this when creating
     * our child window. Moving this field will require a rebuild of AWT!
     */
    int hwnd;

    Hashtable atts;

    /**
     * The document url.
     */
    URL documentURL;

    /**
     * The base url.
     */
    URL baseURL;

    /**
     * The applet (if loaded).
     */
    Applet applet;

    /**
     * The classloader for the applet.
     */
    AppletBaseClassLoader loader;
```

```java
/**
 * The current status. Either: APPLET_DISPOSE, APPLET_LOAD,
 * APPLET_INIT, APPLET_START.
 */
int status;

/**
 * IDispatch interface for applet.
 */
int pdispApplet;

/**
 * The thread for the applet.
 */
Thread handler;

/**
 * The applet size.
 */
Dimension appletSize = new Dimension(0, 0);

/* applet event ids */
public final static int APPLET_DISPOSE = 0;
public final static int APPLET_LOAD = 1;
public final static int APPLET_INIT = 2;
public final static int APPLET_START = 3;
public final static int APPLET_STOP = 4;
public final static int APPLET_DESTROY = 5;

/* Windows messages */
final static int WM_USER = 0x400;
final static int HOSTFRAME_SHOWSTATUS = WM_USER+1;
final static int HOSTFRAME_REPAINTSTATUS = WM_USER+2;
final static int HOSTFRAME_SHOWDOCUMENT = WM_USER+3;
final static int HOSTFRAME_SETDOWNLOADSTATE = WM_USER+4;

/* resource string ids */
final static int STATUS_INITED = 0x100;
final static int STATUS_STARTED = 0x101;
final static int STATUS_STOPPED = 0x102;
final static int STATUS_DESTROYED = 0x103;
final static int STATUS_OPENING_CLASS = 0x104;
final static int STATUS_OPENING_CABINET = 0x105;

/*
 * Hooks to manipulate the applet's IDispatch pointer.
 */

public static native int getAppletDispatch(Applet applet);
public static native void releaseAppletDispatch(int pDispatch);

 // from IJavaObjectLoader
public int deliverJavaObjectDispatch()
{
    if (pdispApplet != 0 && (status == APPLET_START)) {
        return pdispApplet;
```

```
        } else {
            return 0;
        }
    }

    /*
     * Puts the specified name/value pair into the applet's parameter bag.
     */
     // from IJavaObjectLoader
    public void loadParameter(String name, String value)
    {
        if (atts == null)
            atts = new Hashtable();

        // For Netscape compatibility, we must remove leading/trailing spaces.
        value = value.trim();

        // For Netscape compatibility, we must remove any control chars.
        int i;
        int j = 0;
        int len = value.length();
        char buf[] = new char[len];
        for (i = 0; i < len; i++) {
            char ch = value.charAt(i);
            if (ch >= 0x0020) {
                buf[j++] = ch;
            }
        }
        value = new String(buf, 0, j);

        atts.put(name.toLowerCase(), value);
    }
    /**
     * Massages the specified URL specification to conform to what the Java libraries
  ⌐expect.
     */

    String massageURLSpec(String spec)
    {
        // IE gives us encoded URL strings. (A space is %20.)
        // Canonicalize it with the Wininet API. Remember to encode
        // the string again before passing it to Wininet or UrlMon.
        //
        // We'll leave http: URLs encoded. It's up to the applet to deal with
        // encoding issues itself which is compatible with the default Sun
        // http: handler.
        if (!spec.startsWith("http:")) {
            String specNew = URLUtils.canonicalizeURL(spec,
                            URLUtils.ICU_DECODE | URLUtils.ICU_NO_ENCODE);
            if (specNew != null)
                spec = specNew;
        }

        // If the string after the file: starts with two or less forward
        // slashes, then conver this to three slashes. The browser calls
        // InternetCanonicalizeURL which will always return file: URLs with
```

```
        // this format. However, the Java URL parsing code ends up treating
        // the drive letter as a host which breaks a bunch of code including
        // the SecurityManager.
        if (spec.startsWith("file:")) {
            int i;
            int length = spec.length();
            for (i = 5; i < length; i++) {
                if (spec.charAt(i) != '/')
                    break;
            }
            if (i < 8) {
                spec = "file:///" + spec.substring(i);
            }
        }

        // For compatibility with existing Java applets, we'll
        // replace afll backslashes with forward slashes. However, we
        // don't want to lose UNC information, so we need to special
        // case this.
        if (spec.startsWith("file:///\\\\")) {
            spec = "file:///\\\\" + spec.substring(10).replace('\\', '/');
        } else {
            spec = spec.replace('\\', '/');
        }

        return spec;
}

/**
 * Called by JavaObjectLoaderHost after all parameters have been loaded; the applet
 * can now be kicked off.
 */
 // from IJavaObjectLoader
public void init(String document, int hwnd, IJavaObjectLoaderHost host)
{
    String att;

    firstTimeInit();

    jolHost = host;

    this.hwnd = hwnd;

    try {
        com.ms.com.ComLib.declareMessagePumpThread();
    } catch (Throwable t) {
    }

    try {
        documentURL = new URL(massageURLSpec(document));
    } catch (MalformedURLException e) {
    }

    att = getParameter("codebase");

    if (att != null) {
```

```
        if (!att.endsWith("/")) {
            att += "/";
        }
        try {
            baseURL = new URL(massageURLSpec(att));
        } catch (MalformedURLException e) {
        }
    }

    if (baseURL == null) {
        baseURL = documentURL;
    }

    // Netscape's applets have a default background color of light gray.
    // A color related to the page would be preferable but some applets
    // don't paint properly without gray so we'll be compatible.
    setBackground(Color.lightGray);
    try {
        appletSize.width = Integer.valueOf(getParameter("width")).intValue();
    } catch (Exception e) {
        //  appletSize.width set to zero when allocated.
    }

    try {
        appletSize.height = Integer.valueOf(getParameter("height")).intValue();
    } catch (Exception e) {
        //  appletSize.height set to zero when allocated.
    }

    resize(appletSize);

    // Create a thread group for the applet, and start a new
    // thread to load the applet.
    String nm = "applet-" + getParameter("code");
    handler = new Thread(new AppletThreadGroup("group " + nm), this, "thread " + nm);
    handler.start();
}

 // from IJavaObjectLoader2
public void resizeApplet(int width, int height)
{
    if (width != appletSize.width || height != appletSize.height) {
        appletSize.width = width;
        appletSize.height = height;
        resize(appletSize);
    }
}

/**
 * Event Queue
 */
Event queue = null;

/**
 * Send an event.
 */
```

```java
 // from IJavaObjectLoader
public void sendEvent(int id) {
    queueEvent(new Event(null, id, null));
}

/**
 * Send an event. Queue it for execution by the handler thread.
 */
protected synchronized void queueEvent(Event evt) {
    if (queue == null) {
        evt.target = queue;
        queue = evt;
        notifyAll();
    } else {
        Event q = queue;
        for (; q.target != null ; q = (Event)q.target);
        q.target = evt;
    }
}

/**
 * Get an event from the queue.
 */
synchronized Event getNextEvent() throws InterruptedException {
    while (queue == null) {
        wait();
    }
    Event evt = queue;
    queue = (Event)queue.target;
    evt.target = this;
    return evt;
}

static Vector frames = new Vector();

public void run()
{
    frames.addElement(this);

    try {

        // Bump up the priority, so that applet events are processed in
        // a timely manner.
        int priority = Thread.currentThread().getPriority();
        Thread.currentThread().setPriority(priority + 1);

        show();

        while (true) {
            Event evt;
            try {
                evt = getNextEvent();
            } catch (InterruptedException e) {
                // Bailing out...
                return;
            }
```

```
            try {
                switch (evt.id) {
                  case APPLET_LOAD:
                    if (status != APPLET_DISPOSE) {
                        break;
                    }

                    loader = getClassLoader();

                    // Create the applet using the class loader
                    String code = getParameter("code");
                    if (code.endsWith(".class")) {
                        code = code.substring(0, code.length() - 6).replace('/', '.');
                    }
                    if (code.endsWith(".java")) {
                        code = code.substring(0, code.length() - 5).replace('/', '.');
                    }
                    try {
                        try {
                            setDownloadState(true);
                            applet = (Applet)loader.loadClass(code).newInstance();
                        } finally {
                            setDownloadState(false);
                        }
                        pdispApplet = getAppletDispatch(applet);
                    } catch (ClassNotFoundException e) {
                        showAppletStatus("load: class " + code + " not found");
                        showAppletException(e);
                        break;
                    } catch (InstantiationException e) {
                        showAppletStatus("load: " + code + " can't be instantiated");
                        showAppletException(e);
                        break;
                    } catch (IllegalAccessException e) {
                        showAppletStatus("load: " + code + " is not public or has no
public constructor");
                        showAppletException(e);
                        break;
                    } catch (Exception e) {
                        showAppletStatus("exception: " + e );
                        showAppletException(e);
                        break;
                    } catch (ThreadDeath e) {
                        showAppletStatus("killed");
                        return;
                    } catch (Error e) {
                        showAppletStatus("error: " + e );
                        showAppletException(e);
                        break;
                    }

                    // Stick it in the frame
                    applet.setStub(this);
                    applet.hide();
                    add("Center", applet);
                    status = APPLET_LOAD;
```

```
            showAppletStatus(STATUS_INITED);
            validate();
            break;

        case APPLET_INIT:
            if (status != APPLET_LOAD) {
                break;
            }
            try {
                setDownloadState(true);
                applet.resize(appletSize);
                applet.init();
                validate();
            } finally {
                setDownloadState(false);
            }
            status = APPLET_INIT;
            showAppletStatus(STATUS_INITED);
            break;

        case APPLET_START:
            if (status != APPLET_INIT) {
                break;
            }
            applet.resize(appletSize);
            applet.start();
            validate();
            applet.show();
            status = APPLET_START;
            showAppletStatus(STATUS_STARTED);
            break;

        case APPLET_STOP:
            if (status != APPLET_START) {
                break;
            }
            status = APPLET_INIT;
            applet.hide();
            applet.stop();
            showAppletStatus(STATUS_STOPPED);
            break;

        case APPLET_DESTROY:
            if (status != APPLET_INIT) {
                break;
            }
            status = APPLET_LOAD;
            applet.destroy();
            showAppletStatus(STATUS_DESTROYED);
            break;

        case APPLET_DISPOSE:
            if (status != APPLET_LOAD) {
                break;
            }
            status = APPLET_DISPOSE;
```

```
                    remove(applet);
                    return;
                }
            } catch (Exception e) {
                showAppletStatus("exception: " + e );
                showAppletException(e);
            } catch (ThreadDeath e) {
                showAppletStatus("killed");
                return;
            } catch (Error e) {
                showAppletStatus("error: " + e );
                showAppletException(e);
            }
        }
    } finally {
        frames.removeElement(this);
        releaseClassLoader(getCodeBase());
        releaseAppletDispatch(pdispApplet);
        dispose();
        jolHost = null;
    }
}

/**
 * Return true when the applet has been started.
 */
public boolean isActive() {
    return status == APPLET_START;
}

/**
 * Status line. Called by the AppletPanel to provide
 * feedback on the Applet's state.
 */
protected void showAppletStatus(String status) {
    jolHost.showStatus(status);
}

protected void showAppletStatus(int id) {
    jolHost.showSystemStatus(id, false, null);
}

protected void showLoaderStatus(int id, String arg) {
    jolHost.showSystemStatus(id, true, arg);
}

protected void setDownloadState(boolean downloading) {
    jolHost.setDownloadState(downloading);
}

/**
 * Called by the AppletPanel to provide
 * feedback when an exception has happend.
 */
protected void showAppletException(Throwable t) {
    t.printStackTrace();
```

```
}

/**
 * The class loaders
 */
private static Vector classloaders = new Vector();

private static int oldloadersCount = 0;

private final static int CLASSLOADER_KEEP_ALIVE_COUNT = 3;

/**
 * Get a class loader.
 */
AppletBaseClassLoader getClassLoader() throws MalformedURLException
{
        ClassLoaderEntry ce;
    String cabbase = getParameter("cabbase");
    URL codebase = null;

    // Get an URL to the codebase.
    if (cabbase == null) {
        codebase = getCodeBase();
    } else {
        codebase = new URL(getCodeBase(), cabbase);
    }

    // Synchronize on the classloader object.
    synchronized (classloaders) {
        int i;
        int size = classloaders.size();
        for (i = 0; i < size; i++) {
            ce = (ClassLoaderEntry)classloaders.elementAt(i);

            if (codebase.equals(ce.codebase)) {
                if (ce.countRefs == 0)
                    oldloadersCount--;

                ce.countRefs++;
                return ce.loader;
            }
        }

        // Create a new classloader...
        AppletBaseClassLoader abcl;

        if (cabbase == null) {
            abcl = new AppletClassLoader(codebase);
        } else {
            abcl = new CabClassLoader(codebase);
        }

                try {

                        abcl.setSecureState(documentURL.getProtocol(),
```

```
codebase.getProtocol());

                    } catch (Throwable e) {

                    }

        ce = new ClassLoaderEntry( codebase, abcl );

        // ...and add it to the list of classloaders.
        classloaders.addElement(ce);
    }
    return ce.loader;
}

static synchronized void releaseClassLoader(URL codebase) {

    int i;
    int size = classloaders.size();

    for (i = 0; i < size; i++) {

        ClassLoaderEntry ce = (ClassLoaderEntry)classloaders.elementAt(i);

        if (codebase.equals(ce.codebase)) {

            // Push classloaders with a refcount of zero to the end of the
            // array.
            ce.countRefs--;
            classloaders.removeElementAt(i);
            classloaders.addElement(ce);

            if (ce.countRefs == 0)
                oldloadersCount++;

            // If we've exceeded the keep alive count, then remove the
            // first element with a reference count of zero.
            while (oldloadersCount >= CLASSLOADER_KEEP_ALIVE_COUNT) {

                for (i = 0; i < size; i++) {

                    ClassLoaderEntry oldce = (ClassLoaderEntry)
                        classloaders.elementAt(i);
                    if (oldce.countRefs == 0) {
                        classloaders.removeElementAt(i);
                        oldloadersCount--;
                        break;
                    }
                }
            }

            break;
        }
    }
}

/**
```

```
 * Gets the document URL.
 */
public URL getDocumentBase()
{
    return documentURL;
}

/**
 * Gets the base URL.
 */
public URL getCodeBase()
{
    return baseURL;
}

/**
 * Gets a parameter of the applet.
 */
public String getParameter(String name)
{
    return (String)atts.get(name.toLowerCase());
}

/**
 * Context for this applet; one is created on demand per frame.
 */
private BrowserAppletContext appletContext;

/**
 * Gets a handler to the applet's context.
 */
public AppletContext getAppletContext()
{
    if (appletContext == null) {
            appletContext = new BrowserAppletContext(this);
    }
    return appletContext;
}

public void appletResize(int width, int height)
{
}

/**
 * Get an applet by name.
 */
public Applet getApplet(String name)
{
    AppletSecurity security = (AppletSecurity)System.getSecurityManager();
    name = name.toLowerCase();
    for (Enumeration e = frames.elements() ; e.hasMoreElements() ;) {
        BrowserAppletFrame f = (BrowserAppletFrame)e.nextElement();
        String param = f.getParameter("name");
        if (param != null) {
            param = param.toLowerCase();
        }
```

```
        if (name.equals(param) && f.getDocumentBase().equals(getDocumentBase()))) {
            try {
                security.checkConnect(getCodeBase().getHost(),
f.getCodeBase().getHost());
                return f.applet;
            } catch (SecurityException ee) {
            }
        }
    }
    return null;
}


/**
 * Return an enumeration of all the accessible
 * applets on this page.
 */
public Enumeration getApplets()
{
    AppletSecurity security = (AppletSecurity)System.getSecurityManager();
    Vector v = new Vector();
    for (Enumeration e = frames.elements() ; e.hasMoreElements() ;) {
        BrowserAppletFrame f = (BrowserAppletFrame)e.nextElement();
        if (f.getDocumentBase().equals(getDocumentBase())) {
            try {
                security.checkConnect(getCodeBase().getHost(),
f.getCodeBase().getHost());
                v.addElement(f.applet);
            } catch (SecurityException ee) {
            }
        }
    }
    return v.elements();
}

byte[] getDataFileFromLoader( URL url )
{
    String stringBase = baseURL.toString();
    String stringUrl = url.toString();
    String stringFile = null;

        if ( stringBase.length() == stringUrl.length() ) {
        return null;
    }

    if ( stringUrl.startsWith(stringBase) ) {
        stringFile = stringUrl.substring( stringBase.length() );
    } else {
            return null;
        }

    return loader.getDataItem( stringFile );
}

Hashtable audioHash = new Hashtable();

/**
```

```
 * Get a clip from the audio clip cache.
 */
synchronized AudioClip getAudioClipFromCache(URL url)
{
            System.getSecurityManager().checkConnect(url.getHost(), url.getPort());
    AudioClip clip = (AudioClip)audioHash.get(url);
    if (clip != null) {
        return clip;
    }

    if (loader.isDataStore()) {
        byte data[] = getDataFileFromLoader(url);
        if (data != null) {
            clip = new AppletAudioClip(url, data);
        }
    }

    if (clip == null) {
        clip = new AppletAudioClip(url);
    }

    audioHash.put(url, clip );

    return clip;
}

Hashtable imgHash = new Hashtable();

/**
 * Get an image from the static image cache.
 */
synchronized Image getImageFromHash(URL url)
{
    System.getSecurityManager().checkConnect(url.getHost(), url.getPort());

    Image img = (Image)imgHash.get(url);

    if (img != null) {
        return img;
    }

    ImageProducer imgProducer = null;

    try {
        try {
            if (loader.isDataStore()) {
                imgProducer = new ByteArrayImageSource(url.toString(),
getDataFileFromLoader(url));
            }
        } catch (Exception e) {
        }

        if (imgProducer == null) {
            URLConnection conn = url.openConnection();
            conn.setUseCaches(true);
            imgProducer = new URLImageSource(url, conn);
```

```
        }

        if (imgProducer != null) {
            img = Toolkit.getDefaultToolkit().createImage(imgProducer);
            imgHash.put(url, img);
        }
    } catch (Exception e) {
    }

    return img;
}

static boolean isFirstTimeInited = false;

static synchronized void firstTimeInit()
{
    if (isFirstTimeInited)
        return;

    isFirstTimeInited = true;

    //  Install our WININET stream handler factory. If this fails, the
    //  system will fall back on the existing factory or use the default
    //  Sun handlers.
    try {
        URL.setURLStreamHandlerFactory(new WininetStreamHandlerFactory());
    } catch (Exception e) {
    }

    //  Redirect stdout and stderr to a file called javalog.txt in the
    //  user's Java directory. PrintStream's print methods are
    //  synchronized so two threads writing to stdout and stderr will be
    //  okay.
    if ("true".equalsIgnoreCase(System.getProperty("com.ms.applet.enable.logging"))) {
        try {
            String logdir = System.getProperty("java.home");
            PrintStream ps = new PrintStream(new BufferedOutputStream(new
                FileOutputStream(new File(logdir, "javalog.txt"))), true);
            System.out = ps;
            System.err = ps;
        } catch (Exception e) {
        }
    }

    Properties props = new Properties(System.getProperties());

    //  Define which packages can be extended by applets.
    props.put("package.restrict.definition.java", "true");
    props.put("package.restrict.definition.sun", "true");
    props.put("package.restrict.definition.com.ms", "true");

    //  Define properties that Java applets can access. Currently, this
    //  is the same set as available from Sun's AppletViewer.
    props.put("java.version.applet", "true");
    props.put("java.vendor.applet", "true");
    props.put("java.vendor.url.applet", "true");
```

```
            props.put("java.class.version.applet", "true");
            props.put("os.name.applet", "true");
            props.put("os.version.applet", "true");
            props.put("os.arch.applet", "true");
            props.put("file.separator.applet", "true");
            props.put("path.separator.applet", "true");
            props.put("line.separator.applet", "true");
            props.put("browser.applet", "true");

            System.setProperties(props);

            // Because we don't use the Sun HTTP protocol handlers to download
            // data, we may not touch the java.net.InetAddress class and thus not
            // call its class initializer until some later point. At that time,
            // a SecurityManager has been installed, so its class initializer is
            // not able to complete normally-- specifically, it cannot resolve
            // the local host address. Thus, we touch it once here so that the
            // class may initialize BEFORE the SecurityManager is installed.
            try {
                InetAddress.getLocalHost();
            } catch (Exception e) {
            }
            if (System.getSecurityManager() == null) {
                System.setSecurityManager(new AppletSecurity());
            }
        }

    public IJavaObjectLoaderHost getLoaderHost()
    {
        return jolHost;
    }

    IJavaObjectLoaderHost jolHost;

}
```

awt

MenuX.java

```
//
//  BrowserAppletFrame.java
//
//  Copyright (c) 1996, Microsoft Corporation
//

package com.ms.applet;

import java.util.*;
import java.io.*;
import java.awt.*;
import java.awt.image.ImageProducer;
import java.applet.*;
import java.net.*;
```

```
import com.ms.net.wininet.WininetStreamHandlerFactory;
import com.ms.applet.AppletAudioClip;
import com.ms.awt.image.ByteArrayImageSource;
import com.ms.net.wininet.URLUtils;
import sun.awt.image.URLImageSource;

class ClassLoaderEntry {
    int countRefs;
    URL codebase;
    AppletBaseClassLoader loader;

    ClassLoaderEntry(URL codebase, AppletBaseClassLoader loader)
    {
        this.countRefs = 1;
        this.codebase = codebase;
        this.loader = loader;
    }
}

public
class BrowserAppletFrame extends Frame
                implements AppletStub, Runnable, IJavaObjectLoader
{
    /**
     * Parent window to show this applet in. AWT looks at this when creating
     * our child window. Moving this field will require a rebuild of AWT!
     */
    int hwnd;

    Hashtable atts;
    /**
     * The document url.
     */
    URL documentURL;

    /**
     * The base url.
     */
    URL baseURL;

    /**
     * The applet (if loaded).
     */
    Applet applet;

    /**
     * The classloader for the applet.
     */
    AppletBaseClassLoader loader;

    /**
     * The current status. Either: APPLET_DISPOSE, APPLET_LOAD,
     * APPLET_INIT, APPLET_START.
     */
    int status;
```

```java
/**
 * IDispatch interface for applet.
 */
 int pdispApplet;

/**
 * The thread for the applet.
 */
Thread handler;

/**
 * The applet size.
 */
Dimension appletSize = new Dimension(0, 0);

/* applet event ids */
public final static int APPLET_DISPOSE = 0;
public final static int APPLET_LOAD = 1;
public final static int APPLET_INIT = 2;
public final static int APPLET_START = 3;
public final static int APPLET_STOP = 4;
public final static int APPLET_DESTROY = 5;

/* Windows messages */
final static int WM_USER = 0x400;
final static int HOSTFRAME_SHOWSTATUS = WM_USER+1;
final static int HOSTFRAME_REPAINTSTATUS = WM_USER+2;
final static int HOSTFRAME_SHOWDOCUMENT = WM_USER+3;
final static int HOSTFRAME_SETDOWNLOADSTATE = WM_USER+4;

/* resource string ids */
final static int STATUS_INITED = 0x100;
final static int STATUS_STARTED = 0x101;
final static int STATUS_STOPPED = 0x102;
final static int STATUS_DESTROYED = 0x103;
final static int STATUS_OPENING_CLASS = 0x104;
final static int STATUS_OPENING_CABINET = 0x105;

/*
 * Hooks to manipulate the applet's IDispatch pointer.
 */

public static native int getAppletDispatch(Applet applet);
public static native void releaseAppletDispatch(int pDispatch);

 // from IJavaObjectLoader
public int deliverJavaObjectDispatch()
{
    if (pdispApplet != 0 && (status == APPLET_START)) {
        return pdispApplet;
    } else {
        return 0;
    }
}

 /*
```

```
 * Puts the specified name/value pair into the applet's parameter bag.
 */
 // from IJavaObjectLoader
public void loadParameter(String name, String value)
{
    if (atts == null)
        atts = new Hashtable();
    // For Netscape compatibility, we must remove leading/trailing spaces.
    value = value.trim();

    // For Netscape compatibility, we must remove any control chars.
    int i;
    int j = 0;
    int len = value.length();
    char buf[] = new char[len];
    for (i = 0; i < len; i++) {
        char ch = value.charAt(i);
        if (ch >= 0x0020) {
            buf[j++] = ch;
        }
    }
    value = new String(buf, 0, j);

    atts.put(name.toLowerCase(), value);
}


/**
 * Massages the specified URL specification to conform to what the Java
 * libraries expect.
 */

String massageURLSpec(String spec)
{
    // IE gives us encoded URL strings. (A space is %20.)
    // Canonicalize it with the Wininet API. Remember to encode
    // the string again before passing it to Wininet or UrlMon.
    //
    // We'll leave http: URLs encoded. It's up to the applet to deal with
    // encoding issues itself which is compatible with the default Sun
    // http: handler.
    if (!spec.startsWith("http:")) {
        String specNew = URLUtils.canonicalizeURL(spec,
                            URLUtils.ICU_DECODE | URLUtils.ICU_NO_ENCODE);
        if (specNew != null)
            spec = specNew;
    }

    // If the string after the file: starts with two or less forward
    // slashes, then conver this to three slashes. The browser calls
    // InternetCanonicalizeURL which will always return file: URLs with
    // this format. However, the Java URL parsing code ends up treating
    // the drive letter as a host which breaks a bunch of code including
    // the SecurityManager.
    if (spec.startsWith("file:")) {
        int i;
        int length = spec.length();
```

```
        for (i = 5; i < length; i++) {
            if (spec.charAt(i) != '/')
                break;
        }
        if (i < 8) {
            spec = "file:///" + spec.substring(i);
        }
    }

    // For compatibility with existing Java applets, we'll
    // replace afll backslashes with forward slashes. However, we
    // don't want to lose UNC information, so we need to special
    // case this.
    if (spec.startsWith("file:///\\\\\")) {
        spec = "file:///\\\\\" + spec.substring(10).replace('\\', '/');
    } else {
        spec = spec.replace('\\', '/');
    }

    return spec;
}

/**
 * Called by JavaObjectLoaderHost after all parameters have been loaded; the
 * applet can now be kicked off.
 */
 // from IJavaObjectLoader
public void init(String document, int hwnd, IJavaObjectLoaderHost host)
{
    String att;

    firstTimeInit();

    jolHost = host;

    this.hwnd = hwnd;

    try {
        com.ms.com.ComLib.declareMessagePumpThread();
    } catch (Throwable t) {
    }

    try {
        documentURL = new URL(massageURLSpec(document));
    } catch (MalformedURLException e) {
    }

    att = getParameter("codebase");

    if (att != null) {
        if (!att.endsWith("/")) {
            att += "/";
        }
        try {
            baseURL = new URL(massageURLSpec(att));
```

```
            } catch (MalformedURLException e) {
            }
        }

        if (baseURL == null) {
            baseURL = documentURL;
        }

        // Netscape's applets have a default background color of light gray.
        // A color related to the page would be preferable but some applets
        // don't paint properly without gray so we'll be compatible.
        setBackground(Color.lightGray);

        try {
            appletSize.width =
Integer.valueOf(getParameter("width")).intValue();
        } catch (Exception e) {
            //  appletSize.width set to zero when allocated.
        }

        try {
            appletSize.height =
Integer.valueOf(getParameter("height")).intValue();
        } catch (Exception e) {
            // appletSize.height set to zero when allocated.
        }

        resize(appletSize);

        // Create a thread group for the applet, and start a new
        // thread to load the applet.
        String nm = "applet-" + getParameter("code");
        handler = new Thread(new AppletThreadGroup("group " + nm), this, "thread
↳" + nm);
        handler.start();
    }

     // from IJavaObjectLoader2
    public void resizeApplet(int width, int height)
    {
        if (width != appletSize.width || height != appletSize.height) {
            appletSize.width = width;
            appletSize.height = height;
            resize(appletSize);
        }
    }

    /**
     * Event Queue
     */
    Event queue = null;

    /**
     * Send an event.
     */
     // from IJavaObjectLoader
```

```
public void sendEvent(int id) {
    queueEvent(new Event(null, id, null));
}

/**
 * Send an event. Queue it for execution by the handler thread.
 */
protected synchronized void queueEvent(Event evt) {
    if (queue == null) {
        evt.target = queue;
        queue = evt;
        notifyAll();
    } else {
        Event q = queue;
        for (; q.target != null ; q = (Event)q.target);
        q.target = evt;
    }
}
/**
 * Get an event from the queue.
 */
synchronized Event getNextEvent() throws InterruptedException {
    while (queue == null) {
        wait();
    }
    Event evt = queue;
    queue = (Event)queue.target;
    evt.target = this;
    return evt;
}

static Vector frames = new Vector();

public void run()
{
    frames.addElement(this);

    try {

        // Bump up the priority, so that applet events are processed in
        // a timely manner.
        int priority = Thread.currentThread().getPriority();
        Thread.currentThread().setPriority(priority + 1);

        show();

        while (true) {
            Event evt;
            try {
                evt = getNextEvent();
            } catch (InterruptedException e) {
                // Bailing out...
                return;
            }

            try {
```

```
            switch (evt.id) {
              case APPLET_LOAD:
                if (status != APPLET_DISPOSE) {
                    break;
                }

                loader = getClassLoader();

                // Create the applet using the class loader
                String code = getParameter("code");
                if (code.endsWith(".class")) {
                    code = code.substring(0, code.length() -
6).replace('/', '.');
                }
                if (code.endsWith(".java")) {
                    code = code.substring(0, code.length() -
5).replace('/', '.');
                }
                try {
                    try {
                        setDownloadState(true);
                        applet =
(Applet)loader.loadClass(code).newInstance();
                    } finally {
                        setDownloadState(false);
                    }
                    pdispApplet = getAppletDispatch(applet);
                } catch (ClassNotFoundException e) {
                    showAppletStatus("load: class " + code + " not
⌐found");
                    showAppletException(e);
                    break;
                } catch (InstantiationException e) {
                    showAppletStatus("load: " + code + " can't be
⌐instantiated");
                    showAppletException(e);
                    break;
                } catch (IllegalAccessException e) {
                    showAppletStatus("load: " + code + " is not public
⌐or has no public constructor");
                    showAppletException(e);
                    break;
                } catch (Exception e) {
                    showAppletStatus("exception: " + e );
                    showAppletException(e);
                    break;
                } catch (ThreadDeath e) {
                    showAppletStatus("killed");
                    return;
                } catch (Error e) {
                    showAppletStatus("error: " + e );
                    showAppletException(e);
                    break;
                }

                // Stick it in the frame
```

```
                    applet.setStub(this);
                    applet.hide();
                    add("Center", applet);
                    status = APPLET_LOAD;
                    showAppletStatus(STATUS_INITED);
                    validate();
                    break;

                case APPLET_INIT:

                    if (status != APPLET_LOAD) {

                        break;

                    }

                    try {

                        setDownloadState(true);

                        applet.resize(appletSize);

                        applet.init();

                        validate();

                    } finally {

                        setDownloadState(false);

                    }

                    status = APPLET_INIT;

                    showAppletStatus(STATUS_INITED);

                    break;

                case APPLET_START:
                    if (status != APPLET_INIT) {
                        break;
                    }
                    applet.resize(appletSize);
                    applet.start();
                    validate();
                    applet.show();
                    status = APPLET_START;
                    showAppletStatus(STATUS_STARTED);
                    break;

                case APPLET_STOP:
                    if (status != APPLET_START) {
                        break;
                    }
                    status = APPLET_INIT;
                    applet.hide();
```

```
                    applet.stop();
                    showAppletStatus(STATUS_STOPPED);
                    break;

                 case APPLET_DESTROY:
                    if (status != APPLET_INIT) {
                        break;
                    }
                    status = APPLET_LOAD;
                    applet.destroy();
                    showAppletStatus(STATUS_DESTROYED);
                    break;

                 case APPLET_DISPOSE:
                    if (status != APPLET_LOAD) {
                        break;
                    }
                    status = APPLET_DISPOSE;
                    remove(applet);
                    return;
                }
            } catch (Exception e) {
                showAppletStatus("exception: " + e );
                showAppletException(e);
            } catch (ThreadDeath e) {
                showAppletStatus("killed");
                return;
            } catch (Error e) {
                showAppletStatus("error: " + e );
                showAppletException(e);
            }
        }
    } finally {
        frames.removeElement(this);
        releaseClassLoader(getCodeBase());
        releaseAppletDispatch(pdispApplet);
        dispose();
        jolHost = null;
    }
}


/**
 * Return true when the applet has been started.
 */
public boolean isActive() {
    return status == APPLET_START;
}


/**
 * Status line. Called by the AppletPanel to provide
 * feedback on the Applet's state.
 */
protected void showAppletStatus(String status) {
    jolHost.showStatus(status);
}
```

```
protected void showAppletStatus(int id) {
    jolHost.showSystemStatus(id, false, null);
}

protected void showLoaderStatus(int id, String arg) {
    jolHost.showSystemStatus(id, true, arg);
}

protected void setDownloadState(boolean downloading) {
    jolHost.setDownloadState(downloading);
}

/**
 * Called by the AppletPanel to provide
 * feedback when an exception has happend.
 */
protected void showAppletException(Throwable t) {
    t.printStackTrace();
}

/**
 * The class loaders
 */
private static Vector classloaders = new Vector();

private static int oldloadersCount = 0;

private final static int CLASSLOADER_KEEP_ALIVE_COUNT = 3;

/**
 * Get a class loader.
 */
AppletBaseClassLoader getClassLoader() throws MalformedURLException
{
        ClassLoaderEntry ce;
    String cabbase = getParameter("cabbase");
    URL codebase = null;

    // Get an URL to the codebase.
    if (cabbase == null) {
        codebase = getCodeBase();
    } else {
        codebase = new URL(getCodeBase(), cabbase);
    }

    // Synchronize on the classloader object.
      synchronized (classloaders) {
          int i;
          int size = classloaders.size();

          for (i = 0; i < size; i++) {
              ce = (ClassLoaderEntry)classloaders.elementAt(i);

              if (codebase.equals(ce.codebase)) {
                  if (ce.countRefs == 0)
                      oldloadersCount--;
```

```
                  ce.countRefs++;
                  return ce.loader;
            }
      }

      // Create a new classloader...
      AppletBaseClassLoader abcl;

      if (cabbase == null) {
          abcl = new AppletClassLoader(codebase);
      } else {
          abcl = new CabClassLoader(codebase);
      }

              try {

                      abcl.setSecureState(documentURL.getProtocol(),

codebase.getProtocol());

              } catch (Throwable e) {

              }

      ce = new ClassLoaderEntry( codebase, abcl );

      // ...and add it to the list of classloaders.

      classloaders.addElement(ce);

    }

    return ce.loader;
  }

  static synchronized void releaseClassLoader(URL codebase) {

    int i;
    int size = classloaders.size();

    for (i = 0; i < size; i++) {

      ClassLoaderEntry ce = (ClassLoaderEntry)classloaders.elementAt(i);

      if (codebase.equals(ce.codebase)) {

          // Push classloaders with a refcount of zero to the end of the
          // array.
          ce.countRefs--;
          classloaders.removeElementAt(i);
          classloaders.addElement(ce);

          if (ce.countRefs == 0)
              oldloadersCount++;
          // If we've exceeded the keep alive count, then remove the
          // first element with a reference count of zero.
```

```
            while (oldloadersCount >= CLASSLOADER_KEEP_ALIVE_COUNT) {

                for (i = 0; i < size; i++) {

                    ClassLoaderEntry oldce = (ClassLoaderEntry)
                        classloaders.elementAt(i);

                    if (oldce.countRefs == 0) {
                        classloaders.removeElementAt(i);
                        oldloadersCount--;
                        break;
                    }
                }
            }

            break;
        }
    }
}

/**
 * Gets the document URL.
 */
public URL getDocumentBase()
{
    return documentURL;
}

/**
 * Gets the base URL.
 */
public URL getCodeBase()
{
    return baseURL;
}

/**
 * Gets a parameter of the applet.
 */
public String getParameter(String name)
{
    return (String)atts.get(name.toLowerCase());
}

/**
 * Context for this applet; one is created on demand per frame.
 */
private BrowserAppletContext appletContext;

/**
 * Gets a handler to the applet's context.
 */
public AppletContext getAppletContext()
{
    if (appletContext == null) {
        appletContext = new BrowserAppletContext(this);
    }
```

```
            return appletContext;
    }

    public void appletResize(int width, int height)
    {
    }

    /**
     * Get an applet by name.
     */
    public Applet getApplet(String name)
    {
        AppletSecurity security = (AppletSecurity)System.getSecurityManager();
        name = name.toLowerCase();
        for (Enumeration e = frames.elements() ; e.hasMoreElements() ;) {
            BrowserAppletFrame f = (BrowserAppletFrame)e.nextElement();
            String param = f.getParameter("name");
            if (param != null) {
                param = param.toLowerCase();
            }
            if (name.equals(param) &&
f.getDocumentBase().equals(getDocumentBase())) {
                try {
                    security.checkConnect(getCodeBase().getHost(),
f.getCodeBase().getHost());
                    return f.applet;
                } catch (SecurityException ee) {
                }
            }
        }
        return null;
    }

    /**
     * Return an enumeration of all the accessible
     * applets on this page.
     */
    public Enumeration getApplets()
    {
        AppletSecurity security = (AppletSecurity)System.getSecurityManager();
        Vector v = new Vector();
        for (Enumeration e = frames.elements() ; e.hasMoreElements() ;) {
            BrowserAppletFrame f = (BrowserAppletFrame)e.nextElement();
            if (f.getDocumentBase().equals(getDocumentBase())) {
                try {
                    security.checkConnect(getCodeBase().getHost(),
f.getCodeBase().getHost());
                    v.addElement(f.applet);
                } catch (SecurityException ee) {
                }
            }
        }
        return v.elements();
    }

    byte[] getDataFileFromLoader( URL url )
```

```
    {
        String stringBase = baseURL.toString();
        String stringUrl = url.toString();
        String stringFile = null;
            if ( stringBase.length() == stringUrl.length() ) {
            return null;
        }

        if ( stringUrl.startsWith(stringBase) ) {
            stringFile = stringUrl.substring( stringBase.length() );
        } else {
                return null;
            }

        return loader.getDataItem( stringFile );
    }

    Hashtable audioHash = new Hashtable();

    /**
     * Get a clip from the audio clip cache.
     */
    synchronized AudioClip getAudioClipFromCache(URL url)
    {
            System.getSecurityManager().checkConnect(url.getHost(),
url.getPort());
        AudioClip clip = (AudioClip)audioHash.get(url);

        if (clip != null) {
            return clip;
        }

        if (loader.isDataStore()) {
            byte data[] = getDataFileFromLoader(url);
            if (data != null) {
                clip = new AppletAudioClip(url, data);
            }
        }

        if (clip == null) {
            clip = new AppletAudioClip(url);
        }

        audioHash.put(url, clip );

        return clip;
    }

    Hashtable imgHash = new Hashtable();

    /**
     * Get an image from the static image cache.
     */
    synchronized Image getImageFromHash(URL url)
    {
        System.getSecurityManager().checkConnect(url.getHost(), url.getPort());
```

```
        Image img = (Image)imgHash.get(url);

        if (img != null) {
            return img;
        }

        ImageProducer imgProducer = null;
        try {
            try {
                if (loader.isDataStore()) {
                    imgProducer = new ByteArrayImageSource(url.toString(),
getDataFileFromLoader(url));
                }
            } catch (Exception e) {
            }

            if (imgProducer == null) {
                URLConnection conn = url.openConnection();
                conn.setUseCaches(true);
                imgProducer = new URLImageSource(url, conn);
            }

            if (imgProducer != null) {
                img = Toolkit.getDefaultToolkit().createImage(imgProducer);
                imgHash.put(url, img);
            }
        } catch (Exception e) {
        }

        return img;
    }

    static boolean isFirstTimeInited = false;

    static synchronized void firstTimeInit()
    {
        if (isFirstTimeInited)
            return;

        isFirstTimeInited = true;

        //  Install our WININET stream handler factory. If this fails, the
        //  system will fall back on the existing factory or use the default
        //  Sun handlers.
        try {
            URL.setURLStreamHandlerFactory(new WininetStreamHandlerFactory());
        } catch (Exception e) {
        }

        //  Redirect stdout and stderr to a file called javalog.txt in the
        //  user's Java directory. PrintStream's print methods are
        //  synchronized so two threads writing to stdout and stderr will be
        //  okay.
        if
("true".equalsIgnoreCase(System.getProperty("com.ms.applet.enable.logging"))) {
            try {
```

```
            String logdir = System.getProperty("java.home");
            PrintStream ps = new PrintStream(new BufferedOutputStream(new
                FileOutputStream(new File(logdir, "javalog.txt"))), true);
            System.out = ps;
            System.err = ps;
        } catch (Exception e) {
        }
    }

    Properties props = new Properties(System.getProperties());
    // Define which packages can be extended by applets.
    props.put("package.restrict.definition.java", "true");
    props.put("package.restrict.definition.sun", "true");
    props.put("package.restrict.definition.com.ms", "true");

    // Define properties that Java applets can access. Currently, this
    // is the same set as available from Sun's AppletViewer.
    props.put("java.version.applet", "true");
    props.put("java.vendor.applet", "true");
    props.put("java.vendor.url.applet", "true");
    props.put("java.class.version.applet", "true");
    props.put("os.name.applet", "true");
    props.put("os.version.applet", "true");
    props.put("os.arch.applet", "true");
    props.put("file.separator.applet", "true");
    props.put("path.separator.applet", "true");
    props.put("line.separator.applet", "true");
    props.put("browser.applet", "true");

    System.setProperties(props);

    // Because we don't use the Sun HTTP protocol handlers to download
    // data, we may not touch the java.net.InetAddress class and thus not
    // call its class initializer until some later point. At that time,
    // a SecurityManager has been installed, so its class initializer is
    // not able to complete normally-- specifically, it cannot resolve
    // the local host address. Thus, we touch it once here so that the
    // class may initialize BEFORE the SecurityManager is installed.
    try {
        InetAddress.getLocalHost();
    } catch (Exception e) {
    }

    if (System.getSecurityManager() == null) {
        System.setSecurityManager(new AppletSecurity());
    }
}

public IJavaObjectLoaderHost getLoaderHost()
{
    return jolHost;
}


IJavaObjectLoaderHost jolHost;
}
```

MenuItemX.java

```java
//
// MenuItemX.java
//
// Copyright (c) 1996, Microsoft Corporation
//

package com.ms.awt;

import java.awt.CheckboxMenuItem;

public class MenuItemX extends CheckboxMenuItem
{
        int id;
        int flags;

        ///////////////////////////////////////////////////////////////////////

        public void Check(boolean val)
        {
                super.setState(val);
        }

        ///////////////////////////////////////////////////////////////////////

        public boolean isChecked()
        {
                return super.getState();
        }

        ///////////////////////////////////////////////////////////////////////

        public int getID()
        {
                return id;
        }

        ///////////////////////////////////////////////////////////////////////

        public MenuItemX(String s, int i1, int i2)
        {
                super(s);

                id = i1;
                flags = i2;
        }

        ///////////////////////////////////////////////////////////////////////

        public void setState(boolean t)
        {
                return;
        }

        ///////////////////////////////////////////////////////////////////////
```

```java
    public synchronized void addNotify()
    {
                super.addNotify();
    }

        ///////////////////////////////////////////////////////////////////////////////////
}
```

MenuXConstants.java

```java
//
//  MenuXConstants.java
//
//  Copyright (c) 1996, Microsoft Corporation
//

package com.ms.awt;

public interface MenuXConstants
{
        public final int UNCHECKED      = 0;
        public final int BY_COMMAND         = 0;
        public final int POPUP          = 1;
        public final int CHECKED        = 2;
        public final int ENDMENU        = 4;
        public final int SEPARATOR_NEXT = 8;
        public final int BY_POSITION  = 16;
}
//
// FontX.java
//
// Copyright (c) 1996, Microsoft Corporation
//
// notes:
// 1.  cant override getFont.
// 2.  going to have to eventually override ALL methods of java.awt.Font,
//          leave place holders in code now.
//
package com.ms.awt;
import java.awt.Font;

public class FontX extends Font
{
    // public static final int PLAIN = 0;
    // public static final int BOLD  = 1;
        // public static final int ITALIC   = 2;
    // private int pData;
    // private String family;
    // protected String name;
    // protected int style;
    // protected int size;
        public static final int EMBEDDED = 1;
        public static final int STRIKEOUT = 2;
        public static final int UNDERLINE = 4;
        private static final int FONTXFONT = 0x8000;
```

```
    private native static int pNewFontEnumeration();
        private native static String pGetFontEnumeratedFamily(int i);
        private native boolean pIsTypeable(int lang);
        private int flags = FONTXFONT;                 // FONTXFONT is used by the native
side.

    //========================================================================

    public FontX(String name, int style, int size)
    {
       super(name, style, size);
    }

    public FontX(String name, int style, int size, boolean bEmbed)
    {
       super(name, style, size);
       if ( bEmbed )
            flags |= 1;
       else
            flags &= 0xfffe;
    }

    public FontX(String name, int style, int size, int theNewFlags)
    {
       super(name, style, size);
            flags |= theNewFlags;
    }

    //========================================================================

    public boolean isTypeable(int language)
    {
            return pIsTypeable(language);
    }
    //========================================================================
    public int getFlags()
    {
            return flags;
    }

    //========================================================================

/*

* All the following need modifying for the new class - for tt extensions

*

    public String getFamily()

    {

            return super.getFamily();

    }
```

```
    //===================================================================
public String getName()
{
        return super.getName();
}


    //===================================================================
public int getStyle()
{
        return super.getStyle();
}


    //===================================================================
public int getSize()
{
        return super.getSize();
}


    //===================================================================
public boolean isPlain()
{
    return super.isPlain();
}


    //===================================================================
public boolean isBold()
{
        return super.isBold();
}


    //===================================================================
public boolean isItalic()
{
        return super.isItalic();
}


    //===================================================================
    public int hashCode()
{
        return (super.getName()).hashCode() ^ style ^ size;
    }
*/
    //===================================================================

public boolean equals(Object obj)
{
    if( obj instanceof FontX )
        return super.equals(obj);
    else if (obj instanceof Font)
        return super.equals(obj);
    else
            return false;
}


    //===================================================================
```

```java
    public String toString()
    {
            String strStyle;

            if (isBold())
                    strStyle = isItalic() ? "bolditalic" : "bold";

            else
                strStyle = isItalic() ? "italic" : "plain";

            return getClass().getName() +
                                "[family=" + getFamily() +
                                ",name=" + getName() +
                                ",style=" + strStyle +
                                ",size=" + getSize() +
                                (((flags & EMBEDDED) !=0) ?", Embedded" :"") +
                                (((flags & STRIKEOUT) !=0) ?", Strikeout" :"") +
                                (((flags & UNDERLINE) !=0) ?", Underline" :"") +
                                "]";
    }

    //========================================================================

    public static String[] getFontList()
    {
        int listSize = pNewFontEnumeration();

        String list[] = new String[listSize + 6];
        list[0] = "Dialog";
        list[1] = "Helvetica";
        list[2] = "TimesRoman";
            list[3] = "Courier";
        list[4] = "DialogInput";
        list[5] = "ZapfDingbats";

        for(int i=0; i<listSize; i++)
                list[6+i] = pGetFontEnumeratedFamily(i);
                return list;
    }

    //========================================================================
}
```

CaretX.java

```java
//
// CaretX.java
//
// Copyright (c) 1996, Microsoft Corporation
//

package com.ms.awt;

import java.awt.Component;
import java.awt.Point;
```

```
import java.awt.peer.ComponentPeer;
import com.ms.awt.peer.ComponentPeerX;

public class CaretX
{
        private Component theComponent;
        private int hwnd;

        private boolean visible = false;
        private int width ;
        private int height;
        private int x;
        private int y;

        private native void pDispose();
        private native void pSetPos(int x, int y);
        private native void pCreate(int hwnd, int w, int h);
        private native void pShow(int hwnd);
        private native void pHide(int hwnd);

        ////////////////////////////////////////////////////////////////////

        public void finalize()
        {
                pDispose();
        }

        ////////////////////////////////////////////////////////////////////

        public CaretX(Component c, int w, int h)
        {
                theComponent         = c;
                ComponentPeer p      = c.getPeer();
                ComponentPeerX peer = (ComponentPeerX)p;

                hwnd   = peer.gethwnd();
                width  = w;
                height = h;
                pCreate(hwnd,w,h);
        }

        ////////////////////////////////////////////////////////////////////

        public void show()
        {
                visible = true;
                pShow(hwnd);
        }

        ////////////////////////////////////////////////////////////////////

        public void hide()
        {
                visible = false;
                pHide(hwnd);
        }
```

```
        ///////////////////////////////////////////////////////////////////

        public void setPos(Point p)
        {
                setPos(p.x, p.y);
        }

        public void setPos(int px, int py)
        {
                x = px;
                y = py;
                System.out.println("Setting caret to (" + x + "," + y + ")");
                pSetPos(x,y);
        }


        ///////////////////////////////////////////////////////////////////

}
```

ByteArrayImageSource.java

```
//
//  ByteArrayImageSource.java
//
//  Copyright (c) 1996, Microsoft Corporation
//

package com.ms.awt.image;

import java.io.*;
import sun.awt.image.*;

public class ByteArrayImageSource extends InputStreamImageSource
{
    String imagefile;
    byte   data[];

    public ByteArrayImageSource(String filename, byte data[])
    {
        if ( filename == null || data == null ) {
                throw new NullPointerException();
           }
           imagefile = filename;
        this.data = data;
    }

    final boolean checkSecurity(Object context, boolean quiet)
    {
        return true;
    }

    protected ImageDecoder getDecoder()
    {
        InputStream is;

        is = new BufferedInputStream(new ByteArrayInputStream(data));
```

```
        int suffixpos = imagefile.lastIndexOf('.');
        if (suffixpos >= 0) {
            String suffix =
imagefile.substring(suffixpos+1).toLowerCase();
            if (suffix.equals("gif")) {
                return new GifImageDecoder(this, is);
            } else if (suffix.equals("jpeg") || suffix.equals("jpg") ||
                suffix.equals("jpe") || suffix.equals("jfif")) {
                return new JPEGImageDecoder(this, is);
            } else if (suffix.equals("xbm")) {
                return new XbmImageDecoder(this, is);
            }
        }
        return getDecoder(is);
    }
}
```

INDEX

About the Web Site

The Web page (http://www.wiley.com/compbooks/) contains several useful, highly reusable Web components. Among the featured applications and tools on the site, you'll find:

- An ISAPI application for sending email messages from a server application
- An ISAPI filter for automatic file publishing
- Another ISAPI filter to provide IIS with enhanced industrial-strength access control
- A Java applet written using Visual J++'s advanced Resource Wizard capabilities to provide two-dimensional layout
- Another Java applet that interfaces with a COM object to provide a Java-based email client
- An Active Server Page (Denali script) written in VBScript to provide "shopping basket" functionality for a commerce Web site

Full source code is provided for all of these utilities. As new APIs and platforms are delivered, the source code will be updated. Links to additional resources are provided and updated on a regular basis.